# INTRODUCTION TO COMPUTER ORGANIZATION

## An Under-the-Hood Look at Hardware and x86-64 Assembly

by Robert G. Plantz

**no starch press**

San Francisco

Printed in the United States of America

First printing

25 24 23 22 21    1 2 3 4 5 6 7 8 9

ISBN-13: 978-1-7185-0009-9 (print)
ISBN-13: 978-1-7185-0010-5 (ebook)

Publisher: William Pollock
Managing Editor: Jill Franklin
Production Manager: Rachel Monaghan
Production Editor: Paula Williamson
Developmental Editor: Alex Freed
Cover Illustrator: Gina Redman
Interior Design: Octopod Studios
Technical Reviewers: William Young and Mike Lyle
Copyeditor: Kim Wimpsett
Compositor: Jeff Lytle, Happenstance Type-O-Rama
Proofreader: Sharon Wilkey

For information on book distributors or translations, please contact No Starch Press, Inc. directly:

No Starch Press, Inc.
245 8th Street, San Francisco, CA 94103
phone: 1.415.863.9900; info@nostarch.com
www.nostarch.com

*Library of Congress Cataloging-in-Publication Data*

Library of Congress Control Number: 2021950164

## About the Author

After obtaining his PhD in electrical engineering from UC Berkeley, Bob Plantz took a position in a physiology research lab at UC San Francisco where he programmed a Data General minicomputer. Following that, he spent several years in industry where he wrote assembly language on half a dozen different architectures at the software/hardware interface level. He then transitioned into a 21-year university teaching career in computer science.

## About the Technical Reviewers

Dr. William Young is Associate Professor of Instruction in the Department of Computer Science at the University of Texas at Austin. Prior to joining the UT faculty in 2001, he had 20 years of experience in industry. He specializes in formal methods and computer security, but often teaches computer architecture, among other courses.

Mike Lyle got his start designing computers for Hughes Aircraft (which only built one plane) to control radar and sonar systems, and then with Sperry-Univac designing operating systems for telecommunication computers. He then taught computer design at UC Berkeley for seven years, and at Sonoma State University for 15 years.

# BRIEF CONTENTS

# CONTENTS IN DETAIL

## CHAPTER 11: INSIDE THE MAIN FUNCTION       221

## CHAPTER 12: INSTRUCTION DETAILS       245

## CHAPTER 13: CONTROL FLOW CONSTRUCTS       263

# PREFACE

This book introduces the concepts of how computer hardware works from a programmer's point of view. The hardware is controlled by a set of *machine instructions*. The way in which these instructions control the hardware is called the *instruction set architecture (ISA)*. A programmer's job is to design a sequence of these instructions that will cause the hardware to perform operations to solve a problem.

Nearly all computer programs are written in a high-level language. Some of these languages are general purpose, and others are geared toward a specific type of application. But they are all intended to provide a programmer with a set of programming constructs more suitable for solving problems in human terms than working directly with the instruction set architecture and the details of the hardware.

## Who This Book Is For

Have you ever wondered what's going on "under the hood" when you write a program in a high-level language? You know that computers can be programmed to make decisions, but how do they do that? You probably know that data is stored in bits, but what does that mean when storing a decimal number? My goal in this book is to answer these and many other questions about how computers work. We'll be looking at both the hardware components and the machine-level instructions used to control the hardware.

I'm assuming that you know the basics of how to program in a high-level language, but you don't need to be an expert programmer. After discussing the hardware components, we'll look at and write lots of programs in *assembly language*, the language that translates directly into the machine instructions.

Unlike most assembly language books, we won't emphasize writing applications in assembly language. Higher-level languages—like C++, Java, and Python—are much more efficient for creating applications. Writing in assembly language is a tedious, error-prone, time-consuming process, so it should be avoided whenever possible. Our goal here is to study programming concepts, not to create applications.

## About This Book

The guidelines I followed in creating this book are as follows:

Learning is easier if it builds on concepts you already know.

Real-world hardware and software make a more interesting platform for learning theoretical concepts.

The tools used for learning should be inexpensive and readily available.

### The Programming in the Book

This book is based on the *x86-64* instruction set architecture, which is the 64-bit version of the *x86* (32-bit) instruction set architecture. It is also known by the names *AMD64*, *x86_64*, *x64*, and *Intel 64*. All the programming in the book was done using the GNU programming environment running under the Ubuntu Linux operating system. The programs should work with most common Linux distributions with few, if any, modifications.

We're using C as our high-level language, with some C++ in a later chapter. Don't worry if you don't know C/C++. All our C/C++ programming will be very simple, and I'll explain what you need to know as we go.

An important issue that arises when learning assembly language is using the keyboard and terminal screen in an application. Programming input from a keyboard and output to a screen is complex, well beyond the expertise of a beginner. The GNU programming environment includes the *C standard library*. Keeping with the "real-world" criterion of this book, we'll use the functions in that library, which are easily called from assembly language, for using the keyboard and screen in our applications.

The x86-64 instruction set architecture includes some 1,500 instructions. The exact number depends on what you consider to be a different instruction, but there are far too many to memorize. Some assembly language books deal with this issue by inventing an "idealized" instruction set architecture to illustrate the concepts. Again, keeping with the "real-world" nature of this book, we'll use the standard x86-64 instruction set but only a small subset of the instructions that will be sufficient to illustrate the basic concepts.

## Why Read This Book?

Given that there are many excellent high-level languages that allow you to write programs without being concerned with how machine instructions control the hardware, you may wonder why you should learn the material in this book. All high-level languages are ultimately translated into machine instructions that control the hardware. Understanding what the hardware does and how the instructions control it helps you to understand the capabilities and limitations of the computer. I believe that this understanding can make you a better programmer, even when you're working with a high-level language.

If your primary interest is in the hardware, I think it's important to understand how the hardware will be used by a program.

You might enjoy assembly language programming and want to carry on. For example, if your interests take you into *systems programming*—writing parts of an operating system, writing a compiler, or even designing another higher-level language—these endeavors typically require an understanding at the assembly language level.

Many challenging opportunities also exist in programming *embedded systems*, systems in which the computer has a dedicated task. Examples are an integral part of our daily life: cell phones; home appliances; automobiles; heating, ventilation, and air conditioning (HVAC) systems; medical devices; and so forth. Embedded systems comprise an essential component of enabling Internet of Things (IoT) technology. Programming them often requires an understanding of how the computer interacts with various hardware devices at the assembly language level.

If you already know assembly language for another processor, this book could serve as a primer for reading the manuals.

## Chapter Organization

The book is roughly organized into three parts: mathematics and logic, hardware, and software. The mathematics part is intended to give you the necessary language to discuss the concepts. The hardware part is an introduction to the components used to construct a computer.

These two parts provide a background for discussing how software controls the hardware. We'll look at each of the basic programming constructs in the C programming language, with some C++ toward the end of the book. Then we'll look at how the compiler translates the C/C++ code into *assembly language*, a language that directly accesses the instruction set architecture. I also show you how a programmer might program the same construct directly in assembly language.

> **Chapter 1: Setting the Stage**   Describes the three overall subsystems of a computer and how they're connected. It also discusses setting up the programming tools used in the book.
>
> **Chapter 2: Data Storage Formats**   Shows how unsigned integers are stored using the binary and hexadecimal number systems and how characters are stored in the ASCII code. We'll write our first C program and use the gdb debugger to explore these concepts.

**Chapter 3: Computer Arithmetic**    Describes the addition and subtraction of unsigned and signed integers and explains the limits of using a fixed number of bits to represent integers.

**Chapter 4: Boolean Algebra**    Describes Boolean algebra operators and functions, and function minimization using algebraic tools and Karnaugh maps.

**Chapter 5: Logic Gates**    Begins with an introduction to electronics. It then discusses logic gates and how they're built using CMOS transistors.

**Chapter 6: Combinational Logic Circuits**    Discusses logic circuits that have no memory, including adders, decoders, multiplexers, and programmable logic devices.

**Chapter 7: Sequential Logic Circuits**    Discusses clocked and unclocked logic circuits that maintain a memory, as well as circuit design using state transition tables and state diagrams.

**Chapter 8: Memory**    Describes memory hierarchy: cloud, mass storage, main memory, cache, and CPU registers. It also discusses memory hardware designs for registers, SRAM, and DRAM.

**Chapter 9: Central Processing Unit**    Gives an overview of CPU subsystems. The chapter also explains the instruction execution cycle and the main x86-64 registers and shows how to view register contents in the gdb debugger.

**Chapter 10: Programming in Assembly Language**    Looks at the minimal C function, both compiler-generated assembly language and as written directly in assembly language. The chapter covers assembler directives and first instructions. I give an example of using the text user interface of gdb as a learning tool. It includes a brief description of AT&T syntax.

**Chapter 11: Inside the main Function**    Describes passing arguments in registers, position-independent code, and use of the call stack for passing the return address and creating automatic variables.

**Chapter 12: Instruction Details**    Looks at how instructions are coded at the bit level. It also covers addressing modes and conditional jumps, as well as algorithms of assembler and linker programs.

**Chapter 13: Control Flow Constructs**    Covers assembly language implementation of controlling program flow with while, do-while, for, if-else, and switch constructs.

**Chapter 14: Inside Subfunctions**    Describes how functions access external variables: global, pass by value, pass by pointer, and pass by reference. The chapter summarizes the structure of the stack frame.

**Chapter 15: Special Uses of Subfunctions**    Shows how recursion works. The chapter also discusses using assembly language to access CPU hardware features that are not directly accessible in high-level language, using a separate function or inline assembly.

**Chapter 16: Computing with Bitwise Logic, Multiplication, and Division Instructions**    Describes bit masking, shifting bits, and the multiplication and division instructions.

**Chapter 17: Data Structures**    Explains how arrays and records (structs) are implemented and accessed in a program at the assembly language level.

**Chapter 18: Object-Oriented Programming**    Shows how structs are used as objects in C++.

**Chapter 19: Fractional Numbers**    Describes fixed-point and floating-point numbers, the IEEE 754 standard, and a few SSE2 floating-point instructions.

**Chapter 20: Input/Output**    Compares I/O with memory and bus timing. Describes isolated and memory-mapped I/O. This chapter gives a rough sketch of polled I/O programming and discusses interrupt-driven and direct memory access I/O.

**Chapter 21: Interrupts and Exceptions**    Briefly describes how the x86-64 handles interrupts and exceptions. The chapter includes examples of using int 0x80 and syscall to do system calls without using the C run-time environment.

**Appendix A: Using GNU make to Build Programs**    Gives a brief tutorial on using the GNU make program.

## Efficient Use of This Book

Because of the way I have organized this book, you will learn the material more efficiently if you follow a few simple guidelines.

Many sections have exercises at the end that give you the opportunity to practice working with the material presented in the main body of the section. These are intended as exercises, not tests. In fact, I have provided answers and my solutions to most of these exercises online at *https://rgplantz.github.io*.

If you are an instructor using this book, sorry, but you will have to make up your own exam questions. Many exercises have fairly obvious extensions that instructors could make to create class assignments.

To make efficient use of these exercises, I recommend an iterative process:

1. Try to solve the problem on your own. Spend some time on it, but do not let yourself get stuck for too long.
2. If the answer does not come to you, peek at my solution. In some cases, I give a hint before providing the full solution.
3. Return to step 1, armed with some knowledge of how an experienced assembly language programmer might approach the solution.

One thing I strongly urge you to do is to type code in by yourself. I believe this physical activity will help you to learn the material faster. If nothing else, it forces you to read every character in the code. And I do not see any advantage to copying and pasting code from my online solutions. Frankly, none of the programs in this book have any real-world usefulness. The code is provided for your own exercising, so please use it in that spirit.

This hands-on approach also applies to the mathematics in the first few chapters, which includes converting numbers between several number bases. Any good calculator will do that easily, but the actual conversion is not the point. The point is to learn about how data values can be represented in bit patterns. I believe that using paper and pencil to work through the arithmetic will help you to get a feel for these patterns.

In the first chapter, we'll start by taking a high-level overview of the major subsystems of a computer. Then I'll describe how I set up the programming environment on my computer to create and run the programs in this book.

# ACKNOWLEDGMENTS

My work is the result of the help from hundreds of people over the years. The people who helped me most are the many students I've had in my classes during my two decades of teaching. They asked questions that showed where my explanations were lacking. You, the reader of this book, get to judge whether I was successful at improving my explanations.

Next, I would like to specifically thank those who directly helped me in the writing of this book. Working with Bill Pollock, the owner of No Starch Press, has been a pleasure. I agree with his ideas of what makes up a good book. He put together a fantastic team to work with me: Zach Lebowski, Alex Freed, Annie Choi, and Athabasca Witschi were the developmental editors, and Paula Williamson was the production editor. In addition, other people at No Starch Press were working behind the scenes to make this book a reality. I truly appreciate their help.

The technical reviewers from outside No Starch Press, William Young and Michael Lyle, did a great job of finding my errors and suggesting improvements to the book.

I would also like to thank my partner, João Barretto, for his support and encouragement while I spent many hours on my computer.

# 1

## SETTING THE STAGE

We'll start with a brief overview of how computer hardware can be thought of as organized into three subsystems. The goal is to make sure we have a common framework for discussing how things are organized and how they fit together. Working within this framework, you'll learn how a program is created and then executed.

This book contains a fair amount of programming. To help you prepare for doing the programming, this chapter ends with a section describing how to set up a programming environment, using my system as an example.

### Computer Subsystems

You can think of computer hardware as consisting of three separate subsystems: *central processing unit* (*CPU*), *memory*, and *input/output* (*I/O*). They are connected with *buses*, as shown in Figure 1-1.

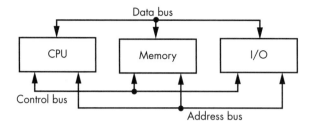

*Figure 1-1: Subsystems of a computer. The CPU, memory, and I/O subsystems communicate with one another via the three buses.*

Let's take each of these pieces in turn:

**Central processing unit (CPU)**   Controls the flow of data to and from memory and I/O devices. The CPU performs arithmetic and logical operations on the data. The CPU can decide the order of operations based on the results of arithmetic and logic operations. It contains a small amount of very fast memory.

**Memory**   Provides storage that is readily accessible to the CPU and I/O devices for the instructions to the CPU and the data they manipulate.

**Input/output (I/O)**   Communicates with the outside world and with mass storage devices (for example, the disk, network, USB, and printer).

**Bus**   A physical communication pathway with a protocol specifying exactly how the pathway is used.

As indicated by the arrows in Figure 1-1, signals can flow in either direction on the buses. The *address bus* is used to specify a specific memory location or an I/O device. Program data and program instructions flow on the *data bus*. The *control bus* carries signals that specify how each of the subsystems should be using the signals on the other buses.

The buses shown in Figure 1-1 indicate logical groupings of the signals that must pass between the three subsystems. A given bus implementation might not have physically separate paths for each of the three types of signals. For example, if you have ever installed a graphics card in a computer, it probably used the Peripheral Component Interconnect Express (PCI-E) bus. The same physical connections on the PCI-E bus carry addresses and data, but at different times.

## Program Execution

A *program* consists of a sequence of instructions stored in memory. When you create a new program, you use an *editor* to write the *source code* for your new program, usually in a high-level language (for example, C, C++, or Java). The editor program sees the source code for your new program as data, which is typically stored in a file on the disk. Then you use a *compiler* to translate the high-level language statements into machine code instructions that are stored in a disk file. Just as with the editor program, the compiler program sees both your source code and the resulting machine instructions as data.

When it comes time to execute the program, the CPU loads the instructions from the machine code disk file into memory. Most programs include some constant data that is also read into memory. The CPU executes the program by reading, often called *fetching*, each instruction from memory and executing it. The data is also fetched as needed by the program.

When the CPU is ready to execute the next instruction in the program, the location of that instruction in memory is placed on the address bus. The CPU also places a *read* signal on the control bus. The memory subsystem responds by placing the instruction on the data bus, where the CPU can then copy it. If the CPU is instructed to read data from memory, the same sequence of events takes place.

If the CPU is instructed to store data in memory, it places the data on the data bus, places the location in memory where the data is to be stored on the address bus, and places a *write* signal on the control bus. The memory subsystem responds by copying the data on the data bus into the specified memory location.

There are variations on this edit-compile-execute scheme. An *interpreter* is a program that translates the programming language into machine instructions, but instead of saving the instructions in a file, they are immediately executed. Another variation is for a compiler to translate the programming language into an intermediate shorthand language that is stored in a file that can be executed by an interpreter.

Most programs also access I/O devices. Some are meant to interact with humans, for example, a keyboard, a mouse, or a screen. Others are meant for machine-readable I/O, for example, a disk. I/O devices are very slow compared to the CPU and memory, and they vary widely in their timing characteristics. Because of their timing characteristics, data transfers between I/O devices and the CPU and memory must be explicitly programmed.

Programming an I/O device requires a thorough understanding of how the device works and how it interacts with the CPU and memory. We'll look at some of the general concepts near the end of the book. Meanwhile, nearly every program we write in the book will use at least the terminal screen, which is an output device. The operating system includes functions to perform I/O, and the C runtime environment provides a library of application-oriented functions to access the operating system I/O functions. We'll use these C library functions to perform most of our I/O operations and leave I/O programming to more advanced books.

These few paragraphs are intended to provide you with a general overall view of how computer hardware is organized. Before exploring many of these concepts in more depth, the next section will help you to set up the tools you'll need for the programming covered in the rest of the book.

# The Programming Environment

In this section, I'll describe how I set up my computer to do all the programming described in this book. You may choose to do things differently, depending on the Linux distribution you are using and your personal preferences.

I used the GNU programming tools that are included with Ubuntu 20.04 LTS running on a desktop computer, both as the primary operating system and running under Windows Subsystem for Linux (*https://docs.microsoft.com/en-us/windows/wsl/install-win10/*), to create and execute the programs in this book. You can download a free copy of Ubuntu at *https://ubuntu.com/*. The installed compilers, gcc and g++, are version 9.3.0, and the assembler, as, is version 2.34.

You may be new to using the Linux command line. As we go through the programs, I'll show you the commands I used to create them, but this will give you just the basics. You'll be much more productive if you take the time to become familiar with using the command line. I found William Shotts's *The Linux Command Line*, Second Edition (No Starch Press, 2019), to be an excellent resource.

You should also become familiar with the documentation provided in Linux for the programming tools we'll be using. The simplest is the help system built into most programs. You access help by typing the name of the program with only the --help option. For example, gcc --help brings up a list of the command line options you can use with gcc with a brief description of what each does.

Most Linux programs include a manual, usually called a *man page*, that provides more complete documentation than the help facility. It can be read by using the man command followed by the name of the program. For example, man man brings up the man page for the man program.

GNU programs come with even more complete documentation that can be read with the info command followed by the name of the program. For example, info info brings up the manual for using info, shown here:

```
Next: Stand-alone Info,   Up: (dir)

Stand-alone GNU Info
********************

This documentation describes the stand-alone Info reader which you can
use to read Info documentation.

    If you are new to the Info reader, then you can get started by typing
'H' for a list of basic key bindings.  You can read through the rest of
this manual by typing <SPC> and <DEL> (or <Space> and <Backspace>) to
move forwards and backwards in it.

* Menu:

* Stand-alone Info::         What is Info?
* Invoking Info::            Options you can pass on the command line.
```

```
* Cursor Commands::              Commands which move the cursor within a node.
* Scrolling Commands::           Commands for reading the text within a node.
* Node Commands::                Commands for selecting a new node.
* Searching Commands::           Commands for searching an Info file.
* Index Commands::               Commands for looking up in indices.
* Xref Commands::                Commands for selecting cross-references.
* Window Commands::              Commands which manipulate multiple windows.
* Printing Nodes::               How to print out the contents of a node.
* Miscellaneous Commands::       A few commands that defy categorization.
* Variables::                    How to change the default behavior of Info.
* Colors and Styles::            Customize the colors used by Info.
* Custom Key Bindings::          How to define your own key-to-command bindings.
* Index::                        Global index.

-----Info: (info-stnd)Top, 31 lines --All-------------------------------------
Welcome to Info version 6.7.  Type H for help, h for tutorial.
```

Items that begin with * and end with :: are hyperlinks to other pages in the manual. Use the arrow keys on your keyboard to put the cursor any place within such an item and press ENTER to bring up that page.

To get the info documentation, I had to install the following Ubuntu packages:

**binutils-doc**   Adds useful documentation for the GNU assembler as (sometimes called gas)

**gcc-doc**   Adds useful documentation for the GNU gcc compiler

The packages you need to get these features may differ depending on the Linux distribution you are using. I have even had to change this list for different releases of Ubuntu over the years.

In most cases, I compiled programs using no optimization (-O0 option) because the goal is to study concepts, not to create the most efficient code. The examples should work in any x86-64 GNU development environment with gcc, g++, and as installed. However, the machine code generated by the compiler may differ depending on its specific configuration and version. You will begin seeing compiler-generated assembly language about halfway through the book. Any differences should be consistent as you continue through the rest of the book.

You will also use a text editor for all your programming. Do not use a word processor. Word processors add a lot of hidden control characters to format the text. These hidden characters confuse compilers and assemblers, causing them not to work.

Several excellent text editors exist for Linux, each with its own personality. My favorite changes from time to time. I recommend trying several that are available to you and deciding which one you prefer.

These are text editors I have used:

**nano**   A simple text editor that is included with most Linux installations. It uses a command line user interface. Text is inserted directly. The CTRL and "meta" keys are used to specify keyboard sequences for manipulating text.

**vi**   Supposed to be installed on all Linux (and Unix) systems. It provides a command line user interface that is mode oriented. Text is manipulated through keyboard commands. Several commands place vi in text-insert mode. The ESC key is used to return to command mode. Most Linux installations include vim (Vi IMproved), which has additional features helpful in editing program source code.

**emacs**   Uses a command line user interface. Text is inserted directly. The CTRL and meta keys are used to specify keyboard sequences for manipulating text.

**gedit**   Probably installed if you are using the GNOME desktop. It uses a graphical user interface that will likely be familiar to you if you're used to using a word processor.

**kate**   Probably installed if you are using the KDE desktop. It uses a graphical user interface that will likely be familiar to you if you're used to using a word processor.

**Visual Studio Code**   A free editor from Microsoft that runs on Windows 7/8/10, Linux, and macOS (*https://code.visualstudio.com/*). It uses a graphical user interface and can be used to edit text files on remote servers and a Windows Subsystem for Linux installation. It also allows you to open a terminal pane for commands.

Graphical user interfaces are also available for both vi and emacs.

Any of these, and many other, text editors would be an excellent choice for the programming covered in this book. Don't spend too much time trying to pick the "best" one.

---

**YOUR TURN**

Make sure that you understand the computer you'll be using for the programming in this book. What CPU does it use? How much memory does it have? What are the I/O devices connected to it? Which editor will you be using?

---

# What You've Learned

**Central processing unit (CPU)**   The subsystem that controls most of the activities of the computer. It also contains a small amount of very fast memory.

**Memory**   The subsystem that provides storage for programs and data.

**Input/output (I/O)**   The subsystem that provides a means of communication with the outside world and with mass storage devices.

**Bus**   A communication pathway between the CPU, memory, and I/O.

**Program execution**   An overview of how the three subsystems and the buses are used when a program is run.

**Programming environment**   An example of how to set up the tools needed to do the programming in this book.

In the next chapter, you will start learning how data is stored in a computer, get an introduction to programming in C, and start learning how to use the debugger as a learning tool.

# 2

## DATA STORAGE FORMATS

In this book, we're going to look at computers in a different way: instead of seeing computers as a collection of programs and files and graphics, we're going to see them as billions of two-state switches and one or more *control units*, devices that can both detect and change the states of the switches. In Chapter 1, we discussed communicating with the world outside the computer by using input and output. In this chapter, we'll begin exploring how computers encode data for storage in memory; then we'll write some programs in C that explore these concepts.

# Describing Switches and Groups of Switches

Everything that happens on your computer—the code you write, the data you use, the images on your screen—is controlled by a series of two-state switches. Each combination of switches represents a possible state the computer is in. If you wanted to describe what was happening on your computer, you could list a combination of switches. In plain English, this would be something like "The first switch is on, the second one is also on, but the third is off, while the fourth is on." But describing the computer this way would be difficult, especially since modern computers use billions of switches. Instead, we'll use a more concise, numeric notation.

## Representing Switches with Bits

You're probably familiar with the *decimal system*, which uses 10 digits, 0 to 9, to write numbers. We want a way to represent switches numerically, but our switches have only 2 states, not 10. Here, the *binary system*—a two-digit system that uses 0 and 1—is going to prove useful.

We'll use a *binary digit*, commonly shortened to *bit*, to represent the state of a switch. A bit can have two values: 0, which represents that a switch is "off," and 1, which represents that it's "on." If we wanted, we could assign the opposite values to these digits—all that matters is that we're consistent. Let's use bits to simplify our statement about switches. In our previous example, we had a computer in which the first switch is on, the second switch is on, the third is off, and the fourth is on. In binary, we would represent this as 1101.

## Representing Groups of Bits

Even with binary, sometimes we have so many bits that the number is unreadable. In those cases, we use *hexadecimal digits* to specify bit patterns. The hexadecimal system has 16 digits, each of which can represent one group of 4 bits.

Table 2-1 shows all 16 possible combinations of 4 bits and the corresponding hexadecimal digit for each combination. After using hexadecimal for a while, you will probably memorize this table, but if you forget it, an online search will quickly bring up a hexadecimal-to-binary converter.

**Table 2-1:** Hexadecimal Representation of Four Bits

| One hexadecimal digit | Four binary digits (bits) |
|---|---|
| 0 | 0000 |
| 1 | 0001 |
| 2 | 0010 |
| 3 | 0011 |

| One hexadecimal digit | Four binary digits (bits) |
|---|---|
| 4 | 0100 |
| 5 | 0101 |
| 6 | 0110 |
| 7 | 0111 |
| 8 | 1000 |
| 9 | 1001 |
| a | 1010 |
| b | 1011 |
| c | 1100 |
| d | 1101 |
| e | 1110 |
| f | 1111 |

Using hexadecimal, we can write 1101, or "on, on, off, on," with a single digit: $d_{16} = 1101_2$.

**NOTE** *When it isn't clear from the context, I will indicate the base of a number in this text with a subscript. For example, $100_{10}$ is in decimal, $100_{16}$ is in hexadecimal, and $100_2$ is in binary.*

The *octal* system, based on the number eight, is less common, but you will encounter it occasionally. The eight octal digits span from 0 to 7, and each one represents a group of three bits. Table 2-2 shows the correspondence between each possible group of three bits and its corresponding one octal digit. If we want, for example, to briefly represent the first three bits in the example we've been using, then we can simply use $6_8$, which is equivalent to $110_2$.

**Table 2-2:** Octal Representation of Three Bits

| One octal digit | Three binary digits (bits) |
|---|---|
| 0 | 000 |
| 1 | 001 |
| 2 | 010 |
| 3 | 011 |
| 4 | 100 |
| 5 | 101 |
| 6 | 110 |
| 7 | 111 |

## Using Hexadecimal Digits

Hexadecimal digits are especially convenient when we need to specify the state of a group of, say, 16 or 32 switches. In place of each group of four bits, we can write one hexadecimal digit. Here are two examples:

$$6c2a_{16} = 0110110000101010_2$$

and

$$0123abcd_{16} = 00000001001000111010101111001101_2$$

A single bit isn't usually useful for storing data. The smallest number of bits that can be accessed at a time in a computer is defined as a *byte*. In most modern computers, a byte consists of eight bits, but there are exceptions to the eight-bit byte. For example, the CDC 6000 series of scientific mainframe computers used a six-bit byte.

In the C and C++ programming languages, prefixing a number with 0x—that's a zero and a lowercase *x*—specifies that the number is expressed in hexadecimal, and prefixing a number with only a 0 specifies octal. C++ allows us to specify a value in binary by prefixing the number with 0b. Although the 0b notation for specifying binary is not part of standard C, our compiler, gcc, allows it. Thus, when writing C or C++ code in this book, these all mean the same thing:

```
100 = 0x64 = 0144 = 0b01100100
```

But if you're using another C compiler, you may not be able to use the 0b syntax to specify binary.

---

**YOUR TURN**

1. Express the following bit patterns in hexadecimal:

   a. 0100 0101 0110 0111

   b. 1000 1001 1010 1011

   c. 1111 1110 1101 1100

   d. 0000 0010 0101 0010

2. Express the following hexadecimal patterns in binary:

   a. 83af

   b. 9001

   c. aaaa

   d. 5555

---

3. How many bits are represented by each of the following?

    a. ffffffff
    b. 7fff58b7def0
    c. $1111_2$
    d. $1111_{16}$

4. How many hexadecimal digits are required to represent each of the following?

    a. 8 bits
    b. 32 bits
    c. 64 bits
    d. 10 bits
    e. 20 bits
    f. 7 bits

# The Mathematical Equivalence of Binary and Decimal

In the previous section, you saw that binary digits are a natural way to show the states of switches within the computer. You also saw that we can use hexadecimal to show the state of four switches with a single character. In this section, I'll go through some of the mathematical properties of the *binary number system* and show how it translates to and from the more familiar *decimal* (base 10) *number system*.

## Getting to Know Positional Notation

By convention, we use a *positional notation* when writing numbers. This means that the value of a symbol depends on its position within a group of symbols. In the familiar decimal number system, we use the symbols 0, 1, …, 9 to represent numbers.

In the number 50, the value of the symbol 5 is 50 because it's in the *tens position*, where any number in that position is multiplied by 10. In the number 500, the value of the symbol 5 is 500 because it's in the *hundreds position*. The symbol 5 is the same in any position, but its *value* depends on the position it occupies within the number.

Taking this a bit further, in the decimal number system, the integer 123 is taken to mean

$$1 \times 100 + 2 \times 10 + 3$$

or

$$1 \times 10^2 + 2 \times 10^1 + 3 \times 10^0$$

In this example, the rightmost digit, 3, is the *least significant digit* because its value contributes the least to the number's total value. The leftmost digit, 1, is the *most significant digit* because it contributes the most value.

---

**ANOTHER NUMBER SYSTEM**

Before positional notations were invented, people used counting systems to keep track of numerical quantities. The *Roman numeral* system is a well-known example of a counting system. It uses the symbols I for 1, V for 5, X for 10, L for 50, and so on. To represent the value 2, you simply use two Is: II. The value 20 is written as XX.

The two main rules of the Roman numeral system are that symbols that represent larger values come first, and if a symbol representing a smaller value is placed before a larger one, then the value of the smaller one is subtracted from the immediately following larger one. For example, IV represents 4 because I (1) is less than V (5), so it is subtracted from the value represented by V.

There is no symbol for 0 in the Roman numeral system because it isn't needed in counting systems. In a positional system, we need a symbol to mark the fact that there is no value in that position, but the position still counts toward the value being represented. For example, the zeros in 500 tell us that there are no values in the tens position or in the ones position. There is just a value of 5 in the hundreds place.

The invention of positional notations greatly simplified arithmetic and led to the mathematics we know today. If you need to convince yourself, divide 60 (LX) by 3 (III) in the Roman numeral system. (Answer: XX.)

---

The *base*, or *radix*, of the decimal number system—the number of unique digits—is 10. This means there are 10 symbols for representing the digits 0 through 9. Moving a digit one place to the left increases its value by a factor of 10. Moving it one place to the right decreases its value by a factor of 10. The positional notation generalizes to any radix $r$ like so:

$$d_{n-1} \times r^{n-1} + d_{n-2} \times r^{n-2} + \ldots + d_1 \times r^1 + d_0 \times r^0$$

where there are $n$ digits in the number, and each $d_i$ is a single digit with $0 \leq d_i < r$.

This expression tells us how to determine the value of each digit in the number. We determine the position of each digit in the number by counting from the right, starting with zero. At each position, we raise the radix, $r$, to the power of its position and then multiply that number by the value of the digit. Adding all the results gives us the value represented by the number.

The radix in the binary number system is 2, so there are only two symbols for representing the digits; this means that $d_i = 0, 1$, and we can write this expression as follows:

$$d_{n-1} \times 2^{n-1} + d_{n-2} \times 2^{n-2} + \ldots + d_1 \times 2^1 + d_0 \times 2^0$$

where there are $n$ digits in the number, and each $d_i = 0$ or $1$.

In the next section, we'll convert binary numbers to and from unsigned decimals. *Signed* numbers can be either positive or negative, but *unsigned* numbers have no sign. We'll discuss signed numbers in Chapter 3.

## Converting Binary to Unsigned Decimal

You can easily convert from binary to decimal by computing the value of 2 raised to the power of the position it is in and then multiplying that by the value of the bit in that position. Here's an example:

$$
\begin{aligned}
10010101_2 &= 1 \times 2^7 + 0 \times 2^6 + 0 \times 2^5 + 1 \times 2^4 + 0 \times 2^3 + 1 \times 2^2 + 0 \times 2^1 + 1 \times 2^0 \\
&= 128 + 16 + 4 + 1 \\
&= 149_{10}
\end{aligned}
$$

The following algorithm summarizes the procedure for converting binary to decimal:

```
Let result = 0
❶ Repeat for each i = 0,...,(n - 1)
    add ❷d_i x ❸2^i to result
```

At each bit position ❶, this algorithm computes the power of 2 ❸ and then multiplies by the respective bit value, either 0 or 1 ❷.

**NOTE**   *Although we're considering only integers at this point, this algorithm does generalize to fractional values. Simply continue the exponents of the radix, r, on to negative values, that is, $r^{n-1}, r^{n-2}, \ldots, r^1, r^0, r^{-1}, r^{-2}, \ldots$. This will be covered in detail in Chapter 19.*

**YOUR TURN**

1.  Looking at the generalized equation in this section, what are the values of r, n, and each $d_i$ for the decimal number 29458254 and the hexadecimal number 29458254?

2.  Convert the following 8-bit binary numbers to decimal:
    a.   1010 1010
    b.   0101 0101
    c.   1111 0000

*(continued)*

    d.   0000 1111
    e.   1000 0000
    f.   0110 0011
    g.   0111 1011
    h.   1111 1111

3.  Convert the following 16-bit binary numbers to decimal:

    a.   1010 1011 1100 1101
    b.   0001 0011 0011 0100
    c.   1111 1110 1101 1100
    d.   0000 0111 1101 1111
    e.   1000 0000 0000 0000
    f.   0000 0100 0000 0000
    g.   0111 1011 1010 1010
    h.   0011 0000 0011 1001

4.  Develop an algorithm to convert hexadecimal to decimal and then convert the following 16-bit numbers to decimal:

    a.   a000
    b.   ffff
    c.   0400
    d.   1111
    e.   8888
    f.   0190
    g.   abcd
    h.   5555

## Converting Unsigned Decimal to Binary

If we want to convert an unsigned decimal integer, $N$, to binary, we set it equal to the previous expression for binary numbers to give this equation:

$$N = d_{n-1} \times 2^{n-1} + d_{n-2} \times 2^{n-2} + \ldots + d_1 \times 2^1 + d_0 \times 2^0$$

where each $d_i = 0$ or 1. We divide both sides of this equation by 2, and the exponent of each 2 term on the right side decreases by 1, giving the following:

$$N_1 + \frac{r_0}{2} = (d_{n-1} \times 2^{n-2} \times d_{n-2} \times 2^{n-3} + \ldots + d_1 \times 2^0) + d_0 \times 2^{-1}$$

where $N_1$ is the integer part, and the remainder, $r_0$, is 0 for even numbers and 1 for odd numbers. Doing a little rewriting, we have the equivalent equation:

$$N_1 + \frac{r_0}{2} = (d_{n-1} \times 2^{n-2} + d_{n-2} \times 2^{n-3} + \cdots + d_1 \times 2^0) + \frac{d_0}{2}$$

All the terms within the parentheses on the right side are integers. The integer part of both sides of an equation must be equal, and the fractional parts must also be equal. That is:

$$N_1 = d_{n-1} \times 2^{n-2} + d_{n-2} \times 2^{n-3} + \dots + d_1 \times 2^0$$

and

$$\frac{r_0}{2} = \frac{d_0}{2}$$

Thus, we see that $d_0 = r_0$. Subtracting $r_0/2$ (which equals $d_0/2$) from both sides of our expanded equation gives this:

$$N_1 = d_{n-1} \times 2^{n-2} + d_{n-2} \times 2^{n-3} + \dots + d_1 \times 2^0$$

Again, we divide both sides by 2:

$$N_2 + \frac{r_1}{2} = d_{n-1} \times 2^{n-3} + d_{n-2} \times 2^{n-4} + \dots + d_2 \times 2^0 + d_1 \times 2^{-1}$$
$$= (d_{n-1} \times 2^{n-3} + d_{n-2} \times 2^{n-4} + \dots + d_2 \times 2^0) + \frac{d_1}{2}$$

Using the same reasoning as earlier, $d_1 = r_1$. We can produce the binary representation of a number by working from right to left, repeatedly dividing by 2, and using the remainder as the value of the respective bit. This is summarized in the following algorithm, where the forward slash (/) is the integer division operator and the percent sign (%) is the modulo operator:

```
quotient = N
i = 0
d_i = quotient % 2
quotient = quotient / 2
While quotient != 0
    i = i + 1
    d_i = quotient % 2
    quotient = quotient / 2
```

Some programming tasks require a specific bit pattern, for example, programming a hardware device. In these cases, specifying a bit pattern—rather than a numerical value—is more natural. We can think of the bits in groups of four and use hexadecimal to specify each group. For example, if our algorithm required the use of zeros alternating with ones, 0101 0101 0101 0101 0101 0101 0101 0101, we could convert this to the decimal value 431655765, or we could express it in hexadecimal as 0x55555555 (shown here in C/C++ syntax). Once you've memorized Table 2-1, you'll find that it's much easier to work with hexadecimal for bit patterns.

The discussion in these two sections has dealt only with unsigned integers. The representation of signed integers depends upon some architectural features of the CPU that we'll discuss in Chapter 3.

## Storing Data in Memory

We now have the language necessary to begin discussing how data is stored in computer memory. You'll first learn how memory is organized. There are two general kinds of memory used for storing program instructions and data in a computer:

*Random access memory* (*RAM*)

Once a bit (switch) is set to either 0 or 1, it stays in that state until the control unit actively changes it or the power is turned off. The control unit can both read the state of a bit and change it.

The name *random access memory* is misleading. Here *random access* means that it takes the same amount of time to access any byte in the memory, not that any randomness is involved when reading the byte. We contrast

RAM with *sequential access memory (SAM)*, where the amount of time it takes to access a byte depends on its position in some sequence. You can think of SAM like tape: the length of time it takes to access a byte depends on the physical location of the byte with respect to the current position of the tape.

*Read-only memory (ROM)*

ROM is also called *nonvolatile memory (NVM)*. The control unit can read the state of each bit but can't change it. You can reprogram some types of ROM with specialized hardware, but the bits remain in the new state when the power is turned off.

## Expressing Memory Addresses

Each byte in memory has a location, or address, much like the room number in an office building. The address of a specific byte never changes. That is, the 957th byte from the beginning of memory will always remain the 957th byte. However, the state (content) of each of the bits—either 0 or 1—in any given byte can be changed.

Computer scientists typically express the address of each byte in memory in hexadecimal, starting the numbering at zero. Thus, we would say that the 957th byte is at address 0x3bc (= 956 in decimal).

The first 16 bytes in memory have the addresses 0, 1, 2, 3, 4, 5, 6, 7, 8, 9, a, b, c, d, e, and f. Using the notation

---

<address>: <content>

---

we can show the content of each of the first 16 bytes of memory like in Table 2-3 (the contents here are arbitrary).

**Table 2-3:** Arbitrary Contents of the First 16 Bytes of Memory

| Address | Content | Address | Content |
|---|---|---|---|
| 0x00000000: | 0x6a | 0x00000008: | 0xf0 |
| 0x00000001: | 0xf0 | 0x00000009: | 0x02 |
| 0x00000002: | 0x5e | 0x0000000a: | 0x33 |
| 0x00000003: | 0x00 | 0x0000000b: | 0x3c |
| 0x00000004: | 0xff | 0x0000000c: | 0xc3 |
| 0x00000005: | 0x51 | 0x0000000d: | 0x3c |
| 0x00000006: | 0xcf | 0x0000000e: | 0x55 |
| 0x00000007: | 0x18 | 0x0000000f: | 0xaa |

The content of each byte is represented by two hexadecimal digits, which specify the exact state of the byte's eight bits.

But what can the state of the byte's eight bits tell us? There are two issues that a programmer needs to consider when storing data in memory:

**How many bits are needed to store the data?**    To answer this question, we need to know how many different values are allowed for the particular data item. Look at the number of different values we can represent in Table 2-1 (four bits) and Table 2-2 (three bits). We can see that we can represent up to $2^n$ different values in $n$ bits. Notice, too, that we might not use all the possible bit patterns we have within an allocated space.

**What is the code for storing the data?**    Most of the data we deal with in everyday life is not expressed in terms of zeros and ones. To store it in computer memory, the programmer must decide how to encode the data in zeros and ones.

In the remaining part of this chapter, we'll see how we can store characters and unsigned integers in memory by using the state of the bits in one or more bytes.

## Characters

When you're programming, you will almost always be manipulating text strings, which are arrays of characters. The first program you ever wrote was probably a "Hello, World!" program. If you wrote it in C, you used a statement like this:

```
printf("Hello, World!\n");
```

or like this in C++:

```
cout << "Hello, World!" << endl;
```

When translating either of these statements into machine code, the compiler must do two things:

- Store each of the characters in a location in memory where the control unit can access them
- Generate the machine instructions to write the characters on the screen

We'll start by considering how a single character is stored in memory.

### Character Encoding

The most common standard for encoding characters for computer storage is *Unicode UTF-8*. It uses from one to four bytes for storing a number called a *code point*, which represents a character. A Unicode code point is written as U+$h$, where $h$ is four to six hexadecimal digits. The operating system and display hardware associate one or more code points with a *glyph*, which is what we see on the screen or on paper. For example, U+0041 is the code point for the Latin capital letter $A$, which has the glyph A in the font used for this book.

UTF-8 is backward compatible with an older standard, the *American Standard Code for Information Interchange* (*ASCII*—pronounced "ask-ee"). ASCII uses seven bits to specify each code point in a 128-character set, which contains the English alphabet (uppercase and lowercase), numerals, special characters, and control characters. In this book, we will use only the characters from the ASCII subset of UTF-8, U+0000 to U+007F, in all our programming.

Table 2-4 shows the Unicode code points for the characters used to represent hexadecimal numbers and the corresponding 8-bit patterns that are stored in memory in our programming environment. You'll have a chance to use this table later in the book, when you learn how to convert from the character representation of an integer to its binary representation. For now, notice that while the numeric characters are organized in a contiguous bit pattern sequence, there is a gap between them and the alphabetic characters.

**Table 2-4:** UTF-8 for the Hexadecimal Characters

| Code point | Character description | Character glyph | Bit pattern |
|------------|----------------------|-----------------|-------------|
| U+0030 | Digit zero | 0 | 0x30 |
| U+0031 | Digit one | 1 | 0x31 |
| U+0032 | Digit two | 2 | 0x32 |
| U+0033 | Digit three | 3 | 0x33 |
| U+0034 | Digit four | 4 | 0x34 |
| U+0035 | Digit five | 5 | 0x35 |
| U+0036 | Digit six | 6 | 0x36 |
| U+0037 | Digit seven | 7 | 0x37 |
| U+0038 | Digit eight | 8 | 0x38 |
| U+0039 | Digit nine | 9 | 0x39 |
| U+0061 | Latin small letter a | a | 0x61 |
| U+0062 | Latin small letter b | b | 0x62 |
| U+0063 | Latin small letter c | c | 0x63 |
| U+0064 | Latin small letter d | d | 0x64 |
| U+0065 | Latin small letter e | e | 0x65 |
| U+0066 | Latin small letter f | f | 0x66 |

Although the hexadecimal numerical portion is the same as the bit pattern for the code points U+0000 to U+007F, this does not necessarily hold true for other characters. For example, U+00B5 is the code point for the micro sign, which is stored in memory as the 16-bit pattern 0xc2b5 and has the glyph μ in the font used for this book.

UTF-8 uses one byte per character to store code points U+0000 to U+007F. Bits 6 and 5 in the byte (recall that bits are numbered from right to left, starting with 0) specify the four groups of characters, shown in

Table 2-5. The special characters are mostly punctuation. For example, the space character is U+0020, and the ; character is U+003B.

**Table 2-5:** Character Groups in Code Points U+0000 to U+007F

| Bit 6 | Bit 5 | Type of character |
|-------|-------|-------------------|
| 0 | 0 | Control |
| 0 | 1 | Numeric and special |
| 1 | 0 | Uppercase alphabetic and special |
| 1 | 1 | Lowercase alphabetic and special |

You can generate a table of the code points that coincide with ASCII characters by typing the command `man ascii` in a Linux terminal window. (You may need to install the ascii program on your computer.) It is quite large and not the sort of thing that you would want to memorize, but it can be helpful to understand roughly how it's organized.

You can learn more about Unicode at *https://www.unicode.org/releases/*. For a more informal discussion of how Unicode came to be, I recommend "The Absolute Minimum Every Software Developer Absolutely, Positively Must Know About Unicode and Character Sets (No Excuses!)" at *https://www.joelonsoftware.com/*.

---

**YOUR TURN**

1. Many people use uppercase for the alphabetic hexadecimal characters. Every programming language I know about accepts either case. Redo Table 2-4, showing the bit patterns for the uppercase hexadecimal characters.

2. Create an ASCII table for the lowercase alphabetic characters.

3. Create an ASCII table for the uppercase alphabetic characters.

4. Create an ASCII table for the punctuation marks.

---

## Storing a Text String

Getting back to Hello, World!\n, the compiler stores this text string as a constant array of characters. To specify the extent of this array, a *C-style string* uses the code point U+0000 (ASCII NUL) at the end of the string as a *sentinel* value, a unique value that indicates the end of a sequence of characters. Thus, the compiler must allocate 13 bytes for this string: 11 for Hello, World!,

1 for the newline \n, and 1 for the NUL. For example, Table 2-6 shows how this text string would be stored starting at location 0x4004a1 in memory.

**Table 2-6:** "Hello, World!" Stored in Memory

| Address | Content | Address | Content |
|---|---|---|---|
| 0x4004a1: | 0x48 | 0x4004a9: | 0x6f |
| 0x4004a2: | 0x65 | 0x4004aa: | 0x72 |
| 0x4004a3: | 0x6c | 0x4004ab: | 0x6c |
| 0x4004a4: | 0x6c | 0x4004ac: | 0x64 |
| 0x4004a5: | 0x6f | 0x4004ad: | 0x21 |
| 0x4004a6: | 0x2c | 0x4004ae: | 0x0a |
| 0x4004a7: | 0x20 | 0x4004af: | 0x00 |

C uses U+000A (ASCII LF) as a single newline character (at address 0x4004ae in this example) even though the C syntax requires that the programmer write two characters, \n. The text string ends with the NUL character at 0x4004af.

In Pascal (another programming language), the length of the string is specified by the first byte in the string, which is taken to be an eight-bit unsigned integer. (This is the reason for the 256-character limit on text strings in Pascal.) The C++ string class has additional features, but the actual text string is stored as a C-style text string within the C++ string instance.

## Unsigned Integers

Since an unsigned integer can be expressed in any radix, probably the most obvious way to store it is to use the binary number system. If we number the bits in a byte from right to left, then the lowest-order bit would be stored in bit 0, the next in bit 1, and so forth. For example, the integer $123_{10} = 7b_{16}$, so the state of the byte where it is stored would be $01111011_2$.

Using only one byte restricts the range of unsigned integers to be from 0 to $255_{10}$, since $ff_{16} = 255_{10}$. The default size for an unsigned integer in our programming environment is four bytes, which allows for a range of 0 to $4,294,967,295_{10}$.

One limitation of using the binary number system is that you need to convert a decimal number from a character string to the binary number system before performing arithmetic operations on it. For example, the decimal number 123 would be stored in character string format as the four bytes 0x31, 0x32, 0x33, and 0x00, while in unsigned integer format it would be stored as the four-byte binary number 0x0000007b. On the other end, binary numbers need to be converted to their decimal character representations for most real-world display purposes.

*Binary Coded Decimal (BCD)* is another code for storing integers. It uses four bits for each decimal digit, as shown in Table 2-7.

**Table 2-7:** Binary Coded Decimal

| Decimal digit | BCD code |
|---|---|
| 0 | 0000 |
| 1 | 0001 |
| 2 | 0010 |
| 3 | 0011 |
| 4 | 0100 |
| 5 | 0101 |
| 6 | 0110 |
| 7 | 0111 |
| 8 | 1000 |
| 9 | 1001 |

For example, in a 16-bit storage location, the decimal number 1234 would be stored in BCD as 0001 0010 0011 0100 (in the binary number system, it would be 0000 0100 1101 0010).

With only 10 of the possible 16 combinations being used, we can see that six bit patterns are wasted. This means that a 16-bit storage location has a range of 0 to 9,999 for values if we use BCD, compared to a range of 0 to 65,535 if we use binary, so this is a less efficient use of memory. On the other hand, the conversions between a character format and an integer format are simpler with BCD, as you will see in Chapter 16.

BCD is important in specialized systems that deal primarily with numerical business data, because they tend to print numbers more often than perform mathematical operations on them. COBOL, a programming language intended for business applications, supports a packed BCD format where two digits (in BCD code) are stored in each eight-bit byte. Here, the *last* (four-bit) digit is used to store the sign of the number, as shown in Table 2-8. The specific codes used depend upon the implementation.

**Table 2-8:** Example Sign Codes for COBOL Packed BCD Format

| Sign | Sign code |
|---|---|
| + | 1010 |
| − | 1011 |
| + | 1100 |
| − | 1101 |
| + | 1110 |
| unsigned | 1111 |

For example, 0001 0010 0011 1010 represents +123, 0001 0010 0011 1011 represents –123, and 0001 0010 0011 1111 represents 123.

Next, we'll explore some of these concepts using the C programming language. If you're new to C, this discussion will provide an introduction to the language.

# Exploring Data Formats with C

In this section, we'll write our first programs with the C programming language. These particular programs illustrate the differences between how numbers are stored in memory and how we humans read them. C allows us to get close enough to the hardware to understand the core concepts, while taking care of many of the low-level details. You shouldn't find the simple C programs used in this book too difficult, especially if you already know how to program in another language.

If you learned how to program in a higher-level language, like C++, Java, or Python, chances are that you learned object-oriented programming. C doesn't support the object-oriented paradigm. C is a *procedural programming language*. C programs are divided into functions. A *function* is a named group of programming statements. Other programming languages also use the terms *procedure* and *subprogram*, with some minor distinctions between them, depending on the language.

## C and C++ I/O Libraries

Most high-level programming languages include a standard library that can be thought of as part of the language. A standard library contains functions and data structures that can be used in the language for doing common things like terminal I/O—writing to the screen and reading from the keyboard. C includes the *C standard library*, and C++ includes the *C++ standard library*.

C programmers use functions in the stdio library, and C++ programmers use functions in the iostream library for terminal I/O. For example, the C code sequence for reading an integer from the keyboard, adding 100 to it, and writing the result to the screen looks like this:

```
int x;
scanf("%i", &x);
x += 100;
printf("%i", x);
```

The C++ code sequence looks something like this:

```
int x;
cin >> x;
x +=100;
cout << x;
```

In both examples, the code reads characters, each as a separate char from the keyboard, and converts the char sequence into the corresponding int format. Then it adds 100 to the int. Finally, the code converts the resulting int into a char sequence and displays it on the screen. The C or C++ I/O library functions in the previous code do the necessary conversions between char sequences and the int storage format.

Figure 2-1 shows the relationship between a C application program, the I/O libraries, and the operating system.

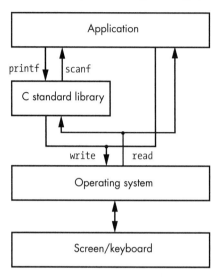

Figure 2-1: Relationship of I/O libraries to application and operating system

When reading from the keyboard, the scanf library function first calls the read *system call* function, a function in the operating system, to read characters from the keyboard. The input on the keyboard is in the form of a string of characters, each in the char data type. The scanf library function performs the conversion of this string to the int data type for the application program. The printf library function converts from the int data type to the corresponding string of characters in the char data type and calls the write system call function to write each character to the screen.

As you can see in Figure 2-1, an application program can call the read and write functions directly to transfer characters. We'll be exploring this in Chapter 16, where we'll be writing our own conversion functions. Although the C/C++ library functions do a much better job of this, the exercise of doing it yourself will give you a better understanding of how data is stored in memory and manipulated by software.

**NOTE**    *If you are not familiar with the GNU make program, I urge you to learn how to use it to build your programs. It may seem like overkill at this point, but it's much easier to learn with simple programs. The manual is available in several formats at* https://www.gnu.org/software/make/manual/, *and I have some comments about using it on my website,* https://rgplantz.github.io/.

## Writing and Executing Your First C Program

Most programming books start with a simple program that just prints "Hello, world" to a computer screen, but we'll start with a program that reads a hexadecimal value, both as an unsigned integer and as a text string (see Listing 2-1).

```
❶ /* intAndString.c
   * Read and display an integer and a text string.
   */

❷ #include <stdio.h>

❸ int main(void)
   {
❹ unsigned int anInt;
     char aString[10];

❺ printf("Enter a number in hexadecimal: ");
❻ scanf("%x", &anInt);
     printf("Enter it again: ");
❼ scanf("%s", aString);
❽ printf("The integer is %u and the string is %s\n", anInt, aString);

❾ return 0;
   }
```

Listing 2-1: Program showing the difference between an integer and a text string

We start our code with some documentation that gives the name of the file ❶ and a brief description of what the program does. When writing your own source files, you should also include your name and the date it was written as part of the documentation (I've omitted them in the example programs in this book to save paper). Everything between the /* and */ is a *comment*. It is there for the human reader and has no effect on the program itself.

The first operation that actually affects the program is the inclusion of another file ❷, the *stdio.h header file*. As you will learn, the C compiler needs to know the type of each data item that is passed to or from a function. A header file is used to provide a *prototype statement* for each function, which specifies these data types. The *stdio.h* header file defines the interface to many of the functions in the C standard library, which allows the compiler to know what to do when calls to any of these functions are encountered in our source code. The *stdio.h* header file is already installed on your computer in a location that the compiler knows.

Next you see the definition of a C main function ❸. All C programs are made up of functions, which have this general format:

```
return_data_type function_name(parameter_list)
{
    function_body
}
```

When a C program is executed, the operating system first sets up a *C runtime environment*, which sets up the resources on your computer to run the program. The C runtime environment then calls the main function, meaning that the program you write must include a function whose *function_name* is main. The main function can call other functions, which in turn can call other functions. But program control normally ends up back in the main function, which then returns to the C runtime environment.

When a function is called in C, the calling function can include a list of *arguments* in the call as inputs to the called function. These inputs serve as *parameters* in the computation performed by the called function. For example, in Listing 2-1, when the program first starts, the main function calls the printf function with one argument, a text string ❺. The printf function uses the text string to determine what to display on the screen. We'll look closely at how arguments get passed to functions, and how they're used as parameters in the function, in Chapter 14. The main function in Listing 2-1 does not need any data from the C runtime environment, which we show in its definition by using void for the *parameter_list*.

Upon completing execution, a function normally returns to the calling function. The called function can pass a data item to the calling function when returning. A main function should return a single integer to the C runtime environment indicating whether the program detected any errors in its execution. Thus, the *return_data_type* for main is int. The main function in Listing 2-1 returns the integer 0 to the C runtime environment ❾, which passes this value to the operating system. The value 0 tells the operating system that everything went smoothly.

In Listing 2-1, we define two variables in the main function at the beginning of the *function_body* ❹, an unsigned integer named anInt and a text string named aString. Most modern programming languages allow us to introduce new variables anywhere in the code, but C requires that they be listed at the beginning of the function. (This rule has some exceptions, but they are beyond the scope of this book.) Think of it as listing the ingredients for a cooking recipe before giving the instructions on how to use them. We *define* a variable by introducing its name and specifying its data type. The [10] notation tells the compiler to allocate an array of 10 chars for the aString variable, which will allow us to store a C-style text string up to 9 characters long. (The 10th char would be the terminating NUL character.) We'll look at arrays in detail in Chapter 17.

The program uses the printf function from the C standard library to display text on the screen. The first argument in the call to printf is a *format string*, which is a text string made up of ordinary characters (except %) to display on the screen.

The simplest format string for printf is just the text that you want printed without any variables to print ❺. If you want to print the values of variables, the format string acts as a template of the text that you want to be printed. The place in the text string where you want the value of a variable to be printed is marked with a *conversion specifier*. Each conversion specifier begins with the % character ❽. The names of the variables are listed after the format string in the same order that their respective conversion specifier appears in the template.

The % character that begins a conversion specifier is immediately followed by one or more conversion code characters to tell printf how to display the value of the variable. Table 2-9 shows some common conversion specifiers.

**Table 2-9:** Common Conversion Specifiers for printf and scanf Format String

| Conversion specifier | Representation |
| --- | --- |
| %u | Unsigned decimal integer |
| %d or %i | Signed decimal integer |
| %f | Float |
| %x | Hexadecimal |
| %s | Text string |

The conversion specifiers can include other characters that specify properties like the field width of the display, whether the value is left or right justified within the field, and more. We won't go into detail here. You can read man page 3 for printf to learn more (do this by typing **man 3 printf** into your shell).

The first argument in the call to the C standard library function, scanf, is also a format string. We use the same conversion specifiers in the format string to tell the scanf function how to interpret the characters typed on the keyboard ❻. We need to tell scanf where to store the input integer by using the *address of* operator on the variable name, &anInt. When passing the name of an array to a function, C sends the address of the array, so we don't use the & operator when calling scanf to read a text string from the keyboard ❼.

Any other character included in the format string for scanf besides these conversion specifiers must be matched exactly by the keyboard input. For example,

```
scanf("1 %i and 2 %i", &oneInt, &twoInt);
```

requires in input like

```
1 123 and 2 456
```

which would read the integers 123 and 456 from the keyboard. You can read man page 3 for scanf to learn more (do this by typing **man 3 scanf** into your shell).

Finally, the main function returns 0 to the C runtime environment ❾, which passes this value to the operating system. The value 0 tells the operating system that everything went smoothly.

Compiling and running the program in Listing 2-1 on my computer gave the following output:

```
$ gcc -Wall -masm=intel -o intAndString intAndString.c
$ ./intAndString
Enter a hexadecimal value: 123abc
Enter it again: 123abc
The integer is 1194684 and the string is 123abc
$
```

The program in Listing 2-1 demonstrates an important concept—hexadecimal is used as a human convenience for stating bit patterns. A number is not inherently binary, decimal, or hexadecimal. It's simply a value. And a specific value can be expressed equivalently in each of these three number bases. For that matter, it can be expressed equivalently in *any* number base (2, 16, 285). But since a computer consists of binary switches, it makes sense to think of numerical values stored in a computer in terms of the binary number base.

---

**YOUR TURN**

1.  Write a hexadecimal-to-decimal converter program in C. Your program will allow a user to enter a number in hexadecimal and print the decimal equivalent. The output should look like this: 0x7b = 123.

2.  Write a decimal-to-hexadecimal converter program in C. Your program will allow a user to enter a number in decimal and print the hexadecimal equivalent. The output should look like this: 123 = 0x7b.

3.  Change %u to %i in the last printf statement in the program in Listing 2-1. What does the program print if you enter ffffffff?

---

# Examining Memory with a Debugger

Now that we've started writing programs, you'll need to learn how to use the GNU debugger, gdb. A *debugger* is a program that allows you to run your program while you observe and control its behavior. When you use a debugger, it's a little like you're a puppeteer, and your program is a carefully controlled puppet. Your main instrument of control is the *breakpoint*; when you set a breakpoint and your program reaches it while running, the program will pause and return control to the debugger program. When control is with the debugger, you can look at the values stored in your program's variables, which can help you figure out where any bugs are.

If all this seems premature—our programs so far are simple and don't seem to require debugging—I promise that it's much better to learn how to use a debugger on a simple example than on a complicated program that does not work.

gdb is also a valuable tool for learning the material in this book, even when you write bug-free programs. For example, in the following gdb session dialog, I'll show you how to determine where a variable is stored in memory and how to see what is stored there, both in decimal and in hexadecimal. You will see how to use gdb on a live program to illustrate the concepts discussed on the previous pages.

The gdb commands listed here should be enough to get you started. You'll see more in Chapter 10.

**b** *source_filename:line_number*   Set a breakpoint at the specified *line_number* in the source file, *source_filename*. The code will stop running at the breakpoint, when *line_number* is encountered, and return control to gdb, allowing you to test various elements of the code.

**c**   Continue program execution from the current location.

**h** *command*   Help on how to use *command*.

**i r**   Show the contents of the CPU registers (*info registers*). (You'll learn about CPU registers in Chapter 9.)

**l** *line_number*   List 10 lines of the source code, centered at the specified *line-number*.

**print** *expression*   Evaluate *expression* and print the value.

**printf** *"format", var1, var2, ...*   Display the values of *var1, var2, ...* in a given format. The *"format"* string follows the same rules as printf in the C standard library.

**r**   Begin execution of a program that has been loaded under control of gdb.

**x/***nfs memory_address*   Display (examine) *n* values in memory in format *f* of size *s* starting at *memory_address*.

## Using Your Debugger

Let's walk through the program in Listing 2-1 using gdb to explore some of the concepts covered thus far. I recommend that you get on your computer and follow along as you read this: it's much easier to understand gdb when you're using it. Note that the addresses you see on your computer will probably be different than those in this example.

Start by compiling the program using the gcc command:

```
$ gcc -g -Wall -masm=intel -o intAndString intAndString.c
```

The -g option tells the compiler to include debugger information in the executable program. The -Wall option tells the compiler to issue warnings about things in your code that are correct C code but still might not be what you intended to write. For example, it will warn you about declaring a variable in your function that is never used, which could mean that you have forgotten something.

Later in the book, when we write assembly language, we'll use the syntax specified in the Intel and AMD documentation, and we'll tell the compiler to use the same syntax with the `masm=intel` option. You don't need this option yet, but I recommend getting used to using it since you'll need it later.

The o option specifies the name of the output file, which is the executable program.

Having compiled the program, we can run it under the control of gdb using this command:

```
$ gdb ./intAndString
--snip--
Reading symbols from ./intAndString…
(gdb) l
1        /* intAndString.c
2         * Using printf to display an integer and a text string.
3         */
4
5        #include <stdio.h>
6
7        int main(void)
8        {
9           unsigned int anInt;
10          char aString[10];
(gdb)
11
12          printf("Enter a number in hexadecimal: ");
13          scanf("%x", &anInt);
14          printf("Enter it again: ");
15          scanf("%s", aString);
16
17          printf("The integer is %u and the string is %s\n", anInt, aString);
18
19          return 0;
20       }
(gdb)
```

The gdb startup message, which I've removed from the previous output to save space, contains information about your debugger and refers you to its usage documentation.

The l command lists 10 lines of source code and then returns control to the gdb program, as shown by the (gdb) prompt. Press ENTER to repeat the previous command, and l displays the next (up to) 10 lines.

A *breakpoint* is used to stop the program and return control to the debugger. I like to set breakpoints where a function is about to call another function so I can examine the values in the argument variables before they are passed on to the called function. This `main` function calls `printf` on line 17, so I set a breakpoint there. Since I'm already looking at the source code in the function where I want to set a breakpoint, I don't need to specify the filename:

```
(gdb)b 17
Breakpoint 1 at 0x11f6: file intAndString.c, line 17.
```

If gdb ever gets to this statement while executing the program, it will pause *before the statement is executed* and return control to the debugger.

Having set my breakpoint, I run the program:

```
(gdb) r
Starting program: /home/bob/progs/chapter_02/intAndString/intAndString
Enter a hexadecimal value: 123abc
Enter it again: 123abc

Breakpoint 1, main () at intAndString.c:17
❶ 17          printf("The integer is %u and the string is %s\n", anInt, aString);
```

The r command starts executing the program from the beginning.
When the program reaches our breakpoint, control returns to gdb, which
displays the next program statement that is ready to be executed ❶. Before
continuing execution, I'll display the content of the two variables that are
being passed to the printf function:

```
(gdb) print anInt
$1 = 1194684
(gdb) print aString
$2 = "123abc\000\177\000>
```

We can use the print command to display the value currently stored in
a variable. gdb knows the data type of each variable from the source code.
It displays int variables in decimal. When displaying char variables, gdb will
do its best to display the character glyph corresponding to the code point
value. When there is no corresponding character glyph, gdb shows the code
point as a \ followed by three *octal* digits. (Refer to Table 2-2.) For example,
there is no character glyph for NUL, so gdb shows \000 at the end of the text
string we entered.

The printf command can format the displayed values. The formatting
string is the same as for the printf function in the C standard library:

```
(gdb) printf "anInt = %u = %#x\n", anInt, anInt
anInt = 1194684 = 0x123abc
(gdb) printf "aString = 0x%s\n", aString
aString = 0x123abc
```

gdb provides another command for examining the content of memory
directly—that is, for examining the actual bit patterns—x. Its help message
is brief, but it tells you everything you need to know:

```
(gdb) h x
Examine memory: x/FMT ADDRESS.
ADDRESS is an expression for the memory address to examine.
FMT is a repeat count followed by a format letter and a size letter.
Format letters are o(octal), x(hex), d(decimal), u(unsigned decimal),
 t(binary), f(float), a(address), i(instruction), c(char) and s(string).
Size letters are b(byte), h(halfword), w(word), g(giant, 8 bytes).
The specified number of objects of the specified size are printed
according to the format.
```

```
Defaults for format and size letters are those previously used.
Default count is 1.  Default address is following last thing printed
with this command or "print".
```

The x command needs the address of the area of memory to show. We can use the print command to find the address of a variable:

```
(gdb) print &anInt
$3 = (unsigned int *) 0x7fffffffde88
```

We'll use the x command to display the content of anInt three different ways: one decimal word (1dw), one hexadecimal word (1xw), and four hexadecimal bytes (4xb).

```
(gdb) x/1dw 0x7fffffffde88
0x7fffffffde88: 1194684
(gdb) x/1xw 0x7fffffffde88
0x7fffffffde88: 0x00123abc
(gdb) x/4xb 0x7fffffffde88
0x7fffffffde88: ❶0xbc    0x3a      0x12      0x00
```

*The size of a* word *depends upon the computer environment you are using. In our environment, it's four bytes.*

The display of the four bytes may look out of order to you. The first byte ❶ is located at the address shown on the left of the row. The next byte in the row is at the subsequent address, 0x7fffffffde89. So, this row displays each of the bytes stored at the four memory addresses 0x7fffffffde88, 0x7fffffffde89, 0x7fffffffde8a, and 0x7fffffffde8b, reading from left to right, that make up the variable, anInt. When displaying these same four bytes separately, the least significant byte appears *first* in memory. This is called *little-endian* storage order; I'll explain further after this tour of gdb.

Similarly, we'll display the content of the aString variable by first getting its address:

```
(gdb) print &aString
$4 = (char (*)[50]) 0x7fffffffde8e
```

Next, we'll look at the content of aString in two ways: 10 characters (10c) and 10 hexadecimal bytes (10xb):

```
(gdb) x/10c 0x7fffffffde8e
0x7fffffffde8e: 49 '1'   50 '2'   51 '3'   97 'a'   98 'b'   99 'c'   0 '\000'
127 '\177'
0x7fffffffde96: 0 '\000'  0 '\000'
(gdb) x/10xb 0x7fffffffde8e
0x7fffffffde8e: 0x31      0x32      0x33      0x61      0x62      0x63      0x00
0x7f
0x7fffffffde96: 0x00      0x00
```

The character display shows the code point in decimal and the character glyph for each character. The hexadecimal byte display shows only the code point in hexadecimal for each byte. Both displays show the NUL character that marks the end of the six-character string that we entered. Since we asked for a 10-byte display, the remaining 3 bytes have random values not related to our text string, often called *garbage values*.

Finally, I continue execution of the program and quit gdb:

```
(gdb)c
Continuing.
The integer is 1194684 and the string is 123abc
[Inferior 1 (process 3165) exited normally]
(gdb)q
$
```

## Understanding Byte Storage Order in Memory

The difference between the full four-byte display and the single-byte display of the integer value at 0x7fffffffde88 in memory illustrates a concept known as *endianness*, or byte storage order. We usually read numbers from left to right. The digits to the left have more significance (count for more) than the digits to the right.

### Little-Endian

Data is stored in memory with the *least* significant byte in a multiple-byte value in the lowest-numbered address. That is, the "littlest" byte (counts the least) comes first in memory.

When we examine memory one byte at a time, each byte is displayed in numerically ascending addresses:

```
0x7fffffffde88: 0xbc
0x7fffffffde89: 0x3a
0x7fffffffde8a: 0x12
0x7fffffffde8b: 0x00
```

At first glance, the value appears to be stored backward, because the least significant ("little end") byte of the value is stored first in memory. When we command gdb to display the entire four-byte value, it knows that ours is a little-endian environment, and it rearranges the display of the bytes in proper order:

```
7fffffffde88: 000123abc
```

### Big-Endian

Data is stored in memory with the *most* significant byte in a multiple-byte value in the lowest-numbered address. That is, the "biggest" byte (counts the most) comes first in memory.

In big-endian storage, the most significant ("biggest") byte is stored in the first (lowest-numbered) memory address. If we ran the previous program on a big-endian computer, such as one using the PowerPC architecture, we would see the following (assuming the variable is located at the same address):

```
(gdb) x/1xw 0x7fffffffde88
0x7fffffffde88: 0x00123abc
(gdb) x/4xb 0x7fffffffde88          [BIG-ENDIAN COMPUTER, NOT OURS!]
0x7fffffffde88: 0x00     0x12     0x3a     0xbc
```

That is, the four bytes in a big-endian computer would be stored as follows:

```
0x7fffffffde88: 0x00
0x7fffffffde89: 0x12
0x7fffffffde8a: 0x3a
0x7fffffffde8b: 0xbc
```

Again, gdb would know that this is a big-endian computer so would display the full four-byte value in proper order.

In the vast majority of programming situations, endianness is not an issue. However, you need to know about it because it can be confusing when examining memory in the debugger. Endianness is also an issue when different computers are communicating with each other. For example, *Transport Control Protocol/Internet Protocol* (*TCP/IP*) is defined to be big-endian, sometimes called *network byte order*. The x86-64 architecture is little-endian. The operating system reorders the bytes for internet communication. But if you're writing communications software for an operating system itself or for an embedded system that may not have an operating system, you need to know about byte order.

---

**YOUR TURN**

Enter the program in Listing 2-1. Follow through the program with gdb. Using the numbers you get, explain where the variables anInt and aString are stored in memory and what is stored in each location.

---

## What You've Learned

**Bits**   A computer is a collection of on/off switches that we can represent with bits.

**Hexadecimal**   A number system based on 16. Each hexadecimal digit, 0 to f, represents four bits.

**Byte**   A group of eight bits. The bit pattern can be expressed as two hexadecimal digits.

**Converting between decimal and binary**   The two number systems are mathematically equivalent.

**Memory addressing**   Bytes in memory are numbered (addressed) sequentially. The byte's address is usually expressed in hexadecimal.

**Endianness**   An integer that is more than one byte can be stored with the highest-order byte in the lowest byte address (big-endian) or with the lowest-order byte in the lowest byte address (little-endian). The x86-64 architecture is little-endian.

**UTF-8 encoding**   A code for storing characters in memory.

**String**   This C-style string is an array of characters terminated by the NUL character.

**printf**   This C library function is used to write formatted data on the monitor screen.

**scanf**   This C library function is used to read formatted data from the keyboard.

**Debugging**   We used the gdb debugger as a learning tool.

In the next chapter, you'll learn about addition and subtraction in the binary number system, for both unsigned and signed integers. Doing so will illuminate some of the potential errors inherent in using a fixed number of bits to represent numerical values.

# 3

## COMPUTER ARITHMETIC

The reality of computing is that we have a finite number of bits. In the previous chapter, you learned that each data item must fit within a fixed number of bits, depending on its data type. This chapter will show that this limit complicates even our most basic mathematical operations. For both signed and unsigned numbers, a limited number of bits is a constraint we don't normally think about when doing math on paper or in our heads.

Fortunately, the *carry flag* (CF) and *overflow flag* (OF) in the *status flags* portion of the CPU's rflags register allow us to detect when adding and subtracting binary numbers yields results that exceed the allocated number of bits for the data type. We'll take a closer look at the carry flag and the overflow flag in subsequent chapters, but for now, let's take a look at how addition and subtraction affect them.

# Adding and Subtracting Unsigned Integers

When computers do arithmetic, they do it in the binary number system. The operations may seem difficult at first, but if you remember the details of performing decimal arithmetic by hand, binary arithmetic becomes much easier. Since most people do addition on a calculator these days, let's review all the steps required to do it by hand. After the review, you'll develop the algorithms to do addition and subtraction in both binary and hexadecimal.

**NOTE**  *Most computer architectures provide arithmetic instructions in other number systems, but these are somewhat specialized. We will not consider them in this book.*

## Adding in the Decimal Number System

Let's start by restricting ourselves to two-digit decimal numbers. Consider two two-digit numbers, $x = 67$ and $y = 79$. Adding these by hand on paper would look like this:

```
    1         ← Carry
    6  7      ← x
+   7  9      ← y
─────────
       6      ← Sum
```

We start by working from the right, adding the two decimal digits in the ones place. $7 + 9 = 16$, which exceeds 10 by 6. We show this by placing a 6 in the ones place in the sum and carrying a 1 to the tens place.

```
 1    1       ← Carries
    6  7      ← x
+   7  9      ← y
─────────
    4  6      ← Sum
```

Next, we add the three decimal digits in the tens place: 1 (the carry from the ones place) $+ 6 + 7$. The sum of these three digits exceeds 10 by 4, which we show by placing a 4 in the sum's tens place and then recording the fact that there is an ultimate carry of 1. Because we're using only two digits, there is no hundreds place.

The following algorithm shows the procedure of adding two decimal integers, $x$ and $y$. In this algorithm, $x_i$ and $y_i$ are the $i^{th}$ digits of $x$ and $y$, respectively, numbering from right to left:

```
Let carry = 0
Repeat for each i = 0,...,(n - 1)   // starting in ones place
    sumᵢ = (xᵢ + yᵢ) % 10           // remainder
    carry = (xᵢ + yᵢ) / 10          // integer division
```

This algorithm works because we use positional notation when writing numbers—a digit one place to the left counts 10 times more. The carry from the current position one place to the left is always 0 or 1.

We use 10 in the / and % operations because there are exactly 10 digits in the decimal number system: 0, 1, 2, ..., 9. Since we are working in an *N*-digit system, we restrict our result to *N* digits. The ultimate carry is either 0 or 1 and is part of the result, along with the *N*-digit sum.

## Subtracting in the Decimal Number System

Let's turn to the subtraction operation. As you remember from subtraction in the decimal number system, you sometimes have to borrow from the next higher-order digit in the *minuend* (the number being subtracted from). We'll do the subtraction with the same numbers we used earlier (67 and 79). We'll go through this in steps so you can see the process. "Scratch" work will be in the borrows row above the two numbers.

```
      6  7   ← x
  -   7  9   ← y
  _____
             ← Difference
```

First, we need to borrow 1 from the 6 in the tens place and add it to the 7 in the ones place; then we can subtract 9 from 17 and get 8:

```
      5  17  ← Borrowing
      6  7   ← x
  -   7  9   ← y
  _____
         8   ← Difference
```

Next, we need to borrow from beyond the two digits, which we mark by placing a 1 in the "carry" position, making 15 in the tens place, from which we subtract 7:

```
  1   15     ← Borrowing
      5
      6  7   ← x
  -   7  9   ← y
  _____
      8  8   ← Difference
```

This is shown in in the following algorithm, where *x* is the minuend and *y* is the number being subtracted from it (the *subtrahend*). If borrow is 1 at the end of this algorithm, it shows that you had to borrow from beyond the *N* digits of the two values, so the *N*-digit result is incorrect. Although it's called the *carry flag*, its purpose is to show when the operation gives a result that will not fit within the number of bits for the data type. Thus, the carry flag shows the value of borrow (from beyond the size of the data type) at the completion of the subtraction operation.

```
Let borrow = 0
Repeat for i = 0,···,(N - 1)
  ❶ If y_i ≤ x_i
        Let difference_i = x_i - y_i
    Else
      ❷ Let j = i + 1
      ❸ While (x_j = 0) and (j < N)
            Add 1 to j
      ❹ If j = N
          ❺ Let borrow = 1
            Subtract 1 from j
            Add 10 to x_j
      ❻ While j > i
            Subtract 1 from x_j
            Subtract 1 from j
            Add 10 to x_j
              ❼ Let difference_i = x_i - y_i
```

This algorithm isn't nearly as complicated as it first looks (but it took me a long time to figure it out!). If the digit we're subtracting from is the same or larger than the one we're subtracting ❶, we're done with that place in the number. Otherwise, we need to borrow from the next place to the left ❷. If the next digit we're trying to borrow from is 0, then we need to continue moving to the left until we find a nonzero digit or until we reach the leftmost end of the number ❸. If we do reach the number of digits allocated for the number ❹, we indicate that by setting borrow to 1 ❺.

After we have borrowed from positions to the left, we work our way back to the position we're dealing with ❻ and perform the subtraction ❼. When you do subtraction on paper, you do all these things automatically, in your head, but that probably won't be as intuitive for you in the binary and hexadecimal systems. (I cheat and write my intermediate borrows in decimal.)

If you're having trouble, don't worry. You don't need a thorough understanding of this algorithm to understand the material in this book. But I think that working through it can help you learn how to develop algorithms for other computing problems. Translating everyday procedures into the logical statements used by programming languages is often a difficult task.

**YOUR TURN**

1. How many bits are required to store a single decimal digit? Invent a code for storing eight decimal digits in 32 bits. Using this code, does binary addition produce the correct results? You'll see such a code later in the book and some reasons for its usefulness.

2. Develop an algorithm for adding fixed-width integers in the binary number system.
3. Develop an algorithm for adding fixed-width integers in the hexadecimal number system.
4. Develop an algorithm for subtracting fixed-width integers in the binary number system.
5. Develop an algorithm for subtracting fixed-width integers in the hexadecimal number system.

## Adding and Subtracting Unsigned Integers in Binary

In this section, you'll learn how to perform addition and subtraction operations on unsigned binary integers, but before going any further, look carefully at Table 3-1, especially the binary bit patterns. You probably won't memorize this table at first, but after you work with the binary and hexadecimal number systems for a while, it will become natural to think of, say, 10, a, or 1010 as being the same numbers, just in different number systems.

**Table 3-1:** Corresponding Bit Patterns and Unsigned Decimal Values for the Hexadecimal Digits

| One hexadecimal digit | Four binary digits (bits) | Unsigned decimal |
|---|---|---|
| 0 | 0000 | 0 |
| 1 | 0001 | 1 |
| 2 | 0010 | 2 |
| 3 | 0011 | 3 |
| 4 | 0100 | 4 |
| 5 | 0101 | 5 |
| 6 | 0110 | 6 |
| 7 | 0111 | 7 |
| 8 | 1000 | 8 |
| 9 | 1001 | 9 |
| a | 1010 | 10 |
| b | 1011 | 11 |
| c | 1100 | 12 |
| d | 1101 | 13 |
| e | 1110 | 14 |
| f | 1111 | 15 |

Now that you've familiarized yourself with Table 3-1, let's discuss unsigned integers. As we do so, don't forget that as far as the value of the number goes, it doesn't matter whether we think of the integers as being in decimal, hexadecimal, or binary—they are all mathematically equivalent. However, we might wonder whether a computer performing arithmetic in binary gets the same results we do when doing the same calculation using decimal arithmetic. Let's take a closer look at some specific operations.

### Adding in the Binary Number System

In the following examples, we use four-bit values. First, consider adding the two unsigned integers, 2 and 4:

$$
\begin{array}{llll}
0 \quad 000 & \leftarrow & \text{Carries} & \\
\quad 0010_2 & = & 2_{16} & = \quad 2_{10} \\
+ \quad 0100_2 & = & 4_{16} & = \quad 4_{10} \\
\hline
\quad 0110_2 & = & 6_{16} & = \quad 6_{10}
\end{array}
$$

The decimal 2 is represented in binary as 0010, and decimal 4 is represented by 0100. The carry flag, or CF, is equal to 0, because the result of the addition operation is also four bits long. We add the digits (shown both in binary and hex here, though the carries are shown only in binary) in the same relative positions, as we do in decimal.

Next, consider two larger integers, keeping our four-bit storage space. We'll add the two unsigned integers, 4 and 14:

$$
\begin{array}{llll}
1 \quad 100 & \leftarrow & \text{Carries} & \\
\quad 0100_2 & = & 4_{16} & = \quad 4_{10} \\
+ \quad 1110_2 & = & e_{16} & = \quad 14_{10} \\
\hline
\quad 0010_2 & = & 2_{16} & \neq \quad 18_{10}
\end{array}
$$

In this case, the carry flag equals 1, because the result of the operation exceeded the four bits that we allocated for storing the integers, and our result is incorrect. If we included the carry flag in the result, we would get a five-bit value, and the result would be $10010_2 = 18_{10}$, which is correct. We'd have to account for the carry flag in software.

### Subtracting in the Binary Number System

Now, let's subtract 14 from 4, or 0110 from 0100:

$$
\begin{array}{llll}
1 \quad 110 & \leftarrow & \text{Borrows} & \\
\quad 0100_2 & = & 4_{10} & \\
- \quad 1110_2 & = & 14_{10} & \\
\hline
\quad 0110_2 & = & 6_{10} & \neq \quad -10_{10}
\end{array}
$$

The CPU indicates that we had to borrow from beyond the four bits by setting the carry flag to 1, which means that the four-bit result in this subtraction is incorrect.

These four-bit arithmetic examples generalize to any size arithmetic performed by the computer. After adding two numbers, the carry flag will always be either set to 0 if there is no ultimate (or final) carry or set to 1 if there is ultimate carry. Subtraction will set the carry flag to 0 if no borrow from the "outside" is required, or 1 if a borrow is required. The CPU always sets the CF flag in the rflags register to the appropriate value, 0 or 1, each time there is an addition or subtraction. When there is no carry, the CPU actively sets CF to 0, regardless of its previously held value.

The results are correct as long as they fit within the allocated number of bits for the data type being used for the computation. The CPU indicates the correctness by setting the carry flag to 0. When the results are incorrect, either because addition would require another bit or subtraction would need to borrow from a higher-order bit, the error is recorded by setting the carry flag to 1.

## Adding and Subtracting Signed Integers

When representing nonzero signed decimal integers, there are two possibilities: positive or negative. With only two options, we just need to use one bit for the sign. We could use a *sign-magnitude code* by simply using the highest-order bit (let's say that 0 means + and 1 means –) for signed numbers, but we'll run into some problems. As an example, consider adding +2 and –2:

$$
\begin{array}{rcl}
0010_2 & = & +2_{10} \\
+\ \underline{1010_2} & = & \underline{-2_{10}} \\
1100_2 & \neq & 0_{10}
\end{array}
$$

The result, $1100_2$, is equal to $-4_{10}$ in our code, which is arithmetically incorrect. The simple addition we used for unsigned numbers will not work correctly for signed numbers when using a sign-magnitude code.

Some computer architectures do use one bit for the sign when using signed decimal integers. They have a special *signed add* instruction that handles cases like this. (A fun aside: such computers have both a +0 and a –0!) But most computers employ a different encoding for signed numbers that allows the use of a simple add instruction.

### Two's Complement

In mathematics, the *complement* of a quantity is the amount that must be added to make it "whole." When applying this concept to numbers, the definition of *whole* depends on the radix (or base) you're working in and the number of digits that you allow to represent the numbers. If $x$ is an

$n$-digit number in radix $r$, its *radix complement*, $\neg x$, is defined such that $x + \neg x = radix^n$, where $radix^n$ is 1 followed by $n$ 0s. For example, if we're working with two-digit decimal numbers, then the *radix* complement of 37 is 63, because $37 + 63 = 10^2 = 100$. Another way of saying this is that adding a number to its radix complement results in 0 with a carry beyond the $n$ digits.

Another useful concept is the *diminished radix complement*, which is defined such that $x + diminished\_radix\_complement = radix^n - 1$. For example, the diminished radix complement of 37 is 62, because $37 + 62 = 10^2 - 1 = 99$. If you add a number to its diminished radix complement, the result is $n$ of the largest digits in the radix—two 9s in this example of two digits in radix 10.

To see how the radix complement can be used to represent negative numbers, say you have an audiotape cassette player. Many cassette players have a four-digit counter that represents tape position. You can insert a tape cassette and push a reset button to set the counter to 0. As you move the tape forward and backward, the counter registers the movement. These counters provide a "coded" representation of the tape position in arbitrary units. Now, assume we can insert a cassette, somehow move it to its center, and push the reset button. Moving the tape forward—in the positive direction—will cause the counter to increment. Moving the tape backward—in the negative direction—will cause the counter to decrement. In particular, if we start at 0 and move to +1, the "code" on the tape counter will show 0001. On the other hand, if we start at 0 and move to –1, the "code" on the tape counter will show 9999.

We can use our tape system to perform the arithmetic in the previous example, (+2) + (–2):

1. Move the tape forward to (+2); the counter shows 0002.
2. Add (–2) by moving the tape backward two steps on the counter; the counter shows 0000, which is 0 according to our code.

Next, we'll perform the same arithmetic starting with (–2) and then adding (+2):

3. Move the tape backward to (–2); the counter shows 9998.
4. Add (+2) by moving the tape forward two steps on the counter; the counter shows 0000, but there is a carry ($9998 + 2 = 0000$ with carry = 1).

If we ignore the carry, the answer is correct. 9998 is the 10's complement (the radix is 10) of 0002. When adding two signed integers using radix complement notation, the carry is irrelevant. Adding two signed numbers can give a result that will not fit within the number of bits allocated for storing the result, just as with unsigned numbers. But our tape example just showed that the carry flag will probably not show us that the result will not fit. We will discuss this issue in the next section.

Computers work in the binary number system, where the radix is 2. So let's look at the two's complement notation for representing signed integers. It uses the same general pattern as the tape counter for representing signed decimal integers in bit patterns. Table 3-2 shows the correspondence between hexadecimal, binary, and signed decimal (in two's complement notation) for four-bit values. In binary, moving the "tape" one place back (negative) from 0 would go from 0000 to 1111.

**Table 3-2:** Four-Bit Two's Complement Notation

| One hexadecimal digit | Four binary digits (bits) | Signed decimal |
|---|---|---|
| 8 | 1000 | –8 |
| 9 | 1001 | –7 |
| a | 1010 | –6 |
| b | 1011 | –5 |
| c | 1100 | –4 |
| d | 1101 | –3 |
| e | 1110 | –2 |
| f | 1111 | –1 |
| 0 | 0000 | 0 |
| 1 | 0001 | +1 |
| 2 | 0010 | +2 |
| 3 | 0011 | +3 |
| 4 | 0100 | +4 |
| 5 | 0101 | +5 |
| 6 | 0110 | +6 |
| 7 | 0111 | +7 |

Here are some important observations about this table:

- The high-order bit of each positive number is 0, and the high-order bit of each negative number is 1.
- Although changing the sign of (*negating*) a number is more complicated than simply changing the high-order bit, it is common to call the high-order bit the *sign bit*.
- The notation allows for one more negative number than positive numbers.
- The range of integers, $x$, that can be represented in this notation (with four bits) is

$$-8_{10} \le x \le +7_{10}$$

or

$$-2^{(4-1)} \le x \le + (2^{(4-1)} - 1)$$

The last observation can be generalized for $n$ bits to the following:

$$-2^{(n-1)} \le x \le +(2^{(n-1)} - 1)$$

When using two's complement notation, the negative of any $n$-bit integer, $x$, is defined as

$$x + (-x) = 2^n$$

Notice that $2^n$ written in binary is 1 followed by $n$ zeros. In other words, in the $n$-bit two's complement notation, adding a number to its negative produces $n$ zeros and a carry equal to 1.

## Computing Two's Complement

Now we'll derive a way to compute the negative of a number by using two's complement notation. Solving the defining equation for $-x$, we get

$$-x = 2^n - x$$

This may look odd to a mathematician, but keep in mind that $x$ in this equation is restricted to $n$ bits, while $2^n$ has $n + 1$ bits (1 followed by $n$ 0s).

For example, if we want to compute $-123$ in binary (using two's complement notation) in eight bits, we perform the arithmetic:

$$\begin{aligned} -123_{10} &= 100000000_2 - 01111011_2 \\ &= 10000101_2 \end{aligned}$$

or in hexadecimal:

$$\begin{aligned} -123_{10} &= 100_{16} - 7b_{16} \\ &= 85_{16} \end{aligned}$$

This subtraction operation is error prone, so let's do a bit of algebra on our equation for computing $-x$. Subtract 1 from both sides and rearrange a little:

$$\begin{aligned} -x - 1 &= 2^n - x - 1 \\ &= (2^n - 1) - x \end{aligned}$$

which gives this:

$$-x = ((2^n - 1) - x) + 1$$

If this looks more complicated than our first equation, don't worry. Let's consider the quantity $(2^n - 1)$. Since $2^n$ is written in binary as 1 followed by $n$ 0s, $(2^n - 1)$ is written as $n$ 1s. For example, for $n = 8$:

$$2^8 - 1 = 11111111_2$$

Thus, we can say:

$$(2^n - 1) - x = 11...1_2 - x$$

where $11...1_2$ designates $n$ 1s.

Though it may not be immediately obvious, you'll see how easy this subtraction is when you consider the previous example of computing $-123$ in eight-bit binary. Let $x = 123$, giving this:

```
    11111111    ← (2ⁿ – 1)
 –  01111011    ← x
 =  10000100    ← One's complement
```

or in hexadecimal giving this:

```
    ff    ← (2ⁿ – 1)
 –  7b    ← x
 =  84    ← One's complement
```

Since all the quantities here have $n$ bits, this computation is easy—simply flip all the bits, giving the diminished radix complement, also called the *one's complement* in the binary number system. A $1$ becomes $0$, and a $0$ becomes a $1$, in the result.

All that remains to compute the negative is to add 1 to the result. Finally, we have the following:

$$\begin{aligned}
-123_{10} &= 84_{16} + 1_{16} \\
&= 85_{16} \\
&= 10000101_2
\end{aligned}$$

**HINT**  *To double-check your arithmetic, pay attention to whether the value you are converting is even or odd. It will be the same in all number bases.*

---

**YOUR TURN**

1. Develop an algorithm to convert signed decimal integers to two's complement binary.

2. Develop an algorithm to convert integers in two's complement binary notation to signed decimal.

*(continued)*

3. The following 16-bit hexadecimal values are stored in two's complement notation. What are the equivalent signed decimal numbers?

   a. 1234

   b. ffff

   c. 8000

   d. 7fff

4. Show how each of the following signed, decimal integers would be stored in 16-bit two's complement notation. Give your answer in hexadecimal.

   a. +1024

   b. −1024

   c. −256

   d. −32767

## Adding and Subtracting Signed Integers in Binary

The number of bits used to represent a value is determined at the time a program is written by the computer architecture and programming language being used. This is why you can't just add more digits (bits) if the result is too large, as you would on paper. For unsigned integers, the solution to this problem is the carry flag, which indicates when the sum of two unsigned integers exceeds the number of bits allocated for it. In this section, you'll see that adding two signed numbers can also produce a result that exceeds the range of values that can be represented by the allocated number of bits, but the carry flag is not used to indicate the error.

The CPU registers when the sum of signed numbers has gotten too big for its bits by using the *overflow flag*, OF, in the flags register, rflags. The value of the overflow flag is given by an operation that may not seem intuitive at first: the *exclusive or (XOR)* of the penultimate and ultimate carries. As an example, let's say we're adding the two eight-bit numbers, $15_{16}$ and $6f_{16}$:

```
Ultimate carry →   0   1        ← Penultimate carry
                 0001 0101    ← x
             +   0110 1111    ← y
                 ─────────────
                 1000 0100    ← Sum
```

In this example, the carry is 0, and the penultimate carry is 1. The OF flag is equal to the XOR of the ultimate carry and penultimate carry, OF = CF $\underline{\vee}$ (penultimate carry), where $\underline{\vee}$ is the XOR operator. In the previous example, OF = 0 $\underline{\vee}$ 1 = 1.

Case by case, we'll see why the OF flag indicates the validity of adding two signed integers in the two's complement representation. In the next three sections, we'll discuss the three possible cases: the two numbers can have opposite signs, both be positive, or both be negative.

## Two Numbers of the Opposite Sign

Let $x$ be the negative number and $y$ the positive number. Then we can express $x$ and $y$ in binary as follows:

$$x = 1..., y = 0...$$

That is, the high-order (sign) bit of one number is 1, and the high-order (sign) bit of the other is 0, regardless of what the other bits are.

$x + y$ always remains within the range of the two's complement representation:

$$-2^{(n-1)} \le x < 0$$
$$0 \le y \le +(2^{(n-1)} - 1)$$
$$-2^{(n-1)} \le x + y \le +(2^{(n-1)} - 1)$$

Now, if we add $x$ and $y$, there are two possible carry results:

- If the penultimate carry is 0:

```
Carry →   0   0      ← Penultimate carry
              1...    ← x
     +    0...        ← y
     _____
              1...    ← Sum
```

This addition produces OF = 0 $\underline{\vee}$ 0 = 0.

- If the penultimate carry is 1:

```
Carry →   1   1      ← Penultimate carry
              1...    ← x
     +    0...        ← y
     _____
              0...    ← Sum
```

This addition produces OF = 1 $\underline{\vee}$ 1 = 0.

Adding two integers of opposite signs always yields 0 for the overflow flag, so the sum is always within the allocated range.

## Two Positive Numbers

Since both are positive, we can express $x$ and $y$ in binary as follows:

$$x = 0..., y = 0...$$

Here the high-order (sign) bit of both numbers is 0, regardless of what the other bits are. Now, if we add *x* and *y*, there are two possible carry results:

- If the penultimate carry is 0:

```
Carry →  0   0      ← Penultimate carry
            0…     ← x
      +     0…     ← y
            0…     ← Sum
```

We'd have OF = 0 $\underline{\vee}$ 0 = 0. The high-order bit of the sum is 0, so it's a positive number, and the sum is in range.

- If the penultimate carry is 1:

```
Carry →  0   1      ← Penultimate carry
            0…     ← x
      +     0…     ← y
            1…     ← Sum
```

Then we'd have OF = 0 $\underline{\vee}$ 1 = 1. The high-order bit of the sum is 1, so it's a negative number. Adding two positive numbers cannot give a negative sum, so the sum must have exceeded the allocated range.

### Two Negative Numbers

Since both are negative, we can express *x* and *y* in binary as follows:

$$x = 1..., y = 1...$$

Because the numbers are negative, the high-order (sign) bit of both numbers is 1, regardless of what the other bits are. Now, if we add *x* and *y*, there are two possible carry results:

- If the penultimate carry is 0:

```
Carry →  1   0      ← Penultimate carry
            1…     ← x
      +     1…     ← y
            0…     ← Sum
```

This gives OF = 1 $\underline{\vee}$ 0 = 1. The high-order bit of this sum is 0, so it's a positive number. But adding two negative numbers cannot give a positive sum, so the sum has exceeded the allocated range.

- If the penultimate carry is 1:

```
Carry →   1    1      ← Penultimate carry
               1...   ← x
          +    1...   ← y
          _____
               1...   ← Sum
```

This addition produces OF = 1 $\vee$ 1 = 0. The high-order bit of the sum is 1, so it is a negative number, and the sum is within range.

We won't go into subtraction here. The same rules apply there, and I invite you to explore them on your own!

Let's take what we just learned, and what we did in "Adding and Subtracting Unsigned Integers in Binary" on page 43, and state some rules for adding or subtracting two $n$-bit numbers:

- When the program treats the result as unsigned, the carry flag, CF, is 0 if and only if the result is within the $n$-bit range; OF is irrelevant.

- When the program treats the result as signed, the overflow flag, OF, is 0 if and only if the result is within the $n$-bit range; CF is irrelevant.

**NOTE**  *Using two's complement notation means that the CPU does not need additional instructions for signed addition and subtraction, thus simplifying the hardware. The CPU just sees bit patterns. Both CF and OF are set according to the rules of binary arithmetic by each arithmetic operation, regardless of how the program treats the numbers. The distinction between signed and unsigned is completely determined by the program. After each addition or subtraction operation, the program should check the state of CF for unsigned integers or OF for signed integers and at least indicate when the sum is in error. Many high-level languages do not perform this check, which can lead to some obscure program bugs.*

## Circular Nature of Integer Codes

The notations used for both unsigned integers and signed integers are circular in nature—that is, for a given number of bits, each code "wraps around." You can see this visually in the "decoder ring" for three-bit numbers shown in Figure 3-1.

To use this decoder ring to add or subtract two integers, follow these steps:

1. Pick the ring corresponding to the type of integer you're using (signed or unsigned).

2. Move to the location on that ring corresponding to the first integer.

3. Move along the ring, moving the number of "spokes" equal to the second integer. Move clockwise to add, and move counterclockwise to subtract.

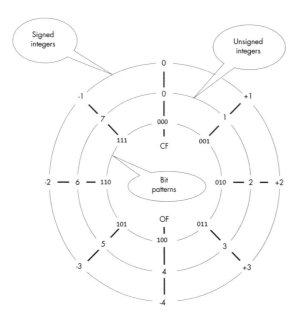

*Figure 3-1: "Decoder ring" for three-bit signed and unsigned integers*

The result is correct if you do not cross the top for unsigned integers or cross the bottom for signed integers.

---

**YOUR TURN**

1.  Use the decoder ring in Figure 3-1 to perform the following arithmetic. Indicate whether the result is "right" or "wrong."

    a.  Unsigned integers: 1 + 3
    b.  Unsigned integers: 3 + 4
    c.  Unsigned integers: 5 + 6
    d.  Signed integers: (+1) + (+3)
    e.  Signed integers: (−3) − (+3)
    f.  Signed integers: (+3) + (−4)

2.  Add the following pairs of eight-bit numbers (shown in hexadecimal) and indicate whether your result is "right" or "wrong." First treat them as unsigned values and then as signed values (stored in two's complement).

    a.  55 + aa
    b.  55 + f0
    c.  80 + 7b
    d.  63 + 7b
    e.  0f + ff
    f.  80 + 80

---

3. Add the following pairs of 16-bit numbers (shown in hexadecimal) and indicate whether your result is "right" or "wrong." First treat them as unsigned values and then as signed values (stored in two's complement).

   a.  1234 + edcc
   b.  1234 + fedc
   c.  8000 + 8000
   d.  0400 + ffff
   e.  07d0 + 782f
   f.  8000 + ffff

## What You've Learned

**Binary arithmetic**   Computers perform addition and subtraction in the binary number system. Addition of two numbers may yield a result that is one bit wider than each of the two numbers. Subtraction of one number from another may require borrowing from one bit beyond the width of the two numbers.

**Representing signed/unsigned**   Bit patterns can be treated as representing either signed or unsigned integers. Two's complement notation is commonly used to represent signed integers.

**Carry flag**   The CPU includes a one-bit carry flag that shows whether the result of addition or subtraction exceeds the number of bits allowed for an unsigned integer.

**Overflow flag**   The CPU includes a one-bit overflow flag that shows whether the result of addition or subtraction exceeds the number of bits allowed for a signed integer using the two's complement notation.

In the next chapter, you'll learn Boolean algebra. Although it may seem a bit strange at first, once we get going, you'll see that it's actually easier than elementary algebra. For one thing, everything evaluates to either 0 or 1!

# 4

## BOOLEAN ALGEBRA

*Boolean algebra* was developed in the 19th century by an English mathematician, George Boole, who was working on ways to use mathematical rigor to solve logic problems. He formalized a mathematical system for manipulating logical values in which the only possible values for the variables are *true* and *false,* usually designated 1 and 0, respectively.

The basic operations in Boolean algebra are *conjunction* (AND), *disjunction* (OR), and *negation* (NOT). This distinguishes it from elementary algebra, which includes the infinite set of real numbers and uses the arithmetic operations addition, subtraction, multiplication, and division. (Exponentiation is a simplified notation for repeated multiplication.)

As mathematicians and logicians were expanding the field of Boolean algebra in increasingly complex and abstract ways, engineers were learning to harness electrical flows using switches in circuits to perform logic operations. The two fields developed in parallel until the mid-1930s, when a graduate student named Claude Shannon proved that electrical switches could be used to implement the full range of Boolean algebraic expressions. (When used to describe switching circuits, Boolean algebra is sometimes called *switching algebra*.) With Shannon's discovery, a world of possibilities was opened, and Boolean algebra became the mathematical foundation of the computer.

This chapter starts with descriptions of the basic Boolean operators. Then you'll learn about their logical rules, which form the basis of Boolean algebra. Next, I'll explain ways to combine Boolean variables and operators into algebraic expressions to form Boolean logic functions. Finally, I'll discuss techniques for simplifying Boolean functions. In subsequent chapters, you'll learn how electronic on/off switches can be used to implement logic functions that can be connected together in logic circuits to perform the primary functions of a computer—arithmetic and logic operations and memory storage.

## Basic Boolean Operators

There are several symbols used to denote each Boolean operator, which I'll include in the description of each of the operators. In this book, I'll present the symbols used by logicians. A Boolean operator acts on a value, or pair of values, called the *operands*.

I'll use *truth tables* to show the results of each operation. A truth table shows the results for all possible combinations of the operands. For example, consider the addition of two bits, $x$ and $y$. There are four possible combinations of the values. Addition will give a sum and a possible carry. Table 4-1 shows how to express this in a truth table.

**Table 4-1:** Truth Table Showing Addition of Two Bits

| $x$ | $y$ | Carry | Sum |
|---|---|---|---|
| 0 | 0 | 0 | 0 |
| 0 | 1 | 0 | 1 |
| 1 | 0 | 0 | 1 |
| 1 | 1 | 1 | 0 |

I'll also provide the electronic circuit representations for the *gates*, the electronic devices that implement the Boolean operators. You'll learn more about these devices in Chapters 5 through 8, where you'll also see that the real-world behavior of the physical devices varies slightly from the ideal mathematical behavior shown in the truth tables.

As with elementary algebra, you can combine these basic operators to define secondary operators. You'll see an example of this when we define the XOR operator near the end of this chapter.

## AND

AND is a *binary operator*, meaning it acts on two operands. The result of AND is 1 if and only if *both* operands are 1; otherwise, the result is 0. In logic, the operation is known as *conjunction*. I'll use ∧ to designate the AND operation. It's also common to use the · symbol or simply AND. Figure 4-1 shows the circuit symbol for an AND gate and a truth table defining the output, with operands $x$ and $y$.

| x | y | x ∧ y |
|---|---|---|
| 0 | 0 | 0 |
| 0 | 1 | 0 |
| 1 | 0 | 0 |
| 1 | 1 | 1 |

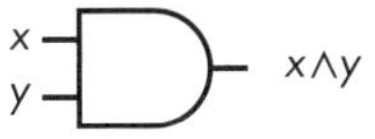

Figure 4-1: The AND gate acting on two variables, x and y

As you can see from the truth table, the AND operator has properties similar to multiplication in elementary algebra, which is why some use the · symbol to represent it.

## OR

OR is also a binary operator. The result of OR is 1 if at least one of the operands is 1; otherwise, the result is 0. In logic, the operation is known as *disjunction*. I'll use ∨ to designate the OR operation. It's also common to use the + symbol or simply OR. Figure 4-2 shows the circuit symbol for an OR gate and a truth table defining the output, with operands $x$ and $y$.

| x | y | x ∨ y |
|---|---|---|
| 0 | 0 | 0 |
| 0 | 1 | 1 |
| 1 | 0 | 1 |
| 1 | 1 | 1 |

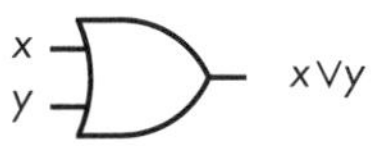

Figure 4-2: The OR gate acting on two variables, x and y

The truth table shows that the OR operator follows rules somewhat similar to addition in elementary algebra, which is why some use the + symbol to represent it.

## NOT

NOT is a *unary operator*, which acts on only one operand. The result of NOT is 1 if the operand is 0, and it is 0 if the operand is 1. Other names for the NOT operation are *complement* and *invert*. I'll use ¬ to designate the NOT operation. It's also common to use the ' symbol, an overscore above the variable, or simply NOT. Figure 4-3 shows the circuit symbol for a NOT gate, and a truth table defining the output, with the operand *x*.

| x | ¬x |
|---|----|
| 0 | 1  |
| 1 | 0  |

*Figure 4-3: The NOT gate acting on one variable, x*

As you'll see, NOT has some properties of the arithmetic negation used in elementary algebra, but there are some significant differences.

It's no accident that AND is multiplicative and OR additive. When George Boole was developing his algebra, he was looking for a way to apply mathematical rigor to logic and use addition and multiplication to manipulate logical statements. Boole developed the rules for his algebra based on using AND for multiplication and OR for addition. In the next section, you'll see how to use these operators, together with NOT, to represent logical statements.

# Boolean Expressions

Just as you can use elementary algebra operators to combine variables into expressions like $(x + y)$, you can use Boolean operators to combine variables into expressions.

There is a significant difference, though. A Boolean expression is created from values (0 and 1) and literals. In Boolean algebra, a *literal* is a single instance of a variable or its complement that's being used in an expression. In the expression

$$x \wedge y \vee \neg x \wedge z \vee \neg x \wedge \neg y \wedge \neg z$$

there are three variables ($x$, $y$, and $z$) and seven literals. In a Boolean expression, you can see a variable in both its complemented form and its uncomplemented form because each form is a separate literal.

We can combine literals by using either the $\wedge$ or $\vee$ operator. Like in elementary algebra, Boolean algebra expressions are made up of *terms*, groups of literals that are acted upon by operators, like $(x \vee y)$ or $(a \wedge b)$. And just like elementary algebra, *operation precedence* (or *order of operations*) specifies how these operators are applied when evaluating the expression. Table 4-2 lists the precedence rules for the Boolean operators. As with elementary algebra, expressions in parentheses are evaluated first, following the precedence rules.

**Table 4-2:** Precedence Rules of Boolean Algebra Operators

| Operation | Notation | Precedence |
|-----------|----------|------------|
| NOT | $\neg x$ | Highest |
| AND | $x \wedge y$ | Middle |
| OR | $x \vee y$ | Lowest |

Now that you know how the three fundamental Boolean operators work, we'll look at some of the rules they obey when used in algebraic expressions. As you'll see later in the chapter, we can use the rules to simplify Boolean expressions, which will allow us, in turn, to simplify the way we implement those expressions in the hardware.

Knowing how to simplify Boolean expressions is an important tool for both those making hardware and those writing software. A computer is just a physical manifestation of Boolean logic. Even if your only interest is in programming, every programming statement you write is ultimately carried out by hardware that is completely described by the system of Boolean algebra. Our programming languages tend to hide much of this through abstraction, but they still use Boolean expressions to implement programming logic.

# Boolean Algebra Rules

When comparing AND and OR in Boolean algebra to multiplication and addition in elementary algebra, you'll find that some of the rules of Boolean algebra are familiar, but some are significantly different. Let's start with the rules that are the same, followed by the rules that differ.

## Boolean Algebra Rules That Are the Same as Elementary Algebra

**AND and OR are associative.**

We say that an operator is *associative* if, when there are two or more occurrences of the operator in an expression, the order of applying the operator does not change the value of the expression. Mathematically:

$$x \wedge (y \wedge z) = (x \wedge y) \wedge z$$

$$x \vee (y \vee z) = (x \vee y) \vee z$$

To prove the associative rule for AND and OR, let's use exhaustive truth tables, as shown in Tables 4-3 and 4-4. Table 4-3 lists all possible values of the three variables $x$, $y$, and $z$, as well as the intermediate computations of the terms $(y \wedge z)$ and $(x \wedge y)$. In the last two columns, we can compute the values of each expression on both sides of the previous equations, which shows that the two equalities hold.

**Table 4-3:** Associativity of the AND Operation

| x | y | z | (y ∧ z) | (x ∧ y) | x ∧ (y ∧ z) | (x ∧ y) ∧ z |
|---|---|---|---------|---------|-------------|-------------|
| 0 | 0 | 0 | 0 | 0 | 0 | 0 |
| 0 | 0 | 1 | 0 | 0 | 0 | 0 |
| 0 | 1 | 0 | 0 | 0 | 0 | 0 |
| 0 | 1 | 1 | 1 | 0 | 0 | 0 |
| 1 | 0 | 0 | 0 | 0 | 0 | 0 |
| 1 | 0 | 1 | 0 | 0 | 0 | 0 |
| 1 | 1 | 0 | 0 | 1 | 0 | 0 |
| 1 | 1 | 1 | 1 | 1 | 1 | 1 |

Table 4-4 lists all possible values of the three variables $x$, $y$, and $z$, as well as the intermediate computations of the terms $(y \lor z)$ and $(x \lor y)$. In the last two columns, we can compute the values of each expression on both sides of the previous equations, which shows that the two equalities hold.

**Table 4-4:** Associativity of the OR Operation

| x | y | z | (y ∨ z) | (x ∨ y) | x ∨ (y ∨ z) | (x ∨ y) ∨ z |
|---|---|---|---------|---------|-------------|-------------|
| 0 | 0 | 0 | 0 | 0 | 0 | 0 |
| 0 | 0 | 1 | 1 | 0 | 1 | 1 |
| 0 | 1 | 0 | 1 | 1 | 1 | 1 |
| 0 | 1 | 1 | 1 | 1 | 1 | 1 |
| 1 | 0 | 0 | 0 | 1 | 1 | 1 |
| 1 | 0 | 1 | 1 | 1 | 1 | 1 |
| 1 | 1 | 0 | 1 | 1 | 1 | 1 |
| 1 | 1 | 1 | 1 | 1 | 1 | 1 |

This strategy will work for each of the rules shown in this section, but I'll go through only the truth table for the associative rule here. You'll do this for the other rules when it's Your Turn at the end of this section.

**AND and OR have identity values.**

An *identity value* is a value specific to an operation such that using that operation on a quantity with the identity value yields the value of the original quantity. For AND and OR, the identity values are 1 and 0, respectively:

$$x \land 1 = x$$

$$x \lor 0 = x$$

## AND and OR are commutative.

We can say that an operator is *commutative* if we can reverse the order of its operands:

$$x \wedge y = y \wedge x$$

$$x \vee y = y \vee x$$

## AND is distributive over OR.

The AND operator applied to quantities OR-ed together can be *distributed* to apply to each of the OR-ed quantities, like so:

$$x \wedge (y \vee z) = (x \wedge y) \vee (x \wedge z)$$

Unlike in elementary algebra, the additive OR *is* distributive over the multiplicative AND. You'll see this in the next section.

## AND has an annulment (also called annihilation) value.

Operating on a value with the operator's *annulment value* yields the annulment value. The annulment value for AND is 0:

$$x \wedge 0 = 0$$

We're used to 0 being the annulment value for multiplication in elementary algebra, but addition has no concept of annulment. You'll learn about the annulment value for OR in the next section.

## NOT shows involution.

An operator shows *involution* if applying it to a quantity twice yields the original quantity:

$$\neg(\neg x) = x$$

Involution is simply the application of a double complement: NOT(NOT true) = true. This is similar to double negation in elementary algebra.

## Boolean Algebra Rules That Differ from Elementary Algebra

Although AND is multiplicative and OR is additive, there are significant differences between these logical operations and the arithmetic ones. The differences stem from the fact that Boolean algebra deals with logic expressions that evaluate to either true or false, while elementary algebra deals with the infinite set of real numbers. In this section, you'll see expressions that might remind you of elementary algebra, but the Boolean algebra rules are different.

**OR is distributive over AND.**

The OR operator applied to quantities AND-ed together can be *distributed* to apply to each of the AND-ed quantities:

$$x \lor (y \land z) = (x \lor y) \land (x \lor z)$$

Because addition is not distributive over multiplication in elementary algebra, you may miss this way of manipulating Boolean expressions.

First, let's look at elementary algebra. Using addition for OR and multiplication for AND in the previous equation, we have this:

$$x + (y \cdot z) \neq (x + y) \cdot (x + z)$$

We can see this by plugging in the numbers $x = 1$, $y = 2$, and $z = 3$. The left-hand side gives

$$1 + (2 \cdot 3) = 7$$

and the right-hand side gives

$$(1 + 2) \cdot (1 + 3) = 12$$

Thus, addition is *not* distributive over multiplication in elementary algebra.

The best way to show that OR is distributive over AND in Boolean algebra is to use a truth table, as shown in Table 4-5.

**Table 4-5:** OR Distributes over AND

| x | y | z | x ∨ (y ∧ z) | (x ∨ y) ∧ (x ∨ z) |
|---|---|---|---|---|
| 0 | 0 | 0 | 0 | 0 |
| 0 | 0 | 1 | 0 | 0 |
| 0 | 1 | 0 | 0 | 0 |
| 0 | 1 | 1 | 1 | 1 |
| 1 | 0 | 0 | 1 | 1 |
| 1 | 0 | 1 | 1 | 1 |
| 1 | 1 | 0 | 1 | 1 |
| 1 | 1 | 1 | 1 | 1 |

Comparing the two right-hand columns, you can see that the variable that is common to the two OR terms, $x$, can be factored out, and thus the distributive property holds.

**OR has an annulment (also called annihilation) value.**

An *annulment value* is a value such that operating on a quantity with the annulment value yields the annulment value. There is no annulment value for addition in elementary algebra, but in Boolean algebra, the annulment value for OR is 1:

$$x \lor 1 = 1$$

**AND and OR both have a complement value.**

The *complement value* is the diminished radix complement of the variable. You saw in Chapter 3 that the sum of a quantity and that quantity's diminished radix complement is equal to (*radix* – 1). Since the radix in Boolean algebra is 2, the complement of 0 is 1, and the complement of 1 is 0. So, the complement of a Boolean quantity is simply the NOT of that quantity, which gives

$$x \land \neg x = 0$$

$$x \lor \neg x = 1$$

The complement value illustrates one of the differences between the AND and OR logical operations and the multiplication and addition arithmetic operations. In elementary algebra:

$$x \cdot (-x) = -x^2$$
$$x + (-x) = 0$$

Even if we restrict $x$ to be 0 or 1, in elementary algebra $1 \cdot (-1) = -1$, and $1 + (-1) = 0$.

**AND and OR are idempotent.**

If an operator is *idempotent*, applying it to two of the same operands results in that operand. In other words:

$$x \land x = x$$

$$x \lor x = x$$

This looks different than in elementary algebra, where repeatedly multiplying a number by itself is exponentiation, and repeatedly adding a number to itself is equivalent to multiplication.

**De Morgan's law applies.**

In Boolean algebra, the special relationship between the AND and OR operations is captured by *De Morgan's law*, which states

$$\neg(x \land y) = \neg x \lor \neg y$$

$$\neg(x \lor y) = \neg x \land \neg y$$

The first equation states that the NOT of the AND of two Boolean quantities is equal to the OR of the NOT of the two quantities. Likewise, the second equation states that the NOT of the OR of two Boolean quantities is equal to the AND of the NOT of the two quantities.

This relationship is an example of the *principle of duality*, which in Boolean algebra states that if you replace every 0 with a 1, every 1 with a 0, every AND with an OR, and every OR with an AND, the equation is still true. Look back over the rules just given and you'll see that all of them except involution have dual operations. De Morgan's law is one of the best examples of duality. Please, when it's Your Turn, prove De Morgan's law so you can see the principle of duality in play.

---

**YOUR TURN**

1. Use truth tables to prove the Boolean algebra rules given in this section.
2. Prove De Morgan's law.

---

## Boolean Functions

The functionality of a computer is based on Boolean logic, which means the various operations of a computer are specified by Boolean functions. A Boolean function looks somewhat like a function in elementary algebra, but the variables can appear in either uncomplemented or complemented form. The variables and constants are connected by Boolean operators. A Boolean function evaluates to either 1 or 0 (true or false).

In "Adding in the Binary Number System" on page 44, you saw that when adding two bits, $x$ and $y$, in a binary number, we have to include a possible carry into their bit position in the number. The conditions that cause carry to be 1 are

$x = 1$, $y = 1$, and there's no carry into the current bit position, or

$x = 0$, $y = 1$, and there's carry into the current bit position, or

$x = 1$, $y = 0$, and there's carry into the current bit position, or

$x = 1$, $y = 1$, and there's carry into the current bit position.

We can express this more concisely with this Boolean function:

$$C_{out}(c_{in}, x, y) = (\neg c_{in} \wedge x \wedge y) \vee (c_{in} \wedge \neg x \wedge y) \vee (c_{in} \wedge x \wedge \neg y) \vee (c_{in} \wedge x \wedge y)$$

where $x$ is one bit, $y$ is the other bit, $c_{in}$ is the carry in from the next-lower-order bit position, and $C_{out}(c_{in}, x, y)$ is the carry resulting from the addition in the current bit position. We'll use this equation throughout this section, but first, let's think about the differences between Boolean and elementary functions.

Like an elementary algebra function, a Boolean algebra function can be manipulated mathematically, but the mathematical operations are different. Operations in elementary algebra are performed on the infinite set of real numbers, but Boolean functions work on only two possible values, 0 or 1. Elementary algebra functions can evaluate to any real number, but Boolean functions can evaluate only to 0 or 1.

This difference means we have to think differently about Boolean functions. For example, look at this elementary algebra function:

$$F(x, y) = x \cdot (-y)$$

You probably read it as, "If I multiply the value of $x$ by the negative of the value of $y$, I'll get the value of $F(x, y)$." However, if you look at the Boolean function

$$F(x, y) = x \wedge (\neg y)$$

there are only four possibilities. If $x = 1$ and $y = 0$, then $F(x, y) = 1$. For the other three possibilities, $F(x, y) = 0$. Whereas you can plug in any numbers in an elementary algebra function, a Boolean algebra function shows you what the values of the variables are that cause the function to evaluate to 1. I think of elementary algebra functions as *asking* me to plug in values for the variables for evaluation, while Boolean algebra functions *tell* me what values of the variables cause the function to evaluate to 1.

There are simpler ways to express the conditions for carry. And those simplifications lead to being able to implement this function in hardware with fewer logic gates, thus lowering the cost and power usage. In this and the following sections, you'll learn how the mathematical nature of Boolean algebra makes function simplification easier and more concise.

## Canonical Sum or Sum of Minterms

A *canonical form* of a Boolean function explicitly shows whether each variable in the problem is complemented or not in each term that defines the function, just as we did with our English statement of the conditions that produce a carry of 1 earlier. This ensures that you have taken all possible combinations into account in the function definition. The truth table, shown in Table 4-6, for the carry equation we saw earlier

$$C_{out}(c_{in}, x, y) = (\neg c_{in} \wedge x \wedge y) \vee (c_{in} \wedge \neg x \wedge y) \vee (c_{in} \wedge x \wedge \neg y) \vee (c_{in} \wedge x \wedge y)$$

should help to clarify this.

**Table 4-6:** Conditions That Cause Carry to Be 1

| Minterm | $c_{in}$ | x | y | $(\neg c_{in} \wedge x \wedge y)$ | $(c_{in} \wedge \neg x \wedge y)$ | $(c_{in} \wedge x \wedge \neg y)$ | $(c_{in} \wedge x \wedge y)$ | $C_{out}(c_{in}, x, y)$ |
|---|---|---|---|---|---|---|---|---|
| $m_0$ | 0 | 0 | 0 | 0 | 0 | 0 | 0 | 0 |
| $m_1$ | 0 | 0 | 1 | 0 | 0 | 0 | 0 | 0 |
| $m_2$ | 0 | 1 | 0 | 0 | 0 | 0 | 0 | 0 |
| $m_3$ | 0 | 1 | 1 | 1 | 0 | 0 | 0 | 1 |
| $m_4$ | 1 | 0 | 0 | 0 | 0 | 0 | 0 | 0 |
| $m_5$ | 1 | 0 | 1 | 0 | 1 | 0 | 0 | 1 |
| $m_6$ | 1 | 1 | 0 | 0 | 0 | 1 | 0 | 1 |
| $m_7$ | 1 | 1 | 1 | 0 | 0 | 0 | 1 | 1 |

Although the parentheses in the equation are not required, I've added them to help you see the form of the equation. The parentheses show four *product terms*, terms where all the literals are operated on only by AND. The four product terms are then OR-ed together. Since the OR operation is like addition, the right-hand side is called a *sum of products*. It's also said to be in *disjunctive normal form*.

Now let's look more closely at the product terms. Each of them includes all the variables in this equation in the form of a literal (uncomplemented or complemented). An equation that has $n$ variables has $2^n$ permutations of the values for the variables; a *minterm* is a product term that specifies exactly one of the permutations. Since there are four combinations of values for $c_{in}$, $x$, and $y$ that produce a carry of 1, the previous equation has four out of the possible eight minterms. A Boolean function that is defined by summing (OR-ing) all the minterms that evaluate to 1 is said to be a *canonical sum*, a *sum of minterms*, or in *full disjunctive normal form*. A function defined by a sum of minterms evaluates to 1 when at least one of the minterms evaluates to 1.

For every minterm, exactly one set of values for the variables makes the minterm evaluate to 1. For example, the minterm $(c_{in} \wedge x \wedge \neg y)$ in the previous equation evaluates to 1 only when $c_{in} = 1$, $x = 1$, $y = 0$. A product term that does not contain all the variables in the problem, either in uncomplemented or in complemented form, will always evaluate to 1 for more sets of values for the variables than a minterm. For example, $(c_{in} \wedge x)$ evaluates to 1 for $c_{in} = 1$, $x = 1$, $y = 0$, and $c_{in} = 1$, $x = 1$, $y = 1$. Because they minimize the number of cases that evaluate to 1, we call them *minterms*.

Rather than write out all the literals in a function, logic designers commonly use the notation $m_i$ to specify the $i$th minterm, where $i$ is the integer represented by the values of the literals in the problem if the values are placed in order and treated as binary numbers. For example, $c_{in} = 1$, $x = 1$, $y = 0$ gives 110, which is the (base 10) number 6; thus, that minterm is $m_6$. Table 4-6 shows all eight possible minterms for a three-variable equation, and the minterm, $m_6 = (c_{in} \wedge x \wedge \neg y)$, in the four-term equation shown earlier evaluates to 1 when $c_{in} = 1$, $x = 1$, $y = 0$.

Using this notation to write Boolean equations as a canonical sum and using the $\Sigma$ symbol to denote summation, we can restate the function for carry:

$$C_{out}(c_{in}, x, y) = (\neg c_{in} \wedge x \wedge y) \vee (c_{in} \wedge \neg x \wedge y) \vee (c_{in} \wedge x \wedge \neg y) \vee (c_{in} \wedge x \wedge y)$$
$$= m_3 \vee m_5 \vee m_6 \vee m_7$$
$$= \Sigma(3,5,6,7)$$

We are looking at a simple example here. For more complicated functions, writing all the minterms out is error-prone. The simplified notation is easier to work with and helps to avoid making errors.

### Canonical Product or Product of Maxterms

Depending on factors like available components and personal choice, a designer may prefer to work with the cases where a function evaluates to 0 instead of 1. In our example, that means a design that specifies when carry is 0. To see how this works, let's take the complement of both sides of the equation for specifying carry, using De Morgan's law:

$$\neg C_{out}(c_{in}, x, y) = (c_{in} \vee \neg x \vee \neg y) \wedge (\neg c_{in} \vee x \vee \neg y) \wedge (\neg c_{in} \vee \neg x \vee y) \wedge (\neg c_{in} \vee \neg x \vee \neg y)$$

Because we complemented both sides of the equation, we now have the Boolean equation for $\neg C_{out}$, the complement of carry. Thus, we are looking for conditions that cause $\neg C_{out}$ to evaluate to 0, not 1. These are shown in the truth table, Table 4-7.

**Table 4-7:** Conditions That Cause the Complement of Carry to Be 0

| Maxterm | $c_{in}$ | $x$ | $y$ | $(c_{in} \vee \neg x \vee \neg y)$ | $(\neg c_{in} \vee x \vee \neg y)$ | $(\neg c_{in} \vee \neg x \vee y)$ | $(\neg c_{in} \vee \neg x \vee \neg y)$ | $\neg C_{out}(c_{in}, x, y)$ |
|---|---|---|---|---|---|---|---|---|
| $M_0$ | 0 | 0 | 0 | 1 | 1 | 1 | 1 | 1 |
| $M_1$ | 0 | 0 | 1 | 1 | 1 | 1 | 1 | 1 |
| $M_2$ | 0 | 1 | 0 | 1 | 1 | 1 | 1 | 1 |
| $M_3$ | 0 | 1 | 1 | 0 | 1 | 1 | 1 | 0 |
| $M_4$ | 1 | 0 | 0 | 1 | 1 | 1 | 1 | 1 |
| $M_5$ | 1 | 0 | 1 | 1 | 0 | 1 | 1 | 0 |
| $M_6$ | 1 | 1 | 0 | 1 | 1 | 0 | 1 | 0 |
| $M_7$ | 1 | 1 | 1 | 1 | 1 | 1 | 0 | 0 |

In this equation, the parentheses are required due to the precedence rules of Boolean operators. The parentheses show four *sum terms*, terms where all the literals are operated on only by OR. The four sum terms are then AND-ed together. Since the AND operation is like multiplication, the right-hand side is called a *product of sums*. It's also said to be in *conjunctive normal form*.

Each of the sum terms includes all the variables in this equation in the form of literals (uncomplemented or complemented). Where a minterm was a *product* term that specified a single permutation of the $2^n$ permutations of possible values for the variables, a *maxterm* is a *sum* term specifying exactly one of those permutations. A Boolean function that is defined by multiplying (AND-ing) all the maxterms that evaluate to 0 is said to be a *canonical product*, a *product of maxterms*, or in *full conjunctive normal form*.

Each maxterm identifies exactly one set of values for the variables in a function that evaluates to 0 when OR-ed together. For example, the maxterm ($\neg c_{in} \lor \neg x \lor y$) in the previous equation evaluates to 0 only when $c_{in} = 1$, $x = 1$, $y = 0$. But a sum term that does not contain all the variables in the problem, either in uncomplemented or complemented form, will always evaluate to 0 for more than one set of values. For example, the sum term ($\neg c_{in} \lor \neg x$) evaluates to 0 for two sets of values for the three variables in this example, $c_{in} = 1$, $x = 1$, $y = 0$ and $c_{in} = 1$, $x = 1$, and $y = 1$. Because they minimize the number of cases that evaluate to 0 and thus *maximize* the number of cases that evaluate to 1, we call them *max*terms.

Rather than write out all the literals in a function, logic designers commonly use the notation $M_i$ to specify the $i^{th}$ maxterm, where $i$ is the integer value of the base 2 number created by concatenating the values of the literals in the problem. For example, stringing together $c_{in} = 1$, $x = 1$, $y = 0$ gives 110, which is the maxterm $M_6$. The truth table, Table 4-7, shows the maxterms that cause carry = 0. Notice that maxterm $M_6 = (\neg c_{in} \lor \neg x \lor y)$ evaluates to 0 when $c_{in} = 1$, $x = 1$, $y = 0$.

Using this notation to write Boolean equations as a canonical sum and using the $\prod$ symbol to denote multiplication, we can restate the function for the complement of carry as follows:

$$\neg C_{out}(c_{in}, x, y) = (c_{in} \lor \neg x \lor \neg y) \land (\neg c_{in} \lor x \lor \neg y) \land (\neg c_{in} \lor \neg x \lor y) \land (\neg c_{in} \lor \neg x \lor \neg y)$$
$$= M_3 \land M_5 \land M_6 \land M_7$$
$$= \prod (3,5,6,7)$$

If you look back at Table 4-7, you'll see that these are the conditions that cause the complement of carry to be 0 and hence carry to be 1. This shows that using either minterms or maxterms is equivalent. The one you use can depend on factors such as what hardware components you have available to implement the function and personal preference.

## Comparison of Canonical Boolean Forms

Table 4-8 shows all the minterms and maxterms for a three-variable problem. If you compare corresponding minterms and maxterms, you can see the duality of minterms and maxterms: one can be formed from the other using De Morgan's law by complementing each variable and interchanging OR and AND.

**Table 4-8:** Canonical Terms for a Three-Variable Problem

| Minterm = 1 | | x | y | z | Maxterm = 0 | |
|---|---|---|---|---|---|---|
| $m_0$ | ¬x ∧ ¬y ∧ ¬z | 0 | 0 | 0 | $M_0$ | x ∨ y ∨ z |
| $m_1$ | ¬x ∧ ¬y ∧ z | 0 | 0 | 1 | $M_1$ | x ∨ y ∨ ¬z |
| $m_2$ | ¬x ∧ y ∧ ¬z | 0 | 1 | 0 | $M_2$ | x ∨ ¬y ∨ z |
| $m_3$ | ¬x ∧ y ∧ z | 0 | 1 | 1 | $M_3$ | x ∨ ¬y ∨ ¬z |
| $m_4$ | x ∧ ¬y ∧ ¬z | 1 | 0 | 0 | $M_4$ | ¬x ∨ y ∨ z |
| $m_5$ | x ∧ ¬y ∧ z | 1 | 0 | 1 | $M_5$ | ¬x ∨ y ∨ ¬z |
| $m_6$ | x ∧ y ∧ ¬z | 1 | 1 | 0 | $M_6$ | ¬x ∨ ¬y ∨ z |
| $m_7$ | x ∧ y ∧ z | 1 | 1 | 1 | $M_7$ | ¬x ∨ ¬y ∨ ¬z |
| ... | | | | | | |

The canonical forms give you a complete, and unique, statement of the function because they take all possible combinations of the values of the variables into account. However, there often are simpler solutions to the problem. The remainder of this chapter is devoted to methods of simplifying Boolean functions.

## Boolean Expression Minimization

When implementing a Boolean function in hardware, each ∧ operator becomes an AND gate, each ∨ operator an OR gate, and each ¬ operator a NOT gate. In general, the complexity of the hardware is related to the number of AND and OR gates used (NOT gates are simple and tend not to contribute significantly to the complexity). Simpler hardware uses fewer components, thus saving cost and space, and uses less power. Cost, space, and power savings are especially important with handheld and wearable devices. In this section, you'll learn how you can manipulate Boolean expressions to reduce the number of ANDs and ORs, thus simplifying their hardware implementation.

### Minimal Expressions

When simplifying a function, start with one of the canonical forms to ensure that you have taken all possible cases into account. To translate a problem into a canonical form, create a truth table that lists all possible combinations of the variables in the problem. From the truth table, it will be easy to list the minterms or maxterms that define the function.

Armed with a canonical statement, the next step is to look for a functionally equivalent *minimal expression*, an expression that does the same thing as the canonical one, but with a minimum number of literals and

Boolean operators. To minimize an expression, we apply the rules of Boolean algebra to reduce the number of terms and the number of literals in each term, without changing the logical meaning of the expression.

There are two types of minimal expressions, depending on whether you use minterms or maxterms:

### Minimal Sum of Products

When starting with a minterms description of the problem, the minimal expression is called a *minimal sum of products*, which is a sum of products expression where all other mathematically equivalent sum of products expressions have at least as many product terms, and those with the same number of product terms have at least as many literals.

As an example of a minimal sum of products, consider these equations:

$$S(x, y, z) = (\neg x \wedge \neg y \wedge \neg z) \vee (x \wedge \neg y \wedge \neg z) \vee (x \wedge \neg y \wedge z)$$
$$S1(x, y, z) = (\neg x \wedge \neg y \wedge \neg z) \vee (x \wedge \neg y)$$
$$S2(x, y, z) = (x \wedge \neg y \wedge z) \vee (\neg y \wedge \neg z)$$
$$S3(x, y, z) = (x \wedge \neg y) \vee (\neg y \wedge \neg z)$$

$S$ is in canonical form as each of the product terms explicitly shows the contribution of all three variables. The other three functions are simplifications of $S$. Although all three have the same number of product terms, $S3$ is a minimal sum of products for $S$ because it has fewer literals in its product terms than $S1$ and $S2$.

### Minimal Product of Sums

When starting with a maxterms description of the problem, the minimal expression is called a *minimal product of sums*, which is a product of sums expression where all other mathematically equivalent product of sums expressions have at least as many sum terms, and those with the same number of sum terms have at least as many literals.

For an example of a minimal product of sums, consider these equations:

$$P(x, y, z)\ \ = (\neg x \vee \neg y \vee z) \wedge (\neg x \vee y \vee z) \wedge (x \vee \neg y \vee z)$$
$$P1(x, y, z) = (x \vee \neg y \vee z) \wedge (\neg x \vee z)$$
$$P2(x, y, z) = (\neg x \vee y \vee z) \wedge (\neg y \vee z)$$
$$P3(x, y, z) = (\neg x \vee z) \wedge (\neg y \vee z)$$

$P$ is in canonical form, and the other three functions are simplifications of $P$. Although all three have the same number of sum terms as $P$, $P3$ is a minimal product of sums for $P$ because it has fewer literals in its product terms than $P1$ and $P2$.

A problem may have more than one minimal solution. Good hardware design typically involves finding several minimal solutions and then assessing each one within the context of the available hardware. This means more than using fewer gates. For example, as you'll learn when we discuss the actual hardware implementations, adding judiciously placed NOT gates can actually reduce hardware complexity.

In the following two sections, you'll see two ways to find minimal expressions.

## Minimization Using Algebraic Manipulations

To illustrate the importance of reducing the complexity of a Boolean function, let's return to the function for carry:

$$C_{out}(c_{in}, x, y) = (\neg c_{in} \wedge x \wedge y) \vee (c_{in} \wedge \neg x \wedge y) \vee (c_{in} \wedge x \wedge \neg y) \vee (c_{in} \wedge x \wedge y)$$

The expression on the right-hand side of the equation is a sum of min-terms. Figure 4-4 shows the circuit to implement this function. It requires four AND gates and one OR gate. The small circles at the inputs to the AND gates indicate a NOT gate at that input.

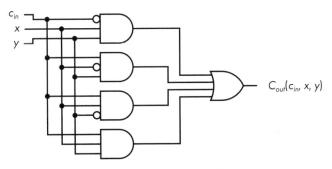

Figure 4-4: Hardware implementation of a function to generate the value of carry when adding two numbers

Now let's try to simplify the Boolean expression implemented in Figure 4-4 to see whether we can reduce the hardware requirements. Note that there may not be a single path to a solution, and there may be more than one correct solution. I'm presenting only one way here.

First, we'll do something that might look strange. We'll use the idempotency rule to duplicate the fourth term twice:

$$C_{out}(c_{in}, x, y) = (\neg c_{in} \wedge x \wedge y) \vee (c_{in} \wedge \neg x \wedge y) \vee (c_{in} \wedge x \wedge \neg y) \vee (c_{in} \wedge x \wedge y)$$
$$\vee (c_{in} \wedge x \wedge y) \vee (c_{in} \wedge x \wedge y)$$

Next, rearrange the product terms slightly to OR each of the three original terms with $(c_{in} \wedge x \wedge y)$:

$$C_{out}(c_{in}, x, y) = ((\neg c_{in} \wedge x \wedge y) \vee (c_{in} \wedge x \wedge y)) \vee ((c_{in} \wedge x \wedge \neg y) \vee (c_{in} \wedge x \wedge y))$$
$$\vee ((c_{in} \wedge \neg x \wedge y) \vee (c_{in} \wedge x \wedge y))$$

Now we can use the rule for distribution of AND over OR to factor out terms that OR to 1:

$$C_{out}(c_{in}, x, y) = (x \wedge y \wedge (\neg c_{in} \vee c_{in})) \vee (c_{in} \wedge x \wedge (\neg y \vee y)) \vee (c_{in} \wedge y \wedge (\neg x \vee x))$$
$$= (x \wedge y \wedge 1) \vee (c_{in} \wedge x \wedge 1) \vee (c_{in} \wedge y \wedge 1)$$
$$= (x \wedge y) \vee (c_{in} \wedge x) \vee (c_{in} \wedge y)$$

Figure 4-5 shows the circuit for this function. Not only have we eliminated an AND gate, but also all the AND gates and the OR gate have one fewer inputs.

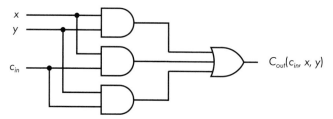

Figure 4-5: Simplified hardware implementation generating carry when adding two numbers

Comparing the circuits in Figures 4-5 and 4-4, Boolean algebra has helped you to simplify the hardware implementation. You can see this simplification from stating the conditions that result in a carry of 1 in English: the original, canonical form of the equation stated that carry, $C_{out}(c_{in}, x, y)$, will be 1 in any of these four cases:

if $c_{in} = 0$, $x = 1$, and $y = 1$

if $c_{in} = 1$, $x = 0$, and $y = 1$

if $c_{in} = 1$, $x = 1$, and $y = 0$

if $c_{in} = 1$, $x = 1$, and $y = 1$

The minimization can be stated much simpler: carry is 1 if at least two of $c_{in}$, $x$, and $y$ are 1.

We arrived at the solution in Figure 4-5 by starting with the sum of minterms; in other words, we were working with the values of $c_{in}$, $x$, and $y$ that generate a 1 for carry. As you saw in "Canonical Product or Product of Maxterms" on page 69, since carry must be either 1 or 0, it's equally as valid to start with the values of $c_{in}$, $x$, and $y$ that generate a 0 for the complement of carry and to write the equation as a product of maxterms:

$$\neg C_{out}(c_{in}, x, y) = (c_{in} \vee \neg x \vee \neg y) \wedge (\neg c_{in} \vee x \vee \neg y) \wedge (\neg c_{in} \vee \neg x \vee y) \wedge (\neg c_{in} \vee \neg x \vee \neg y)$$

To simplify this equation, we'll take the same approach we took with the sum of minterms and start by duplicating the last term twice:

$$\neg C_{out}(c_{in}, x, y) = (c_{in} \vee \neg x \vee \neg y) \wedge (\neg c_{in} \vee x \vee \neg y) \wedge (\neg c_{in} \vee \neg x \vee y) \wedge (\neg c_{in} \vee \neg x \vee \neg y)$$
$$\wedge (\neg c_{in} \vee \neg x \vee \neg y) \wedge (\neg c_{in} \vee \neg x \vee \neg y)$$

Adding some parentheses helps to clarify the simplification process:

$$\neg C_{out}(c_{in}, x, y) = ((c_{in} \vee \neg x \vee \neg y) \wedge (\neg c_{in} \vee \neg x \vee \neg y)) \wedge ((\neg c_{in} \vee x \vee \neg y) \wedge (\neg c_{in} \vee \neg x \vee \neg y))$$
$$\wedge ((\neg c_{in} \vee \neg x \vee y) \wedge (\neg c_{in} \vee \neg x \vee \neg y))$$

Next, use the distribution of OR over AND. Because this is tricky, I'll go over the steps to simplify the first grouping of product terms in this equation—the steps for the other two groupings are similar to this one. Distribution of OR over AND has this generic form:

$$(X \vee Y) \wedge (X \vee Z) = X \vee (Y \wedge Z)$$

Looking at the sum terms in our first grouping, you can see they both share a $(\neg x \vee \neg y)$. So, we'll make these substitutions into the generic form:

$$X = (\neg x \vee \neg y)$$
$$Y = c_{in}$$
$$Z = \neg c_{in}$$

Making the substitutions and using the complement rule for AND, we get

$$(c_{in} \vee \neg x \vee \neg y) \wedge (\neg c_{in} \vee \neg x \vee \neg y) = (\neg x \vee \neg y) \vee (c_{in} \wedge \neg c_{in})$$
$$= (\neg x \vee \neg y)$$

Applying these same manipulations to other two groupings, we get

$$\neg C_{out}(c_{in}, x, y) = (\neg x \vee \neg y) \wedge (\neg c_{in} \vee \neg x) \wedge (\neg c_{in} \vee \neg y)$$

Figure 4-6 shows the circuit implementation of this function. This circuit produces the complement of carry. We would need to complement the output, $\neg C_{out}(c_{in}, x, y)$, to get the value of carry.

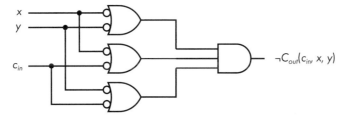

Figure 4-6: Simplified hardware implementation generating the complement of carry when adding two numbers

Compare Figure 4-6 with Figure 4-5, and you can graphically see De Morgan's law: the ORs have become ANDs with complemented values as inputs.

The circuit in Figure 4-5 might look simpler to you because the circuit in Figure 4-6 requires NOT gates at the six inputs to the OR gates. But as you will see in the next chapter, this may not be the case because of the inherent electronic properties of the devices used to construct logic gates. The important point to understand here is that there is more than one way to solve the problem. One of the jobs of the hardware engineer is to decide which solution is best, based on things such as cost, availability of components, and so on.

## Minimization Using Karnaugh Maps

The algebraic manipulations used to minimize Boolean functions may not always be obvious. You may find it easier to work with a graphic representation of the logical statements.

A commonly used graphic tool for working with Boolean functions is the *Karnaugh map*, also called a *K-map*. Invented in 1953 by Maurice Karnaugh, a telecommunications engineer at Bell Labs, the Karnaugh map gives a way to visually find the same simplifications you can find algebraically. They can be used either with a sum of products, using minterms, or a product of sums, using maxterms. To illustrate how they work, we'll start with minterms.

### Simplifying Sums of Products Using Karnaugh Maps

The Karnaugh map is a rectangular grid with a cell for each minterm. There are $2^n$ cells for $n$ variables. Figure 4-7 is a Karnaugh map showing all four possible minterms for two variables, $x$ and $y$. The vertical axis is used for plotting $x$, and the horizontal for $y$. The value of $x$ for each row is shown by the number (0 or 1) immediately to the left of the row, and the value of $y$ for each column appears at the top of the column.

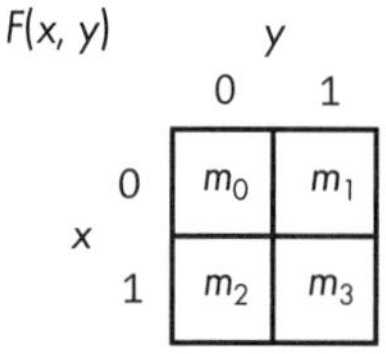

$F(x, y)$

|   | $y$ | |
|---|---|---|
|   | 0 | 1 |
| 0 | $m_0$ | $m_1$ |
| 1 | $m_2$ | $m_3$ |

*Figure 4-7: Mapping of two-variable minterms on a Karnaugh map*

To illustrate how to use a Karnaugh map, let's look at an arbitrary function of two variables:

$$F(x, y) = (x \wedge \neg y) \vee (\neg x \wedge y) \vee (x \wedge y)$$

Start by placing a 1 in each cell corresponding to a minterm that appears in the equation, as shown in Figure 4-8.

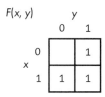

Figure 4-8: Karnaugh
map of the arbitrary
function, F(x, y)

By placing a 1 in the cell corresponding to each minterm that evaluates to 1, we can see graphically when the equation evaluates to 1. The two cells on the right side correspond to the minterms $m_1$ and $m_3$, $(\neg x \wedge y)$ and $(x \wedge y)$. Since these terms are OR-ed together, $F(x, y)$ evaluates to 1 if either of these minterms evaluates to 1. Using the distributive and complement rules, we can see that

$$(\neg x \wedge y) \vee (x \wedge y) = (\neg x \vee x) \wedge y$$
$$= y$$

This shows algebraically that $F(x, y)$ evaluates to 1 whenever $y$ is 1, which you'll see next by simplifying this Karnaugh map.

The only difference between the two minterms, $(\neg x \wedge y)$ and $(x \wedge y)$, is the change from $x$ to $\neg x$. Karnaugh maps are arranged such that only one variable changes between two cells that share an edge, a requirement called the *adjacency rule*.

To use a Karnaugh map to perform simplification, you group two adjacent cells in a sum of products Karnaugh map that have 1s in them. Then you eliminate the variable that differs between them and coalesce the two product terms. Repeating this process allows you to simplify the equation. Each grouping eliminates a product term in the final sum of products. This can be extended to equations with more than two variables, but the number of cells that are grouped together must be a multiple of 2, and you can group only adjacent cells. The adjacency wraps around from side to side and from top to bottom. You'll see an example of that in a few pages.

To see how all this works, consider the grouping in the Karnaugh map in Figure 4-9.

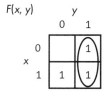

Figure 4-9: Two of
the minterms in F(x, y)
grouped

This grouping is a graphical representation of the algebraic manipulation we did earlier. You can see that $F(x, y)$ evaluates to 1 whenever $y = 1$, regardless of the value of $x$. Thus, the grouping coalesces two minterms into one product term by eliminating $x$.

From the last grouping, we know our final simplified function will have a $y$ term. Let's do another grouping to find the next term. First, we'll simplify the equation algebraically. Returning to the original equation for $F(x, y)$, we can use idempotency to duplicate one of the minterms:

$$F(x,\ y) = (x \wedge \neg y) \vee (\neg x \wedge y) \vee (x \wedge y) \vee (x \wedge y)$$

Now we'll do some algebraic manipulation on the first product term and the one we just added:

$$
\begin{aligned}
(x \wedge \neg y) \vee (x \wedge y)\ &= (\neg y \vee y) \wedge x \\
&= x
\end{aligned}
$$

Instead of using algebraic manipulations, we can do this directly on our Karnaugh map, as shown in Figure 4-10. This map shows that separate groups can include the same cell (minterm).

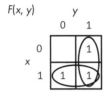

Figure 4-10: A Karnaugh map grouping showing that $(x \wedge \neg y) \vee (\neg x \wedge y) \vee (x \wedge y) = (x \vee y)$

The group in the bottom row represents the product term $x$, and the one in the right-hand column represents $y$, giving us the following minimization:

$$F(x,\ y) = x \vee y$$

Note that the cell that is included in both groupings, $(x \wedge y)$, is the term that we duplicated using the idempotent rule in our algebraic solution previously. You can think of including a cell in more than one group as adding a duplicate copy of the cell, like using the idempotent rule in our algebraic manipulation earlier, and then coalescing it with the other cell(s) in the group, thus removing it.

The adjacency rule is automatically satisfied when there are only two variables in the function. But when we add another variable, we need to think about how to order the cells of a Karnaugh map such that we can use the adjacency rule to simplify Boolean expressions.

### Karnaugh Map Cell Order

One of the problems with both the binary and BCD codes is that the difference between two adjacent values often involves more than one bit being changed. In 1943 Frank Gray introduced a code, the *Gray code*, in which adjacent values differ by only one bit. The Gray code was invented because the switching technology of that time was more prone to errors. If one bit was in error, the value represented by a group of bits was off by only one in the Gray code. That's seldom a problem these days, but this property shows us how to order the cells in a Karnaugh map.

Constructing the Gray code is quite easy. Start with one bit:

| Decimal | Gray code |
| --- | --- |
| 0 | 0 |
| 1 | 1 |

To add a bit, first write the mirror image of the existing pattern:

| Gray code |
| --- |
| 0 |
| 1 |
| 1 |
| 0 |

Then add a 0 to the beginning of each of the original bit patterns and add a 1 to the beginning of each of the mirror image set to give the Gray code for two bits, as shown in Table 4-9.

**Table 4-9:** Gray Code for Two Bits

| Decimal | Gray code |
| --- | --- |
| 0 | 00 |
| 1 | 01 |
| 2 | 11 |
| 3 | 10 |

This is the reason the Gray code is sometimes called *reflected binary code* (*RBC*). Table 4-10 shows the Gray code for four bits.

**Table 4-10:** Gray Code for Four Bits

| Decimal | Gray code | Binary |
| --- | --- | --- |
| 0 | 0000 | 0000 |
| 1 | 0001 | 0001 |
| 2 | 0011 | 0010 |

*(continued)*

**Table 4-10:** Gray Code for Four Bits *(continued)*

| Decimal | Gray code | Binary |
|---|---|---|
| 3 | 0010 | 0011 |
| 4 | 0110 | 0100 |
| 5 | 0111 | 0101 |
| 6 | 0101 | 0110 |
| 7 | 0100 | 0111 |
| 8 | 1100 | 1000 |
| 9 | 1101 | 1001 |
| 10 | 1111 | 1010 |
| 11 | 1110 | 1011 |
| 12 | 1010 | 1100 |
| 13 | 1011 | 1101 |
| 14 | 1001 | 1110 |
| 15 | 1000 | 1111 |

Let's compare the binary codes with the Gray codes for the decimal values 7 and 8 in Table 4-10. The binary codes for 7 and 8 are `0111` and `1000`, respectively; all four bits change when stepping only 1 in decimal value. But comparing the Gray codes for 7 and 8, `0100` and `1100`, respectively, only one bit changes, thus satisfying the adjacency rule for a Karnaugh map.

Notice that the pattern of changing only one bit between adjacent values also holds when the bit pattern wraps around. Only one bit is changed when going from the highest value (15 for four bits) to the lowest (0).

### Karnaugh Map for Three Variables

To see how the adjacency property is important, let's consider a more complicated function. We'll use a Karnaugh map to simplify our function for carry, which has three variables. Adding another variable means that we need to double the number of cells to hold the minterms. To keep the map two-dimensional, we add the new variable to an existing variable on one side of the map. We need a total of eight cells ($2^3$), so we'll draw it four cells wide and two high. We'll add *z* to the *y*-axis and draw our Karnaugh map with *y* and *z* on the horizontal axis, and *x* on the vertical, as shown in Figure 4-11.

*F(x, y, z)*

| *x* \ *yz* | 00 | 01 | 11 | 10 |
|---|---|---|---|---|
| 0 | $m_0$ | $m_1$ | $m_3$ | $m_2$ |
| 1 | $m_4$ | $m_5$ | $m_7$ | $m_6$ |

*Figure 4-11: Mapping of three-variable minterms on a Karnaugh map*

The order of the bit patterns along the top of the three-variable Karnaugh map is 00, 01, 11, 10, which is the Gray code order in Table 4-9, as opposed to 00, 01, 10, 11. The adjacency rule also holds when wrapping around the edges of the Karnaugh map—that is, going from $m_2$ to $m_0$ or going from $m_6$ to $m_4$—which means that groups can wrap around the edges of the map. (Other axis labeling schemes will also work, as you'll see when it's Your Turn at the end of this section.)

You saw earlier in this chapter that carry can be expressed as the sum of four minterms:

$$C_{out}(c_{in}, x, y) = (\neg c_{in} \wedge x \wedge y) \vee (c_{in} \wedge \neg x \wedge y) \vee (c_{in} \wedge x \wedge \neg y) \vee (c_{in} \wedge x \wedge y)$$
$$= m_3 \vee m_5 \vee m_6 \vee m_7$$
$$= \sum (3,5,6,7)$$

Figure 4-12 shows these four minterms on the Karnaugh map.

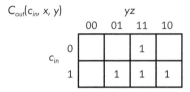

Figure 4-12: Karnaugh map of the function for carry

We look for adjacent cells that can be grouped together to eliminate one variable from the product term. As noted, the groups can overlap, giving the three groups shown in Figure 4-13.

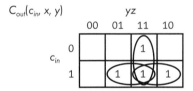

Figure 4-13: A minimum sum of products of the function for carry = 1

Using the three groups in the Karnaugh map in Figure 4-13, we end up with the same equation we got through algebraic manipulations:

$$C_{out}(c_{in}, x, y) = (x \wedge y) \vee (c_{in} \wedge x) \vee (c_{in} \wedge y)$$

### Simplifying Products of Sums Using Karnaugh Maps

It's equally valid to work with a function that shows when the complement of carry is 0. We did that using maxterms:

$$\neg C_{max}(c_{in}, x, y) = (c_{in} \vee \neg x \vee \neg y) \wedge (\neg c_{in} \vee x \vee \neg y) \wedge (\neg c_{in} \vee \neg x \vee y) \wedge (\neg c_{in} \vee \neg x \vee \neg y)$$
$$= M_7 \wedge M_6 \wedge M_5 \wedge M_3$$
$$= \prod (3,5,6,7)$$

Figure 4-14 shows the arrangement of maxterms on a three-variable Karnaugh map.

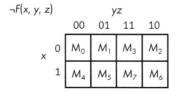

Figure 4-14: Mapping of three-variable maxterms on a Karnaugh map

When working with a maxterm statement of the solution, you mark the cells that evaluate to 0. The minimization process is the same as when working with minterms, except that you group the cells with 0s in them.

Figure 4-15 shows a minimization of $\neg C_{out}(c_{in}, x, y)$, the complement of carry.

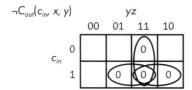

Figure 4-15: A minimum product of sums of the function for NOT carry = 0

The Karnaugh map in Figure 4-15 leads to the same product of sums we got algebraically for the complement of carry = 0:

$$\neg C_{out}(c_{in}, x, y) = (\neg x \lor \neg y) \land (\neg c_{in} \lor \neg x) \land (\neg c_{in} \lor \neg y)$$

If you compare Figures 4-13 and 4-15, you can see a graphic view of De Morgan's law. When making this comparison, keep in mind that Figure 4-13 shows the product terms that get added, and Figure 4-15 shows the sum terms that get multiplied, and the result is complemented. Thus, we exchange 0 and 1 and exchange AND and OR to go from one Karnaugh map to the other.

To further emphasize the duality of minterm and maxterm, compare (a) and (b) in Figure 4-16.

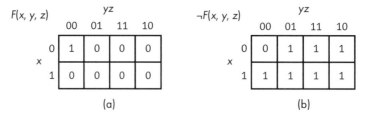

Figure 4-16: Comparison of (a) one minterm and (b) one maxterm

Figure 4-16(a) shows the following function:

$$F(x, y, z) = \neg x \wedge \neg y \wedge \neg z$$

Although it's not necessary and usually not done, we have placed a 0 in each of the cells representing minterms not included in this function.

Similarly, in Figure 4-16(b), we have placed a 0 for the maxterm and a 1 in each of the cells representing the maxterms that are not included in the function:

$$\neg F(x, y, z) = x \vee y \vee z$$

This comparison graphically shows how a minterm specifies the minimum number of 1s in a Karnaugh map, while a maxterm specifies the maximum number of 1s.

### Larger Groupings on a Karnaugh Map

Thus far, we have grouped only two cells together on our Karnaugh maps. Let's look at an example of larger groups. Consider a function that outputs 1 when a three-bit number is even. Table 4-11 shows the truth table. It uses 1 to indicate that the number is even and uses 0 to indicate odd.

**Table 4-11:** Even Values of an Eight-Bit Number

| Minterm | x | y | z | Number | Even(x, y, z) |
|---------|---|---|---|--------|---------------|
| $m_0$ | 0 | 0 | 0 | 0 | 1 |
| $m_1$ | 0 | 0 | 1 | 1 | 0 |
| $m_2$ | 0 | 1 | 0 | 2 | 1 |
| $m_3$ | 0 | 1 | 1 | 3 | 0 |
| $m_4$ | 1 | 0 | 0 | 4 | 1 |
| $m_5$ | 1 | 0 | 1 | 5 | 0 |
| $m_6$ | 1 | 1 | 0 | 6 | 1 |
| $m_7$ | 1 | 1 | 1 | 7 | 0 |

The canonical sum of products for this function is

$$Even(x, y, z) = \sum(0,2,4,6)$$

Figure 4-17 shows these minterms on a Karnaugh map with these four terms grouped together. You can group all four together because they all have adjacent edges.

From the Karnaugh map in Figure 4-17, we can write the equation for showing when a three-bit number is even:

$$Even(x, y, z) = \neg z$$

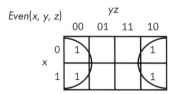

Figure 4-17: Karnaugh map showing
even values of a three-bit number

The Karnaugh map shows that it does not matter what the values of $x$
and $y$ are, only that $z = 0$.

### Adding More Variables to a Karnaugh Map

Each time you add another variable to a Karnaugh map, you need to double
the number of cells. The only requirement for the Karnaugh map to work
is that you arrange the minterms, or maxterms, according to the adjacency
rule. Figure 4-18 shows a four-variable Karnaugh map for minterms. The $y$
and $z$ variables are on the horizontal axis, and $w$ and $x$ are on the vertical.

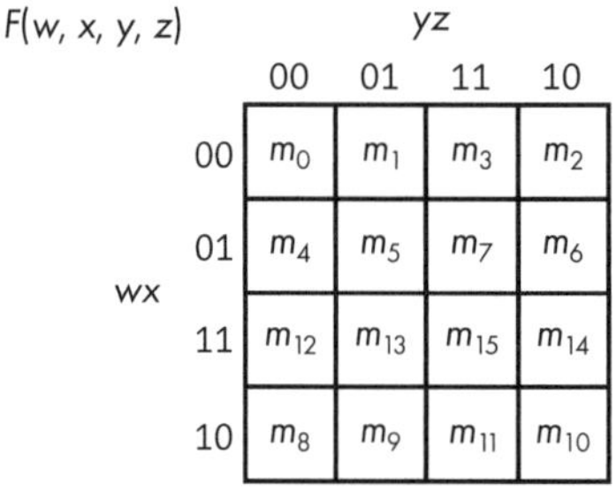

$F(w, x, y, z)$

|  | | yz | | |
| --- | --- | --- | --- | --- |
|  | 00 | 01 | 11 | 10 |
| wx 00 | $m_0$ | $m_1$ | $m_3$ | $m_2$ |
| 01 | $m_4$ | $m_5$ | $m_7$ | $m_6$ |
| 11 | $m_{12}$ | $m_{13}$ | $m_{15}$ | $m_{14}$ |
| 10 | $m_8$ | $m_9$ | $m_{11}$ | $m_{10}$ |

Figure 4-18: Mapping of four-variable
minterms on a Karnaugh map

So far we have assumed that every minterm (or maxterm) is accounted
for in our functions. But design does not take place in a vacuum. We might
have knowledge about other components of the overall design telling us
that some combinations of variable values can never occur. Next, we'll see
how to take this knowledge into account in your function simplification
process. The Karnaugh map provides an especially clear way to visualize
the situation.

### Don't Care Cells

Sometimes, you have information about the values that the variables can
have. If you know which combinations of values will never occur, the minterms (or maxterms) that represent those combination are irrelevant. For

example, you may want a function that indicates whether one of two possible events has occurred, but you know that the two events cannot occur simultaneously. Let's name the events $x$ and $y$, and let 0 indicate that the event has not occurred and 1 indicate that it has. Table 4-12 shows the truth table for our function, $F(x, y)$.

**Table 4-12:** Truth Table for $x$ or $y$ Occurring, but Not Both

| x | y | F(x, y) |
|---|---|---------|
| 0 | 0 | 0 |
| 0 | 1 | 1 |
| 1 | 0 | 1 |
| 1 | 1 | X |

We can show that both events cannot occur simultaneously by placing an X in that row. We can draw a Karnaugh map with an X for the minterm that can't exist in the system, as shown in Figure 4-19. The X represents a *don't care* cell—we don't care whether this cell is grouped with other cells or not.

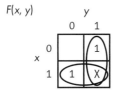

Figure 4-19: Karnaugh map for F(x, y), showing a "don't care" cell

Since the cell that represents the minterm $(x \wedge y)$ is a "don't care" cell, we can include it, or not, in our minimization groupings, leading to the two groupings shown. The Karnaugh map in Figure 4-19 leads us to the solution:

$$F(x, y) = x \vee y$$

which is a simple OR gate. You probably guessed this solution without having to use a Karnaugh map. You'll see a more interesting use of "don't care" cells when you learn about the design of two digital logic circuits at the end of Chapter 7.

## Combining Basic Boolean Operators

As mentioned earlier in this chapter, we can combine basic Boolean operators to implement more-complex Boolean operators. Now that you know how to work with Boolean functions, we'll design one of the more common operators, the *exclusive or*, often called *XOR*, using the three basic operators, AND, OR, and NOT. It's so commonly used that it has its own circuit symbol.

### XOR

The XOR is a binary operator. The result is 1 if one, and only one, of the two operands is 1; otherwise, the result is 0. We'll use $\underline{\vee}$ to designate the XOR operation. It's also common to use the $\oplus$ symbol. Figure 4-20 shows the XOR gate operation with inputs $x$ and $y$.

| x | y | $x \underline{\vee} y$ |
|---|---|---|
| 0 | 0 | 0 |
| 0 | 1 | 1 |
| 1 | 0 | 1 |
| 1 | 1 | 0 |

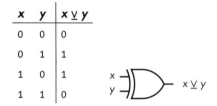

Figure 4-20: The XOR gate acting on two variables, x and y

The minterm implementation of this operation is

$$x \underline{\vee} y = (x \wedge \neg y) \vee (\neg x \wedge y)$$

The XOR operator can be implemented with two AND gates, two NOT gates, and one OR gate, as shown in Figure 4-21.

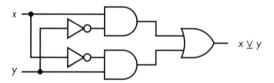

Figure 4-21: XOR gate made from AND, OR, and NOT gates

We can, of course, design many more Boolean operators. But we're going to move on in the next few chapters and see how these operators can be implemented in hardware. It's all done with simple on/off switches.

1. Design a function that will detect all the four-bit integers that are even.

2. Find a minimal sum-of-products expression for this function:

$$F(x, y, z) = (\neg x \wedge \neg y \wedge \neg z) \vee (\neg x \wedge \neg y \wedge z) \vee (\neg x \wedge y \wedge \neg z) \vee (x \wedge \neg y \wedge \neg z)$$
$$\vee (x \wedge y \wedge \neg z) \vee (x \wedge y \wedge z)$$

3. Find a minimal product-of-sums expression for this function:

$$F(x, y, z) = (x \vee y \vee z) \wedge (x \vee y \vee \neg z) \wedge (x \vee \neg y \vee \neg z)$$
$$\wedge (\neg x \vee y \vee z) \wedge (\neg x \vee \neg y \vee \neg z)$$

4. The arrangement of the variables for a Karnaugh map is arbitrary, but the minterms (or maxterms) need to be consistent with the labeling. Show where each minterm is located with this Karnaugh map axis labeling using the notation of Figure 4-11.

$F(x, y, z)$

```
              xy
       00   01   11   10
     ┌────┬────┬────┬────┐
   0 │    │    │    │    │
 z   ├────┼────┼────┼────┤
   1 │    │    │    │    │
     └────┴────┴────┴────┘
```

5. The arrangement of the variables for a Karnaugh map is arbitrary, but the minterms (or maxterms) need to be consistent with the labeling. Show where each minterm is located with this Karnaugh map axis labeling using the notation of Figure 4-11.

$F(x, y, z)$

```
              xz
       00   01   11   10
     ┌────┬────┬────┬────┐
   0 │    │    │    │    │
 y   ├────┼────┼────┼────┤
   1 │    │    │    │    │
     └────┴────┴────┴────┘
```

6. Create a Karnaugh map for five variables. You'll probably need to review the Gray code in Table 4-10 and increase it to five bits.

Design a logic function that detects the single-digit prime numbers. Assume that the numbers are coded in four-bit BCD (see Table 2-7 in Chapter 2). The function is 1 for each prime number.

# What You've Learned

**Boolean operators**   The basic Boolean operators are AND, OR, and NOT.

**Rules of Boolean algebra**   Boolean algebra provides a mathematical way to work with the rules of logic. AND works like multiplication, and OR is similar to addition in elementary algebra.

**Simplifying Boolean algebra expressions**   Boolean functions specify the functionality of a computer. Simplifying these functions leads to a simpler hardware implementation.

**Karnaugh maps**   These provide a graphical way to simplify Boolean expressions.

**Gray code**   This shows how to order the cells in a Karnaugh map.

**Combining basic Boolean operators**   XOR can be created from AND, OR, and NOT.

The next chapter starts with an introduction to basic electronics that will provide a basis for understanding how transistors can be used to implement switches. From there, we'll look at how transistor switches are used to implement logic gates.

# 5

## LOGIC GATES

In the previous chapter, you learned about Boolean algebra expressions and how to implement them using logic gates. In this chapter, you'll learn how to implement logic gates in hardware by using *transistors*, the solid-state electronic devices used to implement the on/off switches we've been discussing throughout this book.

To help you to understand how transistors operate, we'll start with a simple introduction to electronics. From there, you'll see how transistors can be connected in pairs to switch faster and use less electrical power. We'll end the chapter with some practical considerations regarding the use of transistors to construct logic gates.

# Crash Course in Electronics

You don't need to be an electrical engineer to understand how logic gates work, but some understanding of the basic concepts can help. This section provides a brief overview of the fundamental concepts of electronic circuits. We'll begin with two definitions.

*Current* refers to the movement of electrical charge. Electrical charge is measured in *coulombs*. A flow of one coulomb per second is defined as one *ampere*, often abbreviated as *amp*. Current flows through an electrical circuit only if there is a completely connected path from one side of the power source to the other side.

*Voltage* refers to the difference in electrical energy per unit charge, also called *potential difference*, between two points in an electrical circuit. One *volt* is defined as the electrical difference between two points on a *conductor* (the medium the current flows through) when one ampere of current flowing through the conductor dissipates one watt of power.

A computer is constructed from the following electronic components:

- Power source that provides the electrical power
- Passive components that affect current flow and voltage levels, but whose characteristics cannot be altered by another electronic component
- Active components that switch between various combinations of the power source, passive components, and other active components under the control of one or more other electronic components
- Conductors that connect the other components together

Let's look at how each of these electronic components works.

## Power Supplies and Batteries

In almost all countries, electrical power comes in the form of *alternating current (AC)*. For AC, a plot of the magnitude of the voltage versus time shows a sinusoidal wave shape. Computer circuits use *direct current (DC)* power, which, unlike AC, does not vary over time. A power supply is used to convert AC power to DC, as shown in Figure 5-1.

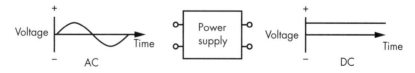

Figure 5-1: AC/DC power supply

Batteries also provide DC electrical power. When drawing circuits, we'll use the symbol for a battery (Figure 5-2) to designate a DC power supply. The power supply in Figure 5-2 provides 5 volts DC.

*Figure 5-2: Circuit symbol for a 5-volt DC power source*

Throughout this book, you've seen that everything that goes on in a computer is based on a system of 1s and 0s. But how are these 1s and 0s physically represented? Computer circuits distinguish between two different voltage levels to provide logical 0 and 1. For example, logical 0 may be represented by 0 volts DC and logical 1 by 5 volts DC. The reverse could also be implemented: 5 volts as logical 0 and 0 volts as logical 1. The only requirement is that the hardware design be consistent. Luckily, programmers don't need to worry about the actual voltages used—that's best left to the computer hardware engineers.

**NOTE** *Electronic devices are designed to operate reliably within a range of voltages. For example, a device designed to operate at a nominal 5 volts typically has a tolerance of ±5%, or 4.75 to 5.25 volts.*

Because computer circuits are constantly switching between the two voltage levels, when the voltage is suddenly switched from one level to another, computer hardware engineers need to consider the time-dependent characteristics of the circuit elements. We'll look at these characteristics in the following section.

## Passive Components

All electrical circuits have resistance, capacitance, and inductance. These electromagnetic properties are distributed throughout any electronic circuit:

**Resistance**    Impedes current flow, thus dissipating energy. The electrical energy is transformed into heat.

**Capacitance**    Stores energy in an electric field. Voltage across a capacitance cannot change instantaneously.

**Inductance**    Stores energy in a magnetic field. Current through an inductance cannot change instantaneously.

It takes time for energy to be stored as an electric field in capacitance, or as a magnetic field in inductance, so these two properties impede *changes* in voltage and current. These two properties are lumped together with resistance and called *impedance*. The impedance to changes slows down the switching that takes place in a computer, and the resistance consumes electrical power. We'll be looking at the general timing characteristics of these properties in the remaining part of this section but will leave a discussion of power consumption to more advanced books on the topic.

To get a feel for the effects of each of these properties, we'll consider the discrete electronic devices that are used to place these properties in a specific location in a circuit: resistors, capacitors, and inductors. They are part of a broader class of electronic components called *passive components*, which cannot be controlled electronically. They simply consume or store the energy.

Figure 5-3 shows the circuit symbols for the passive electronic devices we'll be discussing. Each is described next.

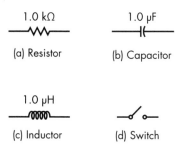

1.0 kΩ
(a) Resistor

1.0 µF
(b) Capacitor

1.0 µH
(c) Inductor

(d) Switch

*Figure 5-3: Circuit symbols for passive devices*

## Switches

A *switch* can be in one of two positions—open or closed. In the open position, there is no connection between the two ends. When closed, the connection between the two ends is complete, thus conducting electricity. The symbol in Figure 5-3 (d) typically indicates a switch that is activated manually. In "Transistors" on page 100, you'll learn that a computer uses transistors for open/closed switches, which are controlled electronically, thus implementing the on/off logic that forms the basis of a computer.

## Resistors

A *resistor* is used to limit the amount of current in a specific location in a circuit. By limiting the current flow into a capacitor or inductor, a resistor affects the time it takes for these other devices to build up their energy storage. The amount of resistance is usually chosen in conjunction with the amount of capacitance or inductance to provide specific timing characteristics. Resistors are also used to limit current flowing through a device to nondestructive levels.

As it limits current flow, a resistor irreversibly transforms the electrical energy into heat. A resistor doesn't store energy, unlike a capacitor or inductor, which can return the stored energy to the circuit at a later time.

The relationship between voltage and current for a single resistor is given by *Ohm's law*,

$$V(t) = I(t) \times R$$

where $V(t)$ is the voltage difference across the resistor at time $t$, $I(t)$ is the current flowing through it at time $t$, and $R$ is the value of the resistor. Resistor values are specified in *ohms*.

The circuit shown in Figure 5-4 shows two resistors connected through a switch to a power supply, which supplies 5 volts. The Greek letter $\Omega$ is used to indicate ohms, and k$\Omega$ indicates $10^3$ ohms. Since current can flow only in a closed path, no current flows until the switch is closed.

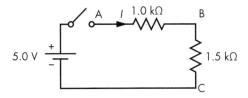

Figure 5-4: Two resistors in series with a power supply and switch

In Figure 5-4, both resistors are in the same path, so when the switch is closed, the same current, $I$, flows through each of them. Resistors that are in the same current flow path are said to be *connected in series*. To determine the amount of current flowing from the battery, we need to compute the total resistance in the current path.

The total resistance in the path of the current is the sum of the two resistors:

$$R = 1.0 \text{ k}\Omega + 1.5 \text{ k}\Omega$$
$$= 2.5 \text{ k}\Omega$$

Thus, the voltage, 5 volts, is applied across a total of 2.5 k$\Omega$. Solving for $I$, and leaving out $t$ because the power supply voltage doesn't vary with time,

$$I = \frac{V}{R}$$
$$= \frac{5.0 \text{ volts}}{2.5 \times 10^3 \text{ ohms}}$$
$$= 2.0 \times 10^{-3} \text{ ohms}$$
$$= 2.0 \text{ ma}$$

where *ma* means milliamps.

We can now determine the voltage difference between points A and B in the circuit in Figure 5-4 by multiplying the resistor value and current:

$$V_{AB} = 1.0 \text{ k}\Omega \times 2.0 \text{ ma}$$
$$= 2.0 \text{ volts}$$

Similarly, the voltage difference between points B and C is

$$V_{BC} = 1.5 \text{ k}\Omega \times 2.0 \text{ ma}$$
$$= 3.0 \text{ volts}$$

Thus, connecting the resistors in series serves as a *voltage divider*, dividing the 5 volts between the two resistors—2.0 volts across the 1.0 k$\Omega$ resistor and 3.0 volts across the 1.5 k$\Omega$ resistor.

Figure 5-5 shows the same two resistors *connected in parallel*.

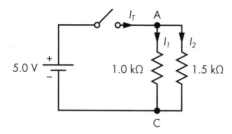

*Figure 5-5: Two resistors in parallel*

In Figure 5-5, the full voltage of the power supply, 5 volts, is applied across points A and C when the switch is closed. Thus, each resistor has 5 volts applied across it, and we can use Ohm's law to compute the current through each:

$$I_1 = \frac{V}{R_1}$$
$$= \frac{5.0 \text{ volts}}{1.0 \text{ k}\Omega}$$
$$= 5.0 \times 10^{-3} \text{ amps}$$
$$= 5.0 \text{ ma}$$

and

$$I_2 = \frac{V}{R_2}$$
$$= \frac{5.0 \text{ volts}}{1.5 \text{ k}\Omega}$$
$$= 3.3 \text{ ma}$$

The total current, $I_T = I_1 + I_2$, supplied by the power supply when the switch is closed is divided at point A to supply both the resistors. It must equal the sum of the two currents through the resistors:

$$I_T = I_1 + I_2$$

$$= 5.0 \text{ ma} + 3.3 \text{ ma}$$
$$= 8.3 \text{ ma}$$

## Capacitors

A *capacitor* stores energy in the form of an *electric field*, which is essentially the electric charge at rest. A capacitor initially allows current to flow into the capacitor. Instead of providing a continuous path for the current flow, a capacitor stores the electric charge, creating an electric field and thus causing the current flow to decrease over time.

Since it takes time for the electric field to build up, capacitors are often used to smooth out rapid changes in voltage. When there is a sudden increase in current flow into the capacitor, the capacitor tends to absorb the electric charge. Then when the current flow suddenly decreases, the stored electric charge is released from the capacitor.

The voltage across a capacitor changes with time according to

$$V(t) = \frac{1}{C}\int_{o}^{t} I(t)dt$$

where $V(t)$ is the voltage difference across the resistor at time $t$, $I(t)$ is the current flowing through it at time $t$, and $C$ is the value of the capacitor in *farads*; the symbol for farads is F.

**NOTE** *In case you haven't studied calculus, the $\int$ symbol represents integration, which can be thought of as "infinitesimal summation." This equation says that the voltage sums up as time increases from 0 to the current time, t. You'll see a graphic view of this in Figure 5-7.*

Figure 5-6 shows a 1.0 µF (microfarad) capacitor being charged through a 1.0 kΩ resistor.

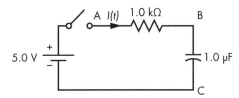

Figure 5-6: Capacitor in series with a resistor. $V_{AB}$ is the voltage across the resistor, and $V_{BC}$ is the voltage across the capacitor.

As you will see later in the chapter, this circuit is a rough simulation of the output of one transistor connected to the input of another. The output of the first transistor has resistance, and the input to the second transistor has capacitance. The switching behavior of the second transistor depends upon the voltage across the (equivalent) capacitor, $V_{BC}(t)$, reaching a threshold value.

Let's look at the time it takes for the voltage across the capacitor to charge up to a threshold value. Assuming the voltage across the capacitor, $V_{BC}$, is 0 volts when the switch is first closed, current flows through the resistor and into the capacitor. The voltage across the resistor plus the voltage across the capacitor must be equal to the voltage available from the power supply. That is,

$$5.0 = I(t)R + V_{BC}(t)$$

Starting with the voltage across the capacitor, $V_{BC}$, at 0 volts, when the switch is first closed, the full voltage of the power supply, 5 volts, will appear across the resistor. Thus, the initial current flow in the circuit will be

$$I_{initial} = \frac{5.0 \text{ volts}}{1.0 \text{ k}\Omega}$$

$$= 5.0 \text{ ma}$$

This initial surge of current into the capacitor causes the voltage across the capacitor to build up toward the power supply voltage. The previous integral equation shows that this buildup exponentially decreases as the voltage across the capacitor approaches its final value. As the voltage across the capacitor, $V_{BC}(t)$, increases, the voltage across the resistor, $V_{AB}(t)$, must decrease. When the voltage across the capacitor finally equals the voltage of the power supply, the voltage across the resistor is 0 volts, and current flow in the circuit becomes zero. The rate of the exponential decrease in current flow is given by the product of the resistor value and the capacitor value, $RC$, called the *time constant*.

For the values of $R$ and $C$ in this example, we get

$$RC = 1.0 \times 10^3 \text{ ohms} \times 1.0 \times 10^{-6} \text{ farads}$$
$$= 1.0 \times 10^{-3} \text{ seconds}$$
$$= 1.0 \text{ msec}$$

Assuming the capacitor in Figure 5-6 has 0 volts across it when the switch is closed, the voltage that develops across the capacitor over time is given by

$$V_{BC}(t) = 5.0 \times (1 - e^{\frac{-t}{10^{-3}}})$$

You can see this graphically in Figure 5-7. The left $y$-axis shows voltage across the capacitor, while the right-side voltage is across the resistor. Note that the scales go in opposite directions.

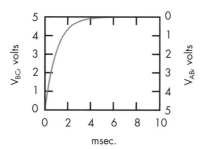

Figure 5-7: Capacitor charging over time in the circuit in Figure 5-6

At the time $t = 1.0$ millisecond (one time constant), the voltage across the capacitor is

$$V_{BC} = 5.0\left(1 - e^{\frac{-10^{-3}}{10^{-3}}}\right)$$
$$= 5.0 \left(1 - e^{-1}\right)$$
$$= 5.0 \times 0.63$$
$$= 3.15 \text{ volts}$$

which is more than the threshold voltage of the typical transistors used in a computer. Again, you'll learn more about this later in the chapter.

After six constants of time have passed, the voltage across the capacitor has reached

$$V_{BC} = 5.0\left(1 - e^{\frac{-6 \times 10^{-3}}{10^{-3}}}\right)$$
$$= 5.0 \left(1 - e^{-1}\right)$$
$$= 5.0 \times 0.63$$
$$= 3.15 \text{ volts}$$

At this time, the voltage across the resistor is essentially 0 volts, and current flow is very low.

## Inductors

An *inductor* stores energy in the form of a *magnetic field*, which is created by electric charge in motion. An inductor initially prevents the flow of electrical charge, requiring time for the magnetic field to build. By providing a continuous path for the flow of electrical charge (current), an inductor creates the magnetic field.

In a computer, inductors are mainly used in the power supply and the circuitry that connects the power supply to the CPU. If you have access to the inside of a computer, you can probably see a small (about 1 cm in diameter) donut-shaped device with wire wrapped around it on the motherboard near the CPU. This is an inductor used to smooth the power supplied to the CPU.

Although either an inductor or a capacitor can be used to smooth the power, the inductor does it by resisting current changes, and the capacitor does it by resisting voltage changes. The choice of which one, or even both, to use for smoothing would take us into a much more complicated discussion of electronics.

The relationship between voltage *V(t)* at time *t* across an inductor and current flow through it, *I(t)*, is given by the equation

$$V(t) = L\frac{dI(t)}{dt}$$

where *L* is the value of the inductor in *henrys*; the symbol for henrys is H.

**NOTE**    *Again, we're using some calculus here. The* $dI(t)/dt$ *notation represents differentiation, which is the rate of change of* $I(t)$ *with respect to time, t. This equation says that the voltage at time, t, is proportional to the rate of change of* $I$ *at that time. (You'll see a graphic view of this later in Figure 5-9.)*

Figure 5-8 shows a 1.0 µH inductor connected in series with a 1.0 kΩ resistor.

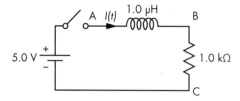

Figure 5-8: Inductor in series with a resistor

When the switch is open, no current flows through this circuit. Upon closing the switch, the inductor initially impedes the flow of current, taking time for a magnetic field to be built up in the inductor. Before the switch is closed, no current is flowing through the resistor, so the voltage across it, $V_{BC}$, is 0 volts. The full voltage of the power supply, 5 volts, appears across the inductor, $V_{AB}$. As current begins to flow through the inductor, the voltage across the resistor, $V_{BC}(t)$, grows. This results in an exponentially decreasing voltage across the inductor. When the voltage across the inductor finally reaches 0 volts, the voltage across the resistor is 5 volts, and current flow in the circuit is 5.0 ma.

The rate of the exponential voltage decrease is given by the time constant $L/R$. Using the values of $R$ and $L$ in Figure 5-8, we get

$$\frac{L}{R} = \frac{1.0 \times 10^{-6} \text{ henrys}}{1.0 \times 10^{3} \text{ ohms}}$$

$$= 1.0 \times 10^{-9} \text{ seconds}$$

$$= 1.0 \text{ nanoseconds}$$

When the switch is closed, the voltage that develops across the inductor over time is given by

$$V_{AB}(t) = 5.0 \times e^{\frac{-t}{10^{-9}}}$$

as shown in Figure 5-9. The left y-axis shows voltage across the resistor, with the right-side voltage across the inductor. Note that the scales go in opposite directions.

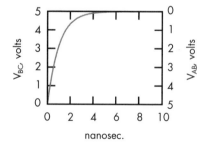

Figure 5-9: Inductor building a magnetic field over time in the circuit in Figure 5-8

At time $t = 1.0$ nanoseconds (one time constant), the voltage across the inductor is

$$V_{AB} = 5.0\ 1 - e^{\frac{-10^{-9}}{10^{-9}}}$$
$$= 5.0\ (1 - e^{-1})$$
$$= 5.0 \times 0.63$$
$$= 3.15 \text{ volts}$$

After about 6 nanoseconds (six time constants), the voltage across the inductor is essentially equal to 0 volts. At this time, the full voltage of the power supply is across the resistor, and a steady current of 5.0 ma flows.

This circuit in Figure 5-8 shows how inductors can be used in a CPU power supply. The power supply in this circuit simulates the computer power supply, and the resistor simulates the CPU, which is consuming the electrical energy from the power supply. The voltage produced by a power supply includes *noise*, which consists of small, high-frequency fluctuations added to the DC level. As shown in Figure 5-9, the voltage supplied to the CPU, $V_{BC}(t)$, changes little over short periods of time. The inductor connected in series between the power supply and the CPU acts to smooth out the voltage that powers the CPU.

## Power Consumption

An important part of hardware design is *power* consumption, especially in battery-powered devices. Of the three electromagnetic properties we've discussed here, resistance is the primary consumer of power.

*Energy* is the ability to cause change, and power is a measure of how fast energy can be used to make the change. The basic unit of energy is a *joule*. The basic unit of power is a *watt*, which is defined as expending one joule per second. For example, I have a backup battery that can store 240 WH. That means it can store enough energy to provide 240 watts for one hour or 120 watts for two hours. It can store 240 WH × 360 seconds/hour = 864,000 joules. The units for volt and ampere are defined such that 1 watt = 1 volt × 1 ampere. This gives rise to the formula for power,

$$P = V \times I$$

where $P$ is the power used, $V$ is the voltage across the component, and $I$ is the current flowing through it.

After a brief charging time, a capacitor prevents current flow, so the amount of power used by a capacitor goes to zero. It simply stores energy in the form of an electrical field. And after a brief field buildup time, the voltage across an inductor goes to zero, so the amount of power used by an inductor goes to zero. An inductor stores energy in the form of a magnetic field.

However, a resistor doesn't store energy. As long as there is a voltage difference across a resistor, current flows through it. The power used by a resistor, $R$, is given by

$$P = V \times I$$
$$= I \times R \times I$$
$$= I^2 \times R$$

This power is converted to heat in the resistor. Since the power consumption increases by the square of the current, a common hardware design goal is to reduce the amount of current flow.

This section has been an idealized discussion of the passive components that computer engineers include in their designs. In the real world, each component includes elements of all three characteristics—resistance, capacitance, and inductance—that the hardware design engineer needs to take into account. These secondary effects are subtle and often troublesome in the design.

The rest of this chapter is devoted to discussing the *active components*, those controlled electronically, that are used to implement the switches that are the basis for a computer. As you will see, the active components include resistance and capacitance, which affect the design of the circuit they're used in.

## Transistors

We have already described a computer as a collection of two-state switches. In previous chapters, we discussed how data can be represented by the settings, 0 or 1, of these switches. Then we moved on to look at how 0s and 1s can be combined using logic gates to implement logical functions. In this section, we'll see how transistors can be used to implement the two-state switches that make up a computer.

A *transistor* is a device whose resistance can be controlled electronically, thus making it an *active component*. The ability to be controlled electronically is what distinguishes the switches made from transistors from the simple on/off switches you saw earlier in the chapter, which could be controlled mechanically. Before describing how a transistor can be used as a switch, let's look at how we'd implement a logic gate using mechanical on/off switches. We'll use the NOT gate for this example.

Figure 5-10 shows two push-button switches connected in series between 5 volts and 0 volts. The top switch is normally closed. When its button is pushed (from the left side), the connection between the two small circles is broken, thus opening the circuit at this point. The bottom switch is normally open. When its button is pushed, a connection is made between the two small circles, thus completing the circuit at this point.

Now we'll let 5 volts represent a 1 and 0 volts a 0. The input to this NOT gate, $x$, pushes the two buttons simultaneously. We will control $x$ in the following way: when $x = 1$, we'll push the two buttons, and when $x = 0$, we will not push the buttons. When the button is not pushed, $x = 0$, the 5 volts are connected to the output, $\neg x$, which represents 1. When the button is pushed, $x = 1$, the 5 volts are disconnected, and the 0 volts, which represent 0, are connected to the output. Thus, an input of 1 gets an output of 0, and an input of 0 gets an output of 1—a NOT gate.

Early computing devices did use mechanical switches to implement their logic, but the results were very slow by today's standards. Modern

computers use *transistors*, which are electronic devices made from semiconductor materials that can be switched between their conducting and non-
conducting states quickly under electronic control.

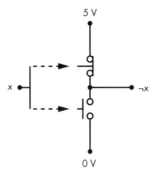

Figure 5-10: NOT gate made
from two push-button switches

Just as with the mechanically controlled push-button example, we use
two different voltages to represent 1 and 0. For example, we might use a
high voltage, say +5 volts, to represent 1, and a low voltage, say 0 volts, to
represent 0. But transistors can be switched on or off electronically, which
makes them much faster than the mechanical switches used in the original
computers. Transistors take up much less space and consume much less
electrical power.

In the following sections, we'll look at two transistors commonly used in
modern computers.

## MOSFET Switch

The most commonly used switching transistor in today's computer logic
circuits is the *metal-oxide-semiconductor field-effect transistor (MOSFET)*. There
are several types of MOSFET that use different voltage levels and polarities.
I'll describe the behavior of the most common type, the *enhancement-mode
MOSFET*, and leave the details of the other variations to more advanced
books on the topic. The brief discussion here should help you to understand the basics of how they work.

The basic material in a MOSFET is typically silicon, which is a *semiconductor*, meaning it conducts electricity, but not very well. Its conductivity is
improved by adding an impurity, a process called *doping*. Depending on the
type of impurity, the electrical conductivity can be either the flow of electrons
or the flow of lack of electrons (called *holes*). Since electrons have a negative
electrical charge, the type that conducts electrons is called *N-type*, and the
type that conducts holes is called *P-type*. The main conduction path through
a MOSFET is the *channel*, which is connected between the *source* and the *drain*
terminals on the MOSFET. The *gate* is made from the opposite type of semiconductor. The gate controls the conductivity through the channel.

Figure 5-11 (a) and (b) shows the two basic types of MOSFET, N-channel and P-channel, respectively. I've shown each MOSFET connected to a 5-volt power source through a resistor.

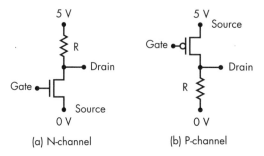

(a) N-channel    (b) P-channel

*Figure 5-11: Two basic types of MOSFETs*

These are simplified circuits so we can discuss how MOSFETs work. Each MOSFET has three connection points, or *terminals*. The gate is used as the input terminal. Voltage applied to the gate, relative to the voltage applied to the source, controls current flow through the MOSFET. The drain is used as the output. The source of an N-channel MOSFET is connected to the lower voltage of the power supply, and the source of a P-channel is connected to the higher voltage.

After learning about complements in Boolean algebra, it probably does not surprise you that the two types of MOSFETs have complementary behavior. You'll see in the following sections how we can connect them in complementary pairs that make for faster, more efficient switches than using only one.

First, we'll look at how each works as a single switching device, starting with the N-channel MOSFET.

### N-Channel MOSFET

In Figure 5-11 (a), the drain of the N-channel MOSFET is connected to the 5-volt side of the power supply through the resistor, R, and the source to the 0-volt side.

When the voltage applied to the gate is positive with respect to the source, the resistance between the drain and the source of the N-channel MOSFET decreases. When this voltage reaches a threshold value, typically in the range of 1 volt, the resistance becomes very low, thus providing a good conduction path for current between the drain and the source. The resulting circuit is equivalent to Figure 5-12 (a).

In this circuit, Figure 5-12 (a), current flows from the 5-volt connection of the power supply to the 0-volt connection through the resistor R. The voltage at the drain will be 0 volts. A problem with this current flow is that the resistor consumes power, simply converting it to heat. In a moment, we'll see the reason we don't want to increase the amount of resistance to limit the current flow to reduce power consumption.

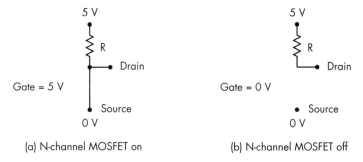

(a) N-channel MOSFET on          (b) N-channel MOSFET off

*Figure 5-12: N-channel MOSFET switch equivalent circuit: (a) switch closed, (b) switch open*

If the voltage applied to the gate is switched to be nearly the same as the voltage applied to the source, 0 volts in this example, the MOSFET turns off, resulting in the equivalent circuit shown in Figure 5-12 (b). The drain is typically connected to another MOSFET's gate, which draws current only briefly as it switches from one state to the other. After this brief switching of state, the connection of the drain to another MOSFET's gate does not draw current. Since no current flows through the resistor, R, there is no voltage difference across it. Thus, the voltage at the drain will be at 5 volts, and the resistor is said to be acting as the *pull-up device*, because when the MOSFET is turned off, the circuit is completed through the resistor, which acts to pull the voltage on the drain up to the higher voltage of the power supply.

### P-channel MOSFET

Now, let's look at the P-channel MOSFET, shown in Figure 5-11 (b). Here the drain is connected to the lower voltage (0 V) through a resistor, and the source is connected to the higher-voltage power supply (5 V). When the voltage applied to the gate is switched to be nearly the same as the voltage applied to the source, the MOSFET turns off. In this case, the resistor, R, acts as a *pull-down device*, to pull the voltage on the drain down to 0 volts. Figure 5-13 (a) shows the equivalent circuit.

When the voltage applied to the gate is negative with respect to the source, the resistance between the drain and source of the P-channel MOSFET decreases. When this voltage reaches a threshold value, typically in the range of –1 volt, the resistance becomes very low, thus providing a good conduction path for current between the drain and the source. Figure 5-13 (b) shows the resulting equivalent circuit when the gate is –5 volts with respect to the source.

There are a couple of problems with both MOSFET types. Looking at the equivalent circuits in Figure 5-12 (a) and 5-13 (b), you can see that the respective MOSFET in its on state acts like a closed switch, thus causing current to flow through the pull-up or pull-down resistor. The current flow through the resistor when the MOSFET is in its on state consumes power that is simply converted to heat.

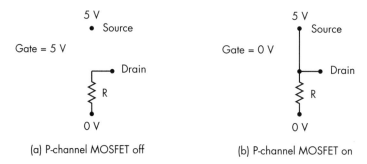

(a) P-channel MOSFET off          (b) P-channel MOSFET on

*Figure 5-13: P-channel MOSFET switch equivalent circuit: (a) switch closed, (b) switch open*

In addition to the pull-up and pull-down resistors using power when a MOSFET is in its on state, there's another problem with this hardware design. Although the gate of a MOSFET draws essentially no current to remain in either an on or off state, a brief burst of current into the gate is required to change the MOSFET's state. That current is supplied by the device connected to the gate, probably from the drain of another MOSFET. We won't go into the details in this book, but the amount of current that can be supplied at the drain from this other MOSFET is largely limited by its pull-up or pull-down resistor. The situation is essentially the same as that in Figures 5-6 and 5-7, where you saw that the time it takes to charge a capacitor is longer for higher-resistance values.

So, there's a trade-off here: the larger the resistors, the lower the current flow, which reduces power consumption when the MOSFET is in the on state. But a larger resistor also reduces the amount of current available at the drain, thus increasing the amount of time it takes to switch a MOSFET connected to the drain. We're left with a dilemma: small pull-up and pull-down resistors increase power consumption, but large resistors slow down the computer.

## CMOS Switch

We can solve this dilemma with *complementary metal-oxide semiconductor (CMOS)* technology. To see how this works, let's eliminate the pull-up and pull-down resistors and connect the drains of a P-channel and an N-channel together. The P-channel will replace the pull-up resistor in the N-channel circuit, and the N-channel will replace the pull-down resistor in the P-channel circuit. We'll also connect the two gates together, giving the circuit shown in Figure 5-14.

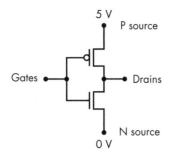

*Figure 5-14: CMOS inverter (NOT) circuit*

Figure 5-15 (a) shows the equivalent circuit with the gates at the higher power supply voltage, 5 volts. The pull-up MOSFET (a P-channel) is off, and the pull-down MOSFET (an N-channel) is on, so the drains are pulled down to the lower power supply voltage, 0 volts. In Figure 5-15 (b) the gates are at the lower power supply voltage, 0 volts, which turns the P-channel MOSFET on and the N-channel MOSFET off. The P-channel MOSFET pulls the drains up to the higher power supply voltage, 5 volts.

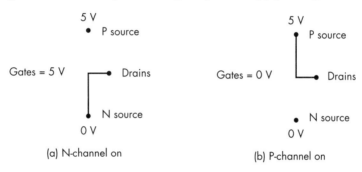

*Figure 5-15: CMOS inverter equivalent circuit: (a) pull-up open and pull-down closed, (b) pull-up closed and pull-down open*

We can summarize this behavior in Table 5-1.

**Table 5-1:** Truth Table for a Single CMOS

| Gates | Drains |
|-------|--------|
| 0 V | 5 V |
| 5 V | 0 V |

If we use the gates connection as the input, we use the drains connection as the output, and we let 5 volts be logical 1 and 0 volts logical 0, then the CMOS implements a NOT gate.

The two main advantages of using CMOS circuits are

- They consume very little power. Because of the switching speed difference between N-channel and P-channel MOSFETs, only a small amount of current flows during the switching period. Less current means less heat, which is often the limiting factor in chip design.
- The circuit responds much faster. A MOSFET can supply the current at its output faster than a resistor, charging the gate of the following MOSFET. This allows us to build faster computers.

Figure 5-16 shows an AND gate implemented with three CMOSs.

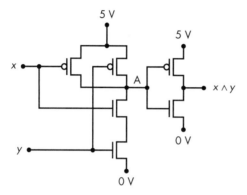

Figure 5-16: AND gate from three CMOS transistors

The truth table, Table 5-2, shows the intermediate output from the first two CMOSs, point A in Figure 5-16.

**Table 5-2:** Truth Table for the AND Gate of Figure 5-16

| x | y | A | x ∧ y |
|---|---|---|-------|
| 0 | 0 | 1 | 0 |
| 0 | 1 | 1 | 0 |
| 1 | 0 | 1 | 0 |
| 1 | 1 | 0 | 1 |

From the truth table, we see that the signal at point A is $\neg(x \wedge y)$. The circuit from point A to the output is a NOT gate. The result at point A is called the *NAND* operation. It requires two fewer transistors than the AND operation. We'll look at the implications of this result in the next section.

## NAND and NOR Gates

As we saw in the previous section, the inherent design of transistors means that most circuits invert the signal. That is, for most circuits, a high voltage at the input produces a low voltage at the output, and vice versa. As a result, an AND gate will typically require a NOT gate at the output to achieve a true AND operation.

You also learned that it takes fewer transistors to produce NOT(AND) than a regular AND. The combination is so common that it has been given the name *NAND gate*. And, of course, we have an equivalent with the OR gate, called the *NOR gate*.

**NAND**  A binary operator that gives a result of 0 if and only if *both* operands are 1 and gives 1 otherwise. We'll use $\neg(x \wedge x)$ to designate the NAND operation. Figure 5-17 shows the hardware symbol for the NAND gate along with a truth table showing its operation on inputs $x$ and $y$.

| x | y | ¬(x ∧ y) |
|---|---|----------|
| 0 | 0 | 1 |
| 0 | 1 | 1 |
| 1 | 0 | 1 |
| 1 | 1 | 0 |

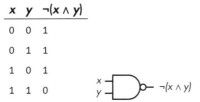

Figure 5-17: The NAND gate acting on two variables, x and y

**NOR**  A binary operator that gives a result of 0 if at least one of the two operands is 1 and gives 1 otherwise. We'll use $\neg(x \vee y)$ to designate the NOR operation. Figure 5-18 shows the hardware symbol for the NOR gate along with a truth table showing its operation on inputs $x$ and $y$.

| x | y | ¬(x ∨ y) |
|---|---|----------|
| 0 | 0 | 1 |
| 0 | 1 | 0 |
| 1 | 0 | 0 |
| 1 | 1 | 0 |

Figure 5-18: The NOR gate acting on two variables, x and y

Notice the small circle at the output of the NAND and NOR gates in Figure 5-18. This signifies *NOT,* just as with the NOT gate (Figure 4-3).

Although in the previous chapter we explicitly showed NOT gates when inputs to gates are complemented, it's common to simply use these small circles at the input to signify the complement. For example, Figure 5-19 shows an OR gate with both inputs complemented.

| x | y | $(\neg x \vee \neg y)$ | $\neg(x \wedge y)$ |
|---|---|---|---|
| 0 | 0 | 1 | 1 |
| 0 | 1 | 1 | 1 |
| 1 | 0 | 1 | 1 |
| 1 | 1 | 0 | 0 |

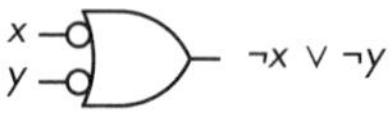

Figure 5-19: An alternate way to draw a NAND gate

As the truth table shows, this is another way to implement a NAND gate. As you learned in Chapter 4, De Morgan's law confirms this:

$$\neg(x \wedge y) = (\neg x \vee \neg y)$$

## NAND as a Universal Gate

One of the interesting properties about NAND gates is that they can be used to build AND, OR, and NOT gates. This means the NAND gate can be used to implement any Boolean function. In this sense, you can think of the NAND gate as a *universal gate*. Recalling De Morgan's law, it probably won't surprise you that a NOR gate can also be used as a universal gate. But the physics of CMOS transistors is such that NAND gates are faster and take less space, so they are almost always the preferred solution.

Let's go through how to use a NAND gate to build AND, OR, and NOT gates. To build a NOT gate using NAND, simply connect the signal to both inputs of a NAND gate, as shown in Figure 5-20.

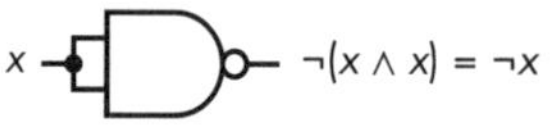

Figure 5-20: A NOT gate built from a NAND gate

To make an AND gate, we can observe that the first NAND gate in Figure 5-21 produces $\neg(x \wedge y)$ and connect it to a NOT gate to produce $(x \wedge y)$.

We can use De Morgan's law to derive an OR gate. Consider the following:

$$\neg(\neg x \wedge \neg y) = \neg(\neg x) \vee \neg(\neg y)$$
$$= x \vee y$$

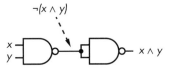

Figure 5-21: An AND gate built
from two NAND gates

So to implement OR, we need three NAND gates, as shown in Figure 5-22. The two NAND gates at the $x$ and $y$ inputs are connected at NOT gates to produce $\neg x$ and $\neg y$, which gives $\neg((\neg x) \vee (\neg y))$ at the output of the third NAND gate.

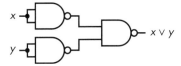

Figure 5-22: An OR gate built from
three NAND gates

It looks like we are creating more complexity to build circuits from NAND gates, but consider this function:

$$F(w, x, y, z) = (w \wedge x) \vee (y \wedge z)$$

Without knowing how logic gates are constructed, it would be reasonable to implement this function with the circuit shown in Figure 5-23.

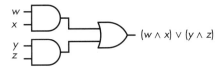

Figure 5-23: F(w, x, y, z) using two AND
gates and one OR gate

The involution property states that $\neg(\neg x) = x$, so we can add two NOT gates in each path, as shown in Figure 5-24.

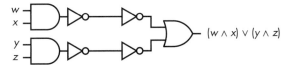

Figure 5-24: F(w, x, y, z) using two AND gates, one
OR gate, and four NOT gates

Comparing the two AND-gate/NOT-gate combinations that operate on the $w$, $x$, $y$, and $z$ inputs with Figure 5-17, we see that each is simply a NAND gate. They will produce $\neg(w \wedge x)$ and $\neg(y \wedge z)$ at the outputs of the two leftmost NOT gates.

We saw from the application of De Morgan's law in Figure 5-19 that $(\neg a) \lor (\neg b) = \neg(a \land b)$. In other words, we can replace the combination of the two rightmost NOT gates and OR gate with a single NAND gate.

$$\neg(\neg(w \land x) \land \neg(y \land z)) = (w \land x) \lor (y \land z)$$

The resulting circuit in Figure 5-25 uses three NAND gates.

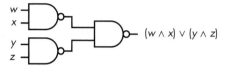

*Figure 5-25: F(w, x, y, z) using only three NAND gates*

From simply viewing the logic circuit diagrams in Figures 5-23 and 5-25, it may seem that we haven't gained anything in this circuit transformation. But we saw in the previous section that a NAND gate (point A in Figure 5-16) requires two fewer transistors than an AND gate. Thus, the NAND gate implementation is less power intensive and faster. Although we don't show it here, the same is true of an OR gate.

The conversion from an AND/OR/NOT gate design to one that uses only NAND gates is straightforward:

1. Express the function as a minimal sum of products.
2. Convert the products (AND terms) and the final sum (OR) to NANDs.
3. Add a NAND gate for any product with only a single literal.

Everything I've said about NAND gates here applies to NOR gates. You simply apply DeMorgan's law to find the complement of everything. But as mentioned, NAND gates are typically faster and take less space than NOR gates, so they are almost always the preferred solution.

As with software, hardware design is an iterative process. Most problems do not have a unique solution, and you often need to develop several designs and analyze each one within the context of the available hardware. As the previous example shows, two solutions that look the same on paper may be very different at the hardware level.

---

**YOUR TURN**

1. Design a NOT gate, AND gate, and OR gate using NOR gates.
2. Design a circuit using NAND gates that detects the "below" condition for two two-bit integers, $x$ and $y$, $F(x, y) = 1$. It's common to use below/above for unsigned integer comparisons and less-than/greater-than for signed integer comparisons.

# What You've Learned

**Basic electronics concepts** Resistance, capacitance, and inductance affect the voltages and current flow in an electronic circuit.

**Transistors** Semiconductor devices that can be used as electronically controlled switches.

**MOSFET** Metal-oxide-semiconductor field-effect transistors are the most commonly used switching device for implementing logic gates in computers. They come in both N-channel and P-channel types.

**CMOS** N-channel and P-channel MOSFETs are paired in a complementary configuration to increase switching speed and reduce power consumption.

**NAND and NOR gates** These require fewer transistors than AND and OR gates because of the inherent electronic characteristics of transistors.

In the next chapter, you'll see how simple logic gates are connected in circuits to implement the complex operations needed to build a computer.

# 6

## COMBINATIONAL LOGIC CIRCUITS

In the previous chapter, you learned about a computer's basic component, the logic gate. Computers are constructed from assemblages of logic gates, called *logic circuits*, that process digital information. In this and the following two chapters, we'll look at how to build some of the logic circuits that make up CPUs, memory, and other devices. We won't describe any of these units in their entirety; instead, we'll look at a few small parts and discuss the concepts behind them. The goal is to provide an introductory overview of the ideas that underlie these logic circuits.

## The Two Classes of Logic Circuits

Logic circuits come in two classes:

**Combinational**   A *combinational logic circuit* has output that depends only on the inputs given at any specific time and not on any previous inputs.

**Sequential**   A *sequential logic circuit* has outputs that depend both on previous and current inputs.

To elucidate these two types, let's consider a TV remote. You can select a specific channel by entering a number on the remote. The channel selection depends only on the number you entered and ignores the channels you were viewing before. Thus, the relationship between the input and the output is combinational.

The remote control also has an input for going up or down one channel. This input depends on the previously selected channel and the previous sequence of up/down button pushes. The channel up/down buttons illustrate a sequential input/output relationship.

We'll explore sequential logic circuits in the next chapter. In this chapter, we'll go through several examples of combinational logic circuits to see how they function.

---

### SIGNAL VOLTAGE LEVELS

Electronic logic circuits represent 1s and 0s with either a high or low voltage. We call the voltage that represents 1 the active voltage. If we use a higher voltage to represent 1, then the signal is called *active-high*. If we use a lower voltage to represent 1, then the signal is called *active-low*.

An active-high signal can be connected to an active-low input, but the hardware designer must take the difference into account. For example, say that the required logical input to an active-low input is 1. Since it is active-low, that means the required voltage is the lower of the two. If the signal to be connected to this input is active-high, then a logical 1 is the higher of the two voltages, and the signal must first be complemented to be interpreted as a 1 at the active-low input.

I will use only logic levels—0 and 1—in the discussions of logic circuits in this book and avoid the actual voltage levels being used in the hardware. But you should know about the terminology because it can come up when talking to others or reading specifications sheets for components.

---

# Adders

We'll start with one of the most fundamental operations performed in the CPU: adding two bits. Our eventual goal is to add two *n*-bit numbers.

Remember from Chapter 2 that the bits in a binary number are numbered from right (the least significant bit) to left (the most significant bit), starting with 0. We will start by showing how to add two bits in the *ith* bit position and complete the discussion showing how to add two four-bit numbers, taking into account the carry from each bit position.

## Half Adder

Addition can be done with several kinds of circuits. We'll start with the *half adder*, which simply adds the two bits in the current bit position of a number (expressed in binary). This is shown by the truth table, Table 6-1. In this table, $x_i$ is the $i^{\text{th}}$ bit of the number $x$. The values in the $y_i$ column represent the $i^{\text{th}}$ bit of the number $y$. $Sum_i$ is the $i^{\text{th}}$ bit of the number, $Sum$, and $Carry_{i+1}$ is the carry from adding bits $x_i$ and $y_i$.

**Table 6-1:** Adding Two Bits, Half-Adder

| $x_i$ | $y_i$ | $Carry_{i+1}$ | $Sum_i$ |
|-------|-------|---------------|---------|
| 0 | 0 | 0 | 0 |
| 0 | 1 | 0 | 1 |
| 1 | 0 | 0 | 1 |
| 1 | 1 | 1 | 0 |

The sum is the XOR of the two inputs, and the carry is the AND of the two inputs. Figure 6-1 shows the logic circuit for a half adder.

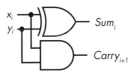

Figure 6-1: A half adder circuit

But there's a flaw here: the half adder works with only two input bits. It can be used to add the two bits from the same bit position of two numbers, but it doesn't take into account a possible carry from the next lower-order bit position. To allow for the carry, we'll have to add a third input.

## Full Adder

Unlike the half adder, a *full adder* circuit has three one-bit inputs, $Carry_i$, $x_i$, and $y_i$. $Carry_i$ is the carry that resulted when you added the two bits in the previous bit position (the bit to the right). For example, if we're adding the two bits in bit position 5, the inputs to the full adder are the two bits in position 5 plus the carry from adding the bits in bit position 4. Table 6-2 shows the results.

**Table 6-2:** Adding Two Bits, Full Adder

| $Carry_i$ | $x_i$ | $y_i$ | $Carry_{i+1}$ | $Sum_i$ |
|---|---|---|---|---|
| 0 | 0 | 0 | 0 | 0 |
| 0 | 0 | 1 | 0 | 1 |
| 0 | 1 | 0 | 0 | 1 |
| 0 | 1 | 1 | 1 | 0 |
| 1 | 0 | 0 | 0 | 1 |
| 1 | 0 | 1 | 1 | 0 |
| 1 | 1 | 0 | 1 | 0 |
| 1 | 1 | 1 | 1 | 1 |

To design a full adder circuit, we start with the function that specifies when $Sum_i$ is 1 as a sum of product terms from Table 6-2.

$$Sum_i(Carry_i, x_i, y_i) = (\neg Carry_i \wedge \neg x_i \wedge y_i) \vee (\neg Carry_i \wedge x_i \wedge \neg y_i)$$
$$\vee (Carry_i \wedge \neg x_i \wedge \neg y_i) \vee (Carry_i \wedge x_i \wedge y_i)$$

There are no obvious simplifications in this equation, so let's look at the Karnaugh map for $Sum_i$ (Figure 6-2).

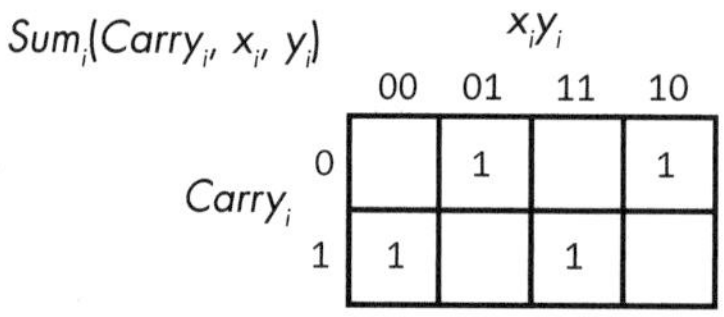

$Sum_i(Carry_i, x_i, y_i)$

Figure 6-2: A Karnaugh map for sum of three bits, $Carry_i$, $x_i$, and $y_i$

There are no obvious groupings in Figure 6-2, so we are left with the four product terms to compute $Sum_i$ in the previous equation.

We saw in Chapter 4 that $Carry_{i+1}$ can be expressed by this equation:

$$Carry_{i+1}(Carry_i, x_i, y_i) = (x_i \wedge y_i) \vee (Carry_i \wedge x_i) \vee (Carry_i \wedge y_i)$$

Together, these two functions give the circuit for a full adder in Figure 6-3.

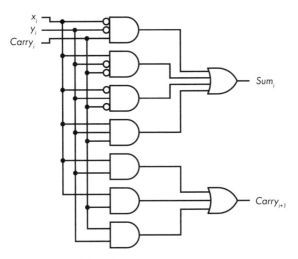

Figure 6-3: A full adder circuit

As you can see, the full adder uses nine logic gates. In the next section, we'll see if we can find a simpler circuit.

## Full Adder from Two Half Adders

To see if we can find a simpler solution for adding two bits and the carry from the next lower-order bit position, let's go back to the equation for $Sum_i$. Using the distribution rule, we can rearrange:

$$Sum_i(Carry_i, x_i, y_i) = \neg Carry_i \wedge ((\neg x_i \wedge y_i) \vee (x_i \wedge \neg y_i))$$
$$\vee\ Carry_i \wedge ((\neg x_i \wedge \neg y_i) \vee (x_i \wedge y_i))$$

In Chapter 4, you learned that the quantity in the parentheses in the first product term is the XOR of $x_i$ and $y_i$:

$$(\neg x_i \wedge y_i) \vee (x_i \wedge \neg y_i) = x_i \veebar y_i$$

Thus, we have this:

$$Sum_i(Carry_i, x_i, y_i) = \neg Carry_i \wedge (x_i \veebar y_i) \vee Carry_i \wedge ((\neg x_i \wedge \neg y_i) \vee (x_i \wedge y_i))$$

Now let's manipulate the quantity in the parentheses in the second product term. Recall that in Boolean algebra $x \wedge \neg x = 0$, so we can write the following:

$$(\neg x_i \wedge \neg y_i) \vee (x_i \wedge y_i) = (x_i \wedge \neg x_i) \vee (\neg x_i \wedge \neg y_i) \vee (x_i \wedge y_i) \vee (y_i \wedge \neg y_i)$$
$$= x_i \wedge (\neg x_i \vee y_i) \vee \neg y_i \wedge (\neg x_i \vee y_i)$$
$$= (x_i \vee \neg y_i) \wedge (\neg x \vee y_i)$$
$$= x_i \veebar y_i$$

Thus,

$$Sum_i(Carry_i, x_i, y_i) = Carry_i \wedge (x_i \veebar y_i) \vee Carry_i \wedge \neg(x_i \veebar y_i)$$
$$= Carry_i \veebar (x_i \veebar y_i)$$

We'll do something to develop a Boolean function for $Carry_{i+1}$ that will probably seem counterintuitive. Let's start with the Karnaugh map for carry when adding three bits, Figure 4-13 from Chapter 4, but remove two of the groupings, as shown by the dotted lines in Figure 6-4.

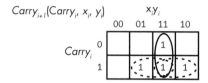

Figure 6-4: The Karnaugh map for carry from Figure 4-13, redrawn without two overlapping groupings (dotted lines)

This will give us the following equation:

$$Carry_{i+1} = (x_i \wedge y_i) \vee (Carry_i \wedge \neg x_i \wedge y_i) \vee (Carry_i \wedge x_i \wedge \neg y_i)$$
$$= (x_i \wedge y_i) \vee Carry_i \wedge ((\neg x_i \wedge y_i) \vee (x_i \wedge \neg y_i))$$
$$= (x_i \wedge y_i) \vee (Carry_i \wedge (x_i \veebar y_i))$$

Notice that two of the terms in this equation, $(x_i \wedge y_i)$ and $(x_i \veebar y_i)$ are already generated by a half adder (see Figure 6-1). So with a second half adder and an OR gate, we can implement a full adder, as shown in Figure 6-5.

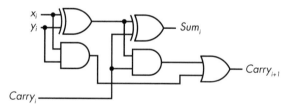

Figure 6-5: Full adder using two half adders

Now you can see where the terms *half adder* and *full adder* come from.

A simple circuit is not always better. In truth, we cannot say which of the two full adder circuits, Figure 6-3 or Figure 6-5, is better just from looking at the logic circuits. Good engineering design depends on many factors, such as how each logic gate is implemented, the cost of the logic gates and their availability, and so forth. The two designs are given here to show that different approaches can lead to different, but functionally equivalent, designs.

## Ripple-Carry Addition and Subtraction Circuits

Now we know how to add the two bits in a given bit position, plus a carry from the next lower-order bit position. But most values that a program works with have many bits, so we need a way to add the corresponding bits in each bit position of two $n$-bit numbers. This can be done with an *n-bit adder*, which can be implemented with $n$ full adders. Figure 6-6 shows a four-bit adder.

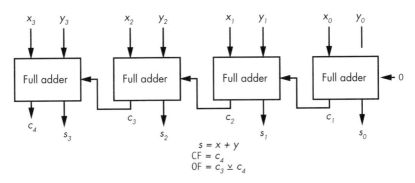

$$s = x + y$$
$$CF = c_4$$
$$OF = c_3 \veebar c_4$$

*Figure 6-6: Four-bit adder*

Addition begins with the full adder on the right receiving the two lowest-order bits, $x_0$ and $y_0$. Since this is the lowest-order bit, there is no carry, and $c_0 = 0$. The bit sum is $s_0$, and the carry from this addition, $c_1$, is connected to the carry input of the next full adder to the left, where it is added to $x_1$ and $y_1$.

Thus, the $i^{th}$ full adder adds the two $i^{th}$ bits of the operands, plus the carry (which is either 0 or 1) from the $(i - 1)^{th}$ full adder. Each full adder handles one bit (often referred to as a *slice*) of the total width of the values being added. The carry from each bit position is added to the bits in the next higher-order bit position. The addition process flows from the lowest-order bit to the highest-order in a sort of rippling effect, which gives this method of adding the name *ripple-carry addition*.

Notice that in Figure 6-6, we have CF and OF, the *carry flag* and *overflow flag*. You learned about carry and overflow in Chapter 3. Whenever the CPU performs an arithmetic operation, addition in this case, it records whether carry and overflow occurred in the rflags register. You will learn about this register in Chapter 9.

Now let's see how we can use a similar idea to implement subtraction. Recall that in two's complement, a number is negated by taking its two's complement, flipping all the bits, and adding 1. Thus, we can subtract $y$ from $x$ by doing this:

$$x - y = x + (two's\ complement\ of\ y)$$
$$= x + ((y's\ bits\ flipped) + 1)$$

Subtraction can be performed with our adder in Figure 6-5 if we complement each $y_i$ and set the initial carry in to 1 instead of 0. Each $y_i$ can be complemented by XORing it with 1. This leads to the four-bit circuit in Figure 6-7, which will add two four-bit numbers when $func = 0$ and subtract them when $func = 1$.

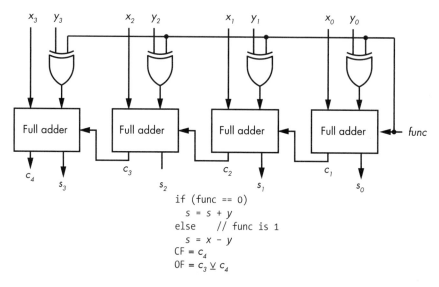

```
if (func == 0)
    s = s + y
else    // func is 1
    s = x - y
CF = c₄
OF = c₃ ∨ c₄
```

$$CF = c_4$$
$$OF = c_3 \veebar c_4$$

Figure 6-7: Four-bit adder/subtractor

There is, of course, a time delay as the sum is computed from right to left. The computation time can be significantly reduced through more complex circuit designs that precompute the values of CF carry and OF, but we won't go into such details in this book. Let's turn to our next type of circuit.

**YOUR TURN**

You learned about the carry flag (CF) and overflow flag (OF) in the rflags register in Chapter 3. The rflags register also contains a zero flag (ZF) and a negative flag (NF). The ZF is 1 when the result of an arithmetic operation is zero, and the NF is 1 when the result is a negative number if the number is considered to be in two's complement notation. Design a circuit that uses the outputs of the full adders in Figure 6-7, $s_0$, $s_1$, $s_2$, $s_3$, $c_3$, and $c_4$, and outputs the CF, OF, NF, and ZF.

# Decoders

Many places in a computer require selecting one of several connections based on a number. For example, as you will see in a few chapters, the CPU has a small amount of memory organized in *registers*, which are used for computations. The x86-64 architecture has sixteen 64-bit registers. If an instruction uses one of the registers, four bits in the instruction must be used to select which of the sixteen registers should be used.

This selection can be done with a *decoder*. The input to the decoder is the four-bit number of the register, and the output is one of sixteen possible connections to the specified register.

A decoder has $n$ binary inputs that can produce up to $2^n$ binary outputs. The most common type of decoder, sometimes called a *line decoder*, selects only one of the output lines to set to 1 for each input bit pattern. It's also common for a decoder to include an Enable input. The truth table for a $3 \times 8$ (3 inputs, 8 outputs) decoder with an enabling input in Table 6-3 shows how this works. When Enable = 0, all the output lines are 0. When Enable = 1, the three-bit number at the input, $x = x_2 x_1 x_0$, selects which output line is set to 1. So this decoder could be used to select one of eight registers with a three-bit number. (I'm not using the sixteen registers in the x86-64 architecture to keep the table a reasonable size here.)

**Table 6-3:** $3 \times 8$ Decoder with Enable

| Input | | | | Output | | | | | | | |
|---|---|---|---|---|---|---|---|---|---|---|---|
| Enable | $x_2$ | $x_1$ | $x_0$ | $y_7$ | $y_6$ | $y_5$ | $y_4$ | $y_3$ | $y_2$ | $y_1$ | $y_0$ |
| 0 | 0 | 0 | 0 | 0 | 0 | 0 | 0 | 0 | 0 | 0 | 0 |
| 0 | 0 | 0 | 1 | 0 | 0 | 0 | 0 | 0 | 0 | 0 | 0 |
| 0 | 0 | 1 | 0 | 0 | 0 | 0 | 0 | 0 | 0 | 0 | 0 |
| 0 | 0 | 1 | 1 | 0 | 0 | 0 | 0 | 0 | 0 | 0 | 0 |
| 0 | 1 | 0 | 0 | 0 | 0 | 0 | 0 | 0 | 0 | 0 | 0 |
| 0 | 1 | 0 | 1 | 0 | 0 | 0 | 0 | 0 | 0 | 0 | 0 |
| 0 | 1 | 1 | 0 | 0 | 0 | 0 | 0 | 0 | 0 | 0 | 0 |
| 0 | 1 | 1 | 1 | 0 | 0 | 0 | 0 | 0 | 0 | 0 | 0 |
| 1 | 0 | 0 | 0 | 0 | 0 | 0 | 0 | 0 | 0 | 0 | 1 |
| 1 | 0 | 0 | 1 | 0 | 0 | 0 | 0 | 0 | 0 | 1 | 0 |
| 1 | 0 | 1 | 0 | 0 | 0 | 0 | 0 | 0 | 1 | 0 | 0 |
| 1 | 0 | 1 | 1 | 0 | 0 | 0 | 0 | 1 | 0 | 0 | 0 |
| 1 | 1 | 0 | 0 | 0 | 0 | 0 | 1 | 0 | 0 | 0 | 0 |
| 1 | 1 | 0 | 1 | 0 | 0 | 1 | 0 | 0 | 0 | 0 | 0 |
| 1 | 1 | 1 | 0 | 0 | 1 | 0 | 0 | 0 | 0 | 0 | 0 |
| 1 | 1 | 1 | 1 | 1 | 0 | 0 | 0 | 0 | 0 | 0 | 0 |

The 3 × 8 line decoder specified in Table 6-3 can be implemented with four-input AND gates, as shown in Figure 6-8.

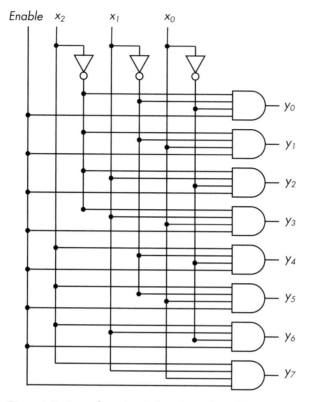

Figure 6-8: Circuit for a 3 × 8 decoder with Enable

Decoders are more versatile than they might seem at first glance. Each possible input can be seen as a minterm (for a refresher on minterms, see Chapter 4). The line decoder in Table 6-3 shows that only a single output is 1 when a minterm evaluates to 1 and Enable is 1. Thus, a decoder can be viewed as a "minterm generator." We know from earlier in the book that any logical expression can be represented as the OR of minterms, so it follows that we can implement any logical expression by ORing the output(s) of a decoder.

For example, if you look back at the Karnaugh maps for the full adder (Figures 6-2 and 6-4), you might see that *Sum* and *Carry* can be expressed as the OR of minterms,

$$Sum_i(Carry_i, x_i, y_i) = m_1 \lor m_2 \lor m_4 \lor m_7$$
$$Carry_{i+1}(Carry_i, x_i, y_i) = m_3 \lor m_5 \lor m_6 \lor m_7$$

where the subscript, $i$, on $x$, $y$, and *Carry* refers to the bit slice, and the subscripts on $m$ are part of the minterm notation. We can implement each bit slice of a full adder with a 3 × 8 decoder and two four-input OR gates, as shown in Figure 6-9.

The decoder circuit in Figure 6-8 requires eight AND gates and three NOT gates. The full adder in Figure 6-9 adds two OR gates, for a total of thirteen logic gates. Comparing this with the full adder design in Figure 6-5, which requires only five logic gates (two XOR, two AND, and one OR), it would seem that using a decoder to construct a full adder increases the complexity of the circuit. But keep in mind that designs are often based on other factors, such as availability of components, cost of components, and so forth.

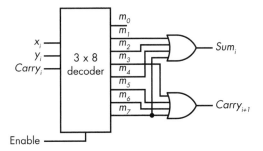

Figure 6-9: One bit slice of a full adder implemented with 3 × 8 decoder. An n-bit adder would require n of these circuits.

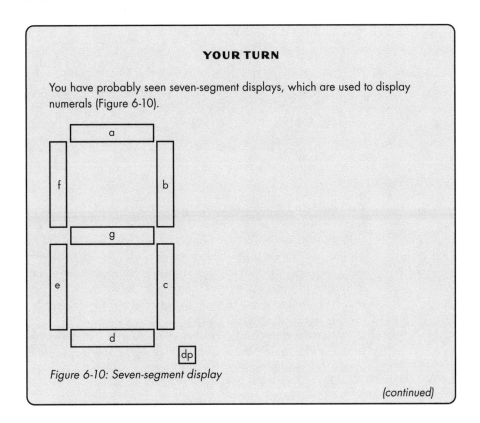

**YOUR TURN**

You have probably seen seven-segment displays, which are used to display numerals (Figure 6-10).

Figure 6-10: Seven-segment display

(continued)

Each segment in a seven-segment display is lit by applying a 1 to the input pin connected to the corresponding segment. I have a seven-segment display with an eight-bit input that lights the segments and the decimal point, as shown in Table 6-4.

**Table 6-4:** Input Bit Assignments for the Seven-Segment Display in Figure 6-10

| Bit | Segment |
|-----|---------|
| 0   | a       |
| 1   | b       |
| 2   | c       |
| 3   | d       |
| 4   | e       |
| 5   | f       |
| 6   | g       |
| 7   | dp      |

For example, we could display a 5 with the bit pattern 0110 1101. However, it would be more convenient for us to write our program to use BCD for individual numerals. Design a decoder that transforms numerals in BCD to segment patterns on our seven-segment display.

## Multiplexers

In the previous section, you learned how an $n$-bit number can be used to select which one of $2^n$ output lines should be set to 1. The opposite situation also occurs, where we need to select which of several inputs should be passed on. For example, when performing arithmetic operations, like addition, the numbers can come from different locations within the CPU. (You will learn more about this in the next few chapters.) The operation itself will be performed by one arithmetic unit, and the CPU needs to select the inputs to the operation from all the possible locations.

A device that can make this selection is called a *multiplexer (MUX)*. It can switch between $2^n$ input lines by using $n$ selection lines. Figure 6-11 shows a circuit for a four-way multiplexer.

The output is given by this:

$$Output = (\neg s_0 \wedge \neg s_1 \wedge w) \vee (\neg s_0 \wedge s_1 \wedge x) \\ \vee (s_0 \wedge \neg s_1 \wedge y) \vee (s_0 \wedge s_1 \wedge z)$$

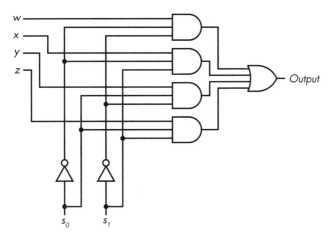

Figure 6-11: A four-way multiplexer

When using AND and OR gates, the number of transistors required to implement a multiplexer gets large as the number of inputs grows. A three-input AND gate is required for each input to the multiplexer, and the number of inputs to the OR gate equals the number of multiplexer inputs. The AND gates are being used to feed only one of the multiplexer inputs to the OR gate. Next we'll see a device that can accomplish the same functionality of the AND and OR gate combination by simply disconnecting the input signal from the output.

## Tristate Buffer

The logic device called a *tristate buffer* has three possible outputs: 0, 1, and "no connection." The "no connection" output is actually a high impedance connection, also called *high Z* or *open*. The "no connection" output lets us physically connect the outputs of many tristate buffers together but select only one to pass its input to the common output line.

A tristate buffer has both a data input and an enabling feature, which behave as shown Table 6-5.

**Table 6-5:** Tristate Buffer
Truth Table

| Enable | In | Out |
| --- | --- | --- |
| 0 | 0 | High Z |
| 0 | 1 | High Z |
| 1 | 0 | 0 |
| 1 | 1 | 1 |

Figure 6-12 shows the circuit symbol for a tristate buffer.

Figure 6-12: Tristate buffer

When Enable = 1, the output, which is equal to the input, is connected to whatever circuit element follows the tristate buffer. But when Enable = 0, the output is essentially disconnected. This is different from 0; being disconnected means it has no effect on the circuit element to which it is connected.

To illustrate how tristate buffers can be used, look back at the four-way multiplexer in "Multiplexers" on page 124. It required four AND gates, two NOT gates, and a four-input OR gate. If we try to scale this up, the $n$-input OR gate will present some technical electronic problems for a large $n$. The use of an $n$-input OR gate can be avoided by using $n$ tristate buffers, as shown by the four-way multiplexer in Figure 6-13.

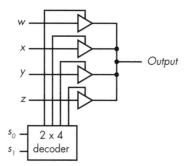

Figure 6-13: Four-way multiplexer built from decoder and tristate buffers

The multiplexer in Figure 6-13 uses a $2 \times 4$ decoder and four tristate buffers. The $2 \times 4$ decoder selects which of the tristate buffers connects one of the inputs, $w$, $x$, $y$, or $z$, to the output.

Figure 6-14 shows the circuit symbol used for a multiplexer, and Table 6-6 shows its behavior.

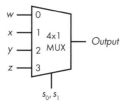

Figure 6-14: Circuit symbol for a four-way multiplexer

**Table 6-6:** Truth Table
for a Four-Way
Multiplexer

| $s_1$ | $s_0$ | Output |
|-------|-------|--------|
| 0 | 0 | w |
| 0 | 1 | x |
| 1 | 0 | y |
| 1 | 1 | z |

As an example of where we might use the four-way multiplexer in Figure 6-14, consider a computer with four registers and one adder. Let's name the registers $w$, $x$, $y$, and $z$. If we connect the bits in the corresponding bit position from each register to a multiplexer, then we can use the two-bit selector, $s_0 s_1$, to choose which register will provide the input to the adder. For example, each bit in position 5, $w_5$, $x_5$, $y_5$, and $z_5$, would be connected one of the inputs in multiplexer 5. If $s_0 s_1 = 10$, the input to the adder would be $y_5$.

## Programmable Logic Devices

So far, we've been discussing hardware designs that use individual logic gates. If the design changes, the logic gate configuration changes. This almost always means that the circuit board that holds the logic gates and connects them will need to be redesigned. A change also often means ordering a different kind of logic gate, which can be expensive and take time. These problems can be reduced by using *programmable logic devices* (*PLDs*) to implement the required logic function.

PLDs contain many AND gates and OR gates, which can be programmed to implement Boolean functions. The inputs, and their complemented value, are connected to the AND gates. The AND gates, taken together, are referred to as the *AND plane*, or *AND array*. The outputs from the AND gates are connected to OR gates, which taken together are referred to as the *OR plane*, or *OR array*. Depending on the type, one or both planes can be programmed to implement combinational logic. When using a PLD, a design change means only changing how the device is programmed, not buying different devices, meaning the circuit board does not need to be redesigned.

PLDs come in several types. Most can be programmed by a user. Some are preprogrammed at the time of manufacture, and some can even be erased and reprogrammed by the user. Programming technologies range from specifying the manufacturing mask (for the preprogrammed devices) to inexpensive electronic programming systems.

There are three general categories of PLDs.

## Programmable Logic Array

In a *programmable logic array* (PLA), both the AND and OR planes are programmable. PLAs are used to implement logic functions. Figure 6-15 gives the general idea for a PLA that has two input variables and two possible output functions of these variables.

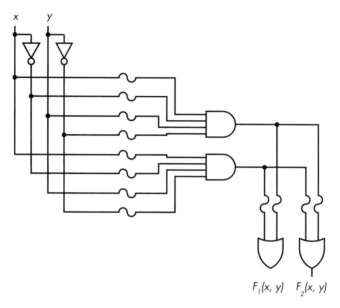

Figure 6-15: Simplified circuit for a programmable logic array

Each input variable, in both its uncomplemented and complemented form, is an input to the AND gates through fuses. A *fuse* is a thin piece of conductor used to protect an electrical circuit. If the current flowing through it is high enough, the conductor melts, thus opening the circuit and stopping current flow. PLDs can be programmed by breaking (or *blowing*) the appropriate fuses, thus removing the input to the logic gate. Some devices use *antifuses* instead of fuses. These are normally open, and programming them consists of completing the connection instead of removing it. Devices that can be reprogrammed have fuses that can be broken and then remade.

In Figure 6-15, the *S*-shaped lines in the circuit diagram represent the fuses. The fuses can be blown or left in place so as to program each AND gate to output a product of the inputs, $x$, $\neg x$, $y$, and $\neg y$. Since every input, plus its complement, is input to each AND gate, any of the AND gates can be programmed to output a minterm.

The products produced by the AND gate plane are all connected to the inputs of the OR gates, also through fuses. Thus, depending on which OR-gate fuses are left in place, the output of each OR gate is a sum of products. There may be additional logic circuitry to select between the different outputs. We have already seen that any Boolean function can be expressed as a sum of products, so this logic device can be programmed to implement any Boolean function by blowing the fuses.

A PLA is typically larger than the one shown in Figure 6-15, which is already complicated to draw. To simplify the drawing, it is typical to use a diagram similar to Figure 6-16 to specify the design.

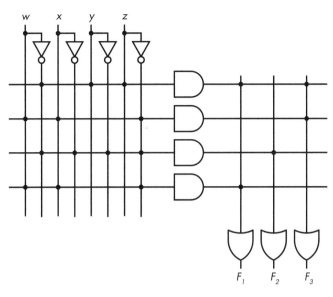

Figure 6-16: Diagram for a programmable logic array. The dots represent connections.

This diagram can be a little tricky to understand. In Figure 6-15, each AND gate has multiple inputs—one for each variable and one for its complement. In Figure 6-16, we use one horizontal line leading to the input of each AND gate to represent multiple wires (variable and complement). So, each AND gate in Figure 6-16 has eight inputs even though we draw only one line.

The dots at the intersections of the vertical and horizontal line represent places where the fuses have been left intact, thus creating a connection. For example, the three dots on the topmost horizontal line indicate that there are three inputs left connected to that AND gate. The output of the topmost AND gate is as follows:

$$\neg w \wedge y \wedge z$$

Referring again to Figure 6-15, we see that the output from each AND gate is connected to each of the OR gates (through fuses). Therefore, the OR gates also have multiple inputs—one for each AND gate—and the vertical lines leading to the OR gate inputs represent multiple wires. The PLA in Figure 6-16 has been programmed to provide these three functions:

$$F_1(w, x, y, z) = (\neg w \wedge y \wedge z) \vee (w \wedge x \wedge \neg z)$$
$$F_2(w, x, y, z) = \neg w \wedge \neg x \wedge \neg y \wedge \neg z$$
$$F_3(w, x, y, z) = (\neg w \wedge y \wedge z) \vee (w \wedge x \wedge \neg z)$$

Since the AND plane can produce all possible minterms and the OR plane can provide any sum of the minterms, a PLA can be used to implement any possible logical function. If we want to change the function, it's a simple matter of programming another PLA and replacing the old one.

## Read-Only Memory

Although PLDs have no memory (meaning the current state isn't affected by previous states of the inputs), they can be used to make *nonvolatile* memory—memory whose contents remain intact when the power is turned off. *Read-only memory* (*ROM*) is used to store bit patterns that can represent data or program instructions. A program can only read the data or program stored in ROM, but the contents of the ROM cannot be changed by writing new data or program instructions to it. ROM is commonly used in devices that have a fixed set of functionalities, like watches, automobile engine control units, and appliances. In fact, our lives are surrounded by devices that are controlled by programs stored in ROM.

ROM can be implemented as a programmable logic device where only the OR gate plane can be programmed. The AND gate plane remains wired to provide all the minterms. We can think of the inputs to the ROM as addresses. Then the OR gate plane is programmed to provide the bit pattern at each address. For example, the ROM diagrammed in Figure 6-17 has two inputs, $a_1$ and $a_0$, which provide a two-bit address.

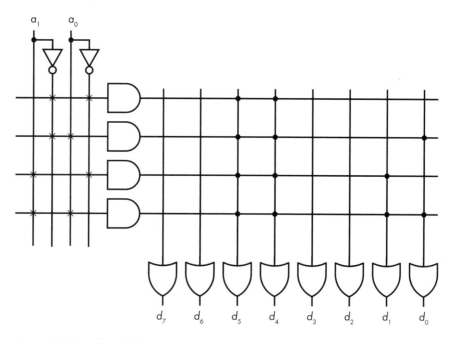

Figure 6-17: Four-byte ROM

The "×" connections in Figure 6-17 represent permanent connections, showing that the AND gate plane is fixed. Each AND gate produces a minterm at each address in this ROM. The OR gate plane produces up to $2^n$ eight-bit bytes, where $n$ is the width, in number of bits, of the address input to the AND gate plane. The connections (dots) to the OR gates represent the bit pattern stored at the corresponding address. Table 6-7 shows a ROM in which the OR gate plane has been programmed to store the four characters, A, B, C, and D (in ASCII code).

**Table 6-7:** A ROM Holding Four ASCII Characters

| Minterm | Address | Contents | ASCII character |
|---------|---------|----------|-----------------|
| $\neg a_1 \neg a_0$ | 00 | 01000001 | A |
| $\neg a_1 a_0$ | 01 | 01000010 | B |
| $a_1 \neg a_0$ | 10 | 01000011 | C |
| $a_1 a_0$ | 11 | 01000100 | D |

Although we have stored only data in this example, computer instructions are bit patterns, so we could just as easily store an entire program in ROM. As with a programmable logic array, if you need to change the program, just program another ROM and replace the old one.

There are several types of ROM. While the bit pattern is set in a ROM during manufacturing, a *programmable read-only memory* (*PROM*) device is programmed by the person who uses it. There are also *erasable programmable read-only memory* (*EPROM*) devices that can be erased with an ultraviolet light and then reprogrammed.

### Programmable Array Logic

In a *programmable array logic* (*PAL*) device, each OR gate is permanently wired to a group of AND gates. Only the AND gate plane is programmable. The PAL diagrammed in Figure 6-18 has four inputs. It provides two outputs, each of which can be the sum of up to four products. The "×" connections in the OR gate plane show that the top four AND gates are OR-ed to produce $F_1(w, x, y, z)$ and the lower four OR-ed to produce $F_2(w, x, y, z)$. The AND gate plane in this figure has been programmed to produce these two functions:

$$F_1(w, x, y, z) = (w \wedge \neg x \wedge z) \vee (\neg w \wedge x) \vee (w \wedge x \wedge \neg y) \vee (\neg w \wedge \neg x \wedge \neg y \wedge \neg z)$$
$$F_2(w, x, y, z) = (\neg w \wedge y \wedge z) \vee (x \wedge y \wedge \neg z) \vee (w \wedge x \wedge y \wedge z) \vee (w \wedge x \wedge \neg y \wedge \neg z)$$

Of the three types of PLD presented here, the PLA is the most flexible, since we can program both the OR and the AND plane, but it is the most expensive of the three devices. The ROM is less flexible. It can be programmed to produce any combination of minterms, which are then OR-ed together. We know that any function can be implemented as the OR of minterms, so we can produce any function with a ROM. However, a ROM doesn't allow us to minimize the function since all the product terms must be minterms.

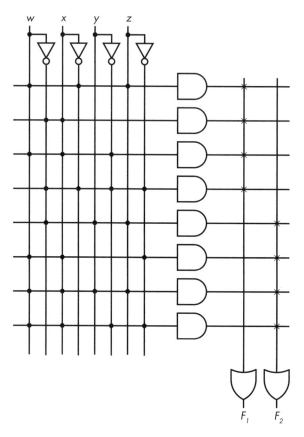

*Figure 6-18: Two-function programmable array logic*

The PAL is the least flexible, because all the product terms programmed in the AND plane will be ORed together. So, we cannot select which minterms are in the function by programming the OR plane. However, PALs allow us to do some Boolean function minimization. If the required function can be implemented in a PAL, it is less expensive than a ROM or PLA.

**YOUR TURN**

Comparing two values to determine which is larger, or whether they are the same, is a common operation in computing. The hardware device to perform such a comparison is called a *comparator*. Use a programmable logic device to design a comparator that compares two two-bit values. Your comparator will have three outputs: equal, greater than, and less than.

# What You've Learned

**Combinational logic circuits**   These depend only on their input at any point in time. They have no memory of previous effects of the inputs. Examples include adders, decoders, multiplexers, and programmable logic devices.

**Half adder**   This circuit has two one-bit inputs. It produces two one-bit outputs: the sum of the inputs and the carry from that sum.

**Full adder**   This circuit has three one-bit inputs. It produces two one-bit outputs: the sum of the inputs and the carry from that sum.

**Ripple-carry adder**   Uses $n$ full adders to add $n$-bit numbers. The carry output from each full adder is one of the three inputs to the full adders in the next higher-order bit position.

**Decoder**   A device used to select one of $n$ outputs based on $2^n$ inputs.

**Multiplexer (MUX)**   A device used to select one of $2^n$ inputs based on an $n$-bit selector signal.

**Programmable logic array (PLA)**   A device used to generate an OR-ed combination of minterms to implement Boolean functions in hardware.

**Read-only memory (ROM)**   Provides nonvolatile memory with the input being the address of the data or instruction.

**Programmable array logic (PAL)**   A device used to implement Boolean functions in hardware. It's less flexible than a PLA or ROM, but it is less expensive.

In the next chapter, you will learn about sequential logic circuits, which use feedback to maintain a memory of their activity.

# 7

## SEQUENTIAL LOGIC CIRCUITS

In the previous chapter, you learned about *combinational logic circuits*, circuits that depend only on their current input. Another way of thinking about this is that combinational logic circuits are instantaneous (except for the time required for the electronics to settle): their output depends only on the input at the time the output is observed. *Sequential logic circuits*, on the other hand, depend on both the current and past inputs. They have a time history, which can be summarized by the current state of the circuit.

Formally, the *system state* is a description of the system such that knowing the state at time $t_0$ and the inputs from time $t_0$ through time $t_1$, uniquely determines the state at time $t_1$ and the outputs from time $t_0$ through time $t_1$. In other words, the system state provides a summary of everything that has affected the system. Knowing the state of a system at any given time, $t$, tells you everything you need to know to specify the system's behavior from that time on. How it got into this state is irrelevant.

The concept of system state is captured in a *finite state machine*, a mathematical model of computation that can exist in any one of a finite number of states. External inputs to a finite state machine cause it to transition from one state to another or to the same state, while possibly producing an output. Sequential logic circuits are used to implement finite state machines. If a sequential logic circuit is designed such that its output depends only on the state it's in, it's called a *Moore state machine*. If the output also depends on the input causing a transition to a state, it's called a *Mealy state machine*.

In this chapter, we'll look at how *feedback* is used in a logic circuit to keep the gates in a particular state over time, thus implementing memory. We'll use *state diagrams* to show how inputs cause a sequential logic circuit to transition between states and what the corresponding outputs are. You'll also learn how sequential logic circuits can be synchronized with a clock to provide reliable results.

## Latches

The first sequential logic circuit we'll look at is a *latch*, a one-bit storage device that can be in one of two states, depending on its input. A latch can be constructed by connecting two or more logic gates such that the output from one gate is fed back into the input of another gate; this keeps the output of both gates in the same state as long as power is applied. The state of a latch does not depend on time. (The term *latch* is also used for a multiple-bit storage device that behaves like the one-bit device described here.)

### SR Latch Using NOR Gates

The most basic latch is the *Set-Reset* (*SR*). It has two inputs (*S* and *R*) and two states, called *Set* and *Reset*. The state is used as the primary output, Q. It's common to also provide the complemented output, ¬Q. The SR latch is said to be in the Set state when the outputs Q = 1 and ¬Q = 0. It's in a Reset state when Q = 0 and ¬Q = 1.

Figure 7-1 shows a simple implementation of an SR latch using NOR gates. The output of each NOR gate is fed into the input of the other. As we describe the behavior of the circuit in this chapter, you'll see that this *feedback* is what keeps the latch in one state.

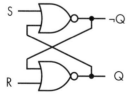

*Figure 7-1: NOR gate implementation of an SR latch*

There are four possible input combinations for an SR. Let's go through them here:

**S = 0, R = 0: Keep current state**

If the latch is in the Set state (Q = 1 and ¬Q = 0), an input of S = 0 and R = 0 will cause ¬Q, the output of the upper NOR gate, to yield ¬(0 ∨ 1) = 0, and Q, the output of the lower NOR gate, to yield ¬(0 ∨ 0) = 1. Conversely, if the latch is in a Reset state (Q = 0 and ¬Q = 1), then the output of the upper NOT gate yields ¬(0 ∨ 0) = 1, and the lower NOR gate yields ¬(1 ∨ 0) = 0. Thus, the cross feedback between the two NOR gates maintains the current state of the latch.

**S = 1, R = 0: Set (Q = 1)**

If the latch is in the Reset state, these inputs cause the output of the upper NOR gate to be ¬(1 ∨ 0) = 0, thus changing ¬Q to 0. This is fed back to the input of the lower NOR gate to yield ¬(0 ∨ 0) = 1. The feedback from the output of the lower NOR gate to the input of the upper keeps the output of the upper NOR gate at ¬(1 ∨ 1) = 0. The latch has then moved into the Set state (Q = 1 and ¬Q = 0).

If the latch is in the Set state, the upper NOR gate yields ¬(1 ∨ 1) = 0, and the output of the lower NOR gate is ¬(0 ∨ 0) = 1. The latch thus remains in the Set state.

**S = 0, R = 1: Reset (Q = 0)**

If the latch is in the Set state, the lower NOR gate yields ¬(0 ∨ 1) = 0, thus changing Q to be 0. This is fed back to the input of the upper NOR gate to yield ¬(0 ∨ 0) = 1. The feedback from the output of the upper NOR gate to the input of the lower keeps the output of the lower NOR gate at ¬(1 ∨ 1) = 0. The latch has then moved into the Reset state (Q = 0 and ¬Q = 1).

If the latch is already in the Reset state, the lower NOR gate yields ¬(1 ∨ 1) = 0, and the output of the upper NOR gate is ¬(0 ∨ 0) = 1, so the latch remains in the Reset state.

**S = 1, R = 1: Not allowed**

If Q = 0 and ¬Q = 1, the upper NOR gate yields ¬(1 ∨ 0) = 0. This is fed back to the input of the lower NOR gate to yield ¬(0 ∨ 1) = 0. This would give Q = ¬Q, which is inconsistent with the laws of Boolean algebra.

If Q = 1 and ¬Q = 0, the lower NOR gate yields ¬(0 ∨ 1) = 0. This is fed back to the input of the upper NOR gate to yield ¬(1 ∨ 0) = 0. This would give Q = ¬Q, which is inconsistent.

Circuits must be designed to prevent this input combination.

To simplify things, we can represent this logic visually. Figure 7-2 introduces a graphic way to show the behavior of a NOR gate SR latch: the *state diagram*. In this state diagram, the current state is shown in the bubbles, with the corresponding primary output below the state. The lines with arrows show the possible transitions between the states and are labeled with the inputs that cause the transition to the next state.

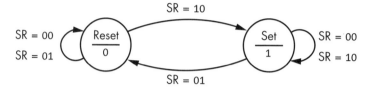

Figure 7-2: State diagram for NOR-gate SR latch

The two circles in Figure 7-2 show the two possible states of the SR latch—Set or Reset. The labels on the lines show the combination of inputs, SR, that causes each state transition. For example, when the latch is in the Reset state, there are two possible inputs, SR = 00 and SR = 01, that cause it to remain in that state. The input SR = 10 causes it to transition to the Set state. Since the output is dependent only on the state, and not on the input, a latch is a Moore state machine.

Those familiar with graph theory will recognize that a state diagram is a directed graph: the states are the vertices, and the inputs that cause transitions are the edges. Although they are beyond the scope of this book, tools from graph theory can be useful in the design process.

As in graph theory, we can also show the same behavior in a tabular form with a *state transition table*, as in Table 7-1. Here S and R are the inputs, Q is the output in the current state, and $Q_{next}$ shows the output in the state that results from the corresponding input. The X in the bottom two rows indicates an impossible condition.

**Table 7-1:** NOR Gate
SR Latch

| S | R | Q | $Q_{next}$ |
|---|---|---|---|
| 0 | 0 | 0 | 0 |
| 0 | 0 | 1 | 1 |
| 0 | 1 | 0 | 0 |
| 0 | 1 | 1 | 0 |
| 1 | 0 | 0 | 1 |
| 1 | 0 | 1 | 1 |
| 1 | 1 | 0 | X |
| 1 | 1 | 1 | X |

Both inputs to a NOR gate SR latch are normally held at 0, which maintains the current state, giving the output Q. Momentarily changing only R to 1 causes the state to go to Reset, which changes the output to $Q = 0$, as shown in the $Q_{next}$ column of the state transition table. And momentarily changing only S to 1 causes the state to go to Set, giving the output $Q = 1$.

As described earlier, the input combination $S = R = 1$ is not allowed because that would cause an inconsistent state for the SR latch. We show this in the state transition table by placing an X in the $Q_{next}$ column in the rows that are prohibited.

## SR Latch Using NAND Gates

The physics of their construction tends to make NAND gates faster than NOR gates. Recalling that NAND and NOR have complementary properties, it probably doesn't surprise you that it's possible to build an SR latch from NAND gates. Since a NAND gate is the logical complement of a NOR gate, we'll use ¬S and ¬R as the inputs, as shown in Figure 7-3. To emphasize the logical duality of the two designs, NAND and NOR, I have drawn the circuit with the output Q at the top and ¬Q on the bottom.

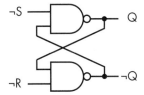

Figure 7-3: NAND gate
implementation of an
SR latch

Like the NOR gate SR latch, the NAND gate SR latch is said to be in the Set state when the outputs are $Q = 1$ and $¬Q = 0$, and in a Reset state when $Q = 0$ and $¬Q = 1$. There are four possible input combinations:

**¬S = 1, ¬R = 1: Keep current state**

If the latch is in the Set state ($Q = 1$ and $¬Q = 0$), the upper NAND gate yields $¬(1 \land 0) = 1$, and the lower NAND gate $¬(1 \land 1) = 0$. If $Q = 0$ and $¬Q = 1$, the latch is in the Reset state, the upper NAND gate yields $¬(1 \land 1) = 0$, and the lower NAND gate $¬(0 \land 1) = 1$. Thus, the cross feedback between the two NAND gates maintains the state of the latch.

**¬S = 0, ¬R = 1: Set (Q = 1)**

If the latch is in the Reset state, the upper NAND gate yields $¬(0 \land 1) = 1$, thus changing Q to be 1. This is fed back to the input of the lower NAND gate to yield $¬(1 \land 1) = 0$. The feedback from the output of the lower NAND gate to the input of the upper keeps the output of the upper NAND gate at $¬(0 \land 0) = 1$. The latch has moved into the Set state ($Q = 1$ and $¬Q = 0$).

If the latch is already in the Set state, then the upper NAND gate yields $\neg(0 \wedge 0) = 1$, and the output of the lower NAND gate is $\neg(1 \wedge 1) = 0$. The latch thus remains in the Set state.

### $\neg S = 1, \neg R = 0$: Reset (Q = 0)

If the latch is in the Set state, the lower NAND gate yields $\neg(1 \wedge 0) = 1$. This is fed back to the input of the upper N gate, making $Q = \neg(1 \wedge 1) = 0$. The feedback from the output of the upper NAND gate to the input of the lower keeps the output of the lower NAND gate at $\neg(0 \wedge 0) = 1$, so the latch moves into the Reset state ($Q = 0$ and $\neg Q = 1$).

If the latch is already in the Reset state, the lower NAND gate yields $\neg(0 \wedge 0) = 1$, and the output of the upper NAND gate is $\neg(1 \wedge 1) = 0$. The latch remains in the Reset state.

### $\neg S = 0, \neg R = 0$: Not allowed

If the latch is in the Reset state, the upper NAND gate yields $\neg(0 \wedge 1) = 1$. This is fed back to the input of the lower NAND gate to yield $\neg(1 \wedge 0) = 1$. This would give $Q = \neg Q$, which is inconsistent.

If the latch is in the Set state, the lower NAND gate yields $\neg(1 \wedge 0) = 1$. This is fed back to the input of the upper NAND gate to yield $\neg(0 \wedge 1) = 1$. This would also give $Q = \neg Q$, which is also inconsistent.

Circuits must be designed to prevent this input combination.

Figure 7-4 shows the behavior of a NAND gate SR latch using a state diagram.

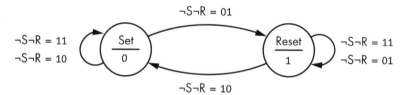

Figure 7-4: NAND gate SR latch

Comparing this with the NOR gate SR latch in Figure 7-2, you can see that they both describe the same behavior. For example, an input of SR = 10 to the NOR gate SR latch will place it in the Set state, while an input of $\neg S \neg R = 01$ to the NAND gate SR latch will also place it in the Set state. I find that I have to think carefully about this when analyzing circuits. An off-by-one error when there are only two choices can cause behavior opposite to what I want.

Table 7-2 is a state transition table for a NAND gate SR latch. Placing 0 on both inputs at the same time causes a problem—namely, that the outputs of both NAND gates would become 1. In other words, $Q = \neg Q = 1$, which is logically impossible. The circuit design must be such to prevent this input combination. The X in two rows indicates an impossible condition.

**Table 7-2:** NAND-Gate
SR Latch

| ¬S | ¬R | Q | Q$_{next}$ |
|----|----|---|------------|
| 1 | 1 | 0 | 0 |
| 1 | 1 | 1 | 1 |
| 1 | 0 | 0 | 0 |
| 1 | 0 | 1 | 0 |
| 0 | 1 | 0 | 1 |
| 0 | 1 | 1 | 1 |
| 0 | 0 | 0 | X |
| 0 | 0 | 1 | X |

The SR latch implemented with two NAND gates can be thought of as the complement of the NOR gate SR latch. The state is maintained by holding both ¬S and ¬R at 1. Momentarily changing ¬S to 0 causes the state to be Set with the output Q = 1, and ¬R = 0 causes it to be Reset with the output Q = 0.

Thus far, we have been looking at a single latch. The problem here is that the state of the latch, and its output, will change whenever the input changes. In a computer, it would be interconnected with many other devices, each changing state with new inputs. It takes time for each device to change state and for its output(s) to propagate to the next device(s), and the precise timing depends on slight manufacturing differences in the devices. The results can be unreliable. We need a means for synchronizing the activity to bring some order to the operations. We'll start by adding an Enable input to the SR latch, which will allow us to control more precisely when the inputs will be allowed to affect the state.

## SR Latch with Enable

We can get better control over the SR latch by adding two NAND gates to provide an Enable input. Connecting the outputs of these two NAND gates to the inputs of an ¬S¬R latch gives us a *gated SR latch*, as shown in Figure 7-5.

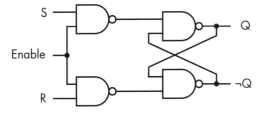

*Figure 7-5: Gated SR latch*

In this circuit, the outputs of both the control NAND gates remain at 1 as long as Enable = 0. This sends ¬S = 1 and ¬R = 1 to the inputs of the ¬S¬R latch portion of this circuit, which causes the state to remain the same. By AND-ing the additional Enable input with the S and R input lines, we can control the time when the state should be changed to the next value.

Table 7-3 shows the state behavior of the SR latch with the Enable control.

**Table 7-3:** Gated SR Latch

| Enable | S | R | Q | $Q_{next}$ |
|---|---|---|---|---|
| 0 | – | – | 0 | 0 |
| 0 | – | – | 1 | 1 |
| 1 | 0 | 0 | 0 | 0 |
| 1 | 0 | 0 | 1 | 1 |
| 1 | 0 | 1 | 0 | 0 |
| 1 | 0 | 1 | 1 | 0 |
| 1 | 1 | 0 | 0 | 1 |
| 1 | 1 | 0 | 1 | 1 |
| 1 | 1 | 1 | 0 | X |
| 1 | 1 | 1 | 1 | X |

In this table, – indicates that an input does not matter, and X indicates a prohibited result. As explained, the design must prevent input combinations that would produce prohibited results. The state of the latch changes only when Enable = 1 and S and R have the opposite values. In the next section, we'll use this observation to simplify the gated SR latch and create a latch that takes a single data input, D, with control over the time when this input will affect the state of the latch.

## The D Latch

A D latch allows us to store the value of one bit. We start with the truth table, Table 7-4, which includes the rows from Table 7-3 where Enable = 1 and R = ¬S. We're looking for a design that will have two inputs—one for Enable, the other for D (short for data). We want D = 1 to set the state, giving the output Q = 1, and D = 0 to reset it, giving the output Q = 0, when the Enable line becomes 1. This design is known as a *D latch*.

**Table 7-4:** D Latch with Enable

| Enable | S | R | D | Q | $Q_{next}$ |
|---|---|---|---|---|---|
| 0 | – | – | – | 0 | 0 |
| 0 | – | – | – | 1 | 1 |
| 1 | 0 | 1 | 0 | 0 | 0 |
| 1 | 0 | 1 | 0 | 1 | 0 |
| 1 | 1 | 0 | 1 | 0 | 1 |
| 1 | 1 | 0 | 1 | 1 | 1 |

We can construct a gated D latch from a gated SR latch by adding a D input and a NOT gate, as shown in Figure 7-6.

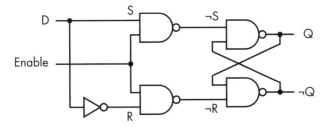

*Figure 7-6: Gated D latch constructed from an SR latch*

The one data input, D, is fed to the S side of the SR latch; the complement of the data value is fed to the R side.

Now we have a circuit that can store one bit of data using the D input and can be synchronized with other operations using the Enable input. However, there are some problems with the D latch. Mainly, there are issues with its reliability when connected with other circuit elements. After the D input has been applied and the circuit has been enabled, it takes a brief period of time for all the electronics to reach the new voltage levels, called the *settling time*. Even after the settling time, the state of a D latch can be affected by the input while the D latch is enabled. Thus, its output can change, making it difficult to synchronize reliably with other devices.

However, this scheme works well when the latch should remain in one state for a long period of time. In general, latches work for operations where we want to select a state and leave it for a period of time that is beyond the control of the computer. An example is an I/O port, where the timing is dependent on the behavior of the device connected to the I/O port. For example, a running program cannot know when the user will press a key on the keyboard. When a key is pressed, the program may not be ready for the character, so the binary code for the character should be latched at the input port. Once the character is stored, the latch would be disabled until the program reads the character code from the latch.

But most of the computing operations within the CPU and main memory must be coordinated in time. You're about to see how sequential logic circuits can be controlled by a clock. Connecting many circuits to the same clock allows us to synchronize their operations.

Let's consider how we might synchronize a D latch connected in a circuit. We feed an input to this D latch and enable it. Even after a brief settling time, its output can change if the input changes, making its output unreliable during the time it is enabled. If the output from our D latch is connected to the input of another device, the input to this second device is unreliable while our D latch is enabled. There is also a *propagation delay* for the output of our D latch to reach the input of the second device due to the physics of the connections. This second device should be disabled until the input to our D latch is reliable and we have allowed for the propagation delay. Once our D latch has settled, it's disabled. After allowing for the propagation delay, the device our D latch is connected to can be enabled.

While the device our D latch is connected to is waiting for a reliable input from our D latch, it is disabled, and its output (from the previous clock cycle) is reliable. So if it's connected to the input of yet another device, this third device can be enabled. This leads to a scheme where every other device is enabled while the alternate devices are disabled. After waiting for a period equal to the sum of the longest settling time and propagation delay time of all the devices connected together, the disabled devices are enabled, and the enabled devices are disabled. The digital 1s and 0s are propagated through this circuit of devices by means of this alternating enable/disable cycle.

As you can probably imagine, coordinating this flipping back and forth between enable and disable can be difficult. We'll give a solution to this problem in the next section.

## Flip-Flops

While a latch could be controlled by a clock signal, its output would be affected by any changes in the input during the portion of time when the clock signal enables the latch. A *flip-flop* circuit is a one-bit storage device designed to accept an input during one portion of the clock signal and then lock the output to a single value throughout the duration of the other portion of the clock signal. This provides the reliability needed to connect many flip-flops in a circuit and synchronize their operations with one clock. We'll start this section with a discussion of clocks and then look at a few examples of flip-flops.

**NOTE** *The terminology varies. Some people also call latches flip-flops. I will use the term* latch *to mean a device that stores one bit, with no timing considerations, and* flip-flop *to mean a device that stores one bit during one-half of a clock cycle and then presents it as an output during the other half of the clock cycle.*

### Clocks

Sequential logic circuits have a time history, summarized in their state. We keep track of time with a *clock*, a device that provides an electronic *clock signal*, typically a square wave that alternates between the 0 and 1 levels, as shown in Figure 7-7. This signal is used as the enabling/disabling input to devices that need to be synchronized.

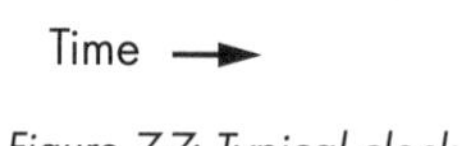

Time ⟶

*Figure 7-7: Typical clock signal to synchronize sequential logic circuits*

The amount of time spent at each level is usually equal. To achieve reliable behavior, most circuits are designed such that a transition of the clock signal triggers the circuit elements to start their respective operations. Either the positive-going (0 to 1) or negative-going (1 to 0) transition may be used. The clock frequency must be slow enough such that all the circuit elements have time to complete their operations before the next clock transition (in the same direction) occurs.

Let's look at a few examples of flip-flop circuits that can be controlled by a clock.

## D Flip-Flop

We'll begin by connecting a clock signal to the Enable input of the gated D latch in Figure 7-6. Here the input affects the output as long as Enable = 1. The problem is that if the input changes while Enable = 1, the output will also change, leading to an unreliable design.

One way to isolate the output from input changes is to connect the outputs of a D latch to the inputs of another D latch in a primary/secondary configuration. The *primary* portion of the circuit processes the input and stores the state, and then it passes its output to the *secondary* portion for final output. This creates a *D flip-flop*, as shown in Figure 7-8. The uncomplemented output of the Primary D latch is fed to the S input, and its complemented output is fed to the R input of the Secondary SR latch, effectively making the Secondary a D latch without requiring a NOT gate at the R input.

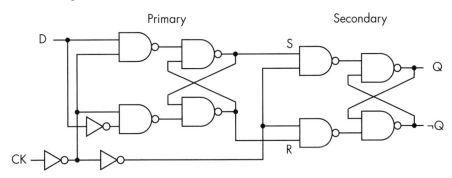

*Figure 7-8: D flip-flop, positive-edge triggering*

In the D flip-flop in Figure 7-8, the bit we want to store, 0 or 1, is fed to the D input of the Primary D latch. The clock signal is fed to the CK input.

Let's walk through how this circuit works, starting with CK = 0. The CK signal passes through a NOT gate, inverting it from 0 to 1 and thus enabling the Primary D latch, placing it in *write mode*. This latch will either Reset or Set, following a D input of 0 or 1, respectively.

While the CK input remains at the 0 level, the second NOT gate inverts the CK signal again, thus presenting the original signal, an enable signal of 0, to the Secondary D latch. This in turn disables it and places it in *read mode*. Any changes in the input to the Primary D latch will affect its output but will have no effect on the Secondary D latch. Therefore, the overall output of this D flip-flop, Q, will be a reliable signal during the entire half-cycle of the clock signal that the secondary portion is in read mode.

When the CK input transitions to the 1 level, the control signal to the Primary D latch becomes 0, disabling it and placing it in read mode. At the same time, the enable input to the Secondary D latch goes to 1, thus placing it in write mode. The output of the Primary D latch is now reliable, providing a reliable input to the Secondary D latch during this entire clock half-cycle. After a brief settling time (in practice, negligible), the output of the Secondary D latch provides a reliable output. Thus, the flip-flop provides a time separation of one-half clock cycle between accepting an input and providing an output. Since the output is available at the 0 to 1 transition, this is called *positive-edge triggering*.

If the first NOT gate connected to the CK signal in Figure 7-8 is removed, that would create a D flip-flop with *negative-edge triggering*.

Sometimes a flip-flop must be set to a known value before the clocking begins—for example, when a computer is first starting up. These known values are input independent of the clock process; hence, they are *asynchronous input*. Figure 7-9 shows a D flip-flop with an asynchronous preset input added to it.

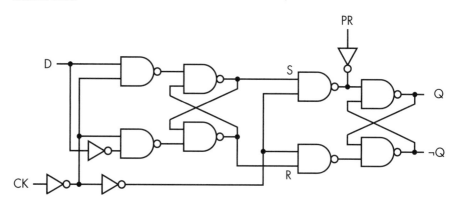

*Figure 7-9: D flip-flop, positive-edge triggering with asynchronous preset*

When a 1 is applied to the PR input, Q becomes 1 and ¬Q becomes 0, regardless of what the other inputs are, even CLK. It is also common to have an asynchronous clear input that sets the state (and output) to 0.

There are more efficient circuits for implementing edge-triggered D flip-flops, but this discussion shows that they can be constructed from ordinary logic gates. They are economical and efficient, so they are widely used in *very-large-scale integration* (*VLSI*) circuits—circuits that include billions of billions of transistor gates on a single semiconductor microchip. Rather than draw the implementation details for each D flip-flop, circuit designers use the symbols shown in Figure 7-10.

The various inputs and outputs are labeled in this figure. Hardware designers typically use $\overline{Q}$ instead of ¬Q. It's common to label the flip-flop as Q$n$ where $n$ = 1, 2, ..., which is used to identify the flip-flop within the overall circuit. The small circle at the clock input in Figure 7-10 (b) means that this D flip-flop is triggered by a negative-going clock transition.

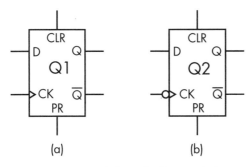

Figure 7-10: Symbols for D flip-flops, including asynchronous clear (CLR) and preset (PR). (a) Positive-edge triggering; (b) negative-edge triggering.

## T Flip-Flop

You're probably familiar with switches that *toggle* between two states each time you activate them. The CAPS LOCK key on your computer is a good example. If the alphabetic keys are in the lowercase mode, pressing the CAPS LOCK key switches to uppercase mode. Press it again, and you're back in lowercase mode. Unlike a set/reset flip-flop, a toggle takes a single input that reverses (or complements) the current state.

We can implement toggleable switches using a flip-flop that simply complements its state, called a *T flip-flop*. To construct a T flip-flop from a D flip-flop, we need to feed the output back and combine it with the input to the D flip-flop. Next, we'll determine exactly how to combine it.

Before tackling the design of the T flip-flop, let's do some Boolean algebra manipulation to get a sense of what direction our design might take. First, take a look at the state diagram for a T flip-flop, in Figure 7-11, and the state transition table, in Table 7-5.

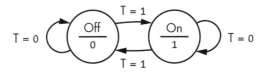

Figure 7-11: T flip-flop state diagram

**Table 7-5:** T Flip-Flop
State Transition Table

| T | Q | $Q_{next}$ |
|---|---|---|
| 0 | 0 | 0 |
| 0 | 1 | 1 |
| 1 | 0 | 1 |
| 1 | 1 | 0 |

Referring to Table 7-4 for a D flip-flop, let's add a column to the state transition table for the T flip-flop, giving Table 7-6, which shows the D values that would cause the same state transitions as T.

**Table 7-6:** D Values That Have the Same Effect as a T Flip-Flop

| T | Q | Q$_{next}$ | D |
|---|---|---|---|
| 0 | 0 | 0 | 0 |
| 0 | 1 | 1 | 1 |
| 1 | 0 | 1 | 1 |
| 1 | 1 | 0 | 0 |

From Table 7-6, it's easy to write the equation for D:

$$D = (\neg T \wedge Q) \vee (T \wedge \neg Q)$$
$$= T \veebar Q$$

Thus, we need to add only a single XOR gate, giving us the design for the T flip-flop shown in Figure 7-12.

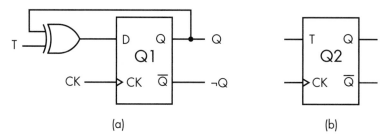

Figure 7-12: T flip-flop. (a) Circuit using a D flip-flop. (b) Symbol for a T flip-flop.

You have seen how we can use a D flip-flop to store one bit in either its 1 (set) or 0 (reset) state, keep the state the same, or, by adding a logic gate, toggle the bit. In the next section, you'll see how we can modify an SR flip-flop to implement all four actions—set, reset, keep, toggle—in a single device.

## JK Flip-Flop

Implementing all four possible actions—set, reset, keep, toggle—requires two inputs, J and K, giving us the *JK flip-flop*. As with the T flip-flop, we'll see if the state diagram and transition table can give us some insight into the design we want. Figure 7-13 shows the state diagram for a JK flip-flop, and Table 7-7 shows its state transition table. The leftmost column in Table 7-7 shows which of the four functions the JK flip-flop performs for each value of JK.

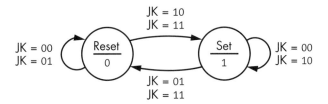

Figure 7-13: JK flip-flop state diagram

**Table 7-7:** JK Flip-Flop State Transition Table

|  | J | K | Q | Q$_{next}$ |
|---|---|---|---|---|
| Keep | 0 | 0 | 0 | 0 |
| Keep | 0 | 0 | 1 | 1 |
| Reset | 0 | 1 | 0 | 0 |
| Reset | 0 | 1 | 1 | 0 |
| Set | 1 | 0 | 0 | 1 |
| Set | 1 | 0 | 1 | 1 |
| Toggle | 1 | 1 | 0 | 1 |
| Toggle | 1 | 1 | 1 | 0 |

The first six rows of the JK flip-flop state transition table are the same as the first six rows on the enabled portion of the SR latch state transition table (Table 7-3). We saw when discussing the SR latch that the condition S = R = 1 is not allowed. Perhaps we can add some logic circuitry so we can use the J = K = 1 condition to implement the toggle function in our JK flip-flop. We'll start with a circuit for an SR flip-flop and add another signal to each of the input NAND gates, as shown in Figure 7-14. The points ¬S and ¬R are labeled to show the inputs to the part of the Primary ¬S¬R latch that is the same, as shown in Figure 7-3.

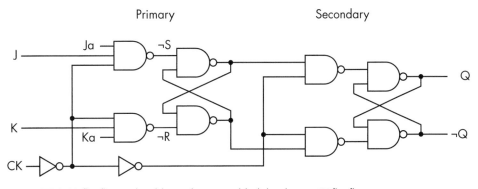

Figure 7-14: SR flip-flop with additional inputs added, leading to JK flip-flop

The Primary SR latch in Figure 7-14 is in its write mode when CK = 0. We want it to toggle the output, Q, when J = K = 1. Given these conditions, Table 7-8 shows how ¬S and ¬R depend on Ja and Ka for the two possible values of Q. We saw how these values of ¬S and ¬R affect Q in Table 7-2, which are copied here into Table 7-8.

**Table 7-8:** Additional Inputs to Add Toggle Function to SR Flip-Flop

| Ja | Ka | ¬S | ¬R | Q | $Q_{next}$ |
|----|----|----|----|---|------------|
| 0 | 0 | 1 | 1 | 0 | 0 |
| 0 | 1 | 1 | 0 | 0 | 0 |
| 1 | 0 | 0 | 1 | 0 | 1 |
| 1 | 1 | 0 | 0 | 0 | X |
| 0 | 0 | 1 | 1 | 1 | 1 |
| 0 | 1 | 1 | 0 | 1 | 0 |
| 1 | 0 | 0 | 1 | 1 | 1 |
| 1 | 1 | 0 | 0 | 1 | X |

The third and sixth rows of Table 7-8 show that JaKa = 10 toggles the state, Q, from 0 to 1, and JaKa = 01 toggles the state from 1 to 0. The leads us to the design in Figure 7-15, with Ja = ¬Q and Ka = Q.

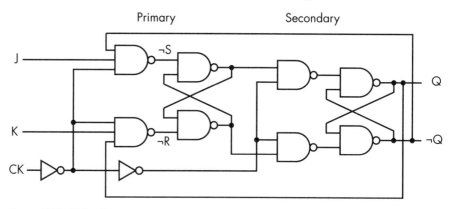

Figure 7-15: JK flip-flop

We should check that the feedback connections made in this circuit preserve the behavior of the other functions of the JK flop-flop. Table 7-9 shows the state transition table for the JK flip-flop in Figure 7-15 with ¬S, ¬R, and ¬Q added. Refer to Table 7-2 for the relationship between ¬S, ¬R, and $Q_{next}$.

**Table 7-9:** JK Flip-Flop State Table for the Circuit in Figure 7-15

|        | J | K | Q | ¬Q | ¬S | ¬R | Q_next |
|--------|---|---|---|----|----|----|--------|
| Keep   | 0 | 0 | 0 | 1  | 1  | 1  | 0      |
| Keep   | 0 | 0 | 1 | 0  | 1  | 1  | 1      |
| Reset  | 0 | 1 | 0 | 1  | 1  | 1  | 0      |
| Reset  | 0 | 1 | 1 | 0  | 1  | 0  | 0      |
| Set    | 1 | 0 | 0 | 1  | 0  | 1  | 1      |
| Set    | 1 | 0 | 1 | 0  | 1  | 1  | 1      |
| Toggle | 1 | 1 | 0 | 1  | 0  | 1  | 1      |
| Toggle | 1 | 1 | 1 | 0  | 1  | 0  | 0      |

Using three-input NAND gates at the input to this JK flip-flop does add some complexity to the circuit. The additional complexity is about the same as adding an XOR gate to a D flip-flop to get a T flip-flop (see Figure 7-12). Although an SR flip-flop is a little less complex than a JK flip-flop if the toggle function is not needed, there are manufacturing cost advantages to having only one design. The JK flip-flop, by providing all four functions, also allows more flexibility, and hence cost savings, in design.

## Designing Sequential Logic Circuits

Now we'll consider a more general set of steps for designing sequential logic circuits. Design in any field is usually iterative, as you have no doubt learned from your programming experience.

You start with a design, analyze it, and then refine the design to make it faster, less expensive, and so forth. After gaining some experience, the design process usually requires fewer iterations. The following steps are a good method for building a first working design:

1.  From the word description of the problem, create a state transition table and state diagram showing what the circuit must do. These form the basic technical specifications for the circuit you will be designing.

2.  Choose a binary code for the states and create a binary-coded version of the state table and/or state diagram. For $N$ states, the code will need $log_2 N$ bits. Any code will work, but some codes may lead to simpler combinational logic in the circuit.

3.  Choose a type of flip-flop. This choice is often dictated by the components you have on hand.

4.  Add columns to the state table that show the input required to each flip-flop to cause each of the required transitions.

5. Simplify the inputs to each flip-flop. Karnaugh maps or algebraic methods are good tools for the simplification process.

6. Draw the circuit.

The simplification step may cause you to rethink your choice of type of flip-flop. These three steps—flip-flop choice, determining inputs, simplification—may need to be repeated several times to get a good design. The following two examples illustrate this process.

## Designing a Counter

Rather than asking you to do all the work at this point, I'll go through two examples. If you have access to a digital circuit simulator, or the required hardware, I suggest that you use those resources to follow along. This is like a guided "Your Turn."

In this example, we want to design a counter that has an Enable input. When Enable = 1, it increments through the sequence 0, 1, 2, 3, 0, 1, ..., incrementing each clock tick. Enable = 0 causes the counter to remain in its current state. The output is the sequence number in two-bit binary.

### Step 1: Create a State Transition Table and State Diagram

At each clock tick, the counter increments by 1 if Enable = 1. If Enable = 0, it remains in the current state. Figure 7-16 shows the four states—0, 1, 2, 3—and the corresponding two-bit output for each state.

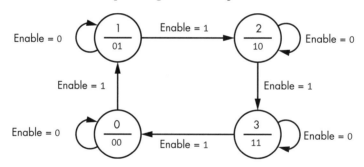

Figure 7-16: State diagram for a counter that cycles through 0, 1, 2, 3, 0, ...

Table 7-10 shows the state transition table.

**Table 7-10:** State Transition Table for a Counter that Cycles Through 0, 1, 2, 3, 0, ...

|  | Enable = 0 | Enable = 1 |
| --- | --- | --- |
| Current $n$ | Next $n$ | Next $n$ |
| 0 | 0 | 1 |
| 1 | 1 | 2 |

| | Enable = 0 | Enable = 1 |
|---|---|---|
| Current $n$ | Next $n$ | Next $n$ |
| 2 | 2 | 3 |
| 3 | 3 | 0 |

When Enable = 0, the counter is essentially turned off, and when Enable = 1, the counter automatically increments by 1, wrapping around to 0 when it reaches its limit of 3.

### Step 2: Create a Binary-Coded Version of the State Table and/or State Diagram

With four states, we need two bits. We will let $n$ be the state, which we represent with the two-bit binary number $n_1 n_0$. The behavior of the counter is shown in the state transition table, Table 7-11.

**Table 7-11:** State Transition Table for Two-Bit Counter

| | Current | | Next | |
|---|---|---|---|---|
| Enable | $n_1$ | $n_0$ | $n_1$ | $n_0$ |
| 0 | 0 | 0 | 0 | 0 |
| 0 | 0 | 1 | 0 | 1 |
| 0 | 1 | 0 | 1 | 0 |
| 0 | 1 | 1 | 1 | 1 |
| 1 | 0 | 0 | 0 | 1 |
| 1 | 0 | 1 | 1 | 0 |
| 1 | 1 | 0 | 1 | 1 |
| 1 | 1 | 1 | 0 | 0 |

### Step 3: Select a Flip-Flop

JK flip-flops are a good place to start because they provide all the functions. After going through the design, we may learn that a simpler flip-flop would work. We could then come back to this step and go through the remaining steps again. An experienced designer may have some insight into the problem that would suggest starting with another type of flip-flop. Often, any potential savings in cost or power consumption do not justify changing to another type of flip-flop.

### Step 4: Add Columns to the State Transition Table Showing the Required Inputs

We need two flip-flops, one for each bit. The columns added to the state transition table show the inputs—Enable, $n_1$, $n_0$—required to each JK flip-flop to cause the correct state transition. From the description of the JK flip-flop earlier in the chapter, we know that JK = 00 keeps the current state, JK = 01 resets it (to 0), JK = 10 sets it (to 1), and JK = 11 toggles the state. We use X when the input can be either 0 or 1, or "don't care." Table 7-12 shows the required JK inputs.

**Table 7-12:** Two-Bit Counter Implemented with JK Flip-Flops

| Enable | Current $n_1$ | $n_0$ | Next $n_1$ | $n_0$ | $J_1$ | $K_1$ | $J_0$ | $K_0$ |
|---|---|---|---|---|---|---|---|---|
| 0 | 0 | 0 | 0 | 0 | 0 | X | 0 | X |
| 0 | 0 | 1 | 0 | 1 | 0 | X | X | 0 |
| 0 | 1 | 0 | 1 | 0 | X | 0 | 0 | X |
| 0 | 1 | 1 | 1 | 1 | X | 0 | X | 0 |
| 1 | 0 | 0 | 0 | 1 | 0 | X | 1 | X |
| 1 | 0 | 1 | 1 | 0 | 1 | X | X | 1 |
| 1 | 1 | 0 | 1 | 1 | X | 0 | 1 | X |
| 1 | 1 | 1 | 0 | 0 | X | 1 | X | 1 |

There are quite a few "don't care" entries for both JK flip-flops in this table. This suggests that we can do quite a bit of simplification. It also suggests that Karnaugh maps will be a good approach, since their graphic presentation tends to make it easier to visualize the effects of "don't care" entries.

### Step 5: Simplify the Required Inputs

We'll use Karnaugh maps to find a simpler solution, using $E$ for Enable, as shown in Figure 7-17.

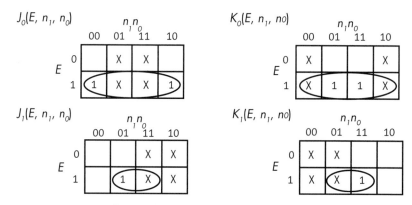

Figure 7-17: Karnaugh maps for two-bit counter implemented with JK flip-flops

We can easily write the equations from the Karnaugh maps to solve this problem, as shown here:

$$J_0(E, n_1, n_0) = E$$
$$K_0(E, n_1, n_0) = E$$
$$J_1(E, n_1, n_0) = E \land n_0$$
$$K_1(E, n_1, n_0) = E \land n_0$$

J = K = 1 causes a JK flip-flop to toggle between states. These equations show that the low-order JK flip-flop toggles with each clock cycle. When it's enabled, its output, $n_0$, changes between 0 and 1 with each clock cycle. That is AND-ed with the Enable input to the high-order JK flip-flop, causing it to toggle between 0 and 1 every two clock cycles. (You will see this timing later in Figure 7-19 in the following step.)

### Step 6: Draw the Circuit

Figure 7-18 shows a circuit to implement this counter. Referring to Table 7-8, we see that both JK flip-flops are being used as toggles in this design.

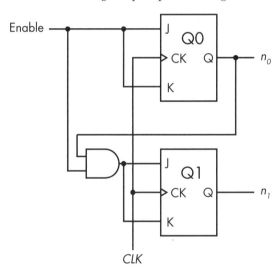

*Figure 7-18: Two-bit counter implemented with two JK flip-flops*

Figure 7-19 shows the timing of the binary counter when counting through the sequence 3, 0, 1, 2, 3 (11, 00, 01, 10, 11).

$Qi$.JK is the input to the $i^{th}$ JK flip-flop, and $n_i$ is its output. (Recall that J = K in this design.) When the $i^{th}$ input, $Qi$.JK, is applied to its JK flip-flop, remember that the output of the flip-flop does not change until the second half of the clock cycle. This can be seen when comparing the trace for the corresponding output, $n_i$, in the figure.

The short delay after a clock transition before the value of each output actually changes represents the time required for the electronics to completely settle to the new values.

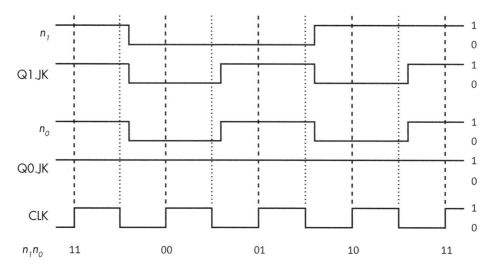

| $n_1 n_0$ | 11 | 00 | 01 | 10 | 11 |

*Figure 7-19: Timing of two-bit counter, implemented with JK flip-flops*

## Designing a Branch Predictor

Let's do another guided "Your Turn" here. This example is a bit more complicated than the previous one.

Except for very inexpensive microcontrollers, most modern CPUs execute instructions in stages. Each stage consists of hardware that is specialized to perform the operations in that stage. An instruction passes through each stage in an assembly-line fashion. For example, if you were to create an assembly line to manufacture wooden chairs, you could do it in three stages: saw the wood to make the parts for the chair, assemble the parts, paint the chair. The hardware needed at each stage would be saw, hammer and screwdriver, and paintbrush.

The arrangement of specialized hardware in the CPU is called a *pipeline*. The hardware in the first stage is designed to fetch an instruction from memory, as you'll see in Chapter 9. After an instruction is fetched from memory, it passes onto the next stage of the pipeline, where the instructions are decoded. Simultaneously, the first stage of the pipeline fetches the next instruction from memory. The result is that the CPU is working on several instructions at the same time. This provides some parallelism, thus improving execution speed.

Almost all programs contain *conditional branch points*—places where the next instruction to be fetched can be in one of two different memory locations. Unfortunately, there is no way to know which of the two instructions to fetch until the decision-making instruction has moved several stages into the pipeline. To maintain execution speed, as soon as a conditional branch instruction has passed on from the fetch stage, it's helpful if the CPU can predict where to fetch the next instruction from. Then the CPU can go ahead and fetch the predicted instruction. If the prediction was wrong, the

CPU simply ignores the work it has done on the predicted instruction by flushing out the pipeline and fetching the other instruction, which enters the beginning of the pipeline.

In this example, we'll design a circuit that predicts whether a conditional branch will be taken. The predictor continues to predict the same outcome, and the branch will be taken, or not taken, until it makes two mistakes in a row.

### Step 1: Create a State Table and State Diagram

We use Yes to indicate when the branch is taken and No to indicate when it's not. The state diagram in Figure 7-20 shows the four possible states.

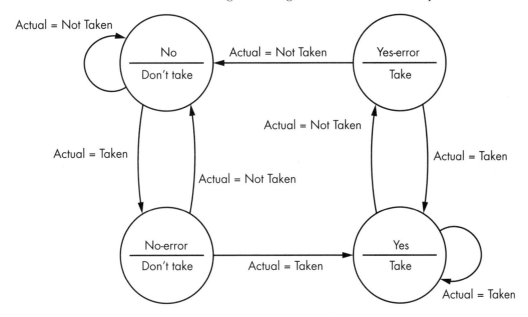

Figure 7-20: Branch predictor

Let's begin in the No state. Here, the branch was not taken at least the last two times this instruction was executed. The output is to predict that it will also not be taken this time. The input to the circuit is whether the branch has actually been taken when the instruction has completed execution.

The arc labeled Actual = Not Taken loops back to the No state, with the prediction (the output) that the branch will not be taken the next time. If the branch is taken, the Actual = Taken arc shows that the circuit moves into the No-error state to indicate one error in the prediction. But because it must be wrong twice in a row to change our prediction, the circuit is still predicting "Don't take" as the output.

From the No-error state, if the branch is not taken (the prediction is correct), the circuit returns back to the No state. However, if the branch is taken, the circuit predicted incorrectly twice in a row, so the circuit moves to the Yes state, and the output is Take.

I'll leave tracing through the remainder of this state diagram as an exercise for you. Once you're satisfied with how it works, take a look at Table 7-13, which provides the technical specifications for our circuit.

**Table 7-13:** Branch Predictor State Table

| | | Actual = Not Taken | | Actual = Taken | |
| --- | --- | --- | --- | --- | --- |
| Current state | Prediction | Next state | Prediction | Next state | Prediction |
| No | Don't take | No | Don't take | No-error | Don't take |
| No-error | Don't take | No | Don't take | Yes | Take |
| Yes-error | Take | No | Don't take | Yes | Take |
| Yes | Take | Yes-error | Take | Yes | Take |

When the result of the conditional branch is determined in the pipeline, taken or not taken, Table 7-13 shows the next state and the corresponding prediction. This prediction would be used to determine which of the two possible addresses—the address of the next instruction or the address of the branch target—to store for use the next time this instruction is encountered in the program.

### Step 2: Represent the States

For this problem, we'll choose a binary code for the state, $s_1 s_0$, as shown in Table 7-14.

**Table 7-14:** States of Branch Predictor

| State | $s_1$ | $s_0$ | Prediction |
| --- | --- | --- | --- |
| No | 0 | 0 | Don't take |
| No-error | 0 | 1 | Don't take |
| Yes-error | 1 | 0 | Take |
| Yes | 1 | 1 | Take |

The Prediction is one bit, $s_1$, which is 0 if the prediction is "Don't take" and 1 if the prediction is Take.

Letting the input, Actual, be 0 when the branch is not taken and 1 when it is taken and using the state notation of Table 7-14, we get the state transition table, Table 7-15.

**Table 7-15:** State Transition Table for Branch Predictor

| | Current | | Next | |
| --- | --- | --- | --- | --- |
| Actual | $s_1$ | $s_0$ | $s_1$ | $s_0$ |
| 0 | 0 | 0 | 0 | 0 |
| 0 | 0 | 1 | 0 | 0 |
| 0 | 1 | 0 | 0 | 0 |
| 0 | 1 | 1 | 1 | 0 |
| 1 | 0 | 0 | 0 | 1 |
| 1 | 0 | 1 | 1 | 1 |
| 1 | 1 | 0 | 1 | 1 |
| 1 | 1 | 1 | 1 | 1 |

When the conditional branch instruction reaches a point in the pipeline where it is determined whether the branch should be taken or not, this information is used as the input, Actual, to the predictor circuit, which transforms the state from Current to Next for the next time this instruction is encountered.

### Step 3: Select a Flip-Flop

For the same reasons as in the counter example, we'll use a JK flip-flop here.

### Step 4: Add Columns to the State Table Showing the Required Inputs

Table 7-16 shows the JK flip-flop inputs required to implement the state transitions in Table 7-15.

**Table 7-16:** JK Flip-Flop Inputs for Branch Predictor

| | Current | | Next | | | | | |
| --- | --- | --- | --- | --- | --- | --- | --- | --- |
| Actual | $s_1$ | $s_0$ | $s_1$ | $s_0$ | $J_1$ | $K_1$ | $J_0$ | $K_0$ |
| 0 | 0 | 0 | 0 | 0 | 0 | X | 0 | X |
| 0 | 0 | 1 | 0 | 0 | 0 | X | X | 1 |
| 0 | 1 | 0 | 0 | 0 | X | 1 | 0 | X |
| 0 | 1 | 1 | 1 | 0 | X | 0 | X | 1 |
| 1 | 0 | 0 | 0 | 1 | 0 | X | 1 | X |
| 1 | 0 | 1 | 1 | 1 | 1 | X | X | 0 |
| 1 | 1 | 0 | 1 | 1 | X | 0 | 1 | X |
| 1 | 1 | 1 | 1 | 1 | X | 0 | X | 0 |

## Step 5: Simplify the Required Inputs

We'll use Karnaugh maps, Figure 7-21, to find a minimal solution. The input is whether the branch was taken: Actual = 0 means it was not taken; Actual = 1 means it was taken.

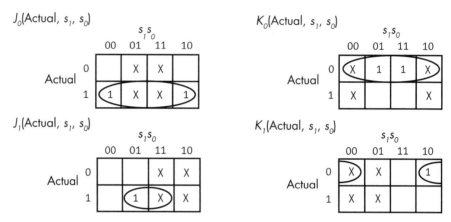

Figure 7-21: Karnaugh maps for branch predictor

We can write the equations directly from these Karnaugh maps:

$$J_0(\text{Actual}, s_1, s_0) = \text{Actual}$$
$$K_0(\text{Actual}, s_1, s_0) = \neg\text{Actual}$$
$$J_1(\text{Actual}, s_1, s_0) = \text{Actual} \land s_0$$
$$K_1(\text{Actual}, s_1, s_0) = \neg\text{Actual} \land \neg s_0$$

For this circuit, then, we'll need two JK flip-flops, two AND gates, and one NOT gate.

## Step 6: Draw the Circuit

In this circuit, the input is Actual = 0 if the branch was not taken the last time, and Actual = 1 if it was taken. We need to add two AND gates and one NOT gate to the inputs of the JK flip-flops, as shown in Figure 7-22.

This example shows the simplest method of branch prediction. More complex methods exist. There is ongoing research into the effectiveness of branch prediction. Although it can speed up some algorithms, the additional hardware required for branch prediction consumes more electrical power, which is of concern in battery-powered devices.

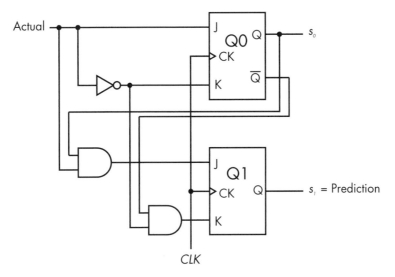

Figure 7-22: Branch predictor circuit using JK flip-flops

## What You've Learned

**SR latch**   The state of an SR latch depends on its input, either set or reset. It can include an Enable input.

**D flip-flop**   A D flip-flop stores one bit of data. By connecting two latches in a primary-secondary configuration, the output is isolated from the input, allowing a flip-flop to be synchronized with a clock signal. The output of a D flip-flop can be changed only once per clock cycle.

**T flip-flop**   The state of a T flip-flop toggles between 0 and 1 with each clock cycle when it is enabled.

**JK flip-flop**   The JK flip-flop is called the *universal flip-flop* because it provides the four primary functions—keep current state, set, reset, toggle.

You also saw two examples of designing sequential logic circuits with JK flip-flops. In the next chapter, you'll learn about some of the various memory structures used in a computer system.

# 8

## MEMORY

In the previous three chapters, we looked at some of the hardware used to implement logical functions. Now we'll look at how this functionality can be used to implement the subsystems that make up a computer, starting with memory.

Every computer user wants lots of memory and fast computing. However, faster memory costs more money, so there are some trade-offs. We'll begin this chapter with a discussion of how different types of memory are used to provide a reasonable compromise between speed and cost. Then we'll discuss a few different ways of implementing memory in hardware.

## The Memory Hierarchy

In general, the closer memory is to the CPU, the faster and more expensive it is. The slowest memory is the cloud. It's also the least expensive. My email account provides 15GB of storage in the cloud and doesn't cost me any money (if I ignore the "cost" of seeing a few advertisements). But its speed is limited by my internet connection. At the other extreme, the memory within the CPU runs at the same speed as the CPU but is relatively expensive. In the x86-64 architecture, there's only about 1KB of memory in the CPU available to the programmer.

Figure 8-1 shows this general hierarchy. As we get closer to the CPU (the top of this figure), memory is faster and costs more money, so there's less of it.

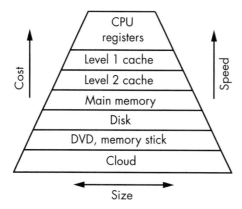

Figure 8-1: Computer memory hierarchy

The top three layers in Figure 8-1 are typically included in the CPU chip in modern computers. There may be one or two more levels of cache before getting to main memory. The main memory and disk are usually in the same enclosure with the CPU, which may include more than one disk.

The next layer away from the CPU represents offline data storage devices. DVDs and memory sticks are only two examples. You may also have an external USB disk, a tape drive, and so forth. These are devices that you usually need to take some physical action, such as inserting a DVD in the player or plugging a memory stick into a USB port, before they are accessible to the computer.

The final layer in this hierarchy is the storage in the cloud. Although most of us set up our computers to log on automatically, it may not always be available.

In this chapter, we'll start with the two layers just above the cloud layer, offline storage and disk, and work our way in to the CPU registers. Then we'll describe the hardware used to build registers and work our way back out to main memory. We'll leave discussion of implementation of the three outermost layers to other books.

## Mass Storage

*Mass storage* is used for keeping programs and large amounts of data in a machine-readable format. This includes hard disks, solid-state drives, memory sticks, optical disks, and so forth. Their contents are *nonvolatile*, meaning that when the power is turned off, the contents remain. They also are slow compared to the CPU. Accessing their contents requires explicit programming.

In Figure 8-2, the input/output (I/O) block includes specialized circuitry that interfaces with mass storage devices.

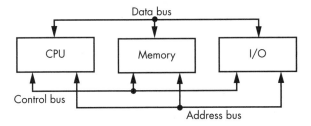

Figure 8-2: Subsystems of a computer. The CPU, memory, and I/O subsystems communicate with one another via the three buses. (Repeat of Figure 1-1.)

For example, my computer has circuitry that implements the Serial Advanced Technology Attachment (SATA) interface protocol. I have an SSD card plugged into one of the SATA ports. The operating system includes software (a *device driver*) that applications call to access the data and applications on my SSD card through the SATA port. We'll discuss I/O programming in Chapter 20, but the specifics of device drivers are beyond the scope of this book.

For the rest of this chapter, we'll look at *volatile* memory, which loses its contents when power is turned off.

## Main Memory

Next, we have *main memory*. This is the RAM that you see in the specifications when you buy a computer. As shown in Figure 8-2, main memory communicates with the CPU using the data, address, and control buses. We'll discuss how these buses work in Chapter 9. Main memory is synchronized in the hardware with the CPU. Thus, a programmer can access items in memory by simply specifying the address and whether to read the item from memory or store a new value there.

Usually, the entire program and dataset are not loaded into main memory. Only the portion currently being worked on is loaded by the operating system from mass storage into main memory. Most mass storage devices in modern computers can be accessed only in *blocks* of predetermined size. For example, the disk block size in my Ubuntu installation is 4KB. When a needed instruction or data item is loaded into main memory, the computer loads the whole block of instructions or data that includes the needed item into memory. Chances are good that the nearby parts of the program (instructions or data) will be needed soon. Since they're already in main memory, the operating system doesn't need to access the mass storage device again, thus speeding up program execution.

The most common organization of main memory is to store both the program instructions and data in main memory. This is referred to as the *von Neumann architecture*, and it was described by John von Neumann ("First Draft of a Report on the EDVAC," Moore School of Electrical Engineering, University of Pennsylvania, 1945), although other computer science pioneers of the day were working with the same concepts.

A downside of the von Neumann architecture is that if an instruction calls for reading data from, or writing data to, memory, the next instruction in the program sequence cannot be read from memory over the same bus until the current instruction has completed the data transfer—this is known as the *von Neumann bottleneck*. This conflict slows program execution, giving rise to another stored-program architecture, the *Harvard architecture*, in which the program and data are stored in different memories, each with its own bus connected to the CPU. This makes it possible for the CPU to access both program instructions and data simultaneously. This specialization reduces the memory usage flexibility that generally increases the total amount of memory needed. It also requires additional memory access hardware. The additional memory and access hardware increase the cost.

Another downside of the von Neumann architecture is that a program can be written to view itself as data, thus enabling a self-modifying program, which is generally a bad idea. GNU/Linux, like most modern, general-purpose operating systems, prohibits applications from modifying themselves.

## Cache Memory

Most of the programs I use take up tens or hundreds of megabytes in main memory. But most of the execution time is taken up by loops, which execute the same few instructions repetitively, access the same few variables, and occupy only tens or hundreds of bytes. Most modern computers include very fast *cache memory* between the main memory and the CPU, which provides a much faster location for the instructions and variables currently being processed by the program.

Cache memory is organized in levels, with Level 1 being the closest to the CPU, and the smallest. The computer I'm using has three levels of cache: 64KB of Level 1, 256KB of Level 2, and 8MB of Level 3. When a program needs to access an instruction or data item, the hardware first checks to see if it's located in the Level 1 cache. If not, it checks the Level 2 cache. If it's in the Level 2 cache, the hardware copies a block of memory that includes the needed instruction or data into the Level 1 cache and then into the CPU, where it stays until the program needs it again, or the Level 1 cache needs to reuse that location for other instructions or data from the Level 2 cache. The amount of memory copied into a cache at a time, called a *line*, is much less than that copied from a mass storage device.

If the required instruction or data is not in the Level 2 cache, the hardware checks the Level 3 cache. If it finds what it needs, it copies the line containing the needed instruction or data into Level 2, then Level 1, and from there into the CPU. If the data is not in Level 3, the hardware checks main memory. In this way, the hardware makes a copy of the portion of the program it's currently working within the Level 3 cache, a smaller portion of what it's working on in the Level 2 cache, and an even smaller portion in the Level 1 cache. It's common for the Level 1 cache to have a Harvard architecture, thus providing separate paths to the CPU for the instructions and the data. The Level 1 cache on my computer has a Harvard architecture with 32KB devoted to instructions and 32KB for data. My Level 1 instruction cache has a line size of 32 bytes, while all the others have a line size of 64 bytes.

When data is written to main memory, it starts with Level 1 cache, then the next cache levels, and finally into main memory. There are many schemes for using caches, which can become rather complex. I'll leave further discussion of caches for more advanced treatments, for example: *https://en.wikibooks.org/wiki/Microprocessor_Design/Cache/.*

The time to access the Level 1 cache is close to the speed of the CPU. Level 2 is about 10 times slower, Level 3 about 100 times slower, and main memory about 1,000 times slower. These values are approximate and differ widely among implementations. Modern processors include cache memory in the same chip as the CPU, and some have more than three levels of cache.

Computer performance is usually limited by the time it takes for the CPU to read instructions and data into the CPU, not by the speed of the CPU itself. Having the instructions and data in Level 1 cache reduces this time. Of course, if they are not in Level 1 cache, and the hardware needs to copy other instructions or data from Level 2, or Level 3, or main memory into Level 3, then Level 2, and finally Level 1, access will take longer than simply getting the instructions or data directly from main memory. The effectiveness of cache depends on the *locality of reference*, which is the tendency of a program to reference nearby memory addresses in a short period of time. This is one of the reasons good programmers break a program, especially repetitive sections, into small units. A small program unit is more likely to fit within a few lines of a cache, where it would be available for succeeding repetitions.

**YOUR TURN**

1.  Determine the cache size(s) on your computer. On my Ubuntu 20.04 LTS system, the command is lscpu. You may need to use another command on your computer.

2.  Determine the line size of each of the caches on your computer. On my Ubuntu 20.04 LTS system, the command is getconf -a| grep CACHE. You may need to use another command on your computer.

### Registers

The fastest memory is within the CPU itself: the *registers*. Registers typically provide about 1KB of storage and are accessed at the same speed as the CPU. They're mainly used for numerical computations, logical operations, temporary data storage, and similar short-term operations—somewhat like how we use scratch paper for hand computation. Many registers are directly accessible by the programmer, while others are hidden. Some are used in the hardware that serves to interface between the CPU and I/O devices. The organization of registers in the CPU is very specific to the particular CPU architecture, and it's one of the most important aspects of programming a computer at the assembly language level. You'll learn about the main registers that a programmer works with in the x86-64 architecture in the next chapter.

But first, let's look at how memory can be implemented in hardware using the logic devices discussed in previous chapters. We'll start with the CPU registers, the top layer in Figure 8-1, and work our way out to main memory. As we work through this hierarchy, you'll learn why faster memory is more expensive, which is the reason for organizing memory in this hierarchical way. We won't cover the implementation of mass storage systems in this book.

## Implementing Memory in Hardware

Now that we're at the top of the hierarchy in Figure 8-1, let's see how we implement the memory in the CPU registers. We'll then work our way back out from the CPU, and you'll see some of the limitations when applying these designs to larger memory systems, like cache and main memory. We'll end the section with designs for the memory in these larger systems.

### Four-Bit Register

Let's begin with a design for a simple *four-bit register*, which might be found in inexpensive CPUs used in price-sensitive consumer products, like coffee makers, remote controls, and so forth. Figure 8-3 shows a design for implementing a four-bit register using a D flip-flop for each bit. Each time the clock does a positive transition, the state (contents) of the register, $r = r_3 r_2 r_1 r_0$, is set to the input, $d = d_3 d_2 d_1 d_0$.

The problem with this circuit is that any changes in any $d_i$ will change the state of the corresponding stored bit, $r_i$, in the next clock cycle, so the contents of the register are essentially valid for only one clock cycle. One-cycle buffering of a bit pattern is sufficient for some applications, but we also need registers that will store a value until it is explicitly changed, perhaps billions of clock cycles later.

Let's add a *Store* signal and feedback from the output, $r_i$, of each bit. We want each $r_i$ to remain unchanged when *Store* = 0 and to follow the input, $d_i$, when *Store* = 1, as shown in Table 8-1.

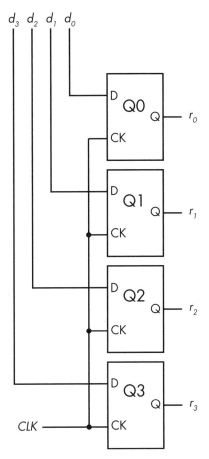

Figure 8-3: A four-bit register using a
D flip-flop for each bit

**Table 8-1:** One-Bit
Storage Using a D
Flip-Flop with *Store*
Signal

| Store | $d_i$ | $r_i$ | D |
|---|---|---|---|
| 0 | 0 | 0 | 0 |
| 0 | 0 | 1 | 1 |
| 0 | 1 | 0 | 0 |
| 0 | 1 | 1 | 1 |
| 1 | 0 | 0 | 0 |
| 1 | 0 | 1 | 0 |
| 1 | 1 | 0 | 1 |
| 1 | 1 | 1 | 1 |

Table 8-1 leads to the Boolean equation for D:

$$D(Store, d_i, r_i) = \neg(\neg(\neg Store \wedge r_i) \wedge \neg(Store \wedge d_i))$$

This equation can be implemented with three NAND gates at the input of each D flip-flop, as shown in Figure 8-4.

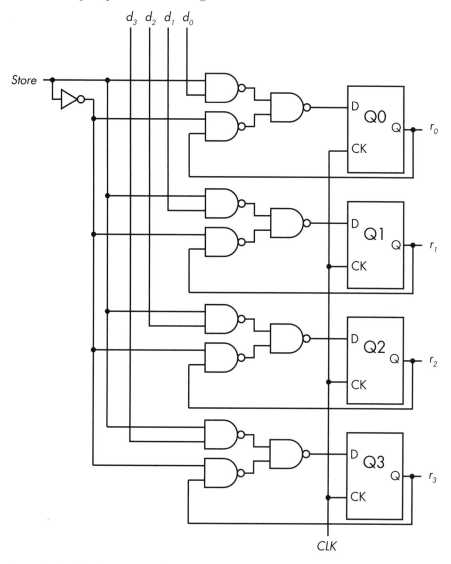

*Figure 8-4: A four-bit register with Store signal*

This design has another important feature that follows from the primary/secondary property of the D flip-flops. The state of the secondary portion does not change until the second half of the clock cycle. So the circuit connected to the output of this register can read the current state during the first half of the clock cycle, while the primary portion is preparing to possibly change the state to the new contents.

We now have a way to store, for example, the results from an adder circuit. The output from the register could be used as the input to another circuit that performs arithmetic or logical operations on the data.

Registers can also be designed to perform simple operations on the data stored in them. We'll look next at a register design that can convert serial data to a parallel format.

## Shift Register

We can use a *shift register* as a *serial-in parallel-out* (*SIPO*) device. A shift register uses a sequence of D flip-flops, like the simple storage register in Figure 8-4, but the output of each flip-flop is connected to the input of the next flip-flop in the sequence, as shown in Figure 8-5.

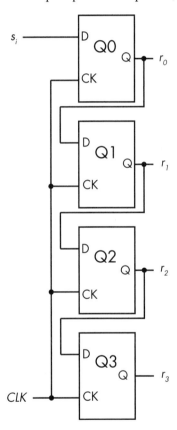

Figure 8-5: Four-bit serial-to-parallel shift register

In the shift register in Figure 8-5, a serial stream of bits is input at $s_i$. At each clock tick, the output of Q0 is applied to the input of Q1, thus copying the previous value of $r_0$ to the new $r_1$. The state of Q0 changes to the value of the new $s_i$, thus copying this to be the new value of $r_0$. The serial stream of bits continues to ripple through the four bits of the shift register. At any time, the last four bits in the serial stream are available in parallel at the four outputs, $r_3$, $r_2$, $r_1$, $r_0$, with $r_3$ being the oldest in time.

The same circuit could be used to provide a time delay of four clock ticks in a serial bit stream. Simply use $r_3$ as the serial output.

## Register File

The registers in the CPU that are used for similar operations are grouped together into a *register file*. For example, as you'll see in the next chapter, the x86-64 architecture includes sixteen 64-bit general-purpose registers that are used for integer computations, temporary storage of addresses, and so forth. We need a mechanism for addressing each of the registers in the register file.

Consider a register file composed of eight four-bit registers, r0–r7, implemented using eight copies of the four-bit register circuit shown in Figure 8-4. To read the four bits of data in one of these eight registers (for example, $r5_3$, $r5_2$, $r5_1$, and $r5_0$ in register r5), we need to specify one of the eight registers using three bits. You learned in Chapter 7 that a multiplexer can select one of several inputs. We can connect a $3 \times 8$ multiplexer to each corresponding bit of the eight registers, as shown in Figure 8-6. The inputs to the multiplexer, $r0_i$–$r7_i$, are the $i^{th}$ bits from each of eight registers, r0–r7. The slash through the *RegSel* line with a 3 next to it is the notation used to show that there are three lines here.

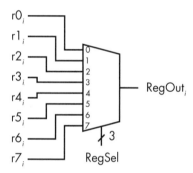

Figure 8-6: Eight-way mux used to select output of register file. This only shows the output of the $i^{th}$ bit; n muxes are required for n-bit registers.

A four-bit register would need four of these multiplexer output circuits. The same *RegSel* would be applied to all four multiplexers simultaneously to output all four bits of the same register. Larger registers would, of course, require correspondingly more multiplexers.

## Read-Write Memory

You saw how to build a four-bit register to store values from D flip-flops in Figure 8-3. We now need to be able to select when to read the value that's stored in the register and disconnect the output when we're not reading it. A tristate buffer allows us to do that, as shown in Figure 8-7. This circuit is for only one four-bit register. We need one of these for each register in the computer. The $addr_j$ line comes from a decoder and selects one of the registers.

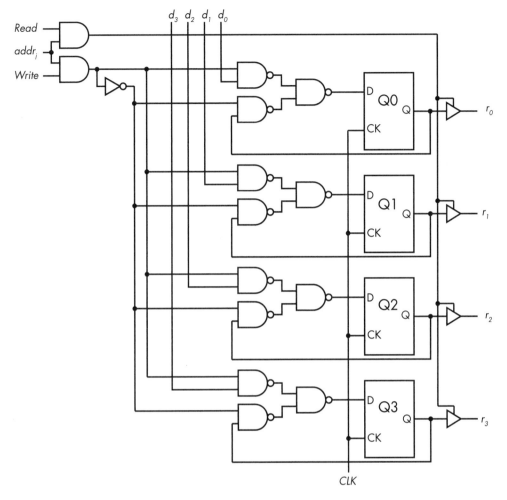

Figure 8-7: Four-bit read-write register

*Write* = 1 causes the four-bit data, $d_3 d_2 d_1 d_0$, to be stored in the D flip-flops Q3, Q2, Q1, and Q0. The four-bit output, $r_3 r_2 r_1 r_0$, remains disconnected from the D flip-flops when *Read* = 0. Setting *Read* = 1 connects the outputs.

We'll continue down the memory hierarchy in Figure 8-1 to cache memory, which is typically constructed from flip-flops, similar to a register file.

## Static Random-Access Memory

The memory we've been discussing that uses flip-flops is called *static random-access memory* (*SRAM*). It's called *static* because it maintains its values so long as power is maintained. As we saw in Chapter 2, it's called *random* because it takes the same amount of time to access any (random) byte in this memory. SRAM is commonly used for cache memory, which can range in size up to several megabytes.

Let's look at ways to address individual bytes in a large memory. Selecting one byte in 1MB of memory requires a 20-bit address. This requires a $20 \times 2^{20}$ address decoder, as shown in Figure 8-8.

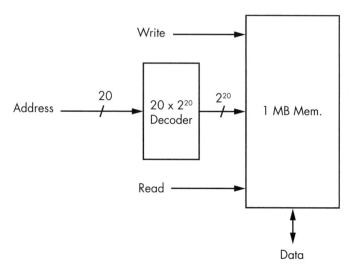

Figure 8-8: Addressing 1MB of memory with one $20 \times 2^{20}$ address decoder

Recall that an $n \times 2^n$ decoder requires $2^n$ AND gates. So a $20 \times 2^{20}$ decoder requires 1,048,576 AND gates. We can simplify the circuitry by organizing memory into a grid of 1,024 rows and 1,024 columns, as shown in Figure 8-9. We can then select a byte by selecting a row and a column, each using a $10 \times 2^{10}$ decoder.

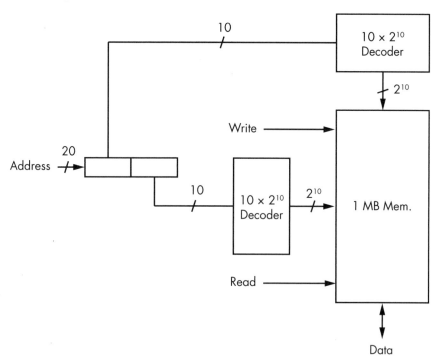

Figure 8-9: Addressing 1MB of memory with two $10 \times 2^{10}$ address decoders

Although two decoders are required, each requires $2^{n/2}$ AND gates, for a total of $2 \times 2^{n/2} = 2^{(n/2)+1} = 2{,}048$ AND gates for each of the two decoders. Of course, accessing individual bytes in memory is slightly more complex, and some complexity is added to split the 20-bit address into two 10-bit portions, but this example should give you an idea of how engineers can simplify designs.

Continuing down the memory hierarchy, we get to main memory, the largest memory unit that is internal to the computer.

## Dynamic Random-Access Memory

Each bit in SRAM requires about six transistors for its implementation. *Dynamic random-access memory (DRAM)*, which is used for main memory, is less expensive.

A bit in DRAM is commonly implemented by a charging a capacitor to one of two voltages. The circuit requires only one transistor to charge the capacitor, as shown in Figure 8-10. These circuits are arranged in a rectangular array.

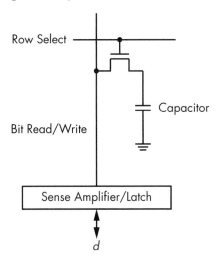

Figure 8-10: One DRAM bit

When the Row Select line is set to 1, all the transistors in that row are turned on, thus connecting the respective capacitor to the Sense Amplifier/Latch. The value stored in the capacitor, high voltage or low voltage, is amplified and stored in the latch. There, it's available to be read. Since this action tends to discharge the capacitors, they must be refreshed from the values stored in the latch. Separate circuitry is provided to do the refresh.

When data is to be stored in DRAM, the new bit value, 0 or 1, is first stored in the latch. Then Row Select is set to 1, and the Sense Amplifier/Latch circuitry applies the voltage corresponding to the logical 0 or 1 to the capacitor. The capacitor is either charged or discharged appropriately.

These operations take more time than simply switching flip-flops, so DRAM is appreciably slower than SRAM. In addition, capacitors lose their charge over time, so each row of capacitors must be read and refreshed in the order of every 60 msec. This requires additional circuitry and further slows memory access.

Now we have a clear picture of how the hierarchical arrangement of memory in a modern computer allows fast program execution while keeping hardware costs at a reasonable level. Although DRAM is much slower than the CPU, its low cost per bit makes it a good choice for main memory. As we move closer to the CPU in the memory hierarchy, the much faster SRAM is used for the cache(s). Since cache is much smaller compared to main memory, the higher cost per bit of SRAM is tolerable. And since the instructions and data needed by the program being executed by the CPU are often in the cache, we see the benefits of the higher speed of the SRAM in program execution.

---

**YOUR TURN**

Derive the equation for $D(Store, d_i, r_i)$ from Table 8-1.

---

## What You've Learned

**Memory hierarchy**   Computer storage is organized such that smaller amounts of faster, more costly memory are located closer to the CPU. Smaller amounts of program instructions and data are copied to the successively faster memory levels as a program executes. This works because there is a very high probability that the next memory location needed by a program will be at an address that is close to the current one.

**Registers**   A few thousand bytes of memory located in the CPU that are accessed at the same speed as the CPU. Implemented in flip-flops.

**Cache**   Thousands to millions of bytes of memory outside the CPU, but often on the same chip. Cache memory is slower than the CPU but synchronized with it. It is often organized in levels, with faster, smaller amounts closer to the CPU. This is usually implemented in SRAM.

**Main memory**   Hundreds of millions to billions of bytes of memory separate from the CPU. It's much slower than the CPU, but synchronized with it. This is usually implemented in DRAM.

**Static random-access memory (SRAM)**   Uses flip-flops to store bits. SRAM is fast, but expensive.

**Dynamic random-access memory (DRAM)**   Uses capacitors to store bits. DRAM is slow, but has a much lower cost.

In the next chapter, you will learn how the x86-64 CPU is organized from a programmer's point of view.

# 9

## CENTRAL PROCESSING UNIT

Now that you've learned about the electronic components used to build a central processing unit (CPU), it's time to learn about some of the specifics of the x86-64 CPU. The two major manufacturers of these CPUs are Intel and AMD. An x86-64 CPU can be run in either 32-bit or 64-bit mode. The 32-bit mode is called the *compatibility mode*, which allows you to run programs that were compiled for either a 32-bit or 16-bit environment.

In this book, we'll focus on the 64-bit mode, which is called *IA-32e* in the Intel manuals and *long mode* in the AMD manuals. I'll refer to it as the *64-bit mode*. I'll point out some of the major differences of the compatibility mode, which I'll refer to as the *32-bit mode*. You cannot mix the two modes in the same program, but most 64-bit operating systems allow you to run either a 32-bit program or a 64-bit program.

We'll begin the chapter with an overview of a typical CPU. Next, we'll look at the registers in the x86-64 CPU and how a programmer accesses them. The chapter concludes with an example of using the gdb debugger to view the contents of the registers.

## CPU Overview

As you probably already know, the CPU is the heart of the computer. It follows the execution path that you specify in your program and performs all the arithmetic and logic operations. It also fetches the instructions and data from memory as they are needed by your program.

We'll begin with a look at the major subsystems of a typical CPU. This will be followed by a description of how the CPU fetches instructions from memory as it executes a program.

### CPU Subsystems

Figure 9-1 shows an overall block diagram of the major subsystems of a typical CPU. The subsystems are connected through internal buses, which include the hardware pathways and the software protocols that control the communications. Keep in mind that this is a highly simplified diagram. Actual CPUs are much more complicated, but the general concepts discussed in this chapter apply to most of them.

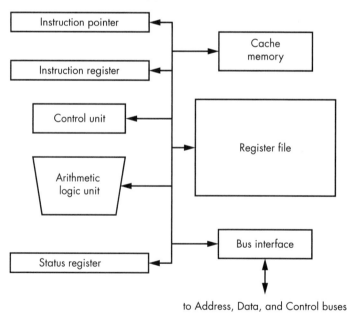

*Figure 9-1: Major subsystems of a CPU*

Let's briefly look at each of the subsystems in Figure 9-1. The descriptions provided here are generic and apply to most CPUs. After this brief introduction, we'll look at the subsystems that a programmer will be most interested in and how they're used in the x86-64 architecture.

**Instruction pointer**   This register always contains the memory address of the next instruction to be executed.

**Cache memory**   Although it could be argued that this is not part of the CPU, most modern CPUs include very fast cache memory on the CPU chip. As you'll see later in this chapter, the CPU fetches each instruction from memory as it executes a program. The CPU can execute instructions much faster than it can fetch them from main memory through the bus interface. The interface with main memory makes it more efficient to fetch several instructions at one time, storing them in cache memory where the CPU has fast access to them.

**Instruction register**   This register contains the instruction currently being executed. Its bit pattern determines what the control unit is causing the CPU to do. Once that action has been completed, the bit pattern in the instruction register will be changed to that of the next instruction, and the CPU will perform the operation specified by this new bit pattern.

**Register file**   A register file is a group of registers used in similar ways. Most CPUs have several register files. For example, the x86-64 CPU has a register file for integer operations and another register file for floating-point operations. Compilers and assemblers have names for each register. Almost all arithmetic and logic operations and data movement operations involve at least one register in a register file.

**Control unit**   The bits in the instruction register are decoded in the control unit. To carry out the action(s) specified by the instruction, the control unit generates the signals that control the other subsystems in the CPU. It's typically implemented as a finite-state machine and contains decoders, multiplexers, and other logic components.

**Arithmetic logic unit (ALU)**   The ALU is used to perform the arithmetic and logic operations you specify in your program. It's also used by the CPU when it needs to do its own arithmetic (for example, add two values to compute a memory address).

**Status register**   Each operation performed by the ALU results in various conditions that must be recorded for possible use by the program. For example, addition can produce a carry. One bit in the status register will be set to either 0 (no carry) or 1 (carry) after the ALU has completed any operation that may produce a carry.

**Bus interface**   This is how the CPU communicates with the other computer subsystems—the memory and input/output (I/O) in Figure 1-1 (see Chapter 1). It contains circuitry to place addresses on the address bus, read and write data on the data bus, and read and write signals on the control bus. The bus interface on many CPUs interfaces with external bus control units that in turn interface with memory and with different types of I/O buses (for example, USB, SATA, or PCI-E).

## Instruction Execution Cycle

In this section, we'll go into more detail about how the CPU executes a program stored in main memory. It does this by fetching the instructions from main memory using the three buses that you learned about in Chapter 1—address, data, and control—through the bus interface.

The address in the *instruction pointer* register, rip, always points to (has the memory address of) the next instruction in a program to be executed. The CPU works its way through a program by fetching the instruction from the memory address in the instruction pointer. When an instruction is fetched, the CPU starts to decode it. The first byte or two, depending on the instruction, tell the CPU the number of bytes in the instruction. The CPU then increments the rip register by this number, causing the rip to contain the address of the next instruction in the program. Thus, the rip marks the current location in a program.

There are instructions that change the address in the rip, thus causing a jump from one place in the program to another. In this case, the address of the next instruction is not known until the instruction that causes the jump is actually executed.

The x86-64 architecture also supports *rip-relative addressing*, which allows the program to access memory locations that are a fixed displacement away from the current address in the rip. This allows us to create a program that can be loaded anywhere in memory for execution, which allows for better security. You'll learn more about this in Chapter 11, as we look into the assembly language details of a function.

When the CPU fetches an instruction from memory, it loads that instruction into the *instruction register*. The bit pattern in the instruction register causes the CPU to perform the operations specified in the instruction. Once that action has been completed, another instruction is automatically loaded into the instruction register, and the CPU will perform the operation specified by this next bit pattern.

Most modern CPUs use an *instruction queue*. Several instructions are waiting in the queue, ready to be executed. Separate electronic circuitry keeps the instruction queue full while the regular control unit is executing the instructions. But this is simply an implementation detail that allows the control unit to run faster. The essence of how the control unit executes a program can be represented by the single instruction register model, which is what I'll describe here.

The steps to fetch each instruction from memory, and thus to execute a program, are as follows:

1. A sequence of instructions is stored in memory.
2. The memory address where the first instruction is located is copied to the instruction pointer.
3. The CPU sends the address in the instruction pointer to memory on the address bus.
4. The CPU sends a "read" signal on the control bus.

5. The memory responds by sending a copy of the state of the bits at that memory location on the data bus, which the CPU then copies into its instruction register.

6. The instruction pointer is automatically incremented to contain the address of the next instruction in memory.

7. The CPU executes the instruction in the instruction register.

8. Go back to step 3.

Steps 3, 4, and 5 are called an *instruction fetch*. Notice that steps 3–8 constitute a cycle, the *instruction execution cycle*. It's shown graphically in Figure 9-2.

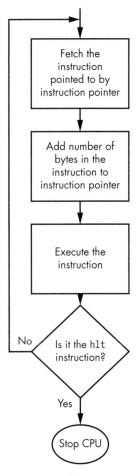

*Figure 9-2: The instruction execution cycle*

Most instructions in a program use at least one register in at least one of the register files. A program typically loads data from memory into a register, operates on the data, and stores the result in memory. Registers are also used to hold addresses of items that are stored in memory, thus serving as pointers to data or other addresses.

The remainder of this chapter is mostly devoted to describing the general-purpose registers in the x86-64 architecture. You'll learn how to view their contents in the gdb debugger. Then in the next chapter, you'll learn how to start using them in assembly language.

# x86-64 Registers

A portion of the memory in the CPU is organized into registers. Machine instructions access CPU registers by their addresses, just like they access main memory. Of course, the register addressing space is separate from the main memory addressing space. Register addresses are placed on the internal CPU bus, not on the address portion of the bus interface, since the registers are in the CPU. The difference from a programmer's point of view is that the assembler has predefined names for the registers, whereas the programmer creates symbolic names for memory addresses. Thus, in each program that you write in assembly language, the following happens:

- CPU registers are accessed by using the names that are predefined in the assembler.
- Memory is accessed by the programmer providing a name for the memory location and using that name in the user program.

Table 9-1 lists the x86-64 architecture registers, which groups them according to their general usage in a program. Within each general category, the columns in the table show the number of registers, the size of each register, and the usage of each register in a program.

**Table 9-1:** The x86-64 Registers

| Basic programming registers | | |
| --- | --- | --- |
| 16 | 64-bit | General-purpose |
| 1 | 64-bit | Flags |
| 1 | 64-bit | Instruction pointer |
| 6 | 16-bit | Segment |
| **Floating-point registers** | | |
| 8 | 80-bit | Floating-point data |
| 1 | 16-bit | Control |
| 1 | 16-bit | Status |
| 1 | 16-bit | Tag |
| 1 | 11-bit | Opcode |
| 1 | 64-bit | FPU instruction pointer |
| 1 | 64-bit | FPU data pointer |

| MMX registers | | |
| --- | --- | --- |
| 8 | 64-bit | MMX |

| XMM registers | | |
| --- | --- | --- |
| 16 | 128-bit | XMM |
| 1 | 32-bit | MXCR |

| Model-specific registers (MSRs) |
| --- |
| Vary depending on implementation. Used only by operating system. |

I've already described the instruction pointer register. Most of the programming concepts presented in this book use only the general-purpose registers. These are used for *integral data types*, such as int and char integer values (signed and unsigned), character representations, Boolean values, and addresses. In the remainder of this section, we'll look at the general-purpose registers and the flags register. We'll discuss the floating-point registers near the end of the book. The MMX and XMM registers are used for more advanced programming techniques that we won't cover.

## General-Purpose Registers

As mentioned, the general-purpose registers deal with integral data types and memory addresses. Each bit in each register is numbered from right to left, beginning with 0. So, the rightmost bit is number 0, the next one to the left is 1, and so on. Since there are 64 bits in each general-purpose register, the leftmost bit is 63.

Each instruction in a computer treats a group of bits as a single unit. In the early days, that unit was called a *word*. Each CPU architecture had a *word size*. In modern CPU architectures, different instructions operate on different numbers of bits, but the terminology has carried over from the early days of the Intel 8086 instruction set architecture to the current 64-bit instruction set architecture, x86-64. Hence, 16 bits is called a *word*, 32 bits a *doubleword*, and 64 bits a *quadword*.

You can access the bits in each general-purpose register by using the following groupings in your programs:

**Quadword**  All 64 bits (63–0)

**Doubleword**  The low-order 32 bits (31–0)

**Word**  The low-order 16 bits (15–0)

**Byte**  The low-order 8 bits (7–0), and in four registers bits (15–8)

The assembler uses a different name for each group of bits in a register. Table 9-2 lists the assembler names for the groups of the bits. Each row in the table represents one register, and each column represents the name for that grouping of bits in the register.

**Table 9-2:** Assembly Language Names for Portions of the General-Purpose CPU Registers

| Bits 63–0 | Bits 31–0 | Bits 15–0 | Bits 15–8 | Bits 7–0 |
|---|---|---|---|---|
| rax | eax | ax | ah | al |
| rbx | ebx | bx | bh | bl |
| rcx | ecx | cx | ch | cl |
| rdx | edx | dx | dh | dl |
| rsi | esi | si | | sil |
| rdi | edi | di | | dil |
| rbp | ebp | bp | | bpl |
| rsp | esp | sp | | spl |
| r8 | r8d | r8w | | r8b |
| r9 | r9d | r9w | | r9b |
| r10 | r10d | r10w | | r10b |
| r11 | r11d | r11w | | r11b |
| r12 | r12d | r12w | | r12b |
| r13 | r13d | r13w | | r13b |
| r14 | r14d | r14w | | r14b |
| r15 | r15d | r15w | | r15b |

In 64-bit mode, writing to an 8-bit or 16-bit portion of a register doesn't affect the other 56 or 48 bits in the register. However, when writing to the low-order 32 bits, the high-order 32 bits are set to 0. (I don't know why the CPU designers chose this behavior, which seems odd to me.) Programs running in 32-bit mode can use only the registers above the line in Table 9-2. 64-bit mode can use of all the registers. The ah, bh, ch, and dh registers (bits 15–8) can't be used in the same instruction with any of the registers below the line. For example, you cannot copy the 8-bit value in the ah register to the sil register with a single instruction, but you could copy it to the dl register.

Most CPU architectures name their registers r0, r1, and so on. When Intel introduced the 8086/8088 instruction set architecture, it used the names above the line in the columns for bits 15–0, 15–8, and 7–0 in Table 9-2. The four 16-bit registers, ax, bx, cx, and dx, were more general-purpose than the other four and were used for most of the computations in the CPU. The programmer could access either the entire register or one-half of each register. The low-order bytes were named al, bl, cl, and dl, and the high-order bytes named ah, bh, ch, and dh.

Access to these 8-bit and 16-bit registers has been maintained in 32-bit mode for backward compatibility but is limited in 64-bit mode. Access to the 8-bit low-order portions of the rsi, rdi, rsp, and rbp registers was added along with the move to 64 bits in the x86-64 architecture but cannot be used in the same instruction with the 8-bit register portions of the ah, bh, ch, or dh registers.

The e prefix on the 32-bit portion of each register name comes from the history of the x86 architecture. The introduction of the 80386 in 1986 brought an increase of register size from 16 bits to 32 bits. There were no new registers; the old ones were simply "extended." In addition to increasing the register size to 64 bits, the introduction of the x86-64 architecture added eight more registers, named r8–r15. Rather than change the names of the first eight registers, I assume that the designers decided to use the r prefix on the historical names.

When using fewer than the entire 64 bits in a register, it's generally bad practice to write code that assumes the remaining portion is in any particular state. Such code is difficult to read and leads to errors during the program's maintenance phase.

Figure 9-3 shows a pictorial representation of the naming of each portion of the general-purpose registers. The three registers shown here are representative of the pattern of all the general-purpose registers.

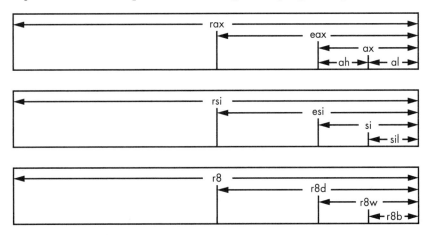

Figure 9-3: General-purpose register naming

Although they're called general-purpose, some instructions use several of these registers in special ways. We'll mostly treat all the general-purpose registers like variables in a high-level language. The important exceptions are the rsp and rbp registers, which hold memory addresses that are key for the proper functioning of a program that's executing.

### Special Pointer Registers

Let's look at two general-purpose registers that are important in a program. The rsp register is used as a stack pointer, and the rbp register is used as a frame pointer. They are used to keep track of the locations of items in an area of memory used as the *call stack*. The call stack is used for temporary storage and passing information between functions when a program is running. Several machine instructions use the rsp register implicitly.

The usage of the rsp and rbp registers must follow a very strict protocol, which I'll describe in detail in subsequent chapters. You need to follow the protocol carefully when writing assembly language.

### Other Restrictions on General-Purpose Registers

Several instructions work only with specific general-purpose registers. For example, the unsigned multiplication and division instructions use the rax and rdx registers. In addition, each operating system and programming environment has a set of rules for using the general-purpose registers. In our programming environment (C under 64-bit GNU/Linux), the first argument to a function is passed in the rdi register, but when using C under 64-bit Windows, the first argument is passed in the rcx register.

You'll learn about these restrictions and conventions (for GNU/Linux, not Windows) in Chapter 11.

## Status Register

Another specialized register in the CPU is the *status register*, which you saw in Figure 9-1. It's given the name rflags. We will be concerned with several bits in this register that are used as *status flags*, which indicate some side effects of many instructions.

Most arithmetic and logical operations affect the status flags. For example, the carry flag, CF, and overflow flag, OF, are in the rflags register. Figure 9-4 shows the bits that are affected. The high-order 32 bits (63–32) are reserved for other use and are not shown here. We also don't show bits 31–12, which are for system flags.

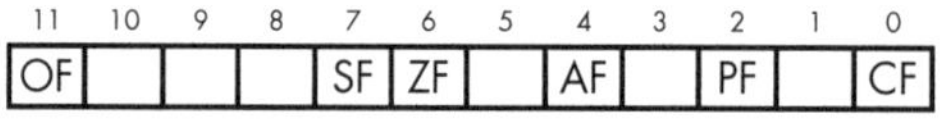

| 11 | 10 | 9 | 8 | 7 | 6 | 5 | 4 | 3 | 2 | 1 | 0 |
|----|----|---|---|----|----|---|----|---|----|---|----|
| OF |    |   |   | SF | ZF |   | AF |   | PF |   | CF |

*Figure 9-4: Status flags portion of the rflags register*

Table 9-3 shows the status flags.

**Table 9-3:** Status Flags in the rflags Register

| Name | Function | Condition that sets flag to 1 |
|------|----------|-------------------------------|
| OF | Overflow flag | Overflow of signed-integer (two's complement) arithmetic |
| SF | Sign flag | Copy of most significant bit of result |
| ZF | Zero flag | Result is 0 |
| AF | Auxiliary carry flag | Shows carry or borrow in binary-coded decimal arithmetic |
| PF | Parity flag | Least significant byte of result has an even number of 1 bits |
| CF | Carry flag | Carry or borrow beyond most significant bit of result |

There are machine instructions for testing the state of the status flags. For example, there's an instruction that will branch to another place in the program if the ZF status flag is 1.

Next, we'll look at some C/C++ data types as they relate to the sizes of the general-purpose registers.

# C/C++ Integral Data Types and Register Sizes

Every piece of data in a computer program has a *data type*, which specifies the following: the possible values for the data type, the bit patterns used to represent those values, operations that can be performed on the data, and the data's semantic usage in the program.

Some programming languages like C, C++, and Java require the programmer to explicitly state the data types of values used in the program. Other languages like Python, BASIC, and JavaScript can determine a data type from the way the value is used. CPU manufacturers specify machine-level data types specific to the CPU architecture, often including specialized data types that are unique to the design.

The C and C++ language specifications provide ranges for values that can be stored in a variable of each data type. For example, an int must be able to store a value in the range −32,767 to + 32,767; thus, it must be at least 16 bits in size. An unsigned int must be at least 0 to 65,525, so it also must be at least 16 bits. Compiler designers are free to exceed the minimums specified in the language specifications.

Table 9-4 gives x86-64 register sizes for C/C++ data types you can expect from our compilers, gcc and g++, but you should be careful not to count on these sizes to always be the same. The *any* notation means a pointer (memory address) to any data type.

**Table 9-4:** Sizes of Some C/C++ Data Types in the x86-64 Architecture

| Data type | Size in 32-bit mode | Size in 64-bit mode |
| --- | --- | --- |
| char | Byte | Byte |
| int | Doubleword | Doubleword |
| long | Doubleword | Quadword |
| long long | Quadword | Quadword |
| float | Doubleword | Doubleword |
| double | Quadword | Quadword |
| *any* | Doubleword | Quadword |

**NOTE** *If your solution to a problem depends on data sizes, C standard libraries often define specific sizes. For example, the GNU C libraries define int16_t to be a 16-bit signed integer and u_int16_t to be an unsigned 16-bit integer. In rare cases, you may want to use assembly language to ensure correctness.*

A value can usually be represented with more than one data type. For example, most people would think of 123 as representing the integer one hundred twenty-three, but this value could be stored in a computer either as an int or as a char[] (a char array where each element of the array holds one code point for a character).

As you can see in Table 9-4, an int in our C/C++ environment is stored in a doubleword, so 123 would be stored with the bit pattern 0x0000007b. As a C-style text string, we'd also need four bytes of memory, but the bit patterns would be 0x31, 0x32, 0x33, and 0x00—that is, the characters 1, 2, 3, and NUL. (Recall that a C-style string is terminated with a NUL character.)

You can learn a lot about how the CPU works by viewing what takes place in the registers. In the next section, you'll learn how to view the registers by using the gdb debugger.

## Using gdb to View the CPU Registers

We'll use the program in Listing 9-1 to show how to use gdb to view the contents of the CPU registers.

```
/* inches2feet.c
 * Converts inches to feet and inches.
 */

#include <stdio.h>
#define inchesPerFoot 12

int main(void)
{
❶  register int feet;
   register int inchesRem;
❷  int inches;
   int *ptr;

   ptr = &inches;

   printf("Enter inches: ");
❸  scanf("%i", ptr);

   feet = inches / inchesPerFoot;
   inchesRem = inches % inchesPerFoot;
   printf("%i\" = %i' %i\"\n", inches, feet, inchesRem);

   return 0;
}
```

Listing 9-1: Simple program to illustrate the use of gdb to view CPU registers

I've used the register storage class modifier ❶ to request that the compiler use a CPU register for the feet and inchesRem variables. The register modifier is advisory only. The C language standard doesn't require the compiler to honor the request. But notice that I didn't request the compiler use a CPU register for the inches variable ❷. The inches variable must be placed in memory since scanf needs a pointer to the location of inches ❸ to store the value read from the keyboard.

You've already seen some gdb commands earlier in the book (review Chapter 2 for a refresher). When you hit a breakpoint in a program that has been running, here are some additional commands that you may find useful for moving through the program under your control and viewing information about the program:

**n** (next) executes the current source code statement; if it's a call to a function, the entire function is executed.

**s** (step) executes the current source code statement; if it's a call to a function, step into the function, arriving at the first instruction of the called function.

**si** (step instruction) executes the current machine instruction; if it's a call to a function, step into the function.

**i r** (info registers) displays the contents of the registers, except the floating-point and vector registers.

Here's how I used gdb to control the execution of the program and observe the register contents. Note that you'll probably see different addresses if you replicate this example on your own, which you're asked to do when it's Your Turn.

```
❶ $ gcc -g -O0 -Wall -masm=intel -o inches2feet inches2feet.c
❷ $ gdb ./inches2feet
GNU gdb (Ubuntu 9.2-0ubuntu1~20.04) 9.2
  --snip--
Reading symbols from ./inches2feet...done.
❸ (gdb) l
1       /* inches2feet.c
2        * Converts inches to feet and inches.
3        */
4
5       #include <stdio.h>
6       #define inchesPerFoot 12
7
8       int main(void)
9       {
10         register int feet;
(gdb) ENTER
11         register int inchesRem;
12         int inches;
13         int *ptr;
14
15         ptr = &inches;
16
17         printf("Enter inches: ");
18         scanf("%i", ptr);
19
20         feet = inches / inchesPerFoot;
(gdb) ENTER
21         inchesRem = inches % inchesPerFoot;
22         printf("%i\" = %i' %i\"\n", inches, feet, inchesRem);
23
24         return 0;
25      }
```

We first compile the program ❶, load it with **gdb** ❷, and then list the source code so we can see where to set breakpoints. Using the ENTER key ❸ (RETURN on some keyboards) repeats the previous command. The debugger starts by printing information about itself, which I have cut out of my display to save space.

We want to follow along as the program processes the data by setting breakpoints at strategic points in the program:

```
(gdb) b 17
Breakpoint 1 at 0x11af: file inches2feet.c, line 17.
(gdb) b 20
Breakpoint 2 at 0x11d8: file inches2feet.c, line 20.
```

We set the first breakpoint where the program is about to prompt the user to enter the input data, line 17, and a second at the statement where the program's computations begin, line 20.

When we run the program, it breaks at the first breakpoint it encounters:

```
(gdb) r
Starting program: /home/progs/chapter_09/inches2feet/inches2feet

Breakpoint 1, main () at inches2feet.c:17
17          printf("Enter inches: ");
```

The program stops at line 17 of the source code, and control returns to gdb. We can see the contents of the registers with the i r command. (Be sure to type a space between i and r.)

```
(gdb) i r
rax            0x7fffffffdeac     140737488346796
rbx            0x555555555260     93824992236128
rcx            0x555555555260     93824992236128
rdx            0x7fffffffdfd8     140737488347096
rsi            0x7fffffffdfc8     140737488347080
rdi            0x1                1
rbp            0x7fffffffded0     0x7fffffffded0
rsp            0x7fffffffdea0     0x7fffffffdea0
r8             0x0                0
r9             0x7ffff7fe0d50     140737354009936
r10            0x7                7
r11            0x2                2
r12            0x5555555550a0     93824992235680
r13            0x7fffffffdfc0     140737488347072
r14            0x0                0
r15            0x0                0
rip            0x5555555551af     0x5555555551af <main+38>
eflags         0x246 [ PF ZF IF ]
cs             0x33   51
ss             0x2b   43
ds             0x0    0
```

| es | 0x0 | 0 |
| fs | 0x0 | 0 |
| gs | 0x0 | 0 |

This display tells us the contents of the registers before the user enters data (you'll see different numbers). We might want to know if the compiler honored our request to use registers for the feet and inchesRem variables. And if it did, which registers did it use?

We'd like to know this information so we can look at the contents of the registers before and after they're used by the program so we can see if the program is storing the correct values in them. We can answer this question by asking gdb to print the addresses of these two variables:

```
(gdb) print &feet
Address requested for identifier "feet" which is in register $r12
(gdb) print &inchesRem
Address requested for identifier "inchesRem" which is in register $rbx
```

When we ask for the address of a variable, gdb will give the memory address associated with a programmer-supplied identifier. But in this program we asked the compiler to use registers, and gdb tells us which register the compiler chose for each variable.

We didn't ask the compiler to use registers for the inches and ptr variables, so gdb should tell us where they are located in memory:

```
(gdb) print &inches
$1 = (int *) 0x7fffffffdeac
(gdb) print &ptr
$2 = (int **) 0x7fffffffdeb0
```

Now that we know r12 is being used for feet and rbx for inchesRem, we can see what's currently stored in these two registers and continue running the program:

```
❶ (gdb) i r rbx r12
rbx          0x555555555260     93824992236128
r12          0x5555555550a0     93824992235680
❷ (gdb) c
Continuing.
Enter inches: 123 ❸
```

Rather than display all the registers, we can specify the two we want to look at ❶. Continuing program's execution ❷, the program asks the user to enter the number of inches, and I responded with 123 ❸. It then breaks back into gdb at the next breakpoint it encounters:

```
Breakpoint 2, main () at inches2feet.c:20
20        feet = inches / inchesPerFoot;
```

Before starting the computations, let's make sure the user's input is stored in the right place:

```
(gdb) print inches
$3 = 123
```

The program is about to compute the number of feet, and then it will compute the remainder of inches. So I'll execute two statements using n:

```
(gdb) n
21          inchesRem = inches % inchesPerFoot;
(gdb) ENTER
22          printf("%i\" = %i' %i\"\n", inches, feet, inchesRem);
```

The program is now ready to print out the results of the computations. I'll check to make sure all the computations were performed correctly and the results are in the proper variables, which we've already determined are in rbx and r12:

```
(gdb) i r rbx r12
rbx              0x3    3
r12              0xa    10
```

There are other ways to see what's stored in feet and inchesRem:

```
(gdb) print $rbx
$4 = 3
(gdb) print $r12
$5 = 10
(gdb) print feet
$6 = 10
(gdb) print inchesRem
$7 = 3
```

When using gdb's print command, you can print only one variable at a time, even if a register is being used to store the variable. The $ prefix on the register name isn't required for the i r command, but it is for the print command.

Before completing execution of the program, I'll take a final look at all the registers:

```
(gdb) i r
rax              0x78            120
rbx              0x3    3
rcx              0xa             10
rdx              0x7b            123
rsi              0x0             0
rdi              0x7ffffffffd960 140737488345440
rbp              0x7ffffffffded0 0x7ffffffffded0
rsp              0x7ffffffffdea0 0x7ffffffffdea0
r8               0xa             10
r9               0x0             0
r10              0x7ffff7f5bac0  140737353464512
```

| | | |
|---|---|---|
| r11 | 0x0 | 0 |
| r12 | 0xa | 10 |
| r13 | 0x7fffffffdfc0 | 140737488347072 |
| r14 | 0x0 | 0 |
| r15 | 0x0 | 0 |
| rip | 0x55555555521e | 0x55555555521e <main+149> |
| eflags | 0x206 [ PF IF ] | |
| cs | 0x33  51 | |
| ss | 0x2b  43 | |
| ds | 0x0   0 | |
| es | 0x0   0 | |
| fs | 0x0   0 | |
| gs | 0x0   0 | |

There's nothing remarkable in this display, but after you gain some experience looking at such displays, you'll learn to sometimes spot that something is not right. Now that I'm satisfied that the program performed all the computations correctly, I'll continue to the end of the program by using cont and then exit with q:

```
(gdb) c
Continuing.
123" = 10' 3"
[Inferior 1 (process 3874) exited normally]
(gdb) q
$
```

The program continues to execute, printing the result and returning control to gdb. Of course, the last thing to do is to exit from gdb.

---

**YOUR TURN**

1.  Modify the program in Listing 9-1 such that registers are used for the variables inches and ptr. Did the compiler allow you to do that? If not, why?

2.  Write a program in C that allows you to determine the endianess of your computer.

3.  Modify the program in the previous exercise so that you can demonstrate, using gdb, that endianess is a property of the CPU. That is, even though a 32-bit int is stored little endian in memory, it will be read into a register in the "proper" order.

---

## What You've Learned

**General-purpose registers**   Sixteen 64-bit registers in the x86-64 provide a small amount of memory for computations in the CPU.

**Status register**   This register contains flags that show whether arithmetic/logic operations produce carry, overflow, or 0.

**Instruction pointer**   This pointer always has the address of the next instruction to be executed.

**Instruction register**   This register holds the instruction currently being executed.

**Arithmetic logic unit**   Performs the arithmetic and logic operations.

**Control unit**   Controls the activity in the CPU.

**Bus interface**   Responsible for interfacing the CPU with the main memory and I/O devices.

**Cache memory**   Cache memory is faster than main memory. It holds portions of the program, both instructions and data, that are currently being worked on by the CPU.

**Instruction execution cycle**   Details how the CPU works its way through a list of instructions.

**C/C++ data type sizes**   Data sizes are closely related to register sizes.

**Debugger**   In addition to helping you find bugs, gdb is useful to help you learn the concepts.

In the next chapter, you'll start programming your computer in assembly language.

# 10

## PROGRAMMING IN ASSEMBLY LANGUAGE

In the previous chapters, you saw how computers can be programmed using 1s and 0s to represent the operations and the data, the *machine language*. Now we'll move on to programming at the machine level, but instead of using machine language, we'll use *assembly language*. Assembly language uses a short *mnemonic* for each machine language instruction. We'll use an *assembler* program to translate the assembly language into the machine language instructions that control the computer.

Creating a program in assembly language is similar to creating one in a higher-level compiled language like C, C++, Java, or FORTRAN. We'll use C as our programming model to explore the primary programming constructs and data structures that are common to essentially all higher-level programming languages. The compiler we're using, gcc, allows us to look at the assembly language it generates. From there, I will show you how I would implement the programming constructs and data structures directly in assembly language.

We'll begin the chapter by looking at the steps the compiler takes to create an executable program from C source code. Next, we'll look at which of these steps apply to assembly language programming and create our own program directly in assembly language that will run in the C runtime environment. You'll also learn about a gdb mode that's useful for learning assembly language.

While reading this chapter, you should also consult the man and info documentation resources available in most GNU/Linux installations for the programs discussed here. (You may need to install the info documentation on your computer as described in Chapter 1.)

## Compiling a Program Written in C

We'll use the GNU compiler, gcc, which creates an *executable program* from one or more source files by performing several distinct steps. Each step results in an intermediate file that serves as input to the next step. The description of each step here assumes a single C source file, *filename.c*.

### Preprocessing

Preprocessing is the first step. This step resolves compiler directives such as #include (file inclusion), #define (macro definition), and #if (conditional compilation) by invoking the program cpp. The compilation process can be stopped at the end of the preprocessing phase with the -E option, which writes the resulting C source code to standard out.

Standard out is usually the terminal window. You can redirect the output to a file with the > operator, like this:

```
$ gcc -Wall -O0 -masm=intel -E filename.c > filename.i
```

The *.i* file extension denotes a file that does not require preprocessing.

### Compilation

Next, the compiler translates the source code that results from preprocessing into assembly language. The compilation process can be stopped at the end of the compilation phase with the -S option (uppercase S), which writes the assembly language source code to *filename.s*.

### Assembly

After the compiler generates the assembly language that implements the C source code, the assembler program, as, translates the assembly language into machine code. The process can be stopped at the end of the assembly phase with the -c option, which writes the machine code to an *object file*, named *filename.o*. Some call this assembler gas, for *GNU assembler*.

**Linking**

The ld program determines where each function and data item will be located in memory when the program is executed. It then replaces the programmer's symbolic names where each of these items is referenced with the memory address of the item. The result of this linking is written to an *executable file*. The default name of the executable file is *a.out*, but you can specify another name with the -o option.

If the called function is in an external library, this is noted where the function is called, and the address of the external function is determined during program execution. The compiler directs the ld program to add the computer code to the executable file that sets up the C runtime environment. This includes operations such as opening paths to standard out (the screen) and standard in (the keyboard) for use by your program.

As you might know, if you don't use any of the gcc options to stop the process at the end of one of these steps (-E, -S, -c), the compiler will perform all four steps and automatically delete the intermediate files, leaving only the executable program as the final result. You can direct gcc to keep all the intermediate files with the -save-temps option.

The complement of being able to stop gcc along the way is that we can supply files that have effectively gone through the earlier steps, and gcc will incorporate those files into the remaining steps. For example, if we write a file in assembly language, gcc will skip the preprocessing and compilation steps and perform the assembly and linking steps. If we supply only object files (*.o*), gcc will go directly to the linking step. An implicit benefit of this is that we can write programs in assembly language that call functions in the C standard library (which are already in object file format), and gcc will automatically link our assembly language with those library functions.

Be careful to use the filename extensions that are specified in the GNU programming environment when naming a file. The default action of the compiler at each step depends upon the filename extension appropriate to that step. To see these naming conventions, type **info gcc** into the command line, select Invoking GCC, and then select Overall Options. If you don't use the specified filename extension, the compiler might not do what you want or even overwrite a required file.

# From C to Assembly Language

Programs written in C are organized into functions. Each function has a name that is unique within the program. After the C runtime environment is set up, the main function is called, so our program starts with main.

Since we can easily look at the assembly language that the compiler generates, that is a good place to start. We'll start off by looking at the assembly language that gcc generates for the minimum C program in Listing 10-1. The program does nothing except return 0 to the operating system. A program can return various numerical error codes to the operating system; 0 indicates that the program did not detect any errors.

**NOTE** *If you are not familiar with the GNU make program, I urge you to learn how to use it to build your programs. It may seem like overkill at this point, but it's much easier to learn with simple programs. The manual is available in several formats at* https://www.gnu.org/software/make/manual/, *and I have some comments about using it on my website,* https://rgplantz.github.io/.

```
/* doNothingProg.c
 * Minimum components of a C program.
 */

int main(void)
{
  return 0;
}
```

*Listing 10-1: Minimum C program*

Even though this program accomplishes very little, some instructions need to be executed just to return 0. To see what takes place, we first translate this program from C to assembly language with the following GNU/Linux command:

```
$ gcc -O0 -Wall -masm=intel -S doNothingProg.c
```

Before showing the result of this command, I'll explain the options I've used. The -O0 (uppercase O and zero) option tells the compiler not to use any optimization. The goal of this book is to show what's taking place at the machine level. Asking the compiler to optimize the code may obscure some important details.

You've already learned that the -Wall option asks the compiler to warn you about questionable constructions in your code. It's not likely in this simple program, but it's a good habit to get into.

The -masm=intel option directs the compiler to generate assembly language using the Intel syntax instead of the default AT&T syntax. I'll explain why we use Intel syntax later in this chapter.

The -S option directs the compiler to stop after the compilation phase and write the assembly language resulting from the compilation to a file with the same name as the C source code file, but with the *.s* extension instead of *.c*. The previous compiler command generates the assembly language shown in Listing 10-2, which is saved in the file *doNothingProg.s*.

```
        .file   "doNothingProg.c"
        .intel_syntax noprefix
        .text
        .globl  main
        .type   main, @function
main:
.LFB0:
    ❶ .cfi_startproc
        endbr64
```

```
                push    rbp
                .cfi_def_cfa_offset 16
                .cfi_offset 6, -16
                mov     rbp, rsp
                .cfi_def_cfa_register 6
                mov     eax, 0
                pop     rbp
                .cfi_def_cfa 7, 8
                ret
                .cfi_endproc
.LFE0:
                .size   main, .-main
                .ident  "GCC: (Ubuntu 9.3.0-17ubuntu1~20.04) 9.3.0"
                .section        .note.GNU-stack,"",@progbits
                .section        .note.gnu.property,"a"
                .align 8
                .long   1f - 0f
                .long   4f - 1f
                .long   5
0:
                .string "GNU"
1:
                .align 8
                .long   0xc0000002
                .long   3f - 2f
2:
                .long   0x3
3:
                .align 8
4:
```

*Listing 10-2: Minimum C program, assembly language generated by compiler*

The first thing you might notice in Listing 10-2 is that many of the identifiers begin with a . character. All of them, except the ones followed by a :, are *assembler directives*, also known as *pseudo-ops*. They are instructions to the assembler program itself, not computer instructions. We won't need all of them for the material in this book. The identifiers that are followed by a : are labels on memory locations, which we'll discuss in a few pages.

### Assembler Directives That We Won't Use

The assembler directives in Listing 10-2 that begin with .cfi ❶ tell the assembler to generate information that can be used for debugging and certain error situations. The identifiers beginning with .LF mark places in the code used to generate this information. A discussion of this is beyond the scope of this book, but their appearance in the listing can be confusing. So, we'll tell the compiler not to include them in the assembly language file with the -fno-asynchronous-unwind-tables option:

```
$ gcc -O0 -Wall -masm=intel -S -fno-asynchronous-unwind-tables doNothingProg.c
```

This produces the file *doNothingProg.s* shown in Listing 10-3.

```
          .file    "doNothingProg.c"
          .intel_syntax noprefix
          .text
          .globl   main
          .type    main, @function
main:
    ❶ endbr64
      push     rbp
      mov      rbp, rsp
      mov      eax, 0
      pop      rbp
      ret
      .size    main, .-main
      .ident   "GCC: (Ubuntu 9.3.0-17ubuntu1~20.04) 9.3.0"
      .section         .note.GNU-stack,"",@progbits
    ❷ .section         .note.gnu.property,"a"
      .align 8
      .long    1f - 0f
      .long    4f - 1f
      .long    5
0:
      .string  "GNU"
1:
      .align 8
      .long    0xc0000002
      .long    3f - 2f
2:
      .long    0x3
3:
      .align 8
4:
```

*Listing 10-3: Minimum C program, assembly language generated by compiler, without* `.cfi` *directives*

Even without the `.cfi` directives, the assembly language still includes an instruction and several directives that we won't use for now. Intel has developed a technique, *Control-flow Enforcement Technology (CET)*, for providing better defense against types of security attacks of computer programs that hijack a program's flow. The technology is supposed to be included in Intel CPUs starting in the second half of 2020. AMD has said they will include an equivalent technology in their CPUs at a later date.

The technology includes a new instruction, `endbr64`, which is used as the first instruction in a function to check whether program flow gets there ❶. The instruction has no effect if the CPU does not include CET.

The compiler also needs to include some information for the linker to use CET. This information is placed in a special section of the file that the assembler will create, denoted with the `.section   .note.gnu.property,"a"` assembler directive ❷, after the actual program code.

The version of gcc used in this book includes the CET feature by default in anticipation of the new CPUs. The details of using CET are beyond the scope of this book. If you're curious, you can read about it at *https://www.intel .com/content/www/us/en/developer/articles/technical/technical-look-control-flow -enforcement-technology.html.* The programs we're writing in this book are not intended for production use, so we won't be concerned about security issues in our programs. We'll use the `-fcf-protection=none` option to tell the compiler not to include CET, and we won't use it when writing directly in assembly language.

To keep our discussion focused on the fundamentals of how a computer works, we'll tell the compiler to generate assembly language with the following command:

```
$ gcc -O0 -Wall -masm=intel -S -fno-asynchronous-unwind-tables \
> -fcf-protection=none doNothingProg1.c
```

This command yields the assembly language file shown in Listing 10-4.

```
❶ .file    "doNothingProg.c"
❷ .intel_syntax noprefix
❸ .text
❹ .globl   main
❺ .type    main, @function
main:
        push     rbp
        mov      rbp, rsp
        mov      eax, 0
        pop      rbp
        ret
❻ .size    main, .-main
❼ .ident   "GCC: (Ubuntu 9.3.0-17ubuntu1~20.04) 9.3.0"
❽ .section .note.GNU-stack,"",@progbits
```

*Listing 10-4: Minimum C program, assembly language generated by compiler, without .cfi directives and CET code*

Now that we've stripped away the advanced features, I'll discuss the assembler directives remaining in Listing 10-4 that we won't need when writing our own assembly language. The `.file` directive ❶ is used by gcc to specify the name of the C source file that this assembly language came from. When writing directly in assembly language, this isn't used. The `.size` directive ❻ computes the size of the machine code, in bytes, that results from assembling this file, and assigns the name of this function, main, to this value. This can be useful information in systems with limited memory but is of no concern in our programs.

I honestly don't know the reasons for using the `.ident` and `.section` directives ❼ ❽. I'm guessing from their arguments that they're being used to provide information to the developers of gcc when users report bugs. Yes, even compilers have bugs! But we won't use these directives in our assembly language.

## Assembler Directives That We Will Use

Now we'll look at the directives that will be required when we write in assembly language. The .text assembler directive ❸ in Listing 10-4 tells the assembler to place whatever follows in the text section. What does *text section* mean?

In GNU/Linux, the object files produced by the assembler are in the *Executable and Linking Format (ELF)*. The ELF standard specifies many types of sections, each specifying the type of information stored in it. We use assembler directives to tell the assembler in which section to place the code.

The GNU/Linux operating system also divides memory into *segments* for specific purposes when a program is loaded from the disk. The linker gathers all the sections that belong in each segment together and outputs an executable ELF file that's organized by segment to make it easier for the operating system to load the program into memory. The four general types of segments are as follows:

**Text (also called code)**   The *text segment* is where program instructions and constant data are stored. The operating system prevents a program from changing anything stored in the text segment, making it read-only.

**Data**   Global variables and static local variables are stored in the *data segment*. Global variables can be accessed by any of the functions in a program. A static local variable can be accessed only by the function it's defined in, but its value remains the same between calls to its function. Programs can both read from and write to variables in the data segment. These variables remain in place for the duration of the program.

**Stack**   Automatic local variables and the information that links functions are stored on the *call stack*. Automatic local variables are created when a function is called, and deleted when the function returns to its calling function. Memory on the stack can be both read from and written to by the program. It's allocated and deallocated dynamically as the program executes.

**Heap**   The *heap* is a pool of memory that's available for a program to use when running. A C program calls the malloc function (C++ calls new) to get a chunk of memory from the heap. It can be both read from and written to by the program. It's used to store data and is explicitly deallocated by calling free (delete in C++) in the program.

This has been a simplistic overview of ELF sections and segments. You can find further details by reading the man page for ELF and reading sources like "ELF-64 Object File Format," which can be downloaded at *https://uclibc.org/docs/elf-64-gen.pdf*, and John R. Levine's *Linkers & Loaders* (Morgan Kaufmann, 1999). The readelf program is also useful for learning about ELF files.

Now look back at Listing 10-4. The .globl directive ❹ has one argument, the identifier main. The .globl directive makes the name globally known so functions that are defined in other files can refer to this name. The code that sets up the C runtime environment was written to call the function named main, so the name must be global in scope. All C/C++ programs start with a main function. In this book, we'll also start our assembly language programs with a main function and execute them within the C runtime environment.

You can write stand-alone assembly language programs that don't depend on the C runtime environment, in which case you can create your own name for the first function in the program. You need to stop the compilation process at the end of the assembly step with the -c option. You then link the object (.o) files using the ld command by itself, not as part of gcc. I'll describe this in more detail in Chapter 20.

The assembler directive, .type, ❺ has two arguments, main and @function. This causes the identifier main to be recorded in the object file as the name of a function.

None of these three directives gets translated into actual machine instructions, and none of them occupies any memory in the finished program. Rather, they're used to describe the characteristics of the statements that follow.

You may have noticed that I haven't yet described the purpose of the .intel_syntax noprefix directive ❷. It specifies the syntax of the assembly language we'll use. You can probably guess that we'll be using the Intel syntax, but that will be easier to understand after I explain the assembly language instructions. We'll do this using the same function from Listing 10-1 but written directly in assembly language.

## Creating a Program in Assembly Language

Listing 10-5 was written in assembly language by a programmer, rather than by a compiler. Naturally, the programmer has added comments to improve readability.

```
❶ # doNothingProg.s
  # Minimum components of a C program, in assembly language.
          .intel_syntax noprefix
          .text
          .globl  main
          .type   main, @function
❷ main:
      ❸ push    rbp         # save caller's frame pointer
      ❹ mov     rbp, rsp    # establish our frame pointer
❺
      ❻ mov     eax, 0      # return 0 to caller

        mov     rsp, rbp    # restore stack pointer
        pop     rbp         # restore caller's frame pointer
        ret                 # back to caller
```

Listing 10-5: Minimum C-style program written in assembly language

## Assembly Language in General

The first thing to notice in Listing 10-5 is that assembly language is organized by lines. Only one assembly language statement is on each line, and none of the statements spans more than one line. This differs from the free-form nature of many high-level languages where the line structure is irrelevant. In fact, good programmers use the ability to write program statements across multiple lines and indentation to emphasize the structure of their code. Good assembly language programmers use blank lines to help separate parts of an algorithm, and they comment almost every line.

Next, notice that the first two lines begin with the # character ❶. The rest of the line is written in English and is easily read. Everything after the # character is a comment. Just as with a high-level language, comments are intended solely for the human reader and have no effect on the program. The comments at the top are followed by the assembler directives we discussed earlier.

Blank lines ❺ are intended to improve readability. Well, they improve readability once you learn how to read assembly language.

The remaining lines are organized roughly into columns. They probably do not make much sense to you at this point because they're written in assembly language, but if you look carefully, each of the assembly language lines is organized into four possible fields:

---

*label:*    *operation*    *operand(s)*    *# comment*

---

Not all the lines will have entries in all the fields. The assembler requires at least one space or tab character to separate the fields. When writing assembly language, your program will be much easier to read if you use the Tab key to move from one field to the next so that the columns line up.

Let's look at each field in some detail:

**Label**    Allows us to give a symbolic name to any line in the program. Each line corresponds to a memory location in the program, so other parts of the program can then refer to the memory location by name.

A label consists of an identifier immediately followed by the : character. You, as the programmer, must make up these identifiers. We'll look at the rules for creating an identifier soon. Only the lines we need to refer to are labeled.

**Operation**    Contains either an *instruction operation code* (*opcode*) or an *assembler directive* (*pseudo op*). The assembler translates the opcode, along with its operands, into machine instructions, which are copied into memory when the program is to be executed.

**Operand**    Specifies the arguments to be used in the operation. The arguments can be explicit values, names of registers, or programmer-created identifiers. The number of operands can be zero, one, two, or three, depending on the operation.

**Comment**   Everything on a line following a # character is ignored by the assembler, thus providing a way for the programmer to provide human-readable comments. Since assembly language is not as easy to read as higher-level languages, good programmers will place a comment on almost every line.

A word about program comments here. Beginners often comment on what the programming statement does, not its purpose relative to solving the problem. For example, a comment like

```
counter = 1;   /* let x = 1 */
```

in C is not very useful. But a comment like

```
counter = 1;   /* need to start at 1 */
```

could be very helpful. Your comments should describe what *you* are doing, not what the computer is doing.

The rules for creating an identifier are similar to those for C/C++. Each identifier consists of a sequence of alphanumeric characters and may include other printable characters such as ., _, and $. The first character must not be a numeral. An identifier may be any length, and all characters are significant. Although the letter case of keyword identifiers (operators, operands, directives) is not significant, it is significant for labels. For example, myLabel and MyLabel are different. Compiler-generated labels begin with the . character, and many system-related names begin with the _ character. It's a good idea to avoid beginning your own labels with the . or the _ character so that you don't inadvertently create one that's already being used by the system.

It's common to place a label on its own line ❷, in which case it applies to the address of the next assembly language statement that takes up memory ❸. This allows you to create longer, more meaningful labels while maintaining the column organization of your code.

Integers can be used as labels, but they have a special meaning. They're used as local labels, which are sometimes useful in advanced assembly language programming techniques. We won't be using them in this book.

## First Assembly Language Instructions

Rather than list all the x86-64 instructions (there are more than 2,000, depending on how you count), I will introduce a few at a time, and only the ones that will be needed to illustrate the programming concept at hand. I will also give only the commonly used variants of the instructions I introduce.

For a detailed description of the instructions and all their variants, you'll need a copy of *Intel® 64 and IA-32 Architectures Software Developer's Manual*, Volume Two, which can be downloaded at *https://software.intel.com/en-us/articles/intel-sdm/*, or *AMD64 Architecture Programmer's Manual*, Volume 3: *General-Purpose and System Instructions*, which can be downloaded at *https://developer.amd.com/resources/developer-guides-manuals/*. These are the instruction set reference manuals from the two major manufacturers of x86-64 CPUs. They can be a little difficult to read, but going back and forth between my descriptions of the instructions in this book and the descriptions in the manuals should help you to learn how to read the manuals.

Assembly language provides a set of mnemonics that correspond directly to the machine language instructions. A *mnemonic* is a short, English-like group of characters that suggests the action of the instruction. For example, mov is used to represent the instruction that copies (moves) a value from one place to another; the machine instruction 0x4889e5 copies the entire 64-bit value in the rsp register to the rbp register. Even if you've never seen assembly language before, the mnemonic representation of this instruction in Listing 10-5 ❹ probably makes much more sense to you than the machine code.

**NOTE** *Strictly speaking, the mnemonics are completely arbitrary, as long as you have an assembler program that will translate them into the desired machine instructions. However, most assembler programs follow the mnemonics used in the manuals provided by CPU vendors.*

The general format of an assembly language instruction in our usage of the assembler (Intel syntax) is

```
operation destination, source1, source2
```

where `destination` is the location where the result of the `operation` will be stored, and `source1` and `source2` are the locations where the input(s) to the `operation` are located. There can be from zero to two sources, and some instructions don't require that you specify a destination. The destination can be a register or memory. A source value can be in a register, in memory, or *immediate data*. Immediate data is stored as part of the machine code implementation of the instruction and is hence a constant value in the program. You'll see how this works in Chapter 12, when we look at how instructions are encoded in the 1s and 0s of machine code.

When describing instructions, I use `reg`, `reg1`, or `reg2` to mean one of the names of a general-purpose register from Table 9-2 in Chapter 9. I use `mem` to mean a label of a memory location and `imm` to mean a literal data value. In most cases, the values specified by the operands must be the same. There are instructions for explicitly converting from one size to another.

Let's start with the most commonly used assembly language instruction, mov. In fact, in Listing 10-5 half the instructions are mov.

### mov—Move

Copies a value from a source to a destination.

mov `reg1, reg2` moves the value in `reg2` to `reg1`.

mov `reg, mem` moves the value in `mem` to `reg`.

mov `mem, reg` moves the value in `reg` to `mem`.

mov `reg, imm` moves `imm` to `reg`.

mov `mem, imm` moves `imm` to `mem`.

The mov instruction does not affect the status flags in the rflags register.

The size (number of bits) of the value moved must be the same for the source and the destination. When the assembler program translates the assembly language instruction to machine code, it can figure out the size from the register name. For example, the mov eax, 0 instruction ❻ in Listing 10-5 will cause the 32-bit integer, 0, to be stored in the eax register, which is the 32-bit portion of the rax register. Recall (from Chapter 9) that when the destination is the 32-bit portion of a register, the high-order 32 bits of that register are set to 0. If I had used mov al, 0, then only an 8-bit representation of 0 would be stored in the al portion of the rax register, and the other bits in the register would not be affected. For 8-bit and 16-bit operations, you should assume that the portion of any register that isn't explicitly modified by an instruction contains an unknown value.

You may have noticed that the variant that moves an immediate value to memory, mov *mem*, *imm*, doesn't use a register. In this case, you have to tell the assembler the data size with a size directive placed before the *mem* operand. Table 10-1 lists the size directives for each data size.

**Table 10-1:** Data Size Directives

| Directive | Data type | Number of bits |
|---|---|---|
| byte ptr | Byte | 8 |
| word ptr | Word | 16 |
| dword ptr | Doubleword | 32 |
| qword ptr | Quadword | 64 |

The size directive includes ptr because it specifies how many bytes the memory address points to. For immediate data, this address is in the rip register. For example,

```
mov     byte ptr x[ebp], 123
mov     qword ptr y[ebp], 123
```

would store 123 in the one-byte variable, x, and 123 in the four-byte variable, y. (This syntax for specifying the memory locations is explained in the next chapter.)

Notice that you can't move data from one memory location directly to another memory location. You have to first move the data into a register from memory and then move it from that register to the other memory location.

The other three instructions used in Listing 10-5 are push, pop, and ret. These three instructions use the call stack. We'll discuss the call stack in detail in the next chapter. For now, you can think of it as a place in memory where you can stack data items one on top of another and then remove them in reverse order. (Think of stacking dinner plates, one at a time, on a shelf and then removing each one as it's needed.) The rsp register always contains the address of the item on the top of the call stack; hence, it's called the *stack pointer*.

### push—**Push onto stack**

Moves a 64-bit source value to the top of the call stack.

push *reg* places the 64-bit value in *reg* on the call stack, changing the rsp register such that it has the memory address of this new item on the stack.

push *mem* places the 64-bit value in *mem* on the call stack, changing the rsp register such that it has the memory address of this new item on the stack.

The push instruction does not affect the status flags in the rflags register.

### pop—**Pop from stack**

Moves a 64-bit value from the top of the call stack to a destination.

pop *reg* copies the 64-bit value at the top of the stack to *reg*, changing the rsp register such that it has the memory address of the next item on the stack.

pop *mem* copies the 64-bit value at the top of the stack to *mem*, changing the rsp register such that it has the memory address of the next item on the stack.

The pop instruction does not affect the status flags in the rflags register.

### ret—**Return from function**

Returns from a function call.

ret has no operands. It pops the 64-bit value at the top of the stack into the instruction pointer, rip, thus transferring program control to that memory address.

The ret instruction does not affect the status flags in the rflags register.

Now that you have an idea of how each of the instructions in Listing 10-5 works, let's see what they're doing in this program. As we walk through this code, keep in mind that this program doesn't do anything for a user. The code here forms a sort of infrastructure for any C-style function that you write. You'll see variations as you continue through the book, but you should take the time to become familiar with the basic structure of this program.

## Minimal Processing in a Function

Aside from the data processing that a function does, it needs to perform some processing just so it can be called and return to the calling function. For example, the function needs to keep track of the address from where it was called so it can return to the correct place when the function has completed. Since there are a limited number of registers, the function needs a place in memory for storing the return address. After completion, the function returns to the calling place and no longer needs the return address, so it can release the memory where the return address was stored.

As you'll learn in the next chapter, the call stack is a great place for functions to temporarily store information. Each function uses a portion of the call stack for storage, which is called a *stack frame*. The function needs a reference to its stack frame, and this address is stored in the rbp register, usually called the *frame pointer*.

Let's walk through the actual processing that takes place in the program in Listing 10-5. I'll repeat the listing here to save you some page flipping (Listing 10-6).

```
# doNothingProg.s
# Minimum components of a C program, in assembly language.
        .intel_syntax noprefix
        .text
        .globl  main
        .type   main, @function
main:
    ❶ push    rbp         # save caller's frame pointer
    ❷ mov     rbp, rsp    # establish our frame pointer

    ❸ mov     eax, 0      # return 0 to caller

    ❹ mov     rsp, rbp    # restore stack pointer
    ❺ pop     rbp         # restore caller's frame pointer
    ❻ ret                 # back to caller
```

*Listing 10-6: Code repeated for your convenience*

The first thing a function must do is to save the calling function's frame pointer so the calling function can use rbp for its own frame pointer and then restore the calling function's frame pointer before returning. It does this by pushing the value onto the call stack ❶. Now that we've saved the calling function's frame pointer, we can use the rbp register as the frame pointer for the current function. The frame pointer is set to the current location of the stack pointer ❷.

**NOTE**    *Remember that we are telling the compiler not to use any code optimization in this book with the -O0 option to gcc. If you tell gcc to optimize the code, it may determine that these values may not need to be saved, so you wouldn't see some of these instructions. After you understand the concepts presented in this book, you can start thinking about how to optimize your code.*

This probably sounds confusing at this point. Don't worry, we'll go into this mechanism in detail in the next chapter. For now, make sure that every function you write in assembly language begins with these two instructions, in this order. Together, they make up the beginning of the *function prologue* that prepares the call stack and the registers for the actual computational work that will be done by the function.

C functions can return values to the calling function. This is the main function, and the operating system expects it to return the 32-bit integer 0 if the function ran without errors. The rax register is used to return up to a 64-bit value, so we store 0 in the eax register ❸ just before returning.

The function prologue prepared the call stack and registers for this function, and we need to follow a strict protocol for preparing the call stack and registers for return to the calling function. This is accomplished with the *function epilogue*. The function epilogue is essentially the mirror image of the function prologue. The first thing to do is to make sure the stack pointer is restored to where it was at the beginning of the prologue ❹. Although we can see that the stack pointer was not changed in this simple function, it will be changed in most functions, so you should get in the habit of restoring it. Restoring the stack pointer is essential for the next step to work.

Now that we've restored the stack pointer from the rbp register, we need to restore the calling function's value in the rbp register. That value was pushed onto the stack in the prologue, so we'll pop it off the top of the stack back into the rbp register ❺. Finally, we can return to the calling function ❻. Since this is the main function, this will return to the operating system.

One of the most valuable uses of gdb is as a learning tool. It has a mode that is especially helpful in learning what each assembly language instruction does. I'll show you how to do this in the next section, using the program in Listing 10-5. This will also help you to become more familiar with using gdb, which is an important skill to have when debugging your programs.

## Using gdb to Learn Assembly Language

This would be a good place for you to run the program in Listing 10-5 so you can follow along with the discussion. It can be assembled, linked, and executed with the following commands:

```
$ as --gstabs -o doNothingProg.o doNothingProg.s
$ gcc -o doNothingProg doNothingProg.o
$ ./doNothingProg
```

The --gstabs option (note the two dashes here) tells the assembler to include debugging information with the object file. The gcc program recognizes that the only input file is already an object file, so it goes directly to the linking stage. There is no need to tell gcc to include the debugging information because it was already included in the object file by the assembler.

As you might guess from the name, you won't see anything on the screen from running this program. We'll need this for later in the chapter when we use gdb to walk through the execution of this program. Then you'll see that this program actually does something.

The gdb debugger has a mode that's useful for seeing the effects of each assembly language instruction as it's executed one step at a time. The *text user interface* (*TUI*) mode splits the terminal window into a display area at the top and the usual command area at the bottom. The display area can be further split into two display areas.

Each display area can show either the source code (src), the registers (regs), or the *disassembled* machine code (asm). Disassembly is the process of translating the machine code (1s and 0s) into the corresponding assembly language. The disassembly process does not know the programmer-defined names, so you will see only the numerical values that were generated by the assembly and linking processes. The asm display will probably be more useful when we look at the details of instructions in Chapter 12.

The documentation for using the TUI mode is in info for gdb. I'll give a simple introduction here of using the TUI mode with the program *doNothingProg.s*, from Listing 10-5. I'll step through most of the instructions. You'll get a chance to single-step through each of them when it's Your Turn.

**NOTE**    *My example here shows gdb being run from the command line. I've been told that this doesn't work well if you try to run gdb under the Emacs editor.*

```
$ gdb ./doNothingProg
--snip--
Reading symbols from ./doNothingProg...
❶ (gdb) set disassembly-flavor intel
❷ (gdb) b main
Breakpoint 1 at 0x1129: file doNothingProg.s, line 8.
(gdb) r
Starting program: /home/bob/progs/chap11/doNothingProg_asm/doNothingProg

Breakpoint 1, main () at doNothingProg.s:8
8               push    rbp                     # save caller's frame pointer
❸ (gdb) tui enable
```

We start the program under gdb the usual way. The default assembly language syntax that gdb uses for disassembly under GNU/Linux is AT&T, so we need to set it to Intel ❶. This syntax issue will be explained at the end of this chapter. It matters if you use the asm display.

Then we set a breakpoint at the beginning of the program ❷. We used source code line numbers for setting breakpoints in C code. But each C statement typically translates into several assembly language instructions, so we can't be sure that gdb will break at a specific instruction. The *label* syntax gives us a way to ensure that gdb will break at a specific instruction if it is labeled.

When we run the program, it breaks at the main label, which is on the first instruction of the function. Next, we enable the TUI mode ❸, which shows the source code, as shown in Figure 10-1.

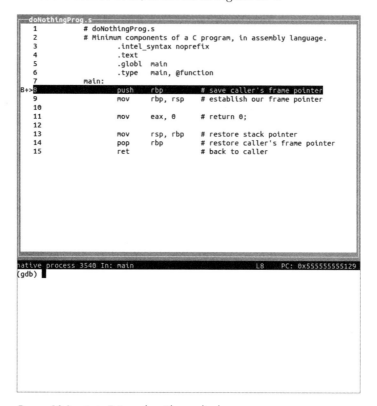

```
 doNothingProg.s
     1          # doNothingProg.s
     2          # Minimum components of a C program, in assembly language.
     3                    .intel_syntax noprefix
     4                    .text
     5                    .globl  main
     6                    .type   main, @function
     7          main:
B+> 8                    push    rbp        # save caller's frame pointer
     9                    mov     rbp, rsp   # establish our frame pointer
    10
    11                    mov     eax, 0     # return 0;
    12
    13                    mov     rsp, rbp   # restore stack pointer
    14                    pop     rbp        # restore caller's frame pointer
    15                    ret                # back to caller




native process 3540 In: main                         L8    PC: 0x555555555129
(gdb)
```

Figure 10-1: gdb in TUI mode with src display

The bottom section of the terminal window shows the usual (gdb) prompt, which is where you enter gdb commands and examine memory contents. The top section shows the source code for this function with the line about to be executed shown in reverse video to highlight it. There's also an indication on the left side that there's a breakpoint at this line (B+) and that the instruction pointer, rip, currently points to this line, >. The display also shows the current address in the rip register, using the name PC, in the lower-right margin of the source display section. (*Program counter* is another name for *instruction pointer*.)

The layout regs command splits the display area of the terminal window and displays the registers, as shown in Figure 10-2. We're about to execute the first instruction in the main function.

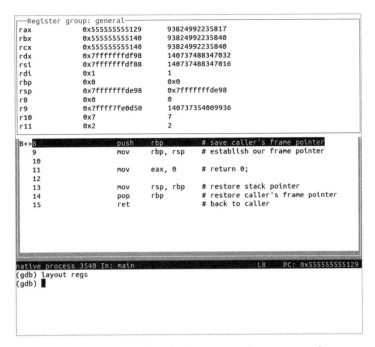

Figure 10-2: gdb in TUI mode with the source and registers windows

The s command executes the current instruction and moves on to the next instruction, which becomes highlighted, as shown in Figure 10-3.

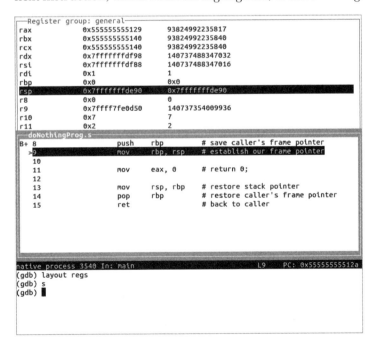

Figure 10-3: Executing an instruction causes any registers that have changed to be highlighted.

Executing the first instruction, push rbp, has caused gdb to highlight the rsp register and its contents in the registers display window shown in Figure 10-3. This instruction has pushed the contents of the rbp register onto the call stack and changed the stack pointer, rsp, accordingly. Pushing a 64-bit register onto the call stack has changed the stack pointer from 0x7fffffffde98 (Figure 10-2) to 0x7fffffffde90; that is, it decremented the stack pointer by the number of bytes (8) pushed onto the stack. You'll learn more about the call stack and its usage in the next chapter.

In Figure 10-3, you can also see that the current location within the program has moved to the next instruction. This instruction is now highlighted; the instruction pointer character, >, has moved to this instruction; and the address in the rip register (PC in lower right) has changed from 0x555555555129 to 0x55555555512a. This change in rip shows that the instruction that was just executed, push rbp, occupies only one byte in memory. You'll learn more about this in Chapter 12.

The TUI enhancement does not provide a data or address view of memory, only a disassembly view. We need to view data and addresses that are stored in memory in the command area. For example, if we want to see what the push rbp instruction stored in memory, we need to use the x command to view the memory pointed to by the stack pointer, rsp. Figure 10-4 shows the giant (64-bit) contents in hexadecimal at the memory address in rsp.

```
┌─Register group: general────────────────────────────────────
│rax            0x555555555129      93824992235817
│rbx            0x555555555140      93824992235840
│rcx            0x555555555140      93824992235840
│rdx            0x7fffffffdf98      140737488347032
│rsi            0x7fffffffdf88      140737488347016
│rdi            0x1                 1
│rbp            0x0                 0x0
│rsp            0x7fffffffde90      0x7fffffffde90
│r8             0x0                 0
│r9             0x7ffff7fe0d50      140737354009936
│r10            0x7                 7
│r11            0x2                 2
┌─doNothingProg.s────────────────────────────────────────────
│B+  8              push    rbp         # save caller's frame pointer
│ > 9              mov     rbp, rsp    # establish our frame pointer
│   10
│   11              mov     eax, 0      # return 0;
│   12
│   13              mov     rsp, rbp    # restore stack pointer
│   14              pop     rbp         # restore caller's frame pointer
│   15              ret                 # back to caller
│
│
│
│
│
│
native process 3540 In: main                        L9   PC: 0x55555555512a
(gdb) layout regs
(gdb) s
(gdb) x/1xg 0x7fffffffde90
0x7fffffffde90: 0x0000000000000000
(gdb) █
```

Figure 10-4: Examining memory in TUI mode is done in the command area.

Executing two more instructions shows that the mov rax, 0 instruction stores 0 in the rax register, as shown in Figure 10-5. Comparing Figures 10-4 and 10-5, you can also see the effects of the mov rbp, rsp instruction.

Figure 10-5: Effects of the mov eax, 0 instruction

Another step takes us to the ret instruction, shown in Figure 10-6, ready to return to the calling function.

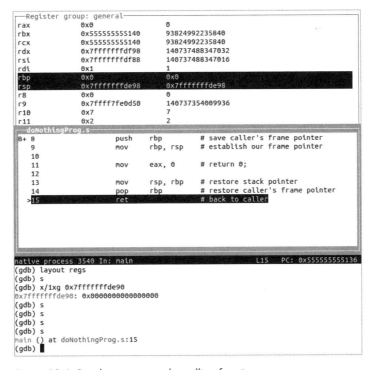

Figure 10-6: Ready to return to the calling function

Comparing Figure 10-6 with Figure 10-2 shows us that the frame pointer, rbp, has been restored to the calling function's value. We can also see that the stack pointer, rsp, has been moved back to the same location it was at when our function first started. If both the frame pointer and stack pointer are not restored before returning to the calling function, it's almost certain that your program will crash. For this reason, I often set a breakpoint at the ret instruction so I can check that my function restored both these registers properly, highlighted in Figure 10-7.

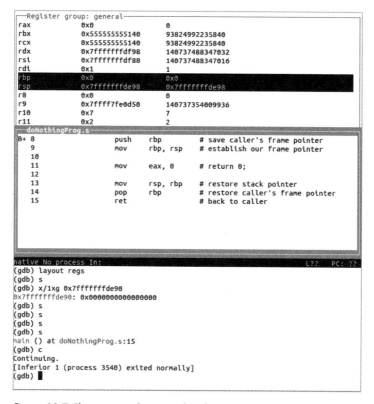

Figure 10-7: The program has completed.

All that remains is to quit gdb.

**YOUR TURN**

1. Enter the program in Listing 10-5 and use gdb to single-step through the code. Notice that when you execute the mov rsp, rbp instruction in the epilogue, TUI does not highlight the registers. Explain. Next, change the program so that it returns the integer 123. Run it with gdb. What number base does gdb use to display the exit code?

2. Enter the program in Listing 10-1 and compile it with debugging turned on (-g option). Set a breakpoint at main. Does gdb break at the entry to the function? Can you follow the actions of the prologue by using the s command? Can you continue through the program and step through the epilogue?

3. Write the following C function in assembly language:

```
/* f.c */
  int f(void) {
  return 0;
}
```

Make sure that it assembles with no errors. Use the -S option to compile f.c and compare gcc's assembly language with yours. Write a main function in C that tests your assembly language function, f, and prints out the function's return value.

4. Write three assembly language functions that do nothing but return an integer. They should each return a different, nonzero integer. Write a main function in C that tests your assembly language functions and prints out the functions' return values by using printf.

5. Write three assembly language functions that do nothing but return a character. Each should return a different character. Write a main function in C that tests your assembly language functions and prints out the functions' return values by using printf.

In the next chapter, we'll take a more detailed look inside the main function. I'll describe how to use the call stack in detail. This will include how to create local variables in a function. But first, I'll give a brief summary of the AT&T assembly language syntax. If you look at any assembly language in a Linux or Unix environment, you'll probably see the AT&T syntax being used.

## AT&T Syntax

I am using the Intel syntax for the assembly language in this book, but for those who might prefer the AT&T syntax, I'll briefly describe it here. AT&T syntax is the default in most Linux distributions.

Listing 10-7 is a repeat of the program in Listing 10-5 but written using the AT&T syntax.

```
# doNothingProg_att.s
# Minimum components of a C program, in assembly language.
        .text
        .globl  main
        .type   main, @function
```

```
main:
    ❶ pushq ❷ %rbp        # save caller's frame pointer
      movq  ❸ %rsp, %rbp  # establish our frame pointer

      movq  ❹ $0, %rax    # return 0;

      movq    %rbp, %rsp  # restore stack pointer
      popq    %rbp        # restore caller's frame pointer
      ret                 # back to caller
```

*Listing 10-7: Minimum C program written in assembly language using AT&T syntax*

The first difference that you probably notice is that a character specifying the size of the operand is added as a suffix to most instruction mnemonics ❶. Table 10-2 lists the size letters. (Yes, this is redundant in the cases where one of the operands is a register, but it's part of the syntax.) The next difference you probably see is that each register is prefixed with the % character ❷.

The most significant difference is that the order of the operands is reversed ❸. Instead of placing the destination first, it's last. If you move between the two syntaxes, Intel and AT&T, it's easy to get the operands in the wrong order, especially with instructions that use two registers. You also need to prefix an immediate data value with the $ character ❹ in the AT&T syntax.

**Table 10-2:** Data Size Suffix for AT&T Syntax

| Suffix letter | Data type | Number of bits |
|---|---|---|
| b | Byte | 8 |
| w | Word | 16 |
| l | Doubleword | 32 |
| q | Quadword | 64 |

As stated in the preface, I chose to use the Intel syntax in this book to be consistent with the Intel and AMD manuals. As far as I know, the GNU assembler, as, is the only one that defaults to the AT&T syntax. All other assemblers use the Intel syntax, and as offers that as an option.

## What You've Learned

**Editor**  A program used to write the source code for a program in the chosen programming language.

**Preprocessor**  The first stage of compilation. It brings other files into the source, defines macros, and so forth, in preparation for actual compilation.

**Compilation**  Translates from the chosen programming language into assembly language.

**Assembly**  Translates assembly language into machine language.

**Linking**   Links separate object code modules and libraries together to produce the final executable program.

**Assembler directives**   Guide the assembler program during the assembly process.

**mov instruction**   Moves values between memory and the CPU and within the CPU.

**push instruction**   Places values on the call stack.

**pop instruction**   Retrieves values from the call stack.

**ret instruction**   Returns program flow to the calling function.

**gdb TUI mode**   Displays changes in registers in real time as you step through a program. It's an excellent learning tool.

**Prologue**   Sets up the call stack for the called function.

**Epilogue**   Restores the call stack for the calling function.

In the next chapter, you'll learn the details about how to pass arguments to functions, how the call stack works, and how to create local variables in functions.

# 11

## INSIDE THE MAIN FUNCTION

As you know, every C program begins by executing a function named main, which is called from a startup function in the C runtime environment. The main function will call other functions (*subfunctions*) to do most of the processing. Even a simple "Hello, World!" program needs to call another function to write the message on the screen.

Most subfunctions need data to be passed to them as arguments from the calling function, and they often pass a result back to the calling function. Arguments to a function can be data or memory addresses. When the function is called, it performs its operations and then returns to the calling function. The calling function needs to send the called function the address to return to. In the x86-64 architecture, the return address is passed on the call stack.

Adding a little more complexity, most functions need their own local variables for storing data and addresses. Registers can be used for variables, but they are global, and we would quickly run out of registers to use. The stack provides a good place to allocate space for local variables in memory.

In this chapter, we'll break down this process. We'll do this by discussing how to write characters on the screen and read characters from the keyboard in our main function. Starting with this chapter, we'll usually bypass the C standard library functions, printf and scanf, and use the system call functions write to output to the screen and read to input from the keyboard.

We'll start by discussing the write and read functions. Then we'll look at how arguments are passed to a function in the CPU registers. We'll next look at how the CPU can determine an address to pass to a function when that's needed. Then we'll look at how a data structure called the *call stack* is used for creating local variables within a function.

## The write and read System Call Functions

In Chapter 2 we used printf and scanf, from the C standard library, for writing to the screen and reading from the keyboard. As shown in Figure 2-1 (in Chapter 2), printf converts data from its memory storage format to a character format and calls the write system call function to display the characters on the screen. When reading characters from the keyboard, scanf calls the read system call function and converts the characters to a memory storage format.

Linux sees the screen and keyboard as files. When a program is first launched, the operating system opens three files—*standard in*, *standard out*, and *standard error*—and assigns an integer to each file that is called a *file descriptor*. The program interacts with each file by using the file descriptor. The C interfaces for calling read and write are specified in the *Portable Operating System Interface* (*POSIX*) standard. The general formats for calling these two functions are

```
int write(int fd, char *buf, int n);
int read(int fd, char *buf, int n);
```

where *fd* is a file descriptor, *buf* is the address of the character storage, and *n* is the number of characters to read or write. You can see more details in the man pages for write and read:

```
man 2 write
man 2 read
```

Table 11-1 shows the file descriptors we'll use and the device each is normally associated with.

**Table 11-1:** File Descriptors for write and read System Call Functions

| Name | Number | Use |
| --- | --- | --- |
| STDIN_FILENO | 0 | Read characters from keyboard |
| STDOUT_FILENO | 1 | Write characters to screen |
| STDERR_FILENO | 2 | Write error messages to screen |

These names are defined in the system header file, *unistd.h*, which is located at */usr/include/unistd.h* on my Ubuntu system. (The location on your system may be different.)

Let's look at how to pass the appropriate arguments to the `write` function to write text on the screen.

## Passing Arguments in Registers

Up to six arguments can be passed in registers from one function to another in our environment. We'll look at how to pass more than six arguments in Chapter 14, and I'll note here that the Windows C environment allows only four arguments to be passed in registers.

Let's start with a program that does something very simple. We'll write "Hello, World!" on the screen by using the `write` system call function (Listing 11-1).

```
/* helloWorld.c
 * Hello World program using the write() system call.
 */

#include <unistd.h>

int main(void)
{

  write(STDOUT_FILENO, "Hello, World!\n", 14);

  return 0;
}
```

*Listing 11-1: "Hello, World!" program using the `write` system call function*

This function passes three arguments to `write`. In principle, the C compiler—or you, when you're writing in assembly language—could use any of the 16 general-purpose registers, except `rsp`, to pass arguments from one function to another. (The reason you can't use `rsp` will be explained in a moment.) Just store the arguments in the registers and call the desired function. Of course, the compiler, or a person writing in assembly language, needs to know exactly which register each argument is in when it comes to the called function.

The best way to avoid making mistakes is to develop a standard set of rules and follow them. This is especially important if more than one person is writing code for a program. Other people have realized the importance of having such standards and have given a good set of standards for passing arguments in *System V Application Binary Interface AMD64 Architecture Processor Supplement (with LP64 and ILP32 Programming Models) Version 1.0*. I found the January 28, 2018, version in PDF format at *https://github.com/hjl-tools/x86-psABI/wiki/x86-64 -psABI-1.0.pdf*. (The latest version is maintained in LaTeX source at *https://gitlab .com/x86-psABIs/x86-64-ABI/*, but you need *pdflatex* to build a PDF version.) The compiler we're using, gcc, follows the rules in the System V standards, and we'll do the same for the assembly language we write.

Table 11-2 summarizes the System V standards for using registers.

**Table 11-2:** General-Purpose Register Usage

| Register | Special usage | Save? |
|---|---|---|
| rax | Return first value from function | No |
| rbx | General-purpose | Yes |
| rcx | Pass fourth argument to function | No |
| rdx | Pass third argument to function; return second value from function | No |
| rsp | Stack pointer | Yes |
| rbp | Optional frame pointer | Yes |
| rdi | Pass first argument to function | No |
| rsi | Pass second argument to function | No |
| r8 | Pass fifth argument to function | No |
| r9 | Pass sixth argument to function | No |
| r10 | Pass function's static chain pointer | No |
| r11 | None | No |
| r12 | None | Yes |
| r13 | None | Yes |
| r14 | None | Yes |
| r15 | None | Yes |

The Save? column shows whether a called function needs to preserve the value in that register for the calling function. You'll learn how to do this in the next few sections.

The first six arguments are passed in registers rdi, rsi, rdx, rcx, r8, and r9, reading from left to right in a C function. Listing 11-2 shows the assembly language generated by gcc for the C function in Listing 11-1. This illustrates how to pass the three required arguments to the write function.

**NOTE** *The compiler did not comment the assembly language code in this listing. I've added my own comments, using ##, to help you to see the relationships with the C source code. I'll do this with most of the compiler-generated assembly language I show in this book.*

```
        .file   "helloWorld.c"
        .intel_syntax noprefix
        .text
    ❶ .section  .rodata
❷ .LC0:
        .string "Hello, World!\n"
        .text
        .globl  main
        .type   main, @function
main:
        push    rbp
```

```
mov     rbp, rsp
mov     edx, ❸14        ## number of chars
lea     rsi, ❹.LC0[rip] ## address of string
mov     edi, ❺1         ## STDOUT_FILENO
call  ❻ write@PLT
mov     eax, 0
pop     rbp
ret
.size   main, .-main
.ident  " GCC: (Ubuntu 9.3.0-17ubuntu1~20.04) 9.3.0"
.section  .note.GNU-stack,"",@progbits
```

*Listing 11-2: Assembly language generated by gcc for program in Listing 11-1*

When programming in assembly language, it's common to store the arguments in the registers starting with the last argument in the argument list, working your way to the first argument. In Listing 11-2, the third argument to write, the number of characters ❸, is stored first in the register for the third argument, edx. The second argument is the address of the first character in the string ❹, which goes in rsi. The first argument, the device to write to ❺, is stored in edi just before the call to write ❻.

This program also introduces two more instructions, lea and call, and some rather odd-looking syntax associated with these instructions. The lea instruction loads the memory address of .LC0 into the rsi register, and the call instruction transfers program control to the address of the write function. Before describing the details of these instructions, we need to look at where the various components of a program are located in memory.

## Position-Independent Code

The job of the linker is to decide where each program component should be located in memory and then fill in the addresses in the program code where the component is referenced. The linker could decide where each component should be located in memory and include these addresses in the executable file, but it's more secure to allow the operating system to decide where to load each component. Let's look at how the assembly language generated by gcc allows the program to be loaded anywhere in memory.

For the program to run correctly when the operating system is given the responsibility to decide where to load it, the linker needs to create a *position-independent executable.* For this to work, each function in the program must consist of *position-independent code,* code that will work correctly no matter where it is loaded into memory. The default for the gcc compiler is usually set to produce position-independent code, and the linking phase produces a position-independent executable.

Linking the functions and global data items in the source code files that we write for our program is straightforward. The linker knows how many bytes are in each function and global data item, so it can compute where each begins relative to the beginning of the program. From there, the linker can compute the number of bytes from where a component is referenced to the relative location of the referenced component, giving an *offset value*. The linker inserts this offset value into the code at the place where the component is referenced.

You've already learned about the execution cycle and how the instruction pointer works its way through the program as it's executed. The result is that at any given point in the program, the current address is in the instruction pointer, rip, regardless of where the program was loaded into memory. During program execution, when the CPU comes to an instruction that references another component, it adds the offset value to the address in the instruction pointer to result in an *effective address* of the referenced component. The effective address is used by both the lea and call instructions.

### lea—Load effective address

Computes an effective address and loads it into a register.

lea *reg, mem* loads the effective address of *mem* into *reg*.

The lea instruction does not affect the status flags in the rflags register.

### call—Call procedure

Saves linking information on the stack and jumps to a procedure.

call *function_name* pushes the address of the next instruction onto the call stack and then transfers control to *function_name*.

The call instruction does not affect the status flags in the rflags register.

In Listing 11-2, the memory location of the text string is labeled .LC0 ❷. The syntax to specify that we need this address relative to the instruction pointer is .LC0[rip] ❹. You can think of this as ".LC0 off of rip." During the linking phase, the linker computes the memory distance between the lea instruction and the .LC0 label, and it uses that value as the offset. To be more precise, the linker uses the memory distance of the instruction immediately following the lea instruction. Recall that during program execution when the CPU fetches an instruction, it increments the address in the rip register to that of the next instruction. So the action of the lea rsi, .LC0[rip] instruction is to add the offset that the linker computed to the address in the rip register, which has now updated to the address of the next instruction, and load that address into the rsi register.

The label .LC0 is in the .rodata section ❶, which is typically loaded into the .text segment by the operating system. Most of what is stored in the .text segment are CPU instructions, so the operating system treats it as a read-only area of memory. The .rodata section contains constant data, which is also read-only.

You'll learn about pushing things onto the stack in the next section, but you can see that the call instruction in Listing 11-2 has @PLT appended to the name of the function being called, write ❻. PLT stands for *procedure linkage table*. The write function is in a C shared library, not in one of source code files that we wrote. The linker has no idea where it will be located relative to our main function, so it includes a procedure linkage table and a *global offset table (GOT)* in the executable file.

The first time our program calls the write function, the *dynamic loader* in the operating system loads the function into memory (if it has not already been loaded by another program), puts the address of the function in the global offset table, and adjusts the procedure linkage table accordingly. If our program calls the write function again, the procedure linkage table uses the value in the global offset table to directly call it. The syntax, write@PLT, says to call the write function, whose address can be found in the procedure linkage table. When we're calling functions that are included when linking our program, we don't need to use the procedure linkage table because the linker can compute the relative address of the function being called.

## The Call Stack

The *call stack*, or simply the *stack*, is used extensively for the interface between a calling function and called function, creating local variables within a function, and saving items within a function. Before describing how these things are done, we need to understand what stacks are and how they are used.

### Stacks in General

A *stack* is a data structure created in memory for storing data items that includes a pointer to the "top" of the stack. Informally, you can think of a stack as being organized very much like a stack of dinner plates on a shelf. We need to be able to access only the item at the top of the stack. (And, yes, if you pull out a plate from somewhere within the stack, you will probably break something.) There are two fundamental operations on a stack:

**push** *data_item*    Places the *data_item* on the top of the stack and moves the stack pointer to point to this latest item.

**pop** *location*    The data item on the top of the stack is moved to *location*, and the stack pointer is moved to point to the next item left on the stack.

The stack is a *last in, first out* (*LIFO*) data structure. The last thing to be pushed onto the stack is the first thing to be popped off.

To illustrate the stack concept, let's continue with our dinner plate example. Say we have three differently colored dinner plates, a red one on the dining table, a green one on the kitchen counter, and a blue one on the bedside table. Now we'll stack them on the shelf in the following way:

1. Push red plate.
2. Push green plate.
3. Push blue plate.

At this point, our stack of plates looks like Figure 11-1.

| Blue plate |
| Green plate |
| Red plate |

*Figure 11-1: Three dinner plates in a stack*

4. Now perform the operation: pop kitchen counter.

We'll have a blue plate on our kitchen counter (recall that the blue plate was on the bedside table) and our stack of dinner plates will be left as shown in Figure 11-2.

| Green plate |
| Red plate |

*Figure 11-2: One dinner plate has been popped from the stack.*

If you have guessed that it's easy to really mess up a stack, you're right. A stack must be used according to a strict discipline. Within any function:

- Always push an item onto the stack before popping anything off.
- Never pop more things off than you have pushed on.
- Always pop everything off the stack.

If you have no use for the item(s) to be popped off, you may simply adjust the stack pointer. This is equivalent to discarding the items that are popped off. (Our dinner plate analogy breaks down here.)

A good way to maintain this discipline is to think of the use of parentheses in an algebraic expression. A push is analogous to a left parenthesis, and a pop is analogous to a right parenthesis. The pairs of parentheses can be nested, but they have to match. An attempt to push too many items onto a stack is called *stack overflow*. An attempt to pop items off the stack beyond the bottom is called *stack underflow*.

We have looked only at the essential operations on a stack here. It's common to add other operations in an implementation of a stack. For example, a *peek* operation allows you to look at the item on the top of the stack without removing it. And as you'll see in subsequent chapters, items not on the top of the stack are often accessed directly without pushing and popping, but in a very well-controlled way.

A stack is implemented by dedicating a contiguous area of main memory to it. Stacks can grow in either direction in memory, into higher addresses or lower. An *ascending stack* grows into higher addresses, and a *descending stack* grows into lower addresses. The stack pointer can point to the top item on the stack, a *full stack,* or to the memory location where the next item will be pushed onto the stack, an *empty stack*. These four possible stack implementations are shown in Figure 11-3 with the integers 1, 2, and 3 pushed onto the stack in that order. Be sure to notice that memory addresses are *increasing downward* in this figure, which is the way we usually view them in the gdb debugger.

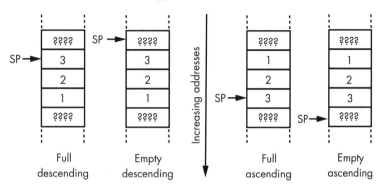

Figure 11-3: Four ways to implement a stack

x86-64 instructions use the stack as a *full-descending stack*. To understand this choice, think about how you might organize things in memory. Recall that the control unit automatically increments the program counter as your program is executed. Programs come in vastly different sizes, so storing the program instructions at low memory addresses allows maximum flexibility with respect to program size.

The stack is a dynamic structure. You do not know ahead of time how much stack space will be required by any given program as it executes. It's impossible to know how much space to allocate for the stack. You would like to allocate as much space as possible, while preventing it from colliding with program instructions. The solution is to start the stack at the highest address and have it grow toward lower addresses.

This is a highly simplified rationalization for implementing stacks such that they grow "downward" in memory. The organization of various program elements in memory is much more complex than the simple description given here. But this may help you to understand that there are some good reasons for what may seem to be a rather odd implementation.

The important point is that we need to write our assembly language accordingly. We'll next look at the details of how the stack is used in the function prologue and epilogue and how arguments to another function in registers, by writing our own "Hello, World!" program directly in assembly language.

### Inside the Function Prologue and Epilogue

My assembly language version of the "Hello, World!" program, Listing 11-3, closely follows the assembly language generated from the C version by the compiler in Listing 11-2, but I've added comments and used a more meaningful label for the string constant. This should make it a little easier to understand how the program uses the stack and passes arguments to the write function.

```
# helloWorld.s
# Hello World program using the write() system call

        .intel_syntax noprefix
# Useful constant
    ❶ .equ    STDOUT, 1

# Constant data
      ❷ .section  .rodata
message:
        .string "Hello, World!\n"
        .equ    ❸ msgLength, .-message-1

# Code
        .text
        .globl  main
        .type   main, @function
main:
        push    rbp             # save caller's frame pointer
        mov     rbp, rsp        # our frame pointer

        mov     edx, MsgLength  # message length
        lea     rsi, message[rip]  # message address
        mov     edi, STDOUT     # the screen
        call    write@plt       # write message

        mov     eax, 0          # return 0

        pop     rbp             # restore caller frame pointer
        ret                     # back to caller
```

Listing 11-3: "Hello, World!" program written in assembly language

Before we get to a discussion of the prologue, notice that I've used another assembler directive, .equ, in Listing 11-3 ❶. The format is

```
.equ symbol, expression
```

Note that we don't need to specify the .text segment for the .rodata section ❷. The assembler and linker produce an .rodata section, and it's up to the operating system to determine where to load it.

The *expression* must evaluate to an integer, and the assembler sets *symbol* equal to that value. You can then use the symbol in your code, making it much easier to read, and the assembler will plug in the value of the expression. The expression is often just an integer. In this program, I have equated the symbol STDOUT to the integer 1.

The . character in an expression means *here* in memory location. Thus, when the assembler gets to the expression ❸, it computes the current location in memory, which is the end of the C-style text string; subtracts the beginning location of the string, the location that the programmer labeled message, and then subtracts 1 for the terminating NUL character. The net result is that MsgLength is equated with the number of printable characters in the text string.

You've learned in Chapter 10 how the caller's frame pointer is saved on the call stack and a new frame pointer is established for this function. But now that you know more about how the call stack works, let's walk through the prologue of this function with gdb.

The first thing we need to do is to set a breakpoint at the beginning of the function:

```
(gdb) b main
Breakpoint 1 at 0x1139: file helloWorld.s, line 18.
```

You can use either the label, main, or the line number. We saw how to use the li command to see the line numbers in Chapter 2. Using the line number may cause gdb to execute the prologue and break after it. (I've seen different behavior in different versions of gdb.)

After setting the breakpoint, when we run the program, it breaks at the first instruction, and we can inspect the contents of the rbp and rsp registers:

```
(gdb) r
Starting program: /home/bob/progs/chap11/helloWorld_asm/helloWorld

Breakpoint 1, main () at helloWorld.s:18
18              push    rbp                    # save caller's frame pointer
(gdb) i r rbp rsp
rbp             0x0                     0x0
rsp             0x7fffffffde88          0x7fffffffde88
```

The i r command gives us the current location of the stack pointer, rsp. The instruction about to be executed will push the eight bytes in the rbp register onto the call stack. To see the effects in memory, we'll examine the current contents of the stack. Since the call stack is full descending, we'll subtract 8 from the current address in the stack pointer for our display so we can get a view of the area of memory that this instruction will change before it's changed:

```
(gdb) x/2xg 0x7fffffffde80
0x7fffffffde80: 0x0000555555555160      0x00007ffff7de70b3
```

The stack pointer is currently pointing to the value 0x00007ffff7de70b3, which is the return address that the call instruction in the calling function (in the C runtime environment, since this is the main function) pushed onto the stack. The rbp register contains 0x0000000000000000. This value is about to be pushed onto the stack at location 0x7fffffffde80, which currently contains 0x0000555555555160.

Next, we execute the two instructions in the function prologue, which will take us to the first instruction after the prologue:

```
(gdb) si
19              mov     rbp, rsp               # our frame pointer
```

```
(gdb) si
21              mov     edx, MsgLength      # message length
```

We'll inspect the values in the rsp and rbp registers:

```
(gdb) i r rbp rsp
rbp             0x7fffffffde80      0x7fffffffde80
rsp             0x7fffffffde80      0x7fffffffde80
```

We can see that the stack pointer has been decremented by 8, and the frame pointer has been set to the top of the stack. Let's look at how the stack has changed by examining the same memory area that we examined earlier:

```
(gdb) x/2xg 0x7fffffffde80
0x7fffffffde80: 0x0000000000000000       0x00007ffff7de70b3
(gdb)
```

We see that the value in the rbp register, 0x0000000000000000, has been nicely saved at the top of the call stack. Next, we'll set a breakpoint at the call write@PLT instruction so we can make sure that the registers have been set up correctly for write:

```
(gdb) b 24
Breakpoint 2 at 0x55555555514e: file helloWorld.s, line 24.
(gdb) c
Continuing.

Breakpoint 2, main () at helloWorld.s:24
24              call    write@plt            # write message
(gdb) i r rdx rsi rdi
rdx             0xe                 14
rsi             0x555555556004      93824992239620
rdi             0x1                 1
```

The rdx register contains the number of characters to be written on the screen, and the rsi register contains the address of the first character. Recall that a C-style text string is terminated with a NUL character, so we'll examine 15 characters at this address:

```
(gdb) x/15c 0x555555556004
0x555555556004: 72 'H'  101 'e' 108 'l' 108 'l' 111 'o' 44 ','  32 ' '  87 'W'
0x55555555600c: 111 'o' 114 'r' 108 'l' 100 'd' 33 '!'  10 '\n' 0 '\000'
```

Next, we'll set a breakpoint at the ret instruction to make sure that the stack pointer and frame pointer have been restored to the caller's values:

```
(gdb) b 29
Breakpoint 3 at 0x555555555159: file helloWorld.s, line 29.
 (gdb) c
Continuing.
Hello, World!
```

```
Breakpoint 3, main () at helloWorld.s:29
29              ret                             # back to caller
(gdb) i r rbp rsp rip
rbp             0x0                 0x0
rsp             0x7fffffffde88      0x7fffffffde88
rip             0x555555555159      0x555555555159 <main+32>
```

I've included the rip register in this display to show the effects of the ret instruction. Executing the ret instruction shows that it pops the value from the top of the stack into the rip register, thus returning to the C runtime environment:

```
(gdb) si
__libc_start_main (main=0x555555555139 <main>, argc=1, argv=0x7fffffffdf78,
    init=<optimized out>, fini=<optimized out>, rtld_fini=<optimized out>,
    stack_end=0x7fffffffdf68) at ../csu/libc-start.c:342
342     ../csu/libc-start.c: No such file or directory.
(gdb) i r rbp rsp rip
rbp             0x0                 0x0
rsp             0x7fffffffde90      0x7fffffffde90
rip             0x7ffff7de70b3      0x7ffff7de70b3 <__libc_start_main+243>
```

Looking back at the displays of the stack shown, we can see that the address that was pushed onto the stack by the function in the C runtime environment that called our main function has been popped back into the rip register.

The protocol that specifies the interaction between functions needs to be followed very precisely, or the program will usually crash.

In the next section, we'll look at how we can create local variables on the stack. You'll see the importance of the frame pointer.

---

**YOUR TURN**

Modify the assembly language program in Listing 11-3 so that it prints Hello, *your_name*! on the screen. Remember to change the documentation so it accurately describes your program.

---

## Local Variables in a Function

Variables that are defined in a C function can be used in the function only where they're defined, making them *local variables*. They are created when the function is called and deleted when the function returns to the calling function, so they are also called *automatic variables*.

You learned in Chapter 9 that CPU registers can be used as variables, but if we were to use CPU registers to hold all of our variables, we'd soon run out of registers in even small program, so we need to allocate space in memory for variables.

We also saw earlier that a function needs to preserve the contents of some registers (the Save? column in Table 11-2) for the calling function. If we want to use such a register in our function, we need to save its content in memory and restore it before returning to the calling function.

We'll next look at how to use the call stack for these two purposes: creating and removing automatic variables and saving and restoring register content.

## Variables on the Stack

From the description of the call stack shown previously, you might guess that it's a good place for saving a register's content—simply push it onto the stack before using the register for something else and then pop the content off into the register before returning to the calling function.

Creating variables on the call stack is more complicated. If we restrict our usage of the stack to pushing and popping, keeping track of where each variable is located on the stack would quickly become messy, if not impossible.

There is, however, an easy way to use the stack for variables. As part of the function prologue, we'll allocate enough memory for the variables on the stack by moving the stack pointer, thus increasing the size of the stack frame for the function. We can use the same addressing technique to access our variables in the stack frame that was used to access the message address in Listing 11-3, except we'll use the frame pointer, rbp, for the address base. We need to be careful not to change rbp so we can use it as a reference point in the stack frame, leaving the stack pointer free to push and pop items as needed.

To illustrate how to use the stack frame for automatic local variables, we'll start with the C program in Listing 11-4, which reads one character from the keyboard and echoes it on the screen.

```
/* echoChar.c
 * Echoes a character entered by the user.
 */

#include <unistd.h>

int main(void)
{
  char aLetter;

  write(STDOUT_FILENO, "Enter one character: ", 21); /* prompt user   */
  read(STDIN_FILENO, &aLetter, 1);                   /* one character */
  write(STDOUT_FILENO, "You entered: ", 13);         /* message       */
  write(STDOUT_FILENO, &aLetter, 1);

  return 0;
}
```

Listing 11-4: Program to echo a single character entered by a user

Listing 11-5 shows the way our compiler does this, which is the assembly language that gcc generates for the C program in Listing 11-4.

```
        .file   "echoChar.c"
        .intel_syntax noprefix
        .text
        .section .rodata
.LC0:
        .string "Enter one character: "
.LC1:
        .string "You entered: "
        .text
        .globl  main
        .type   main, @function
main:
        push    rbp
        mov     rbp, rsp
    ❶ sub     rsp, 16
    ❷ mov     rax, QWORD PTR fs:40
    ❸ mov     QWORD PTR -8[rbp], rax
        xor     eax, eax
        mov     edx, 21          ## prompt message
        lea     rsi, .LC0[rip]
        mov     edi, 1
        call    write@PLT
    ❹ lea     rax, -9[rbp]      ## &aLetter
        mov     edx, 1
        mov     rsi, rax
        mov     edi, 0
        call    read@PLT
        mov     edx, 13          ## response message
        lea     rsi, .LC1[rip]
        mov     edi, 1
        call    write@PLT
        lea     rax, -9[rbp]
        mov     edx, 1
        mov     rsi, rax
        mov     edi, 1
        call    write@PLT
        mov     eax, 0
    ❺ mov     rcx, QWORD PTR -8[rbp]
        xor     rcx, QWORD PTR fs:40
        je      .L3
        call    __stack_chk_fail@PLT
.L3:
        leave
        ret
        .size   main, .-main
        .ident  "GCC: (Ubuntu 9.3.0-17ubuntu1~20.04) 9.3.0"
        .section .note.GNU-stack,"",@progbits
```

Listing 11-5: Assembly language generated by the compiler for the echoChar program in Listing 11-4

The C program defines a local char variable, aLetter, which requires only one byte. However, the compiler allocated 16 bytes on the call stack by simply moving the stack pointer ❶. The x86-64 architecture includes a set of sixteen 128-bit registers that are used by some floating-point and vector instructions. You'll learn more about them in Chapter 18. The stack pointer needs to be aligned at 16-byte address boundaries for these instructions, so most protocol standards specify that the stack pointer be aligned at 16-byte boundaries. This is less error-prone than aligning the stack pointer only where it's needed.

The instruction to move the stack pointer introduces the subtraction instruction, sub. While we're here, we'll also describe the addition and negation instructions, add and neg.

### sub—Subtract

Subtracts source value from destination value, leaving result in destination.

sub *reg1, reg2* subtracts the value in *reg2* from the value in *reg1*, leaving the result in *reg1*.

sub *reg, mem* subtracts the value in *mem* from the value in *reg*, leaving the result in *reg*.

sub *mem, reg* subtracts the value in *reg* from the value in *mem*, leaving the result in *mem*.

sub *reg, imm* subtracts *imm* from the value in *reg*, leaving the result in *reg*.

sub *mem, imm* subtracts *imm* from the value in *mem*, leaving the result in *mem*.

The sub instruction sets the OF, SF, ZF, AF, PF, and CF status flags in the rflags register according to the result.

### add—Add

Adds source value to destination value, leaving result in destination.

add *reg1, reg2* adds the value in *reg2* to the value in *reg1*, leaving the result in *reg1*.

add *reg, mem* adds the value in *mem* to the value in *reg*, leaving the result in *reg*.

add *mem, reg* adds the value in *reg* to the value in *mem*, leaving the result in *mem*.

add *reg, imm* adds *imm* to the value in *reg*, leaving the result in *reg*.

add *mem, imm* adds *imm* to the value in *mem*, leaving the result in *mem*.

The add instruction sets the OF, SF, ZF, AF, PF, and CF status flags in the rflags register according to the result.

### neg—Negate

Performs the two's complement negation of a value.

neg *reg* negates the value in *reg*.

neg *mem* negates the value in *mem*.

The neg instruction sets the OF, SF, ZF, AF, PF, and CF status flags in the rflags register according to the result.

The instructions to multiply and divide are more complex and are described in Chapter 16.

We need to pass the address of the local char variable to the read function so it can store the character entered by the user there. We can do this with the lea (load effective address) instruction ❹. As you can see, the compiler has chosen the byte that's located 9 bytes inside the 16 bytes allocated on the stack. Figure 11-4 shows the location of this variable.

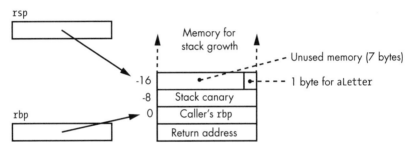

*Figure 11-4: Stack frame for program in Listing 11-5*

One of the items in the stack frame of Figure 11-4 is a *stack canary*, which is used to help detect stack corruption.

## Stack Corruption

The function epilogue restores the caller's frame pointer in the rbp register and returns the stack pointer to point to the return address. However, if either of these values has been changed on the stack, the program will not behave properly. A stack canary can help detect whether either of these values has been changed.

When a program starts, the operating system stores a 64-bit random number in a special place in memory labeled fs:40, which only the operating system can change. We read this value from memory ❷ and store it in the stack frame immediately after the caller's value of rbp ❸. Then, before executing the function epilogue, we check to see if the value of the stack canary has been changed ❺.

**NOTE** *Using a stack canary is an optional feature. In my version of gcc, it's used by default. You can override the default behavior with one of the command line options -fstack -protector, -fstack-protector-strong, or -fstack-protector-all to use a stack canary, and -fno-stack-protector not to use one.*

The code to perform this check introduces two more instructions.

### xor—Exclusive OR

Performs a bitwise exclusive OR between the source value and destination value, leaving the result in the destination.

xor *reg1*, *reg2* performs bitwise exclusive OR between the values in *reg1* and *reg2*, which can be the same or different registers. The result is left in *reg1*.

xor *reg*, *mem* performs bitwise exclusive OR between the values in *reg* and *mem*, leaving the result in *reg*.

xor *mem*, *reg* performs bitwise exclusive OR between the values in *mem* and *reg*, leaving the result in *mem*.

xor *reg*, *imm* performs bitwise exclusive OR between a value in *reg* and *imm*, leaving the result in *reg*.

xor *mem*, *imm* performs bitwise exclusive OR between a value in memory and the constant *imm*, leaving the result in memory.

The xor instruction sets the SF, ZF, and PF status flags in the rflags register according to the result. The OF and CF status flags are cleared to 0, and the value of the AF status flag is undefined.

### je—Jump if equal

Jumps if the zero flag is true, which typically shows equality of two values.

je *label* jumps to the memory location *label* if the ZF is 1 (true).

The je instruction is one of several conditional jump instructions, which will be explained in Chapter 13 when we talk about program flow constructs. The conditional jump instructions test the status flags in the rflags register and transfer program flow accordingly. The je instruction tests the zero status flag and jumps to *label* in the function if the flag is true.

In Listing 11-5, the code to check for a corrupt stack ❺ first retrieves the value that was saved on the stack, the stack canary, and then performs a bitwise exclusive OR with the original value that was generated when the program first started, at memory location fs:40. If the two values are identical, the exclusive OR results in 0, which sets the zero status flag, ZF, to 1 (true), causing the je .L3 instruction to transfer program flow to the leave instruction, thus skipping over the call to the __stack_chk_fail@PLT function. If the exclusive OR operation does not produce a 0, the jump will not occur, and the program will call the __stack_chk_fail@PLT function, which will report the stack corruption error and terminate the program.

You see another new instruction in this program, leave.

**leave—Leave function**

Deletes the stack frame.

leave restores the caller's frame pointer and places the stack pointer at the return address.

The leave instruction performs the same operations as the two instructions:

```
mov    rsp, rbp
pop    rbp
```

Referring to Figure 11-4, you can see that this moves the stack pointer to the place where the caller's rbp is stored and then pops this back into the rbp register, leaving the stack pointer at the return address.

The assembly language generated by gcc in Listing 11-5 includes some additional notation, QWORD PTR ❷❺. In most cases, the assembler can figure out the size of the operand—byte, word, double word, or quadword—from the context of the instruction. If one of the operands is a register, the register name dictates the size of the operand. But if one of the operands is a memory address and the other is a literal constant, the operand size is undeterminable. For example, in Listing 11-5, if the instruction at ❸ had been the following,

```
mov    -8[rbp], 123
```

the integer 123 could be stored in any size from one byte and larger. In this case, you need to tell the assembler the size of the data item, using the notation in Table 10-1 in Chapter 10 (replicated here as Table 11-3).

**Table 11-3:** Assembler Data Item Size Notations

| Modifier | Data type | Number of bits |
|----------|-----------|----------------|
| byte ptr | Byte | 8 |
| word ptr | Word | 16 |
| dword ptr | Doubleword | 32 |
| qword ptr | Quadword | 64 |

Thus, the instruction

```
mov    byte ptr -8[rbp], 123
```

would store 123 as an 8-bit value, while the instruction

```
mov    qword ptr -8[rbp], 123
```

would store 123 as a 64-bit value. I don't know why the compiler writer chose to use this notation in Listing 11-5 since the assembler can figure out the data item size from the names of the register being used, rax, but the redundancy isn't harmful.

Let's put this stuff together and write the echoChar program directly in assembly language. We'll use more meaningful names for the labels, let the assembler compute the length of the text strings, and comment our code, as shown in Listing 11-6.

```
# echoChar.s
# Prompts user to enter a character, then echoes the response
        .intel_syntax noprefix
# Useful constants
        .equ    STDIN,0
        .equ    STDOUT,1
# Stack frame
        .equ    aLetter,-1
        .equ    localSize,-16

# Constant data
        .section  .rodata
prompt:
        .string "Enter one character: "
        .equ    promptSz,.-prompt-1
msg:
        .string "You entered: "
        .equ    msgSz,.-msg-1
        .text
# Code
        .globl  main
        .type   main, @function
main:
        push    rbp           # save caller's frame pointer
        mov     rbp, rsp      # establish our frame pointer
        add     rsp, localSize # for local var.

        mov     rax, fs:40    # get stack canary
        mov     -8[rbp], rax  # and save it

        mov     edx, promptSz # prompt size
        lea     rsi, prompt[rip] # address of prompt text string
        mov     edi, STDOUT   # standard out
        call    write@plt     # invoke write function

        mov     edx, 1        # 1 character
        lea     rsi, ❶aLetter[rbp] # place to store character
        mov     edi, STDOUT   # standard out
        call    write@plt     # invoke write function
```

```
        mov     edx, 1          # 1 character
        lea     rsi, aLetter[rbp] # place to store character
        mov     edi, STDIN      # standard in
        call    read@plt        # invoke read function

        mov     edx, msgSz      # message size
        lea     rsi, msg[rip]   # address of message text string
        mov     edi, STDOUT     # standard out
        call    write@plt       # invoke write function

        mov     edx, 1          # 1 character
        lea     rsi, aLetter[rbp] # place where character stored
        mov     edi, STDOUT     # standard out
        call    write@plt       # invoke write function

        mov     eax, 0          # return 0

        mov     rcx, -8[rbp]    # retrieve saved canary
        xor     rcx, fs:40      # and check it
        je      goodCanary
        call    __stack_chk_fail@PLT    # bad canary
goodCanary:
    ❷ mov     rsp, rbp        # delete local variables
        pop     rbp             # restore caller's frame pointer
        ret                     # back to calling function
```

*Listing 11-6: Program to echo a single character, written directly in assembly language*

When reading the code in Listing 11-6, I think you'll find that giving names to the offsets for variables in the stack frame makes the code much easier to read ❶. I also explicitly undo the stack frame instead of using the leave instruction to emphasize what is taking place ❷.

In subsequent chapters, you'll learn how to use the stack frame for larger and more complex variables. You'll also learn how to use the stack for passing arguments beyond the six that can be passed in registers.

## Not Using the C Runtime Environment

The main purpose of this book is to show what is going on at the instruction set level when writing in higher-level languages, so we'll continue using the C (and later the C++) runtime environment and the POSIX write and read system call functions for the remainder of this book.

Of course, it's possible to write stand-alone programs that do not use the C runtime environment. You'll see how this is done in Chapter 20.

1.  Enter the program in Listing 11-6 and get it to work. Why do you get the extra system prompt when the program ends? Here's an example:

```
$ ./echoChar
Enter one character: a
You entered: a$
$
```

2.  Modify the program to eliminate the extra system prompt. Here's an example:

```
$ ./echoChar
Enter one character: a
You entered: a
$
```

Did your modification cause an error? If so, what do you need to do to fix it?

3.  The following subfunction stores a text string at a memory address passed to it and returns the number of characters stored there:

```c
/* theMessage.c
 * Stores "Hello" for caller and returns
 * number of characters stored.
 */

int theMessage(char *aMessage)
{

    int nChars = 0;
    char *messagePtr = "Hello.\n";

    while (*messagePtr != 0)
    {
      *aMessage = *messagePtr;
      nChars++;
      messagePtr++;
      aMessage++;
    }

    return nChars;
}
```

Write a main function in assembly language that calls this subfunction and displays the text string that was stored. Use a stack canary. Change the message in the subfunction to Greetings.\n. What happens?

## What You've Learned

**write and read functions**   System call functions that bypass the C standard library.

**Passing arguments to a subfunction**   Up to six arguments are passed in registers.

**Position-independent executable**   The operating system can load the program any place in memory, and it will execute correctly.

**Call stack**   An area of memory used for storing program data and addresses that grows and shrinks as needed.

**Function prologue**   Sets up the call stack for the transition from the calling function to the called function.

**Function epilogue**   The complement to the function prologue that restores the call stack to the state it was in when the function was called.

**Automatic variables**   Created anew each time the function is called. They can be easily created on the call stack.

**Stack canary**   A random number is placed at the beginning of the stack area for the current function that can show when important information on the call stack was changed.

In the next chapter, we'll step back from writing programs and look at the translation into machine code performed by the assembler program.

# 12

## INSTRUCTION DETAILS

In Chapters 2 and 3 you learned how bit patterns can be used to represent data, and in Chapters 4–8 you learned how bits can be implemented in hardware and used to perform computations. In this chapter, we'll look at a few details of how instructions are encoded in bit patterns that perform the computations and specify the locations of the data they operate on.

The primary goal of this chapter is to give an overall view of how computer instructions know where the data they operate on is located. The details of machine code for each instruction are not the sort of thing that people memorize. You'll need to consult the manuals for the details. The details have helped me to debug my programs in some cases.

Another reason for learning about how instructions are encoded is that the information is included in the manual's description of each instruction. Having some knowledge about instruction encoding can help you to read the manuals.

We'll examine two of the most common operations in most programs: moving data and branching. We'll look at how the CPU locates the operands of an instruction, what data or addresses it operates on, and how the CPU knows where to branch to when it executes a branching instruction.

## Looking at Machine Code

We can look at the machine code, the 0s and 1s that make up a program, by producing an *assembly listing*, which shows the machine code corresponding to each instruction. We can produce assembly listings by passing the -al options to the assembler. This causes the listing to be written to standard out, which defaults to the screen. We can capture this with the redirection operator. For example, I used this:

```
$ as –gstabs -al -o adressing.o addressing.s > addressing.lst
```

to produce the file shown in Listing 12-1.

```
GAS LISTING register.s                      page 1


   1                  # register.s
   2                  # Some instructions to illustrate machine code.
   3                          .intel_syntax noprefix
   4                          .text
   5                          .globl  main
   6                          .type   main, @function
   7             main:
   8 0000 ❶55          push    rbp         # save caller's frame pointer
   9 0001 4889E5        mov     rbp, rsp    # establish our frame pointer
  10
  11 0004 ❷89C8         mov     eax, ecx    # 32 bits, low reg codes
  12 0006 ❸89F7         mov     edi, esi    # highest reg codes
  13 0008 ❹6689C8       mov     ax, cx      # 16 bits
  14 000b ❺88C8         mov     al, cl      # 8 bits
  15 000d ❻4489C7       mov     edi, r8d    # 32 bits, 64-bit register
  16 0010 ❼4889C8       mov     rax, rcx    # 64 bits
  17
  18 0013 B8000000      mov     eax, 0      # return 0 to os
  18      00
  19 0018 4889EC        mov     rsp, rbp    # restore stack pointer
  20 001b ❽5D           pop     rbp         # restore caller's frame pointer
  21 001c ❾C3           ret                 # back to caller
```

*Listing 12-1: Machine code for some sample instructions*

This program doesn't do anything. It's just a collection of instructions that we'll use to illustrate how instructions are encoded in machine language. I've included a prologue and epilogue so you can assemble and link the program and run it under gdb if you want to see what each instruction does (which you're asked to do when it's Your Turn).

The first column in the assembly listing is the line number in decimal. The next column shows the address, in hexadecimal, of each instruction relative to the beginning of the function. The third column shows the machine code, also in hexadecimal. The remaining part of this listing is the assembly language source code. Since the listing file includes line numbers, we'll refer to them when discussing how the instructions are coded in machine code.

## Instruction Bytes

Both the operation and its operands need to be coded in binary. The number of bytes needed for this encoding dictates the number of possible operation/operand combinations in the computer's instruction set. In the x86-64 architecture, the number of bytes varies, while some other architectures use the same number of bytes for each instruction. We'll consider only x86-64 instructions in this book.

The location of each operand needs to be specified in the machine code for the instruction. An operand could be located in a register, in memory, or in an I/O port. Programming I/O ports is more complicated, so we'll leave that for Chapter 19. The way we specify the location of an operand is called the *addressing mode*. We'll look at several addressing modes and how they're encoded in the instruction.

To give some context to how an x86-64 instruction is encoded, Figure 12-1 shows the general layout of the bytes in an instruction. We'll look at the meaning of each byte afterward.

| Prefix | Opcode | ModR/M | SIB | Offset | Immediate |

*Figure 12-1: General arrangement of an x86-64 machine instruction*

At least one byte is needed for each instruction to specify the operation, usually called the *opcode*. There can be one, two, or three bytes in the opcode.

In the simplest addressing mode, the operand is located in a register. Some instruction opcodes leave enough extra bits in the opcode byte to include the code for a register, but most require an additional byte for this. When an operand is located in memory, the addressing is more complex. These more complex addressing modes necessitate additional bytes in the instruction, shown by the dashed lines in Figure 12-1.

Before getting to operands in memory, let's look at the case when they're located in registers. We'll use the instructions in Listing 12-1 to show how the CPU knows which register(s) to use.

### Opcode Bytes

The ret instruction on line 21 of Listing 12-1 does not explicitly have any operands, but it has two implicit ones—the rsp and rip registers. Since it always affects only these two registers, the instruction doesn't need to specify them and can be encoded in only one opcode byte ❾.

The push and pop instructions on lines 8 and 20 specify a register, rbp, as their operand. The opcode for push is 01010*rrr* ❶, and for pop it's 01011*rrr* ❽, where the three bits *rrr* are used to encode the register. There are only three bits in this single byte available for encoding the register, which limits us to the eight registers rax to rdi. The number of bytes to push or pop is determined by how the operating system sets up the call stack when a program is first loaded into memory. We're working in a 64-bit environment, so these instructions operate on 64-bit values. If we use either of these instructions with one of the registers r8 to r15, the assembler adds a prefix byte that contains the fourth bit, which I'll explain in "REX Prefix Byte" on page 250.

Next, we'll look at the instruction on line 11, which moves the 32-bit value in ecx to eax. The opcode is 0x89 ❷. The mov instruction can move data from register to register, from memory to register, and from register to memory. There are too many permutations to code up in a single byte, so the assembler adds a ModR/M byte to the instruction.

## ModR/M Byte

The *ModR/M* byte is used to extend the possible combinations of operator and operands. Figure 12-2 shows the format of the ModR/M byte.

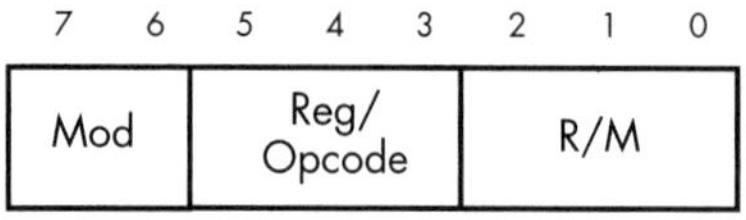

Figure 12-2: ModR/M byte

The two Mod bits specify one of four possible addressing modes. The Reg/Opcode bits specify a register or additional bits of the opcode. The R/M bits specify a register that is used by the instruction in different ways, depending on the addressing mode specified in the Mod bits.

I won't give all the possible cases for the ModR/M byte in this book, since that information is available in the manuals. We'll look at how they're coded in several instructions, which should help you to figure out how to read the manuals.

Tables 12-1 and 12-2 give the codes that are used for the registers in any part of an instruction. Table 12-1 shows the codes used to specify 8-, 16-, and 32-bit portions of the first eight registers, rax–rdi.

**Table 12-1:** 8-, 16-, and 32-Bit Register Codes

| 8-bit register | 16-bit register | 32-bit register | Code |
| --- | --- | --- | --- |
| al | ax | eax | 000 |
| cl | cx | ecx | 001 |
| dl | dx | edx | 010 |
| bl | bx | ebx | 011 |
| ah | sp | esp | 100 |

| 8-bit register | 16-bit register | 32-bit register | Code |
|---|---|---|---|
| ch | bp | ebp | 101 |
| dh | si | esi | 110 |
| bh | di | edi | 111 |

You may wonder how the CPU can distinguish between the three sizes of a registers with the same code. The default operand size is 32 bits. If you use a 16-bit register, the assembler inserts the 0x66 prefix byte before the opcode, which overrides the default and causes that instruction to use 16-bit operands. The distinction between 8-bit and 32-bit operations is made by using different opcodes.

Table 12-2 shows the register codes for the full set of 64-bit registers. As you'll see next section, most 64-bit operations are accomplished by adding a REX prefix byte before the opcode.

**Table 12-2:** 64-Bit Register Codes

| Register | Code | Register | Code |
|---|---|---|---|
| rax | 0000 | r8 | 1000 |
| rcx | 0001 | r9 | 1001 |
| rdx | 0010 | r10 | 1010 |
| rbx | 0011 | r11 | 1011 |
| rsp | 0100 | r12 | 1100 |
| rbp | 0101 | r13 | 1101 |
| rsi | 0110 | r14 | 1110 |
| rdi | 0111 | r15 | 1111 |

The first thing you probably notice about the register codes in Table 12-2 is that they are four bits, but the ModR/M byte allows only three bits for the codes. If the instruction uses only the 32-bit portions of the first eight registers, eax to edi, the high-order bit is 0 and not needed. The remaining three bits fit within the ModR/M byte. You'll see in a moment where the fourth bit is located when an instruction uses any portion of the r8–r15 registers or the full 64 bits of any of the 16 registers, rax–r15.

The instruction on line 12 of Listing 12-1 is another example of using only 32-bit registers. It has the same opcode, 0x89 ❸, as the instruction on line 11 ❷, but they operate on different general-purpose registers. The registers are specified in the ModR/M byte: 11 001 000 for moving from ecx to eax, and 11 110 111 for moving from esi to edi. I inserted spaces in the bit patterns here so you can see the three fields corresponding to Figure 12-2 in each byte. The Mod field, 11, specifies the register-to-register mode for the move. Consulting Table 12-1, we can see that the three bits in the Reg/Opcode field of line 12, 110, specify the source register, esi, and the three bits in the R/M field, 111, specify the destination register, edi.

The instruction on line 13 moves only 16 bits from cx to ax. Instead of using a different opcode, this variance from the 32-bit move is indicated with the prefix byte 0x66 ❹. On line 14, we're moving only 8 bits from cl to al, which uses a different opcode, 0x88 ❺.

Line 15 shows a 32-bit move, but this time we're using one of the registers, r8d, that was added when upgrading from a 32-bit to a 64-bit CPU design. Now we need four bits to specify the r8 register, which requires the assembler to modify the instruction with a REX prefix ❻.

### REX Prefix Byte

A *REX prefix* byte is required for most instructions that involve a 64-bit operand or one of the registers r8 to r15. Figure 12-3 shows the format of the REX prefix.

| 7 | 6 | 5 | 4 | 3 | 2 | 1 | 0 |
|---|---|---|---|---|---|---|---|
| 0 | 1 | 0 | 0 | W | R | X | B |

*Figure 12-3: REX prefix format*

The REX prefix byte starts with the high-order four bits 0100. The W bit is set to 1 for a 64-bit operand or 0 for any other size. If the instruction uses any of the 64-bit registers r8 to r15, the high-order bit for each register (see Table 12-2) is stored in the R, X, or B bits, depending on how the register is used in the instruction. (The remaining three bits are stored in the ModR/M byte, as described earlier.)

We can see the use of the W bit by comparing the instructions on lines 11 ❷ and 16 ❼. They both move from the rcx register to the rax register, but the instruction on line 11 moves 32 bits, while the one on line 16 moves 64 bits. The only difference between the instructions is the addition of the REX prefix byte, 01001000 (W = 1), to the 64-bit instruction ❼.

The instruction on line 15 moves only 32 bits, but the source is one of the registers added for the 64-bit upgrade from the 32-bit CPU. So, the assembler adds the REX prefix, 01000100 ❻. The W bit is 0, indicating a 32-bit move, but the R bit is 1. When executing this instruction, the CPU uses this 1 as the high-order bit of the source register field in the ModR/M byte, 11 000 111, to give 1000, or r8 (see Table 12-2). Since W = 0, the instruction moves only 32 bits.

So far, we've considered only instruction addressing modes used to move a value from one CPU register to another. Of course, there needs to be a way to move a value into a register in the first place. We'll next look at an addressing mode that can be used to move a constant value into a register or memory.

## Immediate Addressing Mode

A single data item up to 64 bits can be stored as part of the instruction. The instruction accesses it using the *immediate addressing* mode (*immediate* because the data item is located at the address immediately after the operation part of the instruction). The data value can be moved into a register or into a memory location. We'll look only at moving into a register here. Listing 12-2 provides some examples of using the immediate addressing mode for storing constants in registers.

GAS LISTING immediate.s                          page 1

```
 1                      # immediate.s
 2                      # Some instructions to illustrate machine code.
 3                              .intel_syntax noprefix
 4                              .text
 5                              .globl  main
 6                              .type   main, @function
 7              main:
 8 0000 55              push    rbp            # save caller's frame pointer
 9 0001 4889E5          mov     rbp, rsp       # establish our frame pointer
10
11 0004 ❶B0AB           mov     al, 0xab       # 8-bit immediate
12 0006 ❷66B8CDAB       mov     ax, 0xabcd     # 16-bit immediate
13 000a ❸B812EFCD       mov     eax, 0xabcdef12  # 32-bit immediate
13      AB
14 000f ❹48B812EF       mov     rax, 0xabcdef12  # to 64-bit reg
14      CDAB0000
14      0000
15 0019 ❺48B88967       mov     rax, 0xabcdef0123456789  # 64-bit immed.
15      452301EF
15      CDAB
16
17 0023 ❻B8000000       mov     eax, 0          # return 0 to os
17      00
18 0028 4889EC          mov     rsp, rbp        # restore stack pointer
19 002b 5D              pop     rbp             # and frame pointer
20 002c C3              ret                     # back to caller
```

*Listing 12-2: Examples of immediate data*

The two opcodes for moving immediate data into a register are 11010*rrr* and 11011*rrr*, where *rrr* is the register number (see Table 12-1). The data itself is stored immediately after the opcode, thus forming part of the instruction. The instruction on line 11 in Listing 12-2 shows an example of moving the value 0xab into the al register ❶. The opcode, 0xb0, includes the coding of the eax register, 000. The byte immediately following the opcode is the data, 0xab, which is stored at the end of the instruction, as shown in Figure 12-1.

Line 13 shows the instruction to move a 32-bit value ❸. It uses the opcode 10111*rrr*, where *rrr* = 000, the same as the 8-bit instruction on line 11. Notice that the constant value, 0xabcdef12, is stored in little-endian format. When reading assembly language listings, it's important to remember that the instruction itself is stored by byte, but any constant data is stored in little-endian format.

Next, let's look at the instruction on line 12. It uses the same opcode as the 32-bit instruction on line 13, but the 0x66 prefix byte tells the CPU to use the other operand size, 16 bits, instead of the default size of 32 bits ❷.

Moving on to line 14, we can see that the assembler inserted a REX prefix, 01001000, with W = 1 to indicate that this is a 64-bit move ❹. The constant value, 0xabcdef12, written in assembly language is only 32 bits, but the assembler filled in the leading zeros to make it a full 64 bits for storage as part of the machine code. The assembly language instruction on line 15 specifies a full 64-bit constant, which can be seen in the machine code ❺.

Now you're able to read the machine code for the instruction on line 17 ❻, mov eax, 0, which we've been using from the beginning of writing assembly language to set the return value from main. Notice that the assembler codes the constant, 0, in 32 bits. Compare this instruction, 0xb800000000, with the instruction on line 13, 0xb812efcdab. They both move a 32-bit constant, which is stored immediately after the opcode, 0xb8, into the eax register.

We can now move on to the addressing modes that direct the CPU to access values stored elsewhere in memory.

## Memory Addressing Modes

Almost any useful program needs to use memory for storing data. In this section, we'll look at the machine code of the addressing modes used to determine a memory address. We'll look only at instructions that read from memory, but the same addressing modes work for writing to memory (which you are asked to do when it's Your Turn).

The x86-64 architecture allows only one of the operands, either the source or the destination, to be a memory location. The simplest case is to move directly to or from memory.

### Direct Memory Addressing

In assembly language, we could label the memory location and simply use that label as an operand to a mov instruction. For example, if my program included a memory location labeled x, the following instruction would store the 32 bits located at location x in the rax register:

```
mov     eax, x
```

The assembler translates this into the machine code, where I have used spaces to separate the different parts of the instruction:

```
8B 04 25 00000000
```

The 0x8b opcode tells the CPU to move a 32-bit value from memory into a register. This is followed by the ModR/M byte, 00 000 100. The Reg/Opcode bits are 000, which designates the eax register. The Mod bits are 00, and the R/M bits are 100, which is a special case telling the CPU to look at the SIB byte (see Figure 12-1) for further details. The format of the SIB byte will be described in a moment, but the 0x25 value in the SIB byte does not follow the usual format. It's another special case telling the CPU that the address of the data is the 32-bit value immediately following this instruction, which is 0x00000000.

This 0x00000000 is simply a placeholder put there by the assembler. The assembler also makes a note in the object file of the location of this placeholder and the name of the memory location it refers to. It's the job of the linker to find this label, determine its address, and insert this address into the placeholder location in the final executable file. In the 64-bit mode, when the CPU executes the instruction, it extends this 32-bit address with leading zeros to be 64 bits.

Since the linker fills in an address here, this instruction is not position-independent code. To make it position independent, we would need to use x relative to the instruction pointer:

```
        mov     eax, x[rip]
```

We'll be using position-independent code throughout this book, so all our memory reads and writes will use a *register indirect* addressing mode, using either the rip or another register as our reference address.

### Register Indirect with Offset

When the CPU is executing an instruction that references memory based on a register, it starts by computing the *effective address.* You've already seen this with the lea instruction, which simply loads the effective address into a register. The mov instruction goes a step further and moves the data stored at the effective address into a register. If the memory address is the destination operand, then the mov instruction stores the data in the register at the effective address.

The simplest indirect addressing mode is just using an address in a register. For example, in the instruction on line 13 of Listing 12-3, the effective address is the address in the rbp register ❷. This instruction moves the four bytes from that memory location into the eax register.

GAS LISTING memory.s                        page 1

```
 1                      # memory.s
 2                      # Some instructions to illustrate machine code.
 3                              .intel_syntax noprefix
 4                              .text
 5                              .globl  main
 6                              .type   main, @function
 7                      main:
 8 0000 55                      push    rbp             # save caller's frame pointer
 9 0001 4889E5                   mov     rbp, rsp        # establish our frame pointer
10 0004 4883EC30                 sub     rsp, 48         # local variables
11
12 0008 48C7C105                 mov     rcx, 5          # for indexing
12      000000
```

```
13 000f ❶8B4500        mov     eax, ❷[rbp]            # indirect
14 0012 ❸8B45D0        mov     eax, ❹-48[rbp]         # indirect + offset
15 0015 8B440DD0       mov     eax, -48[rbp+❺rcx]     # indirect + offset and index
16 0019 8B448DD0       mov     eax, -48[rbp+❻4*rcx]   # and scaled index
17
18 001d B8000000       mov     eax, 0     # return 0 to os
18      00
19 0022 4889EC         mov     rsp, rbp   # restore stack pointer
20 0025 5D             pop     rbp        # and frame pointer
21 0026 C3             ret                # back to caller
```

*Listing 12-3: Register indirect memory addressing*

The next instruction, on line 14, computes the effective address by adding an offset, -48, to the address in the rbp register ❹. The CPU does this computation internally and does not change the contents of rbp. For example, if rbp contained 0x00007fffffffdf60, the effective address would be 0x00007fffffffdf60 + 0xffffffffffffffd0 = 0x00007fffffffdf30. The instruction would move the four bytes at 0x00007fffffffdf30 into eax.

Let's compare the machine code for the instructions on lines 13 and 14:

```
000f 8B4500
0012 8B45D0
```

They both use the opcode 0x8b, which tells the CPU to compute an effective address and move 32 bits from that address to the eax register. They both use the same ModR/M byte, 01 000 101 (45 in hexadecimal). The 01 in the Mod field tells the CPU to compute an effective address by adding an 8-bit offset to the value in the base register. The offset value is in two's complement and can be negative ❸. The CPU extends the 8 bits to 64 bits, preserving the sign by copying the highest-order bit of the 8-bit value into the 56 higher-order bits of the 64-bit value (called *sign extension*), before adding it to the value in the base register. The offset byte is stored at the offset field of the instruction, before any immediate data, as shown in Figure 12-1.

Rather than creating a separate opcode for mov without offset (line 13), the CPU designers chose to simply set the offset to 0 ❶. The base register for this operation is coded in the R/M field—101 in these instructions. The default address size is 64 bits in the x86-64 architecture, so the CPU uses the entire rbp register, and there is no need for a REX prefix byte here.

If this is starting to look complicated to you, don't panic. As you saw in Chapter 11, you'll use the .equ assembler directive to provide meaningful names for these offsets. Then this instruction would look something like this:

```
        mov     eax, numberOfItems[rbp]
```

The assembler will substitute the value of numberOfItems for you, and the CPU will do the arithmetic.

### Register Indirect with Indexing

On line 15, we've added in the *indexing register,* rcx ❺. The effective address is the sum of the values in rcx and rbp plus -48. This addressing mode is useful for working through an array one byte at a time. Notice that both the indexing and base registers must be the same size even though the value in the register you use for indexing would fit into a smaller portion of the register. Thus, on line 15, we've stored a 64-bit value in rcx to ensure that the high-order bits are 0, even though the value would fit within 8 bits. The CPU will add the full 64 bits of the index register to the base register when computing the effective address.

The ModR/M byte of this instruction is 01 000 100. The 01 in the Mod field indicates an 8-bit offset, and the 000 in the Reg/Opcode field specifies that the destination register is eax. The 100 in the R/M field is the number for the stack pointer register, which would never be used for this type of operation. So the CPU designers chose to use this code to indicate that another special byte, the SIB byte, is needed for encoding the rest of this instruction.

### SIB Byte

Figure 12-4 shows the format of the SIB byte.

*Figure 12-4: Format of the SIB byte*

The SIB byte has fields for the Scale, Index register, and Base register. The Scale can be 1, 2, 4, or 8.

The SIB byte in the instruction on line 15 is 00 001 101, which indicates a scale of 1, rcx as the index register, and rbp as the base register. As mentioned, the CPU assumes 64-bit addressing, so three bits are sufficient for encoding the first eight registers, rax to rdi. If we were to use any of r8 to r15, the assembler would need to prefix this instruction with a REX prefix byte so it could use four bits to encode these registers.

Often, the size of the data items in an array is larger than one byte. The instruction on line 16 shows that the value in the index register can be scaled ❻. In this example code, increasing the index value by 1 adds 4 to the effective address. The SIB byte is 10 001 101, showing the same base and index registers but a scale factor of 4.

So far, we've been looking at moving data. Moving data is probably the most common operation in a program. The next most common operation is probably jumping from one place in the program to another.

# Jump Instructions

Nearly every program has multiple branches in its flow of execution. Almost all the jumps are conditional, based on some settings in the status flag. In this section, we'll look at how the jump instruction is coded so that program flow goes to the right location when the jump is taken.

There are some 30 conditional jump instructions that can do either a *short jump* or a *near jump*. The short jump is limited to a distance that can be represented as an 8-bit signed integer (–128 – +127 bytes), whereas a near jump uses a 16-bit or 32-bit signed integer. Most programs are written such that short jumps are sufficient.

A *long jump* (greater than –2,147,483,648 – +2,147,483,647 bytes) requires the use of the jmp (unconditional jump) instruction. We can do this using a conditional jump to jump over the unconditional jump. It's basically a double-negative construct. For example, to do a long jump based on the equal condition, you could use the jne instruction like this:

```
       jne    skip    # skip the jump if equal
       jmp    FarAway # not not equal, so jump
skip:  next instruction
```

We'll look only at the short conditional jump here, whose instruction format is shown in Figure 12-5.

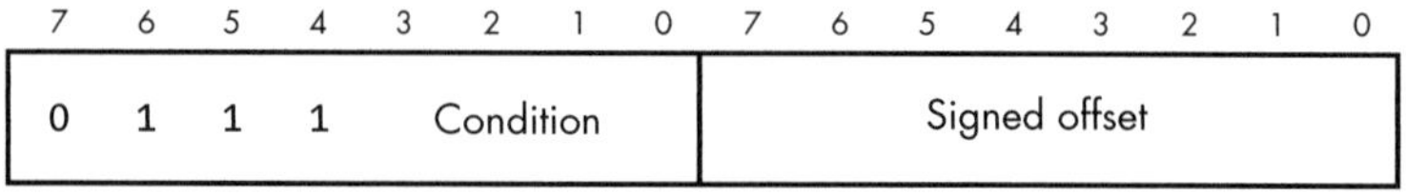

*Figure 12-5: Format of short conditional jump instruction*

The four condition bits in Figure 12-5 direct the CPU to check various combinations of the status flags in the status register. The assembler uses mnemonics for the conditions that suggest what you want to do. The conditional jump instruction should follow immediately after the operation that causes the conditions you want to check, because an intermediate instruction might change the conditions of the status flags.

Listing 12-4 is an example of two short conditional jump instructions that jump based on the results of an xor instruction.

```
GAS LISTING jumps.s                           page 1


   1              # jumps.s
   2              # Some instructions to illustrate machine code.
   3                      .intel_syntax noprefix
   4                      .text
   5                      .globl  main
   6                      .type   main, @function
```

```
 7                       main:
 8 0000 55                       push     rbp             # save caller's frame pointer
 9 0001 4889E5                   mov      rbp, rsp        # establish our frame pointer
10
11 0004 4831D8                   xor      rax, rbx        # sets status flags
12 0007 ❶7506                    jne      ❷forward        # test ZF
13                       back:
14 0009 4D89C8                   mov      r8, r9          # stuff to jump over
15 000c 4889CB                   mov      rbx, rcx
16                       forward:
17 000f 4831D8                   xor      rax, rbx        # sets status flags
18 0012 ❸74F5                    je       back            # test ZF
19
20 0014 B8000000                 mov      eax, 0          # return 0 to os
20      00
21 0019 4889EC                   mov      rsp, rbp        # restore stack pointer
22 001c 5D                       pop      rbp             # and frame pointer
23 001d C3                       ret                      # back to caller
```

*Listing 12-4: Machine code for short jump instructions*

The instruction on line 12 should be read, "Jump to forward if the values in rax and rbx are not equal." The jne instruction checks the ZF in the status register. The results of the xor instruction will be 0 only if the two values in rax and rbx are equal, which would produce ZF = 1 (true). The jne instruction takes the jump when ZF = 0 (false).

The assembler also provides a jnz mnemonic for the same machine instruction. Looking at Figure 12-5, you can see that there are only 16 (four bits) possible conditions that can be tested by a short jump, but there are more than 30 such assembly language instructions. There's usually more than one assembler mnemonic for each conditional jump instruction. You should use the mnemonic that most clearly conveys your intent in the algorithm. We'll discuss the conditional jump instructions when we look at controlling program flow in Chapter 13.

Returning to line 12, the offset byte contains 0x06 ❶. When this instruction is being executed, the instruction pointer has already been incremented to have the address of the next instruction, 0x0009, relative to the beginning of this function. If ZF = 0, this instruction simply adds the offset to the current value in the instruction pointer, giving 0x000f relative to the beginning of this function. If ZF = 1, program execution continues with the instruction at 0x0009 relative to the beginning of this function.

Next, we'll look at the je instruction on line 18. It takes the jump (adds the offset value to the instruction pointer) when ZF = 1 (true). Note that the value of the offset, 0xf5, is a negative number ❸. The CPU sign-extends the offset to 64 bits before adding it to the 64-bit address in the instruction pointer. The result is that it subtracts 0x0b from the instruction pointer, giving 0x0014 − 0x000b = 0x0009 relative to the beginning of this function.

This discussion should give you a brief idea of how these conditional jump instructions work. You will see much more about them, including a list of the commonly used ones, when we talk about some program flow constructs in Chapter 13. But before we move on to more programming, we'll take a quick look at how assembler and linker programs work.

# Assemblers and Linkers

Now that you have an idea of what machine code looks like, let's look at how an assembler program translates assembly language into machine code. The general algorithm is similar for linking functions together, so we'll also look at that. The presentation here is just an overview. It ignores most of the details. My intent is to give you only a rough idea of how an assembler translates the source code into machine language and how a linker connects the different modules that make up an entire program.

## The Assembler

The assembler needs to translate the assembly language into machine code. Since there is a one-to-one correspondence between the two, the simplest approach would be to go through the assembly language source one line at a time, translating that line. This would work fine, except for situations like line 12 in Listing 12-4. This instruction, jne forward ❷, refers to a label that the assembler has not yet encountered. The assembler would have no idea of what the offset is from this instruction to the forward label. As you saw in Figure 12-5, the offset is part of the instruction.

One solution to this problem is to use a *two-pass assembler*. The assembler creates a *local symbol table* associating each symbol with a numerical value during the first pass. Those symbols defined with an .equ directive are entered directly on the table. For the labeled locations in the code, the assembler needs to determine the location of each label relative to the beginning of the module being assembled and then enter that value and the label to the table. A separate local symbol table is created for each .text and .data segment in the file. Algorithm 12-1 gives an overview of creating a local symbol table.

```
Let LocationCounter = 0
do
    Read a line of source code
    if (.equ directive)
        LocalSymbolTable.Symbol = symbol
        LocalSymbolTable.Value = expression value
    else if (line has a label)
        LocalSymbolTable.Symbol = label
        LocalSymbolTable.Value = LocationCounter
    Determine NumberOfBytes required by line when assembled
    LocationCounter = LocationCounter + NumberOfBytes
while(more lines of source code)
```

*Algorithm 12-1: First pass of a two-pass assembler*

Once the local symbol table is created, the assembler does a second pass through the source code file. It uses a built-in *opcode table* to determine the machine code, and when a symbol is used in an instruction, it looks up the value of the symbol on the local symbol table. If it does not find the symbol in the local symbol table, it leaves space in the instruction for a number and records the symbol and its location in the object file. Algorithm 12-2 shows this process.

```
Let LocationCounter = 0
do
    Read a line of source code
    Find machine code from opcode table
    if (symbol is used in instruction)
        if (symbol found in LocalSymbolTable)
            get value of symbol
        else
            Let value = 0
            Write symbol and LocationCounter to object file
        Add symbol value to instruction
    Write assembled instruction to object file
    Determine NumberOfBytes used by the assembled instruction
    LocationCounter = LocationCounter + NumberOfBytes
while(more lines of source code)
```

*Algorithm 12-2: Second pass of a two-pass assembler*

Algorithm 12-1 and Algorithm 12-2 are highly simplified. They ignore many details but are intended to show you the general idea of how an assembler works. As an alternative, we could create a *one-pass assembler*. It would need to maintain a list of the location of each forward reference and, then when the label is found, use the table to go back and fill in the appropriate value.

This has been a brief overview of the assembly process. Chapter 7 in *Structured Computer Organization*, Sixth Edition, by Andrew S. Tanenbaum and Todd Austin (Pearson, 2012) has a section that provides more details about the assembly process. There is a thorough discussion of the design of assembler programs in Chapter 2 in Leland Beck's *System Software: An Introduction to Systems Programming*, Third Edition (Pearson, 1997).

Most functions will contain references to .text segments defined in other files, which cannot be resolved by the assembler. The same is true of any .data segments if they're used. The job of the linker is to resolve these references.

## The Linker

A linker works in much the same way as an assembler, except the basic unit is a block of machine code instead of a line of assembly language. A typical program is made up of many object files, each of which often has more than one .text segment and may have .data segments, all of which must be linked together. As with an assembler, two passes can be used to resolve forward references.

An object file created by the assembler includes the size of each segment in the file together with a list of all the global symbols and where they are used in the segment. During the first pass, the linker reads each object file and creates a *global symbol table*, which contains the relative location of each global symbol from the beginning of the program. In the second pass, the linker creates an executable file that includes all the machine code from the object files with the relative location values from the global symbol table plugged into the locations where they are referenced.

This process will resolve all the references to symbols that are defined in the program, but it will leave references to externally defined references unresolved (for example, names of functions or variables that are defined in libraries). The linker enters these references to external names into the global offset table. If the external reference is a function call, the linker also enters this information into the procedure linkage table (you first saw these two tables in Chapter 11) along with the location in the machine code where the reference is made.

When the program runs, the operating system also loads the global offset table and the procedure linkage table for the program. During execution, if the program accesses an external variable, the operating system loads the library module where the variable is defined and enters its relative address in the global offset table. When the program calls one of the functions in the procedure linkage table, if the function has not already been loaded, the operating system loads it, inserts its address into the program's global offset table, and adjusts the corresponding entry in the procedure linkage table accordingly.

I want to emphasize that this has been a sketchy overview of how assemblers and linkers work. I've omitted the details and given only a rough overview of what is involved. If you would like to learn more about linkers, I recommend John R. Levine's *Linkers & Loaders* (1999).

## What You've Learned

**Assembler listings**   Show the machine code for each instruction.

**Nonuniform instruction length**   x86-64 instructions can be as short as one byte but can have many more bytes, depending on the instruction.

**Instruction prefix bytes**   You will often see the REX prefix byte in a 64-bit instruction.

**ModR/M byte**   Used to specify a register or addressing mode.

**SIB byte**   Used to specify the registers used to index through an array in memory.

**Immediate addressing mode**   Constant data can be stored as part of the instruction.

**Register indirect with offset addressing mode**   The memory location is specified as a fixed offset from the address in a base register.

**Register indirect with indexing addressing mode**   In addition to using an offset from a base register, a second register can be used as an index into a specific location in memory.

**Conditional jumps**   A set of jump instructions can be used to test the status codes and jump to another place in the program depending on the state of status codes.

**Assembler**   A program that translates assembly language to machine code and creates a global symbol table.

**Linker**   This program resolves cross-references between the segments in the program and creates a procedure linkage table that is used by the operating system.

In the next chapter, we'll return to programming and look at the two most common program flow constructs: repetition and two-way branching.

# 13

## CONTROL FLOW CONSTRUCTS

When writing a program in C or assembly language, we specify the order in which each statement or instruction is executed. This order is called the *control flow*. Programming by specifying the control flow is known as *imperative programming*. This is in contrast to *declarative programming*, where we state the logic of the computation and another program figures out the control flow to perform it.

If you have been using make to build your programs, as we recommended in Chapter 2, the statements in a makefile are an example of declarative programming. You specify the logic of the results, and the make program figures out the control flow to produce the results.

There are three fundamental control flow constructs: sequence, iteration, and selection. You've already seen sequence in the programs thus far: each instruction, or subfunction, is executed in the order in which it's written. In this chapter, we'll look at how to alter the control flow from the written order to iterate the same block of written instructions or to select between several blocks of written instructions. We'll look at how each of these control flow constructs is implemented at the assembly language level. (We'll look at the details of higher-level control flow actions, calling functions, in Chapter 14.)

Both iteration and selection depend on altering control flow based on a true/false condition, using a conditional jump. Since they'll be used in the rest of the chapter, we'll start by looking at the jumps, conditional and unconditional, that are available.

# Jumps

A *jump instruction* transfers control flow from one memory location to another. When implementing the iteration and selection flow constructs, we'll need to use conditional jumps and sometimes unconditional jumps.

## Unconditional Jumps

As you learned in Chapter 9, when an instruction is fetched from memory, the CPU automatically increments the instruction pointer to have the address of the next instruction in memory. The unconditional jump instruction changes the instruction pointer, which causes the CPU to continue program execution in some other location.

### jmp—Jump

Unconditionally transfers program control flow to a memory location.

jmp *label* transfers control flow to *label*.

jmp *reg* transfers control flow to the address in *reg*.

The *label* can be on any memory location within –2,147,483,648 to +2,147,483,647 bytes. The CPU sign extends the offset between the jmp instruction and *label* to 64 bits and adds this signed number to the instruction pointer, rip. The *reg* form simply copies the 64 bits in *reg* to the rip register.

The assembler's computation of the offset in the label form of the jmp instruction takes into account that the value in the rip register will point to the next instruction following the jmp during program execution. This offset is simply added to the rip to cause the transfer of control.

The jmp instruction is commonly used together with a conditional jump instruction to skip over blocks of code or to go back to the beginning of a block of code and execute it again.

## Conditional Jumps

There are two groups of conditional jump instructions. The first group works by evaluating a logical combination of some of the status flags in the rflags register. If the logical expression evaluates to true, the instruction changes the value in the instruction pointer, rip. Otherwise, the instruction pointer does not change, and control flow continues with the instruction immediately after the conditional jump instruction.

The general form for this group of conditional jump instructions is as follows:

### jcc—Jump if condition

Transfers control flow to a memory location if the condition *cc* is met.

jcc *label* transfers control flow to *label* when *cc* is true.

The jcc instruction reads the status flags in the rflags register. None of the conditional jump instructions changes the status flags. The distance from the jcc instruction, *after the CPU fetches the instruction*, to *label* must be within –2,147,483,648 to +2,147,483,647 bytes.

The second group of conditional jump instructions have the same behavior as those in the jcc group, but they are based on the content of the rcx register instead of the rflags register:

### jcxz—Jump if cx is zero

Transfers control flow to a memory location if the content of the cx register is 0.

jcxz *label* transfers control flow to *label* when the content of the cx register is 0.

### jecxz—Jump if ecx is zero

Transfers control flow to a memory location if the content of the ecx register is 0.

jecxz *label* transfers control flow to *label* when the content of the ecx register is 0.

### jrcxz—Jump if rcx is zero

Transfers control flow to a memory location if the content of the rcx register is 0.

jrcxz *label* transfers control flow to *label* when the content of the rcx register is 0.

The jcxz, jecxz, and jrcxz instructions evaluate only the respective bits in the rcx register, *not the status flags*. They jump to *label*, which must be within –128 to +127 bytes of the instruction, relative to the current value of the instruction pointer *after the CPU fetches the instruction*, if the bits are 0.

There are 16 condition combinations of the *cc* portion of the jcc instruction. Some of the conditions have more than one assembly language mnemonic, giving 30 different jcc instructions. They are listed in Table 13-1, along with the status flags that each tests.

**Table 13-1:** Conditional Jumps

| cc | Condition | Status flags | cc | Condition | Status flags |
|---|---|---|---|---|---|
| jz | Zero | ZF | je | Equal | ZF |
| jnz | Not zero | ¬ZF | jne | Not equal | ¬ZF |
| ja | Above | ¬CF ∧ ¬ZF | jg | Greater than | ¬SF ∧ ¬ZF |
| jae | Above or equal | ¬CF | jge | Greater than or equal | SF = OF |
| jna | Not above | CF ∨ ZF | jng | Not greater than | ZF ∧ SF ≠ OF |
| jnae | Not above or equal | CF | jnge | Not greater than or equal | SF ≠ OF |
| jb | Below | CF | jl | Less than | SF ≠ OF |
| jbe | Below or equal | CF ∨ ZF | jle | Less than or equal | ZF ∧ SF ≠ OF |
| jnb | Not below | ¬CF | jnl | Not less than | SF = OF |
| jnbe | Not below or equal | ¬CF ∧ ¬ZF | jnle | Not less than or equal | ¬SF ∧ ¬ZF |
| jc | Carry | CF | jo | Overflow | OF |
| jnc | No carry | ¬CF | jno | No overflow | ¬OF |
| jp | Parity | PF | js | Sign | SF |
| jnp | No parity | ¬PF | jns | No sign | ¬SF |
| jpe | Parity even | PF | jno | Parity odd | ¬PF |

I have arranged the codes in Table 13-1 in the order you are likely to use them. The codes on the left apply roughly to unsigned values, and those on the right to signed. Make special note of the difference between above and greater than, and between below and less than. *Above* and *below* refer to unsigned values, and *greater than* and *less than* refer to signed values. For example, 0xffffffff is above 0x00000001 with respect to the bit patterns. But if these bit patterns represent signed integers, then 0xffffffff = −1 and 0x00000001 = +1 and thus 0xffffffff is less than 0x00000001.

It's important to use the conditional jump instructions immediately after the instruction whose result you want to base the jump on. An intervening instruction might change the states of the status flags, thus introducing a bug into your program.

Before moving on to the flow constructs that use conditional jumps, I'll share a hint with you. When using a relational conditional jump like jg or jl, I usually forget the order of the test—source compared to destination, or destination compared to source. So when testing my program, I almost always start by using gdb and putting a breakpoint at the conditional jump instruction. When the program breaks, I check the values. Then I use the s step command to see which way the jump went.

# Iteration

Many algorithms use *iteration*, also called *looping*, which is the repeated execution of a block of instructions until the value(s) of the *loop control variable*(s) meet a *termination condition*. There are two ways to implement controlled repetition: *looping* and *recursion*. With a looping construct, the value(s) of the loop control variable(s) must be changed within the block of instructions. In recursion, the block of instructions is repeatedly invoked with differing values of the control variable(s). Recursion is implemented using a separate function, which we'll discuss in Chapter 15 when we talk about subfunctions. In this chapter, we'll look at looping constructs within a function.

**NOTE**    *Although the loop termination condition can be dependent on more than one variable, I'll use just one loop control variable to clarify the discussion.*

## *while Loop*

The while loop is a fundamental form of looping. Here is the form in C:

```
initialize loop control variable
while (expression)
{
    body
    change loop control variable
}
next_statement
```

Before entering the while loop, you need to initialize the loop control variable. At the beginning of the while loop, the *expression* is evaluated in a Boolean context. If it evaluates to false, 0 in C, control flow continues to the *next_statement*. If the *expression* evaluates to true, nonzero in C, the body is executed, the loop control variable is changed, and control flow continues at the top with the reevaluation of the *expression*. Figure 13-1 shows the flow graphically.

We used the write system call function in Chapter 11 to write a text message on the screen (Listing 11-1). In that program, we explicitly told the write function how many characters were in the text string. In this chapter, we'll see how to use looping to avoid having to determine the number of characters in the text string. We'll use the write function to write one character at a time on the screen, looping until we reach the NUL character that terminates a C-style text string.

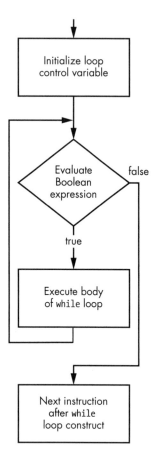

*Figure 13-1: Control flow of the* while *loop*

We'll start with a C while loop, shown in Listing 13-1.

```c
/* helloWorld.c
 * Hello World program using the write() system call
 * one character at a time.
 */
#include <unistd.h>
❶ #define NUL '\0'

int main(void)
{
❷ char *stringPtr = ❸ "Hello, World!\n";

    while ❹ (*stringPtr != NUL)
    {
    ❺ write(STDOUT_FILENO, stringPtr, 1);
    ❻ stringPtr++;
```

```
        }

    return 0;
}
```

*Listing 13-1: Writing a text string to the terminal window one character at a time*

We use the #define directive to give a symbolic name to the NUL character ❶. The stringPtr variable is defined to be a pointer to a char type ❷. As
you'll see when we look at the assembly language, the compiler will store
the text string ❸ in a read-only part of memory and store the address of the
first character in that text string in the stringPtr pointer variable.

The while statement first checks to see if the pointer variable, stringPtr,
is pointing to the NUL character ❹. If it's not the NUL character, program flow
enters the while loop body and writes the character pointed to by stringPtr
on the screen ❺. The pointer variable is then incremented to point to the
next character in the text string ❻. Program flow returns to the top of the
loop where this next character is checked to see if it's the NUL character ❹.
This loop terminates when the character pointer, stringPtr, is pointing to
the NUL character. By testing for this condition first, we wouldn't even enter
the body of the while loop if stringPtr were to point to an empty string,
because there would be nothing to do.

The compiler generated the assembly language shown in Listing 13-2
for this program.

```
            .file   "helloWorld.c"
            .intel_syntax noprefix
            .text
            .section        .rodata
    .LC0:
            .string "Hello, World!\n"
            .text
            .globl  main
            .type   main, @function
    main:
            push    rbp
            mov     rbp, rsp
            sub     rsp, 16
            lea     rax, .LC0[rip]          ## address of text string
            mov     QWORD PTR -8[rbp], rax
        ❶ jmp     .L2                     ## jump to bottom
    ❷ .L3:
            mov     rax, QWORD PTR -8[rbp]   ## address of current character
            mov     edx, 1                  ## one character
            mov     rsi, rax                ## pass address
            mov     edi, 1                  ## STDOUT_FILENO
            call    write@PLT
            add     QWORD PTR -8[rbp], 1    ## increment pointer
    .L2:
            mov     rax, QWORD PTR -8[rbp]   ## address of current character
            movzx   eax, BYTE PTR [rax]     ## load character
        ❸ test    al, al                  ## NUL character?
            jne     .L3                     ## no, continue looping
```

```
        mov     eax, 0                      ## yes, all done
        leave
        ret
        .size   main, .-main
        .ident  "GCC: (Ubuntu 9.3.0-17ubuntu1~20.04) 9.3.0"
        .section        .note.GNU-stack,"",@progbits
```

*Listing 13-2: Assembly language for the C program in Listing 13-1*

Although this assembly language seems to be testing for the termination condition at the end of the loop, it follows the logical flow shown in Figure 13-1. It jumps down to .L2 ❶ and tests for the terminating condition ❸ before jumping up to .L3 ❷ to start execution of the body of the while loop.

This code introduces two more instructions:

**movzx—Move with zero-extend**
Copies (moves) a source value from memory or a register to a wider register and zero-extends the value in the destination register.

movzx *reg, reg* moves from a register to a register.

movzx *reg, mem* moves from a memory location to a register.

An 8-bit source value can be extended to 16, 32, or 64 bits, and a 16-bit value can be extended to 32 or 64 bits. The additional high-order bits in the destination are all 0. If the extension is to 32 bits, the high-order 32-bit portion of the destination register is also all 0. Recall (from Chapter 9) that a mov of 32 bits into a register will zero the high-order 32 bits of the register, thus zero-extending 32 bits to 64 bits. The movzx instruction does not affect the status flags in the rflags register.

**test—Test bits**
Performs a bitwise AND between the source and destination operands, without changing either and sets status flags accordingly.

test *reg, reg* tests between two registers.

test *mem, reg* tests between a register and a memory location.

test *reg, imm* tests between an explicit number and a register.

test *mem, imm* tests between an explicit number and a memory location.

The test instruction sets the status flags in the rflags register to show the result of AND-ing the source and destination operands. Neither operand is changed.

In my assembly language version of this program, Listing 13-3, I've organized the code so that the conditional test is at the top of the while loop ❶.

```
# helloWorld.s
# Hello World program using the write() system call
# one character at a time.
```

```
        .intel_syntax noprefix
# Useful constants
        .equ    STDOUT,1
# Stack frame
        .equ    aString,-8
        .equ    localSize,-16
# Read only data
        .section  .rodata
theString:
        .string "Hello, World!\n"
# Code
        .text
        .globl  main
        .type   main, @function
main:
        push    rbp             # save frame pointer
        mov     rbp, rsp        # set new frame pointer
        add     rsp, localSize  # for local var.

        lea     rax, theString[rip]
        mov     aString[rbp], rax  # *aString = "Hello World.\n";
whileLoop:
        mov     rsi, aString[rbp]  # current char in string
    ❶ cmp     byte ptr [rsi], 0  # null character?
    ❷ je      allDone            # yes, all done

        mov     edx, 1          # one character
        mov     edi, STDOUT     # to standard out
        call    write@plt

    ❸ inc     qword ptr aString[rbp]  # aString++;
    ❹ jmp     whileLoop          # back to top
allDone:
        mov     eax, 0          # return 0;
        mov     rsp, rbp        # restore stack pointer
        pop     rbp             # and caller frame pointer
        ret
```

*Listing 13-3: Writing one character at a time to the screen, in assembly language*

I have also used two more new instructions, cmp ❶ and inc ❸, which are detailed next.

### cmp—Compare

Compares first operand with second operand and, without changing either, sets the status flags accordingly.

cmp *reg, reg* compares the value in a first register with the value in a second register.

cmp *mem, reg* compares the value in memory with the value in a register.

cmp *reg, imm* compares the value in a register with the explicit number.

cmp *mem, imm* compares the value in memory with the explicit number.

The `cmp` instruction sets the status flags in the `rflags` register to show the result of subtracting the first operand from the second operand. Neither operand is changed.

### inc—Increment

Adds 1 to a variable.

inc *reg* adds 1 to the value in a register.

inc *mem* adds 1 to the value in memory.

The `inc` instruction does set the status flags in the `rflags` register according to the result.

It might seem that my assembly language solution is less efficient than what the compiler generated (Listing 13-2) because the `jmp` instruction ❹ is executed in addition to the conditional `je` instruction ❷ with each iteration of the loop. Most modern CPUs use a technique known as *branch prediction*, in which they assume that a conditional jump will always go one way. We won't go into the details in this book, but the technique greatly speeds up the execution of the conditional jump instruction when the jump is not taken.

A `while` loop works well when a *sentinel value*, a unique value that marks the end of a data sequence, is used as the termination condition. For example, the `while` loop in Listing 13-1 works for any length of text string. The loop continues writing one character at a time on the screen until it reaches the sentinel value, a `NUL` character. C has another looping construct, the `for` loop, that many programmers find to be more natural in some algorithms.

## for Loop

Although their C syntax differs, the two looping constructs, `while` and `for`, are semantically equivalent. The syntactical difference is that the *for loop* allows you to group all three control elements—loop control variable initialization, checking, and changing—within the parentheses. The general form of a `for` loop is as follows:

```
for (initialize loop control variable; expression; change loop control
variable)
{
  body
}
next_statement
```

But placing all the control elements within the parentheses is not required. In fact, we could also write the `for` loop as follows:

```
initialize loop control variable
for (; expression;)
{
  body
```

```
          change loop control variable
}
next_statement
```

The for loop syntax does require both semicolons in the parentheses.

We could rewrite the program in Listing 13-1 using a for loop, as shown in Listing 13-4.

```
/* helloWorld-for.c
 * Hello World program using the write() system call
 * one character at a time.
 */
#include <unistd.h>
#define NUL '\x00'

int main(void)
{
  char *stringPtr;

  for (stringPtr = "Hello, World!\n"; *stringPtr != NUL; stringPtr++)
  {
    write(STDOUT_FILENO, stringPtr, 1);
  }

  return 0;
}
```

*Listing 13-4: Using a for loop to write a text string in the terminal window one character at a time*

You may wonder if either looping construct is better than the other. Here's where your knowledge of assembly language becomes useful. When I used gcc to generate the assembly language for Listing 13-4, I got the same assembly language code as for the while loop version in Listing 13-1. Since the assembly language for the for loop is shown in Listing 13-2, I won't repeat it here.

**NOTE**  *Since the for statement in this program controls only one C statement, you really don't need the curly brackets around that statement. But I usually include them because if I later modify the program and add another statement, I often forget that I then need the curly brackets.*

A for loop is often used for a *count-controlled loop*, in which the number of iterations is known before the loop is started. You'll see an example of this usage in a moment when we look at the selection constructs.

The conclusion we can reach from this comparison of a for loop with a while loop is that you should use the high-level language looping construct that feels natural for the problem you're solving. And, yes, this is usually a subjective choice.

The third looping construct in C does provide a different behavior. Both the while loop and for loop constructs will skip the body of the loop if the termination conditions are met by the initial value of the loop control variable. The do-while loop will always execute the loop body at least once.

## do-while Loop

In some situations, the algorithm will execute the body of the loop at least once. In these cases, the *do-while loop* may be more natural. It has this general form:

```
initialize loop control variable
do
{
  body
  change loop control variable
} while (expression)
next_statement
```

In the do-while looping construct, the value of the expression is computed at the end of executing the loop body. Looping continues until this evaluation results in a Boolean false. We can rewrite our "Hello, World!" program using a do-while loop, as shown in Listing 13-5.

```
/* helloWorld-do.c
 * Hello World program using the write() system call
 * one character at a time.
 */
#include <unistd.h>
#define NUL '\x00'

int main(void)
{
  char *stringPtr = "Hello, World!\n";

  do
  {
    write(STDOUT_FILENO, stringPtr, 1);
    stringPtr++;
  }
  while (*stringPtr != NUL);

  return 0;
}
```

*Listing 13-5: Writing one character at a time on the screen with a do-while loop*

The assembly language generated by gcc, Listing 13-6, shows the difference between the do-while and the while and for constructs.

```
                    .file    "helloWorld-do.c"
                    .intel_syntax noprefix
                    .text
                    .section  .rodata
        .LC0:
                    .string "Hello, World!\n"
                    .text
                    .globl   main
                    .type    main, @function
        main:
                    push     rbp
                    mov      rbp, rsp
                    sub      rsp, 16
                    mov      QWORD PTR -8[rbp], 0
                    lea      rax, .LC0[rip]          ## address of text string
                    mov      QWORD PTR -8[rbp], rax
   ❶ .L2:
                    mov      rax, QWORD PTR -8[rbp]  ## address of current character
                    mov      edx, 1                 ## one character
                    mov      rsi, rax               ## pass address
                    mov      edi, 1                 ## STDOUT_FILENO
                    call     write@PLT
                    add      QWORD PTR -8[rbp], 1    ## increment pointer
                    mov      rax, QWORD PTR -8[rbp]  ## address of current characte
                    movzx    eax, BYTE PTR [rax]     ## load character
              ❷ test     al, al                 ## NUL character?
                    jne      .L2                    ## no, continue looping
                    mov      eax, 0
                    leave
                    ret
                    .size    main, .-main
                    .ident   "GCC: (Ubuntu 9.3.0-17ubuntu1~20.04) 9.3.0"
                    .section  .note.GNU-stack,"",@progbits
```

*Listing 13-6: Assembly language for the do-while loop in Listing 13-5*

Comparing the assembly language in Listing 13-6 with that in
Listing 13-2 (the while and for loops), the only difference is that the do-while
doesn't jump down to perform the loop control check ❷ before executing
the loop the first time ❶. It may seem that do-while is more efficient, but
looking at the assembly language, we can see the only savings is a single
jump the first time the loop is executed.

**WARNING**     *The do-while loop construct will always execute the body of the loop at least once.
Make sure this is the correct algorithm to solve the problem. For example, the algorithm
in Listing 13-5 is incorrect for an empty text string: it would write the NUL character to
the screen and then check the byte in memory immediately following the NUL character,
which is unspecified in this program.*

Next, we'll look at how to select whether to execute a block of code.

## Selection

Another common flow construct is selection, where we determine whether to execute a block of code. We'll start with the simplest case—determining whether to execute a single block based on a Boolean conditional statement. Then we'll look at using a Boolean conditional statement to select one of two blocks. We'll end the chapter by discussing ways to select between several blocks based on an integral value.

### if Conditional

The general form of an *if conditional* in C is as follows:

```
if (expression)
{
  block
}
next_statement
```

The *expression* is evaluated in a Boolean context. If it evaluates to false, 0 in C, control flow continues to the *next_statement*. If the *expression* evaluates to true, nonzero in C, the block of code is executed, and control flow continues to the *next_statement*.

Listing 13-7 shows an example of an if statement that simulates flipping a coin 10 times and showing when it comes up heads.

```
/* coinFlips1.c
 * Flips a coin, heads.
 */

#include <stdio.h>
#include <stdlib.h>

int main()
{
  register int randomNumber;
  register int i;
```

```
❶ for (i = 0; i < 10; i++)
  {
    randomNumber = ❷ random();
    if ❸ (randomNumber < RAND_MAX/2)
    {
    ❹ puts("heads");
    }
  }

  return 0;
}
```

*Listing 13-7: Flipping a coin, showing when it comes up heads*

This program uses a count-controlled for loop to simulate flipping a
coin 10 times ❶. The simulation involves calling the random function in the
C standard library ❷. If the random number is in the lower half of all possible values from the random function ❸, we call that heads. We use the puts
function in the C standard library, which prints a simple text string on the
screen with an appended newline character ❹. The compiler generated the
assembly language shown in Listing 13-8.

```
        .file    "coinFlips1.c"
        .intel_syntax noprefix
        .text
        .section  .rodata
.LC0:
        .string "heads"
        .text
        .globl  main
        .type   main, @function
main:
        push    rbp
        mov     rbp, rsp
        push    r12
        push    rbx
        mov     ebx, 0
        jmp     .L2             ## jump to bottom of for loop
.L4:
        call    random@PLT      ## get random number
        mov     r12d, eax       ## save random number
        cmp     r12d, 1073741822 ## compare with half max
    ❶  jg      .L3             ## greater, skip block
        lea     rdi, .LC0[rip]  ## less or equal, execute block
        call    puts@PLT
❷ .L3:
        add     ebx, 1
.L2:
        cmp     ebx, 9
        jle     .L4
        mov     eax, 0
        pop     rbx
        pop     r12
        pop     rbp
        ret
```

```
        .size   main, .-main
        .ident  "GCC: (Ubuntu 9.3.0-17ubuntu1~20.04) 9.3.0"
        .section    .note.GNU-stack,"",@progbits
```

Listing 13-8: Assembly language for a simple if statement

The if statement is implemented with a simple conditional jump ❶. If the condition is true (in this case, greater than), program flow jumps over the block of code that is controlled by the if statement ❷.

We often need to select between two different blocks of code, which we'll discuss next.

### if-then-else Conditional

The general form of an *if-then-else conditional* in C is as follows (C does not use a then keyword):

```
if (expression)
{
    then-block
}
else
{
    else-block
}
next_statement
```

The *expression* is evaluated in a Boolean context. If the *expression* evaluates to true, nonzero in C, the *then-block* is executed, and control flow jumps to the *next_statement*. If it evaluates to false, 0 in C, control flow jumps to the *else-block* and then continues to the *next_statement*. Figure 13-2 shows the control flow of the if-then-else conditional.

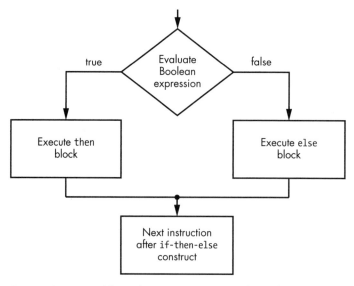

Figure 13-2: Control flow of an *if-then-else* conditional

One of the problems with the coin-flipping program in Listing 13-7 is that the user doesn't know the total number of times the coin was flipped. We can improve the program by using an if-then-else conditional to print a message stating when the coin came up tails, as shown in Listing 13-9.

```
/* coinFlips2.c
 * Flips a coin, heads or tails.
 */

#include <stdio.h>
#include <stdlib.h>

int main()
{
  register int randomNumber;
  register int i;

  for (i = 0; i < 10; i++)
  {
    randomNumber = random();
    if (randomNumber < RAND_MAX/2)
    {
      puts("heads");
    }
    else
    {
      puts("tails");
    }
  }

  return 0;
}
```

Listing 13-9: Flipping a coin, heads or tails

Listing 13-10 shows the compiler-generated assembly language.

```
        .file   "coinFlips2.c"
        .intel_syntax noprefix
        .text
        .section        .rodata
.LC0:
        .string "heads"
.LC1:
        .string "tails"
        .text
        .globl  main
        .type   main, @function
main:
        push    rbp
        mov     rbp, rsp
        push    r12
        push    rbx
        mov     ebx, 0
        jmp     .L2
```

```
.L5:
        call    random@PLT          ## get random number
        mov     r12d, eax           ## save random number
        cmp     r12d, 1073741822    ## less than half max?
        jg      .L3                 ## no, else block
        lea     rdi, .LC0[rip]      ## yes, then block
        lea     rdi, .LC0[rip]
        call    puts@PLT
    ❶ jmp     .L4
  .L3:
        lea     rdi, .LC1[rip]      ## else block
        call    puts@PLT
❷ .L4:
        add     ebx, 1
  .L2:
        cmp     ebx, 9
        jle     .L5
        mov     eax, 0
        pop     rbx
        pop     r12
        pop     rbp
        ret
        .size   main, .-main
        .ident  "GCC: (Ubuntu 9.3.0-17ubuntu1~20.04) 9.3.0"
        .section        .note.GNU-stack,"",@progbits
```

*Listing 13-10: Assembly language that implements if-else construct*

When writing in assembly language, you need an unconditional jump at the end of the *then-block* ❶ to jump over the *else-block* ❷.

My assembly language design of the coin-flipping program differs slightly, as shown in Listing 13-11.

```
# coinFlips2.s
# flips a coin, heads/tails
        .intel_syntax noprefix

# Useful constants
        .equ    MIDDLE, 1073741823  # half of RAND_MAX
        .equ    STACK_ALIGN, 8

# Constant data
        .section .rodata
headsMsg:
        .string "heads"
tailsMsg:
        .string "tails"

# The code
        .text
        .globl  main
        .type   main, @function
```

```
main:
        push    rbp                     # save frame pointer
        mov     rbp, rsp                # set new frame pointer
    ❶ push    r12                     # save, use for i
    ❷ sub     rsp, STACK_ALIGN

        mov     r12, 0                  # i = 0;
for:
        cmp     r12, 10                 # any more?
        jae     done                    # no, all done

        call    random@plt              # get a random number
        cmp     eax, MIDDLE             # which half?
        jg      tails
        lea     rdi, headsMsg[rip]      # it was heads
        call    puts@plt
        jmp     next                    # jump over else block
tails:
        lea     rdi, tailsMsg[rip]      # it was tails
        call    puts@plt
next:   inc     r12                     # i++;
        jmp     for
done:
    ❸ add     rsp, STACK_ALIGN        # realign stack ptr
    ❹ pop     r12                     # restore for caller
        mov     rsp, rbp                # restore stack pointer
        pop     rbp                     # and caller frame pointer
        ret
```

*Listing 13-11: An assembly language design for the coin-flipping program*

The primary difference between my design and what the compiler generated is that I use only the r12 register for the variable i, while the compiler used both rbx and r12. When deciding which registers to use for variables in a function, it's important that you check the rules in Table 11-1 in Chapter 11. That table says that a function must preserve the value in r12 for the calling function. A good way to do this is to push it onto the stack after setting up the stack frame ❶ and then pop it back off before undoing the stack frame ❹. You can probably see the importance of having agreed-upon rules here. Not only must our function return to the calling function with its value in r12 preserved, but we can assume that the functions our function calls also preserve our value in r12. So, it's safe to assume that the value remains the same through a function call.

One of the stack-handling rules that's easy to violate when saving registers on the stack is keeping the stack pointer on 16-byte addressing boundaries between function calls. The registers are 8 bytes wide, so I've followed this rule by subtracting 8 from the stack pointer ❷ after saving r12 by pushing it onto the stack. It's important to remember to add the same value back before popping the value of r12 off the stack ❸, thus restoring the register's value for the calling function.

I won't go into the details here, but if you need to select one of several blocks of code to execute, you can use the if-else statement in a *ladder construct*. The general form is as follows:

```
if (expression1)
{
  block1
}
else if (expression2)
{
  block2
}
⋮
else (expression_n)
{
  block_n
}
next_statement
```

The if-then-else selection is based on a Boolean evaluation of the controlling expression, but as you'll see next section, there are algorithms in which the selection is based on a discrete value, which is used to select one of several cases.

### switch Conditional

C provides a *switch conditional*, where control flow jumps to a place in a list of code blocks depending on the value of an expression. The general form of the switch is as follows:

```
switch (selector)
{
  case selector_1:
    block_1
  case selector_2:
    block_2
  ⋮
  case selector_n:
    block_n
  default:
    default_block
}
```

The *selector* variable must evaluate to an integral value. If the value equals one of the integral values specified by case—*selector_1*, *selector_2*, . . . , or *selector_n*—control flow jumps to that location in the list of code blocks, and all the remaining code blocks in the list of cases will be executed. Since we often want to execute only one block of code, it's common to use a break statement at the end of each block, which causes control flow to exit the switch statement. If the value of the *selector* does not match any case values, control flow exits the switch statement or jumps to the optional default case if it exists.

Listing 13-12 gives a simple example of using a switch to show whether the index of a for loop is 1, 2, 3, or greater than 3.

```
/* switch.c
 * Three-way selection.
 */

#include <stdio.h>

int main(void)
{
  register int selector;
  register int i;

  for (i = 1; i <= 10; i++)
  {
    selector = i;
    switch (selector)
    {
      case 1:
        puts("i = 1");
        break;
      case 2:
        puts("i = 2");
        break;
      case 3:
        puts("i = 3");
        break;
      default:
        puts("i > 3");
    }
  }

  return 0;
}
```

*Listing 13-12: Selecting one of three cases*

The compiler implemented this switch statement in assembly language as a ladder of if-else statements. I'll let you run the compiler to look at it on your own. As you might guess, it consists of code sequences like this:

```
        cmp     r12d, 2
        je      .L4
        ⋮
.L4:
        lea     rdi, .LC1[rip]
        call    puts@PLT
        jmp     .L7
```

where .L7 is a label at the end of the switch construct.

Instead, I'll show you another way to implement a switch, using a *jump table*, as shown in Listing 13-13.

```
# switch.s
# Three-way switch using jump table
        .intel_syntax noprefix
# Useful constants
        .equ    LIMIT, 10
# Constant data
        .section  .rodata
oneMsg:
        .string "i = 1"
twoMsg:
        .string "i = 2"
threeMsg:
        .string "i = 3"
overMsg:
        .string "i > 3"
# Jump table
        .align  8
jumpTable:
        .quad ❶ one         # addresses where messages are
        .quad    two        # printed
        .quad    three
        .quad    over
        .quad    over
        .quad    over
        .quad    over
        .quad    over
        .quad    over        # need an entry for
        .quad    over        # each possibility
# Program code
        .text
        .globl  main
        .type   main, @function
main:
        push    rbp         # save frame pointer
        mov     rbp, rsp    # set new frame pointer
        push    rbx
        push    r12         # save, use for i

        mov     r12, 1      # i = 1;
for:
        cmp     r12, LIMIT  # at limit?
        je      done        # yes, all done
# List of cases
      ❷ lea     rax, jumpTable[rip]
        mov     rbx, r12    # current location in loop
      ❸ sub     rbx, 1      # count from 0
      ❹ shl     rbx, 3      # multiply by 8
        add     rax, rbx    # location in jumpTable
      ❺ mov     rax, [rax]  # get address from jumpTable
        jmp     rax         # jump there
one:
        lea     rdi, oneMsg[rip]
        call    puts@plt    # display message
        jmp     endSwitch
```

```
two:
        lea     rdi, twoMsg[rip]
        call    puts@PLT
        jmp     endSwitch
three:
        lea     rdi, threeMsg[rip]
        call    puts@plt
        jmp     endSwitch
over:
        lea     rdi, overMsg[rip]
        call    puts@plt
endSwitch:
        inc     r12             # i++;
        jmp     for             # loop back
done:
        mov     eax, 0          # return 0;
        pop     r12             # restore regs
        pop     rbx
        mov     rsp, rbp        # restore stack pointer
        pop     rbp             # and caller frame pointer
        ret
```

*Listing 13-13: Jump table*

Each entry in the jump table is the address of the code block to execute for the corresponding value of the selector variable ❶. The .quad directive allocates 8 bytes, the proper space for an address.

In the program code, we need to compute which of the addresses in the jump table to use. I start by loading the beginning address of the table ❷. I make a copy of the index variable so I can perform some arithmetic operations without disrupting the index. To start, I subtract 1 because the first address on the table is zero bytes from the beginning ❸. We'll look at shift instructions in more detail in Chapter 16, but the shl rbx, 3 instruction ❹ shifts the value in the rbx register three bits to the left, thus multiplying it by 8, the number of bytes in each address on our jump table.

The rbx register now contains the relative location of the address of the selected code block from the beginning of the table. Adding rax to rbx gives the location in the table where the address we want is stored. The mov rax, [rax] instruction ❺ may look strange to you, but it simply replaces the address in rax with the address that's stored in the table. Now all I need to do is to jump to the address in the rax register.

You need to be careful that there is an entry in the jump table for every possible read from the table. When the CPU executes the mov rax, [rax] instruction, it will fetch the 8 bytes located at whatever address is in rax. The jmp rax instruction will jump to wherever this new value is. You'll get a chance to explore this when it's Your Turn.

It's difficult to say whether a jump table is more efficient than an if-else ladder. The efficiency depends on several factors, like cache usage and the internal CPU design. This could vary among different CPU implementations that use the same instruction set. But now you know two ways to implement a switch construct.

## What You've Learned

**Unconditional jump**   Changes the instruction pointer to alter control flow.

**Conditional jump**   Evaluates Boolean combinations of the status flags in the rflags register and alter control flow if the combination evaluates to true.

**while loop**   Checks for a Boolean condition and then iterates a block of code until the condition becomes false.

**for loop**   Checks for a Boolean condition and then iterates a block of code until the condition becomes false.

**do-while loop**   Executes a block of code once and iterates it until a Boolean condition becomes false.

**if conditional**   Checks for a Boolean condition and then executes a block of code if the condition is true.

**if-else conditional**   Checks for a Boolean condition and then executes one of two blocks of code depending on whether the condition is true or false.

**switch conditional**   Evaluates an expression and then jumps to a location in a list of blocks of code depending on the integral value of the expression.

Now that you know about control flow constructs, we'll move on to a discussion of how to write your own subfunctions. You'll learn how to pass arguments and how to access those arguments in the subfunction.

# 14

## INSIDE SUBFUNCTIONS

Good engineering practice generally includes breaking problems down into functionally distinct subproblems. In software, this approach leads to programs with many functions, each of which solves a subproblem. This "divide and conquer" approach has distinct advantages:

It's easier to solve a small subproblem.

Previous solutions to subproblems are often reusable.

Several people can be working on different parts of the overall problem simultaneously.

When breaking down a problem like this, it's important to coordinate the many partial solutions so that they work together to provide a correct overall solution. In software, this translates to making sure that the data interface between a calling function and a called function works correctly. To ensure correct operation of the interface, it must be specified in an explicit way.

We'll first discuss how to place data items in a global location so that all the functions in the program can have direct access to them. Then we'll look at restricting the passage of data items as arguments to a function, which gives us better control over the data that the function works with.

In the previous chapters, you learned how to pass arguments to a function in registers. In this chapter, you'll learn how to store these arguments in memory so that the registers can be reused inside the called function. You'll also learn how to pass more arguments to a function than can be done with the six registers specified in Table 11-2 in Chapter 11.

We'll also look in more detail at the creation of variables within a function. Our discussion will include variables that exist only when program flow is in the function, as well as variables that stay in memory for the duration of the program but are accessible only within their defining function.

Before discussing the inner workings of functions, let's take a look at some of the rules that govern the use of variable names in C.

## Scope of Variable Names in C

This is not a book on C, so I'm not going to cover all the rules here, but enough to help us to see how programs are organized. *Scope* refers to the places in our code where the name is *visible*, meaning where we can use the name. There are four kinds of scope in C: *file*, *function*, *block*, and *function prototype*.

In C, a *declaration* of a variable introduces its name and data type into the current scope. A *definition* of a variable is a declaration that also allocates memory for the variable. A variable can be defined in only one place in a program, but as we'll see in the "Global Variables" section, it might be declared in more than one scope.

Variables that are defined inside a function definition, including its parameter list, have function scope and are called *local variables*. Their scope extends from the point of definition to the end of the function.

A *block* in C is a group of C statements enclosed in a matched pair of curly brackets, {...}. The scope of variables defined inside a block extends from the point of definition to the end of that block, including any enclosed blocks.

A function prototype is only a declaration of the function, not its definition. The scope of variables defined in a function prototype is limited to their own prototype. This limit allows us to use the same names in different function prototypes. For example, the C standard library includes functions for computing sine and cosine, whose prototypes are as follows:

```
double sin(double x);
double cos(double x);
```

We can use both function prototypes in the same function without having to use different names for the arguments.

We'll look at file scope after a brief overview of the reasons for passing arguments to a function.

## Overview of Passing Arguments

As you read through this section, be careful to distinguish between data input/output from a called function and data input/output by a user. User input typically comes from an input device, such as the keyboard or touch screen, and user output is typically sent to an output device, such as the screen or speaker.

To illustrate the difference, consider the C program statement from Listing 2-1 in Chapter 2.

```
scanf("%x", &anInt);
```

The scanf function has one data input from the main function, the address of the formatting text string, "%x". The scanf function reads user data that is input from the keyboard and outputs data, an unsigned integer, to anInt variable in the main function. In this chapter, we'll discuss the inputs and outputs between functions within a program, not the inputs from and outputs to the user of the program.

Functions can interact with the data in other parts of the program in four ways:

**Global**   The data is directly accessible from any function in the program.

**Input**   The data comes from another part of the program and is used by the function, but the original copy is not modified.

**Output**   The function provides new data to another part of the program.

**Update**   The function modifies a data item that is held by another part of the program. The new value is based on the value before the function was called.

All four interactions can be performed if the called function also knows the location of the data item, but this exposes the original copy of the data and allows it to be changed even if it's intended only as input to a called function.

We can output data from a function by placing the output in a globally known location, like a register or globally known address. We can also pass the called function the address of the place to store the output. Updates require the called function to know the address of the data being updated.

We'll start the discussion by looking at how global variables are created and how they are accessed in a subfunction.

# Global Variables

*Global variables* are those that are defined outside any functions and have *file scope*. They can be accessed from the point of their definition to the end of the file. Global variables can also be accessed from another file by declaring them with the extern modifier. This only introduces the name and data type of the variable into the scope of the declaration, without allocating memory.

Listing 14-1 shows how to define global variables.

```
/* sumIntsGlobal.c
 * Adds two integers using global variables
 */

#include <stdio.h>
#include "addTwoGlobal.h"

/* Define global variables. */
int x = 0, y = 0, z;

int main(void)
{
  printf("Enter an integer: ");
  scanf("%i", &x);
  printf("Enter an integer: ");
  scanf("%i", &y);
  addTwo();
  printf("%i + %i = %i\n", x, y, z);

  return 0;
}
```

Listing 14-1: A main function that defines three global variables

This program defines the variables x and y, both initialized to 0, and also defines z for the result. Note we initialized the first two of the variables and not the third; this is simply so we can show two different ways to define global variables in the following assembly language.

Placing the definitions outside the function body makes the variables global. This main function calls the addTwo function, which will add x and y and store the sum in z. Listing 14-2 shows the assembly language produced by the compiler for this main function.

```
.file   "sumIntsGlobal.c"
        .intel_syntax noprefix
    ❶ .text
        .globl  x
    ❷ .bss            ## bss section
    ❸ .align 4
    ❹ .type   x, @object
        .size   x, 4    ## 4 bytes
```

```
x:
      ❺ .zero    4         ## initialize to 0
        .globl   y
        .align 4
        .type    y, @object
        .size    y, 4
y:
        .zero    4         ## initialize to 0
      ❻ .comm    z,4,4
        .section .rodata
.LC0:
        .string "Enter an integer: "
.LC1:
        .string "%i"
.LC2:
        .string "%i + %i = %i\n"
        .text
        .globl   main
        .type    main, @function
main:
        push     rbp
        mov      rbp, rsp
        lea      rdi, .LC0[rip]
        mov      eax, 0
        call     printf@PLT
      ❼ lea      rsi, x[rip]      ## globals are relative to rip
        lea      rdi, .LC1[rip]   ## format string
        mov      eax, 0
        call     __isoc99_scanf@PLT
        lea      rdi, .LC0[rip]
        mov      eax, 0
        call     printf@PLT
        lea      rsi, y[rip]
        lea      rdi, .LC1[rip]
        mov      eax, 0
        call     __isoc99_scanf@PLT
        call     addTwo@PLT
        mov      ecx, DWORD PTR z[rip] ## load globals
        mov      edx, DWORD PTR y[rip]
        mov      eax, DWORD PTR x[rip]
        mov      esi, eax
        lea      rdi, .LC2[rip]
        mov      eax, 0
        call     printf@PLT
        mov      eax, 0
        pop      rbp
        ret      .size    main, .-main
        .ident   "GCC: (Ubuntu 9.3.0-17ubuntu1~20.04) 9.3.0"
        .section .note.GNU-stack,"",@progbits
```

*Listing 14-2: Compiler-generated assembly language for the function in Listing 14-1*

I don't know the reason the compiler added the first .text directive ❶, but it's not needed. Its effect is immediately overridden by the .bss directive ❷.

The .bss directive designates a data segment that is uninitialized by the program source code but is initialized to 0 when the program is loaded into memory for execution. This program aligns the beginning of its bss segment at a multiple of four using the .align directive ❸. The program then defines the label, x, to be an object of size four bytes using the .type and .size directives ❹. The .zero directive here says to skip four bytes and make sure they are set to 0 when the program is loaded ❺. It's probably redundant since we're in a bss section. The y variable is defined in the same way.

Since the z variable is not initialized, it is defined with the .comm directive ❻. The first argument to .comm is the name of the variable, z. The second argument is the number of bytes to allocate in the data segment for this variable, and the third argument specifies the address alignment of the beginning of the variable. In this case, four bytes will be allocated for z, and the address of the first byte will be a multiple of four.

The compiler has generated position-independent code for the main function, which accesses the global variables relative to the instruction pointer ❼. This works because the loader will locate the data and bss segments adjacent to the text segment when running a position-independent executable.

Next, let's look at how the subfunction accesses the global variables in this program. Listing 14-3 shows the header file for this function.

```
/* addTwoGlobal.h
 * Adds two integers and determines overflow.
 */

#ifndef ADDTWOGLOBAL_H
#define ADDTWOGLOBAL_H
void addTwo(void);
#endif
```

Listing 14-3: Header file for the addTwo function version that uses global variables

The header file has the *function prototype statement* for the addTwo function, which declares the function. It gives the name of the function and tells the compiler the data types for any arguments and the return value. In this case, there are no arguments, nor is there a return value.

You need a prototype statement for each function you'll call in a file, but you can have only one prototype statement for each function. When you include this file in another file using #include, the C compiler directive #ifndef ADDTWOGLOBAL_H will cause the compiler preprocessor to skip down to the #endif if ADDTWOGLOBAL_H has already been defined during this compilation. Otherwise, the preprocessor will execute the #define ADDTWOGLOBAL_H statement, which defines it. It's common to use #include to include other header files in header files, and the #ifndef technique protects against duplicating prototype statements. Using the uppercase of the header filename gives us a unique identifier to #define.

Listing 14-4 gives the C code for defining the addTwo function.

```
/* addTwoGlobal.c
 * Adds two integers and determines overflow.
 */

❶ #include "addTwoGlobal.h"

/* Declare global variables defined elsewhere. */
❷ extern int x, y, z;

void addTwo(void)
{
  z = x + y;
}
```

*Listing 14-4: The addTwo subfunction using global variables*

The header file for a function should be included with (#include ❶) in the file where the function is defined to make sure that the function prototype in the header file matches the definition. The global variables are defined in only one place, but they need to be declared in any other file that uses them ❷.

Listing 14-5 shows the assembly language generated by the compiler.

```
        .file   "addTwoGlobal.c"
        .intel_syntax noprefix
        .text
        .globl  addTwo
        .type   addTwo, @function
addTwo:
        push    rbp
        mov     rbp, rsp
        mov     edx, DWORD PTR ❶x[rip] ## names are global
        mov     eax, DWORD PTR  y[rip] ## relative to rip
        add     eax, edx
        mov     DWORD PTR z[rip], eax
        nop
        pop     rbp
        ret
        .size   addTwo, .-addTwo
        .ident  "GCC: (Ubuntu 9.3.0-17ubuntu1~20.04) 9.3.0"
        .section  .note.GNU-stack,"",@progbits
```

*Listing 14-5: Assembly language generated by the compiler for the subfunction in Listing 14-4*

Just as in the main function, the global variables are accessed relative to the instruction pointer ❶.

Although global variables are simple to work with in small programs, managing them quickly becomes unwieldly in large programs. You need to keep track of exactly what each function in the program is doing with the variables. Managing variables is much easier if you define them within a function and pass only what is needed to each subfunction. In the next section, we'll look at how to maintain good control over what gets passed to and from a subfunction.

## Explicitly Passing Arguments

When we restrict each function to using only those variables it needs, it's much easier to isolate the inner workings of a function from other functions, a principle called *information hiding.* You, the programmer, need to deal only with those variables and constants that the subfunction needs in order to do its specific job. Of course, most subfunctions will need to interact with some of the variables in its calling function as inputs, outputs, or updates. In this section, we'll look at how the arguments explicitly passed to a function are used by that function to accept input, produce output, or update a variable.

When a value serves only as input to the called function, we can pass a copy of the value to the called function; this is called *pass by value.* Passing by value prevents the called function from possibly changing the value in the calling function.

Receiving output from the called function is a bit more complex. One way is to use a *return value,* which in our environment is placed in the eax register. Using the eax register assumes the return value is an int; there are other rules for returning larger values, which we won't go into in this book. You've seen this technique used in most of the example programs in this book. The main function almost always returns a 0 to the function in the operating system that called it.

The other techniques for the called function to receive an output from the calling function require that the calling function pass the called function the address of the place to store the output. This can be implemented in the higher-level language as either *pass by pointer* or *pass by reference.* The difference is that with pass by pointer, the program can change the pointer to point to another object, while in pass by reference, the pointer cannot be changed by the program. C and C++ both support pass by pointer, but only C++ supports pass by reference. These are the same at the assembly language level—the address of the place to store the output is passed to the called function. The difference is enforced by the high-level language.

### Passing Arguments in C

We'll write the same program as in Listings 14-1, 14-3, and 14-4, but this time we'll define the variables as locals in the main function and pass them as arguments to the subfunction, as in Listing 14-6.

```
/* sumInts.c
 * Adds two integers using local variables
 */

#include <stdio.h>
#include "addTwo.h"
```

```
int main(void)
{
❶ int x = 0, y = 0, z;

  printf("Enter an integer: ");
  scanf("%i", &x);
  printf("Enter an integer: ");
  scanf("%i", &y);
  addTwo(x, y, ❷&z);
  printf("%i + %i = %i\n", x, y, z);

  return 0;
}
```

*Listing 14-6: Sum two integers, local variables*

Defining the variables inside the body of the function ❶ makes them visible only to this function. The values of the x and y variables are inputs to the addTwo function, so we pass copies of these variables. The addTwo function will store its result at the address we pass in as the third argument, &z ❷.

Listing 14-7 shows the header file for the addTwo function.

```
/* addTwo.h
 * Adds two integers and outputs sum.
 */

#ifndef ADDTWO_H
#define ADDTWO_H
void addTwo(int a, int b, int *c);
#endif
```

*Listing 14-7: Header file for the addTwo function*

Listing 14-8 shows the definition of the function.

```
/* addTwo.c
 * Adds two integers and outputs sum.
 */

#include "addTwo.h"

void addTwo(int a, int b, int *c)
{
  int temp;

  temp = a + b;
  *c = temp;
}
```

*Listing 14-8: The addTwo function*

The third argument to this function, c, is a pointer to an int. We need to dereference the variable, *c, to store the result of the computation at the address passed in c.

## What's Going On in Assembly Language

Listing 14-9 shows the assembly language by the compiler for the main function in sumInts.

```
        .file   "sumInts.c"
        .intel_syntax noprefix
        .text
        .section        .rodata
.LC0:
        .string "Enter an integer: "
.LC1:
        .string "%i"
.LC2:
        .string "%i + %i = %i\n"
        .text
        .globl  main
        .type   main, @function
main:
        push    rbp
        mov     rbp, rsp
        sub     rsp, 32
        mov     rax, QWORD PTR fs:40
        mov     QWORD PTR -8[rbp], rax
        xor     eax, eax
        mov     DWORD PTR -20[rbp], 0   ## x = 0;
        mov     DWORD PTR -16[rbp], 0   ## y = 0;
        lea     rdi, .LC0[rip]
        mov     eax, 0
        call    printf@PLT
        lea     rax, -20[rbp]           ## address of x
        mov     rsi, rax
        lea     rdi, .LC1[rip]
        mov     eax, 0
        call    __isoc99_scanf@PLT
        lea     rdi, .LC0[rip]
        mov     eax, 0
        call    printf@PLT
        lea     rax, -16[rbp]           ## address of y
        mov     rsi, rax
        lea     rdi, .LC1[rip]
        mov     eax, 0
        call    __isoc99_scanf@PLT
        mov     ecx, DWORD PTR -16[rbp] ## load y
        mov     eax, DWORD PTR -20[rbp] ## load x
        lea   ❶ rdx, -12[rbp]           ## address of z
        mov     esi, ecx                ## y
        mov     edi, eax                ## x
        call    addTwo@PLT
        mov     ecx, DWORD PTR -12[rbp] ## z
        mov     edx, DWORD PTR -16[rbp] ## y
        mov     eax, DWORD PTR -20[rbp] ## x
        mov     esi, eax
        lea     rdi, .LC2[rip]
        mov     eax, 0
```

```
        call     printf@PLT
        mov      eax, 0
        mov      rsi, QWORD PTR -8[rbp]
        xor      rsi, QWORD PTR fs:40
        je       .L3
        call     __stack_chk_fail@PLT
.L3:
        leave
        ret
        .size    main, .-main
        .ident   "GCC: (Ubuntu 9.3.0-17ubuntu1~20.04) 9.3.0"
        .section         .note.GNU-stack,"",@progbits
```

*Listing 14-9: Assembly language generated by compiler for the* main *function in* sumInts

From Table 11-2 in Chapter 11, we learned that the third argument is passed in register rdx. We can see that the compiler has allocated space at −12 off of rbp when it loads this address into rdx ❶.

Next, we'll look at the compiler-generated assembly language for the addTwo function, as shown in Listing 14-10.

```
        .file    "addTwo.c"
        .intel_syntax noprefix
        .text
        .globl   addTwo
        .type    addTwo, @function
addTwo:
        push     rbp
        mov      rbp, rsp
❶ mov      DWORD PTR -20[rbp], edi   ## store a
        mov      DWORD PTR -24[rbp], esi   ## store b
        mov      QWORD PTR -32[rbp], rdx   ## address of c
        mov      edx, DWORD PTR -20[rbp]
        mov      eax, DWORD PTR -24[rbp]
        add      eax, edx                  ## a + b
        mov      DWORD PTR -4[rbp], eax    ## sum = a + b;
❷ mov      rax, QWORD PTR -32[rbp]   ## address of c
        mov      edx, DWORD PTR -4[rbp]    ## load sum
❸ mov      DWORD PTR [rax], edx      ## *c = sum;
❹ nop
        pop      rbp
        ret
        .size    addTwo, .-addTwo
        .ident   "GCC: (Ubuntu 9.3.0-17ubuntu1~20.04) 9.3.0"
        .section         .note.GNU-stack,"",@progbits
```

*Listing 14-10: Assembly language generated by compiler for the* addTwo *function*

The first thing you might notice about this function is that it does not allocate space on the stack for local variables, but it is using an area on the stack for the sum local variable. In addition, it's storing the three input arguments in the stack area where local variables are usually placed ❶. The *System V Application Binary Interface* defines the 128 bytes beyond the stack pointer—that is, the 128 bytes at addresses lower than the one in the rsp register—as a *red zone*. The operating system is not allowed to use this area, so the function can use it for temporary storage of values that do not need to be saved when another function is called. In particular, *leaf functions*, functions that do not call other functions, can store local variables in this area without moving the stack pointer.

Figure 14-1 gives a pictorial view of addTwo's stack frame.

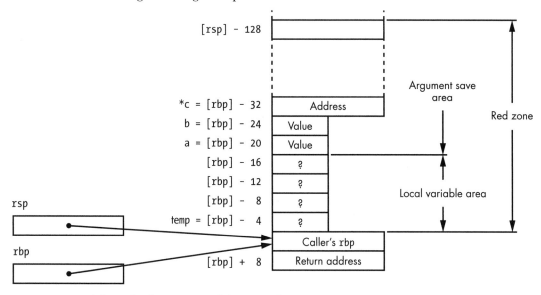

Figure 14-1: Stack frame for the C version of the addTwo function

The address of each item in the stack frame is given on the left side. For example, the temp local variable is stored at the address in rbp minus 4. Although the rules in the System V Application Binary Interface specify only that the stack pointer must be at a 16-byte address boundary, the compiler has followed that rule for separating the local variable area from the argument save area. Notice that the red zone is defined relative to the stack pointer, rsp, while the variables and saved arguments are accessed relative to the frame pointer, rbp.

After performing the computation using the input data, the function loads the address of the place to store the result from where it was stored in the stack area ❷. It then stores the result at that address ❸.

The compiler has inserted another instruction, nop, after the instruction that stores the result ❹.

### nop—No operation

Performs no operation, but uses one byte.

The nop instruction is used to fine-tune hardware implementation details to improve efficiency. It has no effect on the logic of the program.

The nop instruction does not affect the status flags in the rflags register.

Most functions take fewer than the six arguments we can pass in registers, but sometimes you want to pass more arguments. In the next section, you'll see how the stack comes to our rescue.

# Handling More Than Six Arguments

When a calling function needs to pass more than six arguments to another function, the additional arguments beyond the first six in registers are passed on the call stack. They are pushed onto the stack in 8-byte chunks before the call. Because the return address will be pushed onto the stack after the arguments when the subfunction is called, the arguments are read directly from the stack instead of popping them off.

## Pushing Arguments onto the Stack

The order of pushing is from right to left in the C argument list. Since these arguments are on the call stack, they are within the called function's stack frame, so the called function can access them.

We'll use the main function in Listing 14-11 to show how this works.

```c
/* sum9Ints.c
 * Sums the integers 1 - 9.
 */
#include <stdio.h>
#include "addNine.h"

int main(void)
{
  int total;
  int a = 1;
  int b = 2;
  int c = 3;
  int d = 4;
  int e = 5;
  int f = 6;
  int g = 7;
  int h = 8;
  int i = 9;

  total = addNine(a, b, c, d, e, f, g, h, i);
  printf("The sum is %i\n", total);
  return 0;
}
```

Listing 14-11: Passing more than six arguments to a subfunction

The values of the first six arguments—a, b, c, d, e, and f—will be passed in the registers edi, esi, edx, ecx, r8d, and r9d. The remaining three arguments will be pushed onto the stack. Listing 14-12 shows the treatment of the variables.

```asm
        .file   "sum9Ints.c"
        .intel_syntax noprefix
        .text
        .section        .rodata
.LC0:
        .string "The sum is %i\n"
        .text
```

```
        .globl  main
        .type   main, @function
main:
        push    rbp
        mov     rbp, rsp
        sub     rsp, 48
        mov     DWORD PTR -40[rbp], 1   ## a = 1
        mov     DWORD PTR -36[rbp], 2   ## b = 2
        mov     DWORD PTR -32[rbp], 3   ## c = 3
        mov     DWORD PTR -28[rbp], 4   ## d = 4
        mov     DWORD PTR -24[rbp], 5   ## e = 5
        mov     DWORD PTR -20[rbp], 6   ## f = 6
        mov     DWORD PTR -16[rbp], 7   ## g = 7
        mov     DWORD PTR -12[rbp], 8   ## h = 8
        mov     DWORD PTR -8[rbp], 9    ## i = 9
        mov     r9d, DWORD PTR -20[rbp] ## load f
        mov     r8d, DWORD PTR -24[rbp] ## load e
        mov     ecx, DWORD PTR -28[rbp] ## load d
        mov     edx, DWORD PTR -32[rbp] ## load c
        mov     esi, DWORD PTR -36[rbp] ## load b
❶ mov     eax, DWORD PTR -40[rbp] ## load a
❷ sub     rsp, 8                  ## for stack alignment
        mov     edi, DWORD PTR -8[rbp]
❸ push    rdi                     ## push i
        mov     edi, DWORD PTR -12[rbp]
        push    rdi                     ## push h
        mov     edi, DWORD PTR -16[rbp]
        push    rdi                     ## push g
❹ mov     edi, eax
        call    addNine@PLT
❺ add     rsp, 32                 ## remove 3 ints and alignment
        mov     DWORD PTR -4[rbp], eax
        mov     eax, DWORD PTR -4[rbp]
        mov     esi, eax
        lea     rdi, .LC0[rip]
        mov     eax, 0
        call    printf@PLT
        mov     eax, 0
        leave
        ret
        .size   main, .-main
        .ident  "GCC: (Ubuntu 9.3.0-17ubuntu1~20.04) 9.3.0"
        .section        .note.GNU-stack,"",@progbits
```

*Listing 14-12: Pushing three arguments onto the stack for the call to addNine*

The first argument, a, is stored at -40[rbp] and must be placed in edi before calling the subfunction. This algorithm temporarily stores the value of a in eax ❶, uses rdi for pushing the three values of i, h, and g onto the stack ❸, and then places the value of the first argument, a, in edi ❹, where it is needed at the first argument to addNine. I do not know why the compiler didn't place the value of a in edi and then use rax for the pushing operations, which would have made this mov instruction unnecessary.

You may notice that when the values are passed in the registers, only the 32-bit portions of the registers are used, but when passed on the stack, the full 64 bits are used. The size of an int in our C environment is 32 bits. But the stack is 64 bits wide, so a push or pop moves a 64-bit value. Recall that moving a 32-bit value into a register zeros the high-order 32 bits in the register; thus, the original 32 bits are preserved in the 64-bit push operations in this function.

Recall that our protocol for using the stack is to make sure that the stack pointer is on a 16-byte address boundary before calling a function. Three 8-byte values will be pushed onto the stack, so the algorithm subtracts 8 from the stack pointer before pushing the three values ❷. After returning from the call to the subfunction, all 32 bytes are effectively removed from the stack by adjusting the stack pointer ❺. Figure 14-2 shows the argument area of the stack just before the call to addNine.

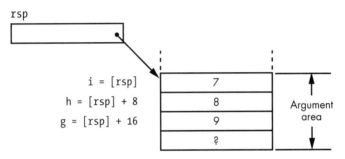

Figure 14-2: Arguments pushed on stack by the main function

Next, let's turn our attention to the addNine function. Listing 14-13 shows the header file.

```
/* addNine.h
 * Returns sum of nine integers.
 */
#ifndef ADDNINE_H
#define ADDNINE_H
int addNine(int one, int two, int three, int four, int five,
          int six, int seven, int eight, int nine);
#endif
```

Listing 14-13: Header file for the addNine function

Listing 14-14 shows the C source code defining the function.

```
/* addNine.c
 * Sums nine integers and returns the sum.
 */

#include <stdio.h>
#include "addNine.h"

int addNine(int one, int two, int three, int four, int five,
          int six, int seven, int eight, int nine)
{
```

```
      int sum;

      sum = one + two + three + four + five + six
              + seven + eight + nine;
      return sum;
}
```

*Listing 14-14: The addNine function, in C*

The compiler generated the assembly language shown in Listing 14-15
for the addNine function.

```
          .file   "addNine.c"
          .intel_syntax noprefix
          .text
          .globl  addNine
          .type   addNine, @function
addNine:
          push    rbp
    ❶ mov     rbp, rsp
    ❷ mov     DWORD PTR -20[rbp], edi   ## store a locally
          mov     DWORD PTR -24[rbp], esi   ## store b locally
          mov     DWORD PTR -28[rbp], edx   ## store c locally
          mov     DWORD PTR -32[rbp], ecx   ## store d locally
          mov     DWORD PTR -36[rbp], r8d   ## store e locally
          mov     DWORD PTR -40[rbp], r9d   ## store f locally
          mov     edx, DWORD PTR -20[rbp]   ## sum = a
          mov     eax, DWORD PTR -24[rbp]
          add     edx, eax                  ## sum += b
          mov     eax, DWORD PTR -28[rbp]
          add     edx, eax                  ## sum += c
          mov     eax, DWORD PTR -32[rbp]
          add     edx, eax                  ## sum += d
          mov     eax, DWORD PTR -36[rbp]
          add     edx, eax                  ## sum += e
          mov     eax, DWORD PTR -40[rbp]
          add     edx, eax                  ## sum += f
    ❸ mov     eax, DWORD PTR 16[rbp]    ## from arg list
          add     edx, eax                  ## sum += g
          mov     eax, DWORD PTR 24[rbp]
          add     edx, eax                  ## sum += h
          mov     eax, DWORD PTR 32[rbp]
          add     eax, edx                  ## sum += i
          mov     DWORD PTR -4[rbp], eax
          mov     eax, DWORD PTR -4[rbp]
          pop     rbp
          ret
          .size   addNine, .-addNine
          .ident  "GCC: (Ubuntu 9.3.0-17ubuntu1~20.04) 9.3.0"
          .section        .note.GNU-stack,"",@progbits
```

*Listing 14-15: Compiler-generated assembly language for the addNine function*

After the prologue for the addNine function establishes its frame
pointer ❶, its stack frame is in the state shown in Figure 14-3.

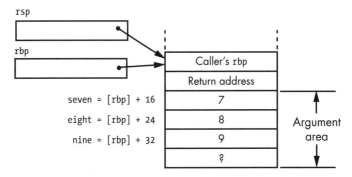

Figure 14-3: Stack frame for addNine function

The addNine function stores the arguments passed in registers in the red zone of the stack ❷. Then it starts its computation of the sum. When it gets to the arguments that were passed on the stack, it loads each one into the eax register as needed ❸. The offsets from the rbp register for each stack argument are obtained from the drawing in Figure 14-3.

**WARNING** *Knowing the exact location of each argument passed on the stack is essential when designing a subfunction. I learned many years ago that I need to draw diagrams like the ones in Figures 14-2 and 14-3 to get this right.*

You have seen that the subfunction accesses arguments directly on the stack instead of popping them off. They can be placed directly on the stack by the calling function instead of pushing them. In the next section, I'll show how this is done when I write the sumNine program directly in assembly language.

## Storing Arguments Directly on the Stack

The push operation is somewhat inefficient. It performs two operations: subtract 8 from the rsp register and store a value at the address in the updated rsp register. When placing several values on the stack, it's a little more efficient to subtract enough from the stack pointer to make room for all the values and then store each value directly on the stack. We'll use this technique when writing the sumNine program directly in assembly language.

Listing 14-16 shows the main function for our assembly language version of the sumNine program.

```
# sum9Ints.s
# Sums the integers 1 - 9.
        .intel_syntax noprefix

# Stack frame
#    passing arguments on stack (rsp)
#    need 3x8 = 24 -> 32 bytes
    ❶ .equ    seventh,0
      .equ    eighth,8
      .equ    ninth,16
      .equ    argSize,-32
```

```
#   local vars (rbp)
#      need 10x4 = 40 -> 48 bytes for alignment
        .equ    i,-4
        .equ    h,-8
        .equ    g,-12
        .equ    f,-16
        .equ    e,-20
        .equ    d,-24
        .equ    c,-28
        .equ    b,-32
        .equ    a,-36
        .equ    total,-40
        .equ    localSize,-48
# Read only data
        .section  .rodata
format:
        .string "The sum is %i\n"
# Code
        .text
        .globl  main
        .type   main, @function
main:
        push    rbp                 # save frame pointer
        mov     rbp, rsp            # set new frame pointer
        add     rsp, localSize      # for local var.

        mov     dword ptr a[rbp], 1 # initialize values
        mov     dword ptr b[rbp], 2 #     etc...
        mov     dword ptr c[rbp], 3
        mov     dword ptr d[rbp], 4
        mov     dword ptr e[rbp], 5
        mov     dword ptr f[rbp], 6
        mov     dword ptr g[rbp], 7
        mov     dword ptr h[rbp], 8
        mov     dword ptr i[rbp], 9

  ❷ add     rsp, argSize        # space for arguments
        mov     eax, i[rbp]         # load i
  ❸ mov     ninth[rsp], rax     #    9th argument
        mov     eax, h[rbp]         # load h
        mov     eighth[rsp], rax    #    8th argument
        mov     eax, g[rbp]         # load g
        mov     seventh[rsp], rax   #    7th argument
        mov     r9d, f[rbp]         # f is 6th
        mov     r8d, e[rbp]         # e is 5th
        mov     ecx, d[rbp]         # d is 4th
        mov     edx, c[rbp]         # c is 3rd
        mov     esi, b[rbp]         # b is 2nd
        mov     edi, a[rbp]         # a is 1st
        call    addNine
  ❹ sub     rsp, argSize        # remove arguments
        mov     total[rbp], eax     # total = sumNine(...)

        mov     esi, total[rbp]     # show result
        lea     rdi, format[rip]
```

```
        mov     eax, 0
        call    printf@plt

        mov     eax, 0          # return 0;
        mov     rsp, rbp        # restore stack pointer
        pop     rbp             # and caller frame pointer
        ret
```

*Listing 14-16: The main function for the sumNine program written directly in assembly language*

We'll start the design by using the diagram of the stack in Figure 14-2 to figure out the values of the identifiers for the seventh, eighth, and ninth arguments ❶. It's also convenient to create an identifier for the amount of space we'll need on the stack for the arguments, making sure that it's a multiple of 16.

We start the call to addNine by first allocating space on the stack for the three arguments beyond the six we'll pass on registers by subtracting the appropriate amount from rsp ❷. Having created identifiers for each argument, it's then a simple matter to directly store each of the three arguments in the area we've just allocated ❸. Then when the addNine subfunction returns to our function, we need to effectively delete the argument area from the top of the stack by adding the same amount that we subtracted from rsp when starting the call sequence ❹.

Next, let's look at how the addNine function, Listing 14-17, accesses the arguments passed on the stack.

```
# addNine.s
# Sums nine integer arguments and returns the total.
        .intel_syntax noprefix
# Calling sequence:
#       edi <- one, 32-bit int
#       esi <- two
#       ecx <- three
#       edx <- four
#       r8d <- five
#       r9d <- six
#       push seven
#       push eight
#       push nine
#       returns sum
# Stack frame
#    arguments in stack frame
    ❶ .equ    seven,16
      .equ    eight,24
      .equ    nine,32
#    local variables
      .equ    total,-4
      .equ    localSize,-16

# Code
      .text
      .globl  addNine
      .type   addNine, @function
```

```
addNine:
        push    rbp              # save frame pointer
        mov     rbp, rsp         # set new frame pointer
        add     rsp, localSize   # for local var.

        add     edi, esi         # add two to one
        add     edi, ecx         # plus three
        add     edi, edx         # plus four
        add     edi, r8d         # plus five
        add     edi, r9d         # plus six
    ❷ add     edi, seven[rbp]  # plus seven
        add     edi, eight[rbp]  # plus eight
        add     edi, nine[rbp]   # plus nine
        mov     total[rbp], edi  # save total

        mov     eax, total[rbp]  # return total;
        mov     rsp, rbp         # restore stack pointer
        pop     rbp              # and caller frame pointer
        ret
```

Listing 14-17: The addNine function written directly in assembly language

The offsets of the arguments seven, eight, and nine are defined using the diagram in Figure 14-3 ❶. Using these identifiers, adding the values passed to the addNine function is straightforward ❷.

## Summary of Stack Frame Usage

When calling a function, it's essential that you follow the register usage and argument passing disciplines precisely. Any deviation can cause errors that are difficult to debug. The rules are as follows.

In the calling function:

1. Assume that the values in the rax, rcx, rdx, rsi, rdi, and r8–r11 registers will be changed by the called function.

2. The first six arguments are passed in the rdi, rsi, rdx, rcx, r8, and r9 registers in left-to-right order.

3. Arguments beyond argument 6 are stored on the stack as though they had been pushed onto the stack in right-to-left order.

4. Use the call instruction to invoke the function you want to call.

Upon entering the called function:

5. Save the caller's frame pointer by pushing rbp onto the stack.

6. Establish a frame pointer for the called function at the current top of the stack by copying rsp to rbp.

7. Allocate space on the stack for all the local variables, plus any required register save space, by subtracting the number of bytes required from rsp; this value must be a multiple of 16.

8. If a called function changes any of the values in the rbx, rbp, rsp, or r12–r15 registers, they must be saved in the register save area and then restored before returning to the calling function.

9.  If the function calls another function, save the arguments passed in registers on the stack.

Within the called function:

10. The rsp register is pointing to the current bottom of the stack that is accessible to this function. Observe the usual stack discipline; do not use the stack pointer to access arguments or local variables.

11. Arguments passed in registers to the function and saved on the stack are accessed by negative offsets from the frame pointer, rbp.

12. Arguments passed on the stack to the function are accessed by positive offsets from the frame pointer, rbp. Local variables are accessed by negative offsets from the frame pointer, rbp.

When leaving the called function:

13. Place the return value, if any, in eax.

14. Restore the values in the rbx, rbp, rsp, and r12–r15 registers from the register save area in the stack frame.

15. Delete the local variable space and register save area by copying rbp to rsp.

16. Restore the caller's frame pointer by popping rbp off the stack save area.

17. Return to the calling function with ret.

Figure 14-4 shows what the stack frame looks like.

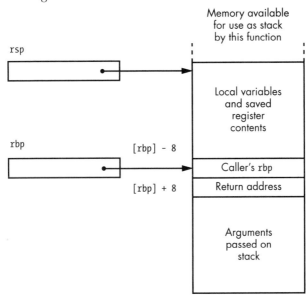

*Figure 14-4: Overall pattern of a stack frame*

As explained, a stack frame may not include all these parts. If no more than six arguments are passed to the function, then the lower box in this diagram does not exist. And some functions may not have any local variables or saved register contents. In certain cases, the function may not even need to save the caller's rbp. The only box in this diagram that will always exist is the return address.

In the next section, we'll look at how to create a local variable that keeps its value between calls to its defining subfunction.

---

**YOUR TURN**

1.  Modify the assembly language program in Listings 14-16 and 14-17 so that all nine arguments are passed on the stack.

2.  Write a program in assembly language that sums all the integers between two integers entered by the user.

3.  Write the two functions, writeStr and readLn, in assembly language. You will use these functions in exercises later in the book.

    a.  writeStr writes text in the terminal window using the write system call. It takes one argument and returns the number of characters written.

    b.  readLn reads characters from the keyboard using the read system call and stores them in memory as a C-style text string. It takes two arguments, a pointer to the memory location to store the text and the number of bytes available in that location. If the number of characters entered exceeds the available storage space, it reads the remaining input but does not store it. It returns the number of characters entered, less the NUL terminating character.

    c.  Test your functions with the following C main function. Don't forget to write the C header files for your assembly language functions. Hint: Use a much smaller number for MAX when testing your readLn function.

```c
/* echo.c
 * Prompts user to enter text and echoes it.
 */

#include "writeStr.h"
#include "readLn.h"
#define MAX 50

int main(void)
{
  char text[MAX];

  writeStr("Enter some text: ");
  readLn(text, MAX);
  writeStr("You entered: ");
  writeStr(text);
  writeStr("\n");

  return 0;
}
```

## Static Local Variables

We learned in Chapter 11 (also see Figures 14-1 and 14-4) that automatic local variables are created in a function's prologue and get deleted in the function's epilogue. This means the value stored in an automatic local variable will be lost in subsequent calls to a subfunction. We might want to keep the value of a variable between function calls while still providing the information-hiding advantage of a local variable. For example, we might have a function that is called from several other functions and want to maintain a count of how many times it's called. We could use a global variable, but a global variable doesn't provide the information-hiding properties of a local variable.

A local variable in a program has one of two possible *lifetimes* in memory. An automatic local variable is created in memory during the prologue of the function it's defined in, and it's deleted in the epilogue of the function. A *static local variable* also has local scope like an automatic local variable, but like a global variable, it remains in memory throughout the lifetime of the entire program.

We'll see where static local variables are created in memory when we discuss the program in Listings 14-18, 14-20, and 14-21, which illustrates the differences between the visibility and persistence of an automatic local variable, a static local variable, and a global variable.

```
/* varLife.c
 * Compares scope and lifetime of automatic, static,
 * and global variables.
 */

#include <stdio.h>
#include "addConst.h"
#define INITx 12
#define INITy 34
#define INITz 56

❶ int z = INITz;

int main(void)
{
❷ int x = INITx;
  int y = INITy;

  printf("            automatic   static   global\n");
  printf("                 x         y       z\n");
  printf("In main:%12i %8i %8i\n", x, y, z);
❸ addConst();
  addConst();
  printf("In main: %12i %8i %8i\n", x, y, z);
  return 0;
}
```

*Listing 14-18: Program to compare automatic local, static local, and global variables*

The main function for this program first initializes a global variable ❶ and then two local variables ❷. It then calls a function to add a constant value to each of three variables ❸. As you will see, even though the variables in addConst have the same names as the ones in main, only the global variable is the same physical object. Thus, this program has five variables: x and y in main, x and y in addConst, and z, which is accessible by both main and addConst.

The compiler generates a little different assembly language for the global variable, z, in this program than it generated for the global variables in Listing 14-2. Let's look at the compiler-generated assembly language for main; see Listing 14-19.

```
          .file    "varLife.c"
          .intel_syntax noprefix
          .text
          .globl   z
❶ .data
          .align 4
          .type    z, @object
          .size    z, 4
z:
❷ .long    56                          ## int z = INITz;
          .section       .rodata
          .align 8
.LC0:
          .string "            automatic   static   global"
          .align 8
.LC1:
          .string "                      x      y      z"
.LC2:
          .string "In main:%12i %8i %8i\n"
          .text
          .globl   main
          .type    main, @function
main:
          push     rbp
          mov      rbp, rsp
          sub      rsp, 16
          mov      DWORD PTR -8[rbp], 12   ## int x = INITx;
          mov      DWORD PTR -4[rbp], 34   ## int y = INITy;
          lea      rdi, .LC0[rip]
          call     puts@PLT
          lea      rdi, .LC1[rip]
          call     puts@PLT
          mov      ecx, DWORD PTR z[rip]
          mov      edx, DWORD PTR -4[rbp]
          mov      eax, DWORD PTR -8[rbp]
          mov      esi, eax
          lea      rdi, .LC2[rip]
          mov      eax, 0
          call     printf@PLT
          call     addConst@PLT
          call     addConst@PLT
```

```
        mov     ecx, DWORD PTR z[rip]
        mov     edx, DWORD PTR -4[rbp]
        mov     eax, DWORD PTR -8[rbp]
        mov     esi, eax
        lea     rdi, .LC2[rip]
        mov     eax, 0
        call    printf@PLT
        mov     eax, 0
        leave
        ret
        .size   main, .-main
        .ident  "GCC: (Ubuntu 9.3.0-17ubuntu1~20.04) 9.3.0"
        .section        .note.GNU-stack,"",@progbits
```

*Listing 14-19: Compiler-generated assembly language for the main function in Listing 14-1*

Most of the assembly language in Listing 14-19 is probably familiar to you, but the implementation of the global variable, z, differs from the way we saw for the x and y global variables in the program in Listing 14-2, which were both placed in the data segment and initialized to 0.

In Listing 14-19, we see that the global variable in this program, z, is placed in the .data section ❶, so it will also be placed in the data segment when the program is executed. But the nonzero value for the global variable in this program must be stored in the executable program file. The compiler has used the .long assembler directive to specify this value ❷. An advantage of using .bss for memory that should be initialized to 0 in a program is that it doesn't require space in the program file, which would be needed to store nonzero values.

The header file for the addConst function, Listing 14-20, shows that it takes no arguments and does not return a value.

```
/* addConst.h
 * Adds constant to automatic, static, global variables.
 */

#ifndef ADDCONST_H
#define ADDCONST_H
void addConst(void);
#endif
```

*Listing 14-20: Header file for addConst function*

Listing 14-21 shows the addConst function.

```
/* addConst.c
 * Adds constant to automatic, static, global variables.
 */

#include <stdio.h>
#include "addConst.h"
❶ #define INITx 78
#define INITy 90
#define ADDITION 1000
```

```
❷ extern int z;            /* global */

void addConst(void)
{
❸ int x = INITx;           /* every call */
❹ static int y = INITy;    /* first call only */

  x += ADDITION;    /* add to each */
  y += ADDITION;
  z += ADDITION;

  printf("In addConst: %8i %8i %8i\n", x, y, z);
}
```

*Listing 14-21: Function to add a constant value to three variables*

We'll use different constants in addConst so we can clearly see the differences in scope and persistence of the five variables in this program when we run it ❶.

The x variable in addConst is defined to be an automatic local variable ❸. It gets created and assigned an initial value, INITx, each time this function is called. This x variable is different from the variable also named x in the main function because each is defined within its respective function, making them local variables. Changing the value of this x does not affect the x variable in main.

The y variable in addConst is defined to be static ❹. A static local variable can be given an initial value when it is defined, as I've done here. If no value is given, it's initialized to numerical zero by the operating system. A local static variable has this initial value the first time the function where it's defined is called. If the variable is changed in the function, the new value persists for the next time the function is called, effectively skipping the initialization. Like x, the y variable is also local, so it is different from the variable also named y in the main function. Changing the value of this y does not affect the y variable in main.

The z variable was defined outside the main function. But because it was defined in another file, we need to declare it as extern in this file so we can access it ❷. As you learned in Chapter 14, changing it in this function changes the only copy in this program, so main will also see the changes to z in addConst.

Listing 14-22 shows the assembly language that the compiler generated for the addConst function.

```
        .file   "addConst.c"
        .intel_syntax noprefix
        .text
        .section        .rodata
.LC0:
        .string "In addConst:%8i %8i %8i\n"
        .text
        .globl  addConst
        .type   addConst, @function
```

```
addConst:
        push    rbp
        mov     rbp, rsp
        sub     rsp, 16
        mov     DWORD PTR ❶-4[rbp], 78       ## int x = INITx;
        add     DWORD PTR -4[rbp], 1000      ## x += ADDITION;
        mov     eax, DWORD PTR ❷y.2319[rip]  ## load y
        add     eax, 1000                    ## y += ADDITION;
        mov     DWORD PTR y.2319[rip], eax   ## store new y
        mov     eax, DWORD PTR ❸z[rip]       ## load z
        add     eax, 1000                    ## z += ADDITION;
        mov     DWORD PTR z[rip], eax        ## store new z
        mov     ecx, DWORD PTR z[rip]
        mov     edx, DWORD PTR y.2319[rip]
        mov     eax, DWORD PTR -4[rbp]
        mov     esi, eax
        lea     rdi, .LC0[rip]
        mov     eax, 0
        call    printf@PLT
        nop
        leave
        ret
        .size   addConst, .-addConst
❹ .data
        .align 4
        .type   y.2319, @object
        .size   y.2319, 4
❺ y.2319:
        .long   90                           ## static int y = INITy;
        .ident  "GCC: (Ubuntu 9.3.0-17ubuntu1~20.04) 9.3.0"
        .section        .note.GNU-stack,"",@progbits
```

*Listing 14-22: Assembly language generated by the compiler for the addConst function in Listing 14-21*

From the assembly language in Listing 14-22, we can see that automatic local variables are allocated in the stack frame. The compiler accesses them using an offset from the frame pointer, rbp ❶. And as we saw earlier in this chapter, global variables are accessed by their global name relative to rip ❸.

Static local variable are also accessed by name relative to rip, but the name is not specified as .global. Furthermore, the compiler adds a number to the name, separated by a . character ❷. This embellishment of our given name for the variable is called *name mangling*. The compiler needs to do name mangling to distinguish this static local variable from possibly another static local variable with the same given name in another function defined in the same file.

As you probably already guessed, a static local variable cannot exist in the stack frame. Like the global variable, z, defined in the main function (see Listing 14-2), the static local variable, y, is allocated in the .data section and initialized with a .long assembler directive ❹. It is labeled with the mangled name so it can be accessed only by its function ❺.

Figure 14-5 shows a run of this program.

| | Automatic | Static | Global |
|---|---|---|---|
| | x | y | z |
| In main: | 12 | 34 | 56 |
| In addConst: | 1078 | 1090 | 1056 |
| In addConst: | 1078 | 2090 | 2056 |
| In main: | 12 | 34 | 2056 |

*Figure 14-5: Scope and lifetime of three classes of C variables*

The program shows that the x and y variables in main are different from the x and y variables in addConst. We can also see that the x in addConst is newly initialized each time the function is called. But the y variable in addConst is given its initial value only the first time the function is called, and the addition of 1,000 to the variable persists between the two calls to the function. We can also see that both main and addConst are using the same (global) z.

My assembly language solution to the varLife program, Listings 14-23 and 14-24, is similar to what the compiler generated, but I use more meaningful labels and names to make the code easier for a human to read.

```
# varLife.s
# Compares scope and lifetime of automatic, static, and global variables.
        .intel_syntax noprefix

# Stack frame
        .equ    x,-8
        .equ    y,-4
        .equ    localSize,-16
# Useful constants
        .equ    INITx,12
        .equ    INITy,34
        .equ    INITz,56
        .section    .rodata
        .align  8
tableHead1:
        .string "            automatic    static    global"
tableHead2:
        .string "                  x         y         z"
format:
        .string "In main:%12i %8i %8i\n"
# Define global variable
        .data
        .align  4
        .globl  z
        .type   z, @object
z:
    ❶ .int    INITz   # initialize the global
# Code
        .text
        .globl  main
        .type   main, @function
main:
        push    rbp                     # save frame pointer
```

```
        mov     rbp, rsp                    # set new frame pointer
        add     rsp, localSize              # for local var.

        mov     ❷ dword ptr x[rbp], INITx # initialize locals
        mov     dword ptr y[rbp], INITy

        lea     rdi, tableHead1[rip]        # print heading
        call    puts@plt
        lea     rdi, tableHead2[rip]
        call    puts@plt
        mov     ❸ ecx, z[rip]             # print variables
        mov     edx, y[rbp]
        mov     esi, x[rbp]
        lea     rdi, format[rip]
        mov     eax, 0
        call    printf@plt

        call    addConst                    # add to variables
        call    addConst

        mov     ecx, z[rip]                 # print variables
        mov     edx, y[rbp]
        mov     esi, x[rbp]
        lea     rdi, format[rip]
        mov     eax, 0
        call    printf@plt

        mov     eax, 0                      # return 0;
        mov     rsp, rbp                    # restore stack pointer
        pop     rbp                         # and caller frame pointer
        ret
```

*Listing 14-23: Assembly language version of the main function for the varLife program*

The .int directive is the same as the .long used by the compiler. In our environment, both emit a 32-bit integer in little endian order. I prefer using the .int directive rather than .long to specify an int value ❶, but this is just personal style.

Since x and y in this function are automatic local variables, they are in the stack frame and accessed relative to the frame pointer ❷, while z is a global so accessed relative to the instruction pointer ❸.

When we write the addConst function in assembly language, we'll use a more meaningful identifier to mangle the static local variable, as shown in Listing 14-24.

```
# addConst.s
# Adds constant to automatic, static, global variables.
        .intel_syntax noprefix

# Stack frame
        .equ    ❶ x,-4
        .equ    localSize,-16
```

```
# Useful constants
        .equ    ADDITION,1000
        .equ    INITx,78
        .equ    INITy,90
# Constant data
        .section .rodata
        .align  8
format:
        .string "In addConst:%8i %8i %8i\n"
# Define static variable
        .data
        .align  4
        .type ❷ y_addConst, @object
y_addConst:
      ❸ .int    INITy


# Code
        .text
        .globl  addConst
        .type   addConst, @function
addConst:
        push    rbp                      # save frame pointer
        mov     rbp, rsp                 # set new frame pointer
        add     rsp, localSize           # for local var.
        mov     dword ptr x[rbp], INITx # initialize

        add     dword ptr x[rbp], ADDITION # add to vars
        add   ❹ dword ptr y_addConst[rip], ADDITION
        add     dword ptr z[rip], ADDITION

        mov     ecx, z[rip]              # print variables
        mov     edx, y_addConst[rip]
        mov     esi, x[rbp]
        lea     rdi, format[rip]
        mov     eax, 0                   # no floats
        call    printf@plt

        mov     eax, 0                   # return 0;
        mov     rsp, rbp                 # restore stack pointer
        pop     rbp                      # and caller frame pointer
        ret
```

*Listing 14-24: Assembly language version of the addConst function*

Be careful to notice that the automatic local variable, x, here is created in the stack frame for addConst ❶ so is different from the x that was created in the stack frame for main. I have chosen to mangle the static local variable, y, by appending the function name to the name of the variable, thus assuring a unique name to the variable ❷. Since y is static, it's placed in the .data section ❸ and accessed relative to the instruction pointer ❹.

Table 14-1 summarizes the memory characteristics of some of the most common components for a program.

**Table 14-1:** Memory Characteristics of Some Components of a Program

| Role in the program | Memory segment | Access | Lifetime |
|---|---|---|---|
| Automatic local variable | Stack | Read and write | Function |
| Constant | Text | Read only | Program |
| Instruction | Text | Read only | Program |
| Static local variable | Data | Read and write | Program |
| Global variable | Data | Read and write | Program |

The memory segment in Table 14-1 refers to the segments created by the operating system. Constants are placed in a text segment because the operating system prohibits a program from writing to a text segment. Variables need to be in a segment that can be both read from and written to.

Table 14-2 summarizes some of the more common assembler directives used to control where program components go in memory.

**Table 14-2:** Some Common Assembler Memory Directives

| Directive | Memory segment | Effect |
|---|---|---|
| .text | Text | Instructions follow |
| .rodata | Text | Constant data follows |
| .string "*string*", ... | Text | Arrays of characters, each terminated by NUL |
| .ascii "*string*", ... | Text | Arrays of characters |
| .asciz "*string*", ... | Text | Arrays of characters, each terminated by NUL |
| .data | Data | Variable data follows |
| .bss | Data | Following data memory initialized to zero |
| .comm *label*, *size* | Data | Allocates *size* bytes of uninitialized data memory |
| .byte *expression*, ... | Data | Initialize memory, one byte for each expression |
| .int *expression*, ... | Data | Initialize memory, one int for each expression |
| .long *expression*, ... | Data | Initialize memory, one int for each expression |

The .string, .ascii, and .asciz directives can allocate more than one text string, each separated by a comma. The .string and .asciz directives add a NUL character to the end of the text string, while .ascii does not.

The first byte of memory allocated by the .comm directive is named *label*, which has global scope in the program. The operating system zeros the *size* bytes of memory associated with *label* when the program is first loaded.

The .int and .long directives do the same thing—allocate 32 bits in our environment set to the value of *expression*, which must be an integral value. The .byte directive must also evaluate to an integral value. These directives can allocate multiple *expression*s, each separated by a comma.

This is only a summary of these directives. You need to consult the info page for as to read the details.

---

**YOUR TURN**

1.  Modify the program in Listings 14-23 and 14-24 so that the addConst function prints the number of times it has been called.

2.  Modify the program in Listings 14-23 and 14-24 so that there are two functions in the same file, addConst0 and addConst1, that add different constants to the variables. Each of these two subfunctions will print the number of times it has been called.

---

## What You've Learned

**Global variables**   Accessible from any function in the program and persist during the entire life of the program.

**Automatic local variables**   Accessible only from within the function where they are defined and last only during the execution of their function.

**Static local variables**   Accessible only from within the function where they are defined and persist between calls to their function.

**Passing arguments**   The first six are passed in registers. Any additional arguments are passed on the stack.

**Pass by value**   A copy of the value is passed.

**Pass by pointer**   The address of the variable is passed. The address can be changed.

**Pass by reference**   The address of the variable is passed. The address cannot be changed.

**Stack frame**   Creation of the stack frame begins in the calling function and is completed in the called function.

**Frame pointer**   Items placed in the stack frame by the calling function are accessed using positive offset from the frame pointer. Items placed in the stack frame by the called function are accessed using negative offsets.

Now that you know how to write functions, we'll look at a couple of specialized uses of subfunctions in the next chapter.

# 15

## SPECIAL USES OF SUBFUNCTIONS

As we saw in Chapter 14, the most common use of a subfunction is to break a problem into smaller, easier-to-solve subproblems. This is the foundation of recursion, the subject of the first half of this chapter. After we cover recursion, we'll take a look at another use of subfunctions: directly accessing hardware features in assembly language that may not be easily accessible in a higher-level language.

### Recursion

Many computer solutions involve repetitive actions. We saw how to use iteration—while, for, and do-while loops—to perform repetitive actions in Chapter 14. While iteration can be used to solve any repetitive problem, some solutions are described more succinctly using *recursion*. A *recursive algorithm* is an algorithm that calls itself to compute a simpler case of the problem and uses that result to compute the more complex case at hand. The recursive calls continue until the simpler case reaches a *base case*. At this point, the recursive algorithm returns the base case value to the next more complex case where the value is used in that computation. This return/compute process continues, performing the increasingly complex computations along the way, until we're back at the original case.

Let's look at an example. In mathematics, we denote the factorial operation on positive integers with an !, which can be defined recursively:

$$n! = n \times (n - 1)!$$
$$0! = 1$$

The first equation shows that $n!$ is defined by computing a simpler case of itself, $(n - 1)!$. This computation is performed repetitively until we reach the base case of $n = 0$. Then we work our way back out, computing each $n!$ along the way.

For comparison, the iterative definition of the factorial operation is as follows:

$$n! = n \times (n - 1) \times (n - 2) \times \cdots 1$$
$$0! = 1$$

Although both forms of defining the factorial operation involve the same number of computations, the recursive form is more concise and perhaps more intuitive to some people.

Listings 15-1, 15-2, and 15-3 show a program that uses a function, factorial, to compute 3!. You'll see the reason for using a small, fixed value when we use gdb to examine the behavior of the following function:

```
/* threeFactorial.c
 */
#include <stdio.h>
#include "factorial.h"

int main(void)
{
  unsigned int x = 3;
  unsigned int y;

  y = factorial(x);
  printf("%u! = %u\n", x, y);
  return 0;
}
```

*Listing 15-1: Program to compute 3!*

The mathematical factorial function is defined for non-negative integers, so we use unsigned ints.

There is nothing remarkable about the header file for the factorial function, shown in Listing 15-2.

```
/* factorial.h
 */

#ifndef FACTORIAL_H
#define FACTORIAL_H
unsigned int factorial(unsigned int n);
#endif
```

*Listing 15-2: Header file for factorial function*

Listing 15-3 shows that the factorial function calls itself to perform a
simpler computation, $(n - 1)$, so it can easily compute $n!$.

```
/* factorial.c
 */
#include "factorial.h"

unsigned int factorial(unsigned int n)
{
  unsigned int current = 1; /* assume base case */
  if ❶(n != 0)
  {
    current = ❷n * factorial(n - 1);
  }
  return current;
}
```

*Listing 15-3: Function to compute n!*

The factorial function first checks for the base case of $n = 0$ ❶. If we're
at the base case, the current result is 1. If we're not at the base case, the
factorial function calls the factorial function to compute $(n - 1)!$ and multiplies that by $n$ to get $n!$ ❷.

The assembly language for the main function is unremarkable, but let's
look at the assembly language the compiler generated for the factorial
function; see Listing 15-4.

```
        .file   "factorial.c"
        .intel_syntax noprefix
        .text
        .globl  factorial
        .type   factorial, @function
factorial:
        push    rbp
        mov     rbp, rsp
        sub     rsp, 32
     ❶ mov     DWORD PTR -20[rbp], edi ## store n
        mov     DWORD PTR -4[rbp], 1    ## current = 1;
        cmp     DWORD PTR -20[rbp], 0   ## base case?
        je      .L2                     ## yes, current good
        mov     eax, DWORD PTR -20[rbp] ## no, compute n - 1
        sub     eax, 1
     ❷ mov     edi, eax
        call    factorial               ## compute (n - 1)!
```

```
        mov     edx, DWORD PTR -20[rbp] ## load n
❸ imul     eax, edx               ## n * (n - 1)!
        mov     DWORD PTR -4[rbp], eax  ## store in current
.L2
        mov     eax, DWORD PTR -4[rbp]  ## load current
        leave
        ret
        .size   factorial, .-factorial
        .ident  "GCC: (Ubuntu 9.3.0-17ubuntu1~20.04) 9.3.0"
        .section        .note.GNU-stack,"",@progbits
```

*Listing 15-4: Compiler-generated assembly language for the factorial function in Listing 15-3*

The algorithm used in the factorial function is a simple if-then construct that we learned about in Chapter 13. The important part of a recursive function is that we need to save any arguments that are passed to it in registers so that the registers can be reused to pass arguments in the recursive call to the function.

For example, the factorial function takes one argument, n, which is passed in the rdi register. (Only the edi portion of the register is used because an int in our environment is 32 bits.) In Table 11-2 in Chapter 11, we see that we don't need to save the content of rdi in our function, but we need to use rdi for the recursive call with the new value, (n - 1) ❷. And when the recursive call returns, we need the original value of n. The compiler has allocated space in the stack frame for saving n ❶.

We haven't discussed the imul instruction ❸. As you might guess, the instruction here multiplies the integer in eax by the one in edx, leaving the product in eax. The details of multiplication instructions are somewhat complex. We'll discuss them in Chapter 16.

We can simplify the factorial function a bit by writing it directly in assembly language, as shown in Listing 15-5.

```
# factorial.s
# Computes n! recursively.
# Calling sequence:
#       edi <- n
#       call    readLn
# returns n!
        .intel_syntax noprefix
# Stack frame
        .equ    n,-4
        .equ    localSize,-16

        .text
        .globl  factorial
        .type   factorial, @function
factorial:
        push    rbp                     # save frame pointer
        mov     rbp, rsp                # set new frame pointer
        add     rsp, localSize          # for local var.

❶ mov     n[rbp], edi             # save n
❷ mov     eax, 1                  # assume at base case
```

```
        cmp     dword ptr n[rbp], 0  # at base case?
❸ je     done                 # yes, done
        mov     edi, n[rbp]          # no,
❹ sub    edi, 1               # compute (n - 1)!
        call    factorial
❺ mul    dword ptr n[rbp]     # n! = n * (n - 1)!
done:
        mov     rsp, rbp             # restore stack pointer
        pop     rbp                  # and caller frame pointer
        ret
```

*Listing 15-5: Assembly language version of factorial function*

One of the simplifications in our assembly language version of factorial is to use eax as the local variable for storing the current result ❷. We also start by assuming that we're at the base case. If this is true, the result is in eax, where it should be for the return ❸. If not, then we call factorial recursively, passing (n - 1) as the argument ❹. Since the input argument is needed after the return from the recursive call for the n * (n - 1)! computation ❺, we need to save the input argument on the stack ❶.

Instead of the signed multiply instruction, imul, used by the compiler, since all the numbers in this function are unsigned, I chose to use the unsigned multiplication instruction, mul ❺. The mul instruction assumes that the multiplicand is already in eax, which it is upon the return from the recursive call to factorial. After the multiplication operation, the mul instruction replaces the multiplicand in eax with the product, where it needs to be for the return. Again, the details of using both the mul and imul instructions are explained in Chapter 16.

Recursive algorithms can be simple and elegant, but they make heavy use of the stack. I used the assembly language version of factorial (and the C header file in Listing 15-2) with the main function of Listing 15-1 and ran the program under gdb so we can take a look at stack usage.

```
(gdb) li factorial
11
12              .text
13              .globl  factorial
14              .type   factorial, @function
15      factorial:
16              push    rbp               # save frame pointer
17              mov     rbp, rsp          # set new frame pointer
18              add     rsp, localSize    # for local var.
19
20              mov     n[rbp], edi       # save n
(gdb)
21              mov     eax, 1            # assume at base case
22              cmp     dword ptr n[rbp], 0  # at base case?
23              je      done              # yes, done
24              mov     edi, n[rbp]       # no,
25              sub     edi, 1            # compute (n - 1)!
26           ❶ call    factorial
27              imul    eax, n[rbp]       # n! = n * (n - 1)!
28      done:
```

```
29          ❷ mov    rsp, rbp        # restore stack pointer
30            pop    rbp             # and caller frame pointer
(gdb) b 26
Breakpoint 1 at 0x118c: file factorial.s, line 26.
(gdb) b 29
Breakpoint 2 at 0x1195: file factorial.s, line 29.
(gdb) r
Starting program: /home/bob/chap15/factorial_asm/threeFactorial

Breakpoint 2, factorial () at factorial.s:26
26              call    factorial
```

I set two breakpoints, one at the recursive call to factorial ❶ and the second at the point where the function returns ❷. When the program breaks back into gdb, let's look at the input value and stack frame for the first recursive call to factorial.

```
(gdb) i r rax rdi rbp rsp
rax            0x1                1
rdi          ❶ 0x2                2
rbp            0x7fffffffde40     0x7fffffffde40
rsp            0x7fffffffde30     0x7fffffffde30
(gdb) x/4xg 0x7fffffffde30
0x7fffffffde30: 0x00007ffff7fb1fc8   ❷0x00000003555551b0
0x7fffffffde40: 0x00007fffffffde60   ❸0x0000555555555156
```

We see that the first recursive call to factorial is passing 2 as the argument ❶, which is (n - 1) in this program. The stack frame for factorial is 32 bytes, which I'm displaying in 8-byte groups here. The first value that was pushed onto the stack when factorial was called from main is the return address to main ❸.

Keep in mind that memory storage in our environment is little endian, so we need to be careful when reading the value of n stored in the stack frame. The code in Listing 15-5 shows that the variable n is stored −4 from rbp, or at memory location 0x7fffffffde3c in my run of the program here. Since our environment is little endian and we're displaying 8-byte values, the 8 bytes that include memory location 0x7fffffffde3c are displayed with the byte at 0x7fffffffde38 in the rightmost position, and the byte at 0x7fffffffde3f in the leftmost position. So the variable n is the fifth byte from the right of this 8-byte display, 0x03 ❷.

Since the input to factorial is 3 (see Listing 15-1), the function will be recursively called two more times before reaching the base case:

```
(gdb) c
Continuing.

Breakpoint 1, factorial () at factorial.s:26
26              call    factorial
(gdb) c
Continuing.

Breakpoint 1, factorial () at factorial.s:26
```

```
26            call    factorial
(gdb) i r rax rdi rbp rsp
rax           0x1                  1
rdi         ❶ 0x0                  0
rbp           0x7fffffffde00       0x7fffffffde00
rsp           0x7fffffffddf0       0x7fffffffddf0
(gdb) x/12xg 0x7fffffffddf0
0x7fffffffddf0: 0x0000000000000000    0x0000000100000000
0x7fffffffde00: 0x00007fffffffde20  ❷0x0000555555555519a
0x7fffffffde10: 0x00000000000000c2    0x00000002ffffde47
0x7fffffffde20: 0x00007fffffffde40  ❸0x0000555555555519a
0x7fffffffde30: 0x00007ffff7fb1fc8    0x00000003555551b0
0x7fffffffde40: 0x00007fffffffde60  ❹0x0000555555555156
```

Now we're at the point where the recursive call to factorial passes in the base case value, 0 ❶. We can see that factorial has created three stack frames, one above the other. The two most recent stack frames show the return address is to the same place ❷❸, which is in factorial. The oldest stack frame shows the return address to main ❹.

Continuing four more times unwinds the stack frames and takes us back to the first one created when main called factorial.

```
(gdb) c
Continuing.

Breakpoint 2, done () at factorial.s:29
29            mov    rsp, rbp              # restore stack pointer
(gdb) c
Continuing.

Breakpoint 2, done () at factorial.s:29
29            mov    rsp, rbp              # restore stack pointer
(gdb) c
Continuing.

Breakpoint 2, done () at factorial.s:29
29            mov    rsp, rbp              # restore stack pointer
(gdb) c
Continuing.

Breakpoint 2, done () at factorial.s:29
29            mov    rsp, rbp              # restore stack pointer
(gdb) i r rax rdi rbp rsp
rax           0x6               ❶6
rdi         ❷ 0x0                0
rbp           0x7fffffffde40     0x7fffffffde40
rsp           0x7fffffffde30     0x7fffffffde30
(gdb) x/4xg 0x7fffffffde30
0x7fffffffde30: 0x00007ffff7fb1fc8    0x00000003555551b0
0x7fffffffde40: 0x00007fffffffde60    0x0000555555555156
(gdb) c
Continuing.
3! = 6
[Inferior 1 (process 2373) exited normally]
```

Now that we're back in the first call to factorial, the call that will return to main, the argument to this call is the base case, 0 ❷, and it's returning the result, 6 ❶.

As you can see, recursive function calls use a lot of stack space. And since they call a function in each repetition, they can be time-consuming. Every recursive solution has an equivalent iterative solution, which is usually more efficient, both in time and stack usage. The iterative algorithm to compute the factorial of an integer, for example, is simple. But although it doesn't show in this simple example, many problems (for example, some sorting algorithms) lend themselves more naturally to a recursive solution. In such problems, the simplicity of the code is often worth the costs of recursion.

Now that we know how to store data items in a function and move data back and forth between functions in assembly language, we'll look at using assembly language to access hardware features that might not be accessible in the high-level language we're using.

---

**YOUR TURN**

Run the C program in Listings 15-1, 15-2, and 15-3 under gdb. Set a breakpoint at the statement that calls factorial recursively, current = n * factorial(n - 1);, and another breakpoint at the next line, }. You can find the line numbers for setting these breakpoints in factorial by first using the li factorial command in gdb. When the program reaches the call with n = 1, identify the three stack frames. Hint: Use the compiler-generated assembly language in Listing 15-4 to determine the size of a stack frame.

---

## Accessing CPU Features in Assembly Language

In Chapter 14, it may have seemed a bit silly to create a whole subfunction just to add two integers (see Listing 14-8), which can be done with a single instruction. But as we saw in Chapter 3, even simple addition can produce carry or overflow, which is indicated by flags in the rflags register in the CPU.

C and C++ do not provide a way to check the overflow or carry flags in the rflags register. In this section, we'll look at two ways to tell our C function whether there is overflow from addition: we can either write a separate function in assembly language that is callable from our C code or embed assembly language within our C code.

### A Separate Function Written in Assembly Language

We'll start by rewriting the sumInts program in C so that it warns the user if the addition produces overflow. We'll check for overflow in the subfunction, addTwo, and pass the result back to the main function by using the return mechanism.

Listing 15-6 shows our modified main function that checks the return value for overflow.

```
/* sumInts.c
 * Adds two integers using local variables
 * Checks for overflow
 */

#include <stdio.h>
#include "addTwo.h"

int main(void)
{
  int x = 0, y = 0, z;
  int overflow;

  printf("Enter an integer: ");
  scanf("%i", &x);
  printf("Enter an integer: ");
  scanf("%i", &y);
❶ overflow = addTwo(x, y, &z);
  printf("%i + %i = %i\n", x, y, z);
  if ❷(overflow)
  {
    printf("    *** Overflow occurred ***\n");
  }

  return 0;
}
```

Listing 15-6: Program to sum two integers and check for overflow

We'll rewrite the addTwo function such that it returns 0 if there's no over-flow and 1 if there is overflow, which we assign to the variable, overflow ❶. In C, zero is logically false, while nonzero is true ❷.

Listing 15-7 shows our header file for our new addTwo function.

```
/* addTwo.h
 * Adds two integers and determines overflow.
 */

#ifndef ADDTWO_H
#define ADDTWO_H
int addTwo(int a, int b, int *c);
#endif
```

Listing 15-7: Header file for addTwo function that checks for overflow

The only change in the function declaration is returning an int instead of void. We need to add a check for overflow in the definition of the addTwo function, as shown in Listing 15-8.

```
/* addTwo.c
 * Adds two integers and determines overflow.
 */

#include "addTwo.h"
```

```
int addTwo(int a, int b, int *c)
{
  int temp;
  int overflow = 0;   /* assume no overflow */

  temp = a + b;
  if ❶(((a > 0) && (b > 0) && (temp < 0)) ||
      ((a < 0) && (b < 0) && (temp > 0)))
  {
    overflow = 1;
  }
  *c = temp;
  return overflow;
}
```

*Listing 15-8: Adds two integers and checks for overflow*

We learned in Chapter 3 that if adding two integers of the same sign gives a result of the opposite sign, we have overflow, so we use this logic as the check for overflow ❶. Listing 15-9 shows the assembly language generated by the compiler from this C source.

```
        .file   "addTwo.c"
        .intel_syntax noprefix
        .text
        .globl  addTwo
        .type   addTwo, @function
addTwo:
        push    rbp
        mov     rbp, rsp
        mov     DWORD PTR -20[rbp], edi   ## store a
        mov     DWORD PTR -24[rbp], esi   ## store b
        mov     QWORD PTR -32[rbp], rdx   ## address of c
     ❶  mov     DWORD PTR -8[rbp], 0      ## overflow = 0;
        mov     edx, DWORD PTR -20[rbp]
        mov     eax, DWORD PTR -24[rbp]
        add     eax, edx                 ## a + b
        mov     DWORD PTR -4[rbp], eax    ## temp = a + b;
     ❷  cmp     DWORD PTR -20[rbp], 0     ## a <= 0?
        jle     .L2                      ## yes
        cmp     DWORD PTR -24[rbp], 0     ## b <= 0?
        jle     .L2                      ## yes
        cmp     DWORD PTR -4[rbp], 0      ## temp < 0?
        js      .L3                      ## yes, overflow
.L2:
        cmp     DWORD PTR -20[rbp], 0     ## a == 0?
     ❸  jns     .L4                      ## yes, no overflow
        cmp     DWORD PTR -24[rbp], 0     ## b == 0?
        jns     .L4                      ## yes, no overflow
        cmp     DWORD PTR -4[rbp], 0      ## temp == 0?
        jle     .L4                      ## yes, no overflow
.L3:
     ❹  mov     DWORD PTR -8[rbp], 1
.L4:
        mov     rax, QWORD PTR -32[rbp]   ## address of c
```

```
        mov     edx, DWORD PTR -4[rbp]      ## temp
        mov     DWORD PTR [rax], edx        ## *c = temp;
        mov     eax, DWORD PTR -8[rbp]      ## return overflow;
        pop     rbp
        ret
        .size   addTwo, .-addTwo
        .ident  "GCC: (Ubuntu 9.3.0-17ubuntu1~20.04) 9.3.0"
        .section        .note.GNU-stack,"",@progbits
```

*Listing 15-9: Assembly language generated by the compiler for addTwo in Listing 15-8*

The algorithm starts by assuming there will not be overflow ❶. After adding the two integers, it checks to see if a ≤ 0 ❷. If it is, it then checks to see a is negative by comparing a to 0 and checking the sign flag in the rflags register ❸. If it is 0, there is no overflow, so the algorithm jumps past the instruction that would change the overflow variable to 1 ❹.

The algorithm for determining overflow in C (Listing 15-8) is somewhat complicated, so we'll take advantage of the fact that the CPU makes that determination during addition and sets the status flags in the rflags register accordingly. We can use the results in the rflags register by writing addTwo directly in assembly language, as shown in Listing 15-10.

```
# addTwo.s
# Adds two integers and returns OF
# Calling sequence:
#       edi <- x, 32-bit int
#       esi <- y, 32-bit int
#       rdx <- &z, place to store sum
#       returns value of OF
        .intel_syntax noprefix
# Stack frame
        .equ    temp,-4
        .equ    overflow,-8
        .equ    localSize,-16
# Code
        .text
        .globl  addTwo
        .type   addTwo, @function
addTwo:
        push    rbp         # save frame pointer
        mov     rbp, rsp    # set new frame pointer
        add     rsp, localSize # for local var.

        add     edi, esi    # x + y
❶      seto    al          # OF T or F
        movzx   eax, al     # convert to int for return
        mov     [rdx] , edi # *c = sum

        mov     rsp, rbp    # restore stack pointer
        pop     rbp         # and caller frame pointer
        ret
```

*Listing 15-10: Assembly language version of addTwo returns the value of the OF flag*

We're using another instruction in Listing 15-10, seto ❶. The setcc instructions are used to tell when various conditions, as shown in the condition codes, are true or false:

**setcc—Byte on Condition**

Sets an 8-bit register to 0 or 1 depending on the condition *cc*.

setcc *reg* stores 1 in 8-bit *reg* when *cc* is true, 0 when *cc* is false.

The setcc instructions use the same *cc* codes as those in the jcc group, as shown in Table 13-1 in Chapter 13. *reg* is an 8-bit register, except ah, bh, ch, and dh cannot be used in 64-bit mode. C treats 1 as true and 0 as false.

Another difference in our assembly language version of addTwo is that we won't use the red zone for local variables. It's a matter of personal programming style, but I prefer to create a full stack frame so I don't have to worry about using the stack if I change the function. I also have not saved the input arguments. The values in the registers used for passing arguments do not need to be preserved for the calling function (see Table 11-2 in Chapter 11).

If we use the C version of the main function (Listing 15-6) to call our assembly language version of addTwo, we still need to #include the C header file (Listing 15-7) to tell the compiler how to call addTwo.

Comparing our assembly language solution (Listing 15-10) with what the compiler did (Listing 15-9) shows that we used about half as many instructions.

**NOTE** *We need to be careful about such comparisons. The speed of program execution depends as much on the internal CPU architecture as on the number of instructions. I think the real savings in this example comes from not having to use somewhat complex C code to tell us about overflow.*

Our assembly language version of the main function for this program, as shown in Listing 15-11, is similar to what the compiler generates from the C version, but our use of symbolic names for offsets in the stack frame and labels makes it easier to read.

```
# sumInts.s
# Adds two integers using local variables
# Checks for overflow
        .intel_syntax noprefix

# Stack frame
        .equ    x,-24
        .equ    y,-20
        .equ    z,-16
        .equ    overflow,-12
        .equ    canary,-8
        .equ    localSize,-32
# Read only data
        .section  .rodata
```

```
askMsg:
        .string "Enter an integer: "
readFormat:
        .string "%i"
resultFormat:
        .string "%i + %i = %i\n"
overMsg:
        .string "    *** Overflow occurred ***\n"
# Code
        .text
        .globl  main
        .type   main, @function
main:
        push    rbp                     # save frame pointer
        mov     rbp, rsp                # set new frame pointer
        add     rsp, localSize          # for local var.
        mov     rax, fs:40              # get stack canary
        mov     canary[rbp], rax        # and save it

        mov     dword ptr x[rbp], 0 # x = 0
        mov     dword ptr y[rbp], 0 # y = 0

        lea     rdi, askMsg[rip]        # ask for integer
        mov     eax, 0
        call    printf@plt
        lea     rsi, x[rbp]             # place to store x
        lea     rdi, readFormat[rip]
        mov     eax, 0
        call    __isoc99_scanf@plt

        lea     rdi, askMsg[rip]        # ask for integer
        mov     eax, 0
        call    printf@plt
        lea     rsi, y[rbp]             # place to store y
        lea     rdi, readFormat[rip]
        mov     eax, 0
        call    __isoc99_scanf@plt

        lea     rdx, z[rbp]             # place to store sum
        mov     esi, x[rbp]             # load x
        mov     edi, y[rbp]             # load y
        call    addTwo
        mov     overflow[rbp], eax # save overflow
        mov     ecx, z[rbp]             # load z
        mov     edx, y[rbp]             # load y
        mov     esi, x[rbp]             # load x
        lea     rdi, resultFormat[rip]
        mov     eax, 0                  # no floating point
        call    printf@plt

        cmp     dword ptr overflow[rbp], 0 # overflow?
        je      noOverflow
        lea     rdi, overMsg[rip]       # yes, print message
        mov     eax, 0
        call    printf@plt
```

```
noOverflow:
        mov     eax, 0                  # return 0

        mov     rcx, canary[rbp]        # retrieve saved canary
        xor     rcx, fs:40              # and check it
        je      goodCanary
        call    __stack_chk_fail@plt  # bad canary
goodCanary:
        mov     rsp, rbp                # restore stack pointer
        pop     rbp                     # and caller frame pointer
        ret
```

*Listing 15-11: Assembly language version of the main function for the sumIntegers program*

This example shows one of the reasons for writing a subfunction in assembly language—we were able to access a feature of the CPU, the OF in the rflags register, which is not accessible in the higher-level language we're using, C. And we needed to check for overflow immediately after the operation that we are checking is performed (addition, in this example).

This example also illustrates a common use of the return value. Inputs and outputs are often passed in the argument list, with supplemental information about the computation carried in the return value.

That said, calling a function to simply add two numbers is inefficient. In the next section, we'll look at a common extension to C that allows us to insert assembly language directly in our C code.

### Inline Assembly Language

Like many C compilers, gcc includes an extension to the standard C language that allows us to embed assembly language in our C code, *inline assembly*. Doing so can be complex. We'll look at a simple case here. You can read the details at *https://gcc.gnu.org/onlinedocs/gcc/Using-Assembly-Language-with-C.html*, or you can use the **info gcc** shell command and select **C Extensions ▸ Using Assembly Language with C ▸ Extended Asm**.

The general form for embedding assembly language in C is as follows:

```
asm asm-qualifiers (assembly language statements
                : output operands
                : input operands
                : clobbers);
```

The *asm-qualifiers* are used to help the compiler optimize the C code, a topic that is beyond the scope of this book. We're not asking the compiler to optimize our C code, so we won't use *asm-qualifiers*.

The *output operands* are the C variables that could be changed by the *assembly language statements*, thus acting as outputs from the *assembly language statements*. The *input operands* are the C variables that are used by the *assembly language statements* but are not changed, thus acting as inputs to the *assembly language statements*. The *clobbers* are the registers that get explicitly changed by the *assembly language statements*, thus telling the compiler about the possible changes in these registers.

In Listing 15-12, we use inline assembly language to check for overflow in our addition.

```c
/* sumInts.c
 * Adds two integers
 */

#include <stdio.h>

int main(void)
{
  int x = 0, y = 0, z, overflow;

  printf("Enter an integer: ");
  scanf("%i", &x);
  printf("Enter an integer: ");
  scanf("%i", &y);

  asm("mov edi, ❶%2❷\n"
      "❸add edi, %3\n"
      "seto al\n"
      "movzx eax, al\n"
      "mov %1, eax\n"
      "mov %0, edi"
      : ❹"=rm" (z), "=rm" (overflow)
      : ❺"rm" (x), "rm" (y)
      : "rax", "rdx", ❻"cc");

  printf("%i + %i = %i\n", x, y, z);
  if (overflow)
    printf("*** Overflow occurred ***\n");

  return 0;
}
```

*Listing 15-12: Using inline assembly language to check for overflow when adding*

The first thing to note about our code here is that it's important to place the add instruction in the assembly language ❸ so that we can check for overflow immediately after the instruction is executed. If we were to do the addition in C and then just check for overflow in our assembly language, the compiler might insert an instruction before our assembly language that might change the overflow flag.

We need to specify the constraints on each of our C variables. The "=rm" (z) ❹ says that our assembly language will assign a value to the z C variable (=) and that the compiler can use either a register (r) or memory (m) for z. We would use "+rm" if the value of the variable is updated in our assembly language. Our inline assembly language code only reads the values in the x and y C variables, so the constraints on them are "rm" ❺.

We specify the C variables in our assembly language by using the syntax %*n* ❶, where *n* is the relative position in the ouputs:inputs list, starting from 0. In our program, z is in position 0, overflow in 1, x in 2, and y in 3. So the instruction mov edi, %2 loads the value in the C variable y into the edi register.

Remember that assembly language source code is line-oriented, so it's important to place a newline character at the end of each assembly language statement ❷. The newline is not needed at the end of the last assembly language statement.

We need to be careful when using inline assembly language. The compiler could generate assembly language for our C code that does not work well with our assembly language. It's a good idea to generate the assembly language for the entire function (using the -S compiler option) and read it carefully to make sure the function is doing what you intend.

---

**YOUR TURN**

1.  Modify the functions in Listings 15-6, 15-7, and 15-10 to use unsigned ints and tell the user when the addition produces carry. Write the main function in C. It will declare the variables as follows:

    ```
    unsigned int x = 0, y = 0, z;
    ```

    The formatting code for reading and printing the values of the unsigned ints is %u. Here's an example:

    ```
    scanf("%u", &x);
    ```

2.  Modify the program in Listing 15-12 to use unsigned ints and tell the user when the addition produces carry.

---

## What You've Learned

**Recursion**  Allows for simple and elegant solutions to some problems, but uses lots of stack space.

**Accessing hardware features.**  Most programming languages do not allow direct access to all the hardware features in a computer. An assembly language subfunction, or inline assembly language, may be the best solution.

**Inline assembly**  Allows us to embed assembly language in our C code.

Now that you know some common ways to use functions in a program, we'll move on to multiplication, division, and logic operations. You'll learn how to convert a string of numerals in ASCII code to the integer they represent.

# 16

## COMPUTING WITH BITWISE LOGIC, MULTIPLICATION, AND DIVISION INSTRUCTIONS

Now that we've learned about program organization, let's turn our attention to computation. We'll start by looking at the logic operators, which can be used to change individual bits in a value by using a technique called *masking*. Then we'll move on to shift operations, which provide a way to multiply or divide by powers of two. In the last two sections of this chapter, we'll cover arithmetic multiplication and division by arbitrary integers.

### Bit Masking

It's often better to think of data items as patterns of bits rather than numerical entities. For example, if you look back at Table 2-5 in Chapter 2, you'll see that the only difference between uppercase and lowercase alphabetic characters in the ASCII code is bit number 5. It's 1 for lowercase and 0 for uppercase. For example, the ASCII code for m is 0x6d, and for M it's 0x4d. If you wanted to write a function that changed the case of a string of alphabetic characters from lowercase to uppercase, you could view this as a numerical difference of 32. You would need to determine the current case of the character and then decide whether to change it by subtracting 32.

But there's a faster way. We can change bit patterns by using logical bitwise operations and a *mask*, or *bitmask*. A mask is a specific pattern of bits that can be used to make specified bits in a variable either 1 or 0, or to invert them. For example, to make sure an alphabetic character is uppercase, we need to make sure its bit number 5 is 0, giving the mask 11011111 = 0xdf. Then, using the previous example of m, 0x6d ∧ 0xdf = 0x4d, which is M. And if the character is already uppercase, then 0x4d ∧ 0xdf = 0x4d, leaving it as uppercase. This solution avoids checking for the case before the conversion.

We can use similar logic for other operations. If you want to make a bit 1, you place a 1 in the appropriate bit position in the mask and use the bitwise OR operation. To produce a 0 in a bit position, place a 0 in that position and a 1 in each of the other bit positions in the mask and then use the bitwise AND operation. You can invert bits by placing a 1 in each bit position you want to invert, placing 0 in all other positions, and using the bitwise XOR operation.

## Bit Masking in C

As you saw earlier, uppercase and lowercase alphabetic characters in the ASCII code are distinguished by bit 5, which is 0 for uppercase and 1 for lowercase. The program in Listings 16-1, 16-2, and 16-3 shows how to use a mask to convert all lowercase alphabetic characters in a text string to uppercase.

**NOTE** *This program, and many that follow in the book, use the* readLn *and* writeStr *functions that you were asked to write in "Your Turn" at the end of Chapter 14. If you want, you could use the* gets *and* puts *functions, respectively, in the C standard library, but you would need to make the appropriate changes in the book's functions that call them because their behavior is a little different.*

```
/* upperCase.c
 * Converts alphabetic characters to uppercase
 */

#include <stdio.h>
#include "toUpper.h"
#include "writeStr.h"
#include "readLn.h"
❶ #define MAX 50

int main()
{
❷ char myString[MAX];

    writeStr("Enter up to 50 alphabetic characters: ");
```

```
❸ readLn(myString, MAX);

❹ toUpper(myString, myString);
  writeStr("All upper: ");
  writeStr(myString);
  writeStr("\n");

  return 0;
}
```

*Listing 16-1: Program to convert lowercase alpha characters to uppercase*

The main function in this program allocates a char array ❷ to hold user input. We use #define to give a symbolic name to the length of the array ❶, which allows us to easily change the length in one place and make sure the correct value gets passed to the readLn function ❸.

Passing the name of an array in C passes the address of the beginning of the array, so we *don't* use the & (address of) operator ❹. You'll learn more about how arrays are implemented in Chapter 17. Nothing else is new in this main function, so we'll move on to the subfunction, toUpper.

Since we're passing the same array as both the source and destination arrays to toUpper, it will replace the characters stored in the array with the new values.

```
/* toUpper.h
 * Converts alphabetic letters in a C string to uppercase.
 */

#ifndef TOUPPER_H
#define TOUPPER_H
int toUpper(char *srcPtr, char *destPtr);
#endif
```

*Listing 16-2: Header file for the toUpper function*

```
/* toUpper.c
 * Converts alphabetic letters in a C string to uppercase.
 */

#include "toUpper.h"
#define UPMASK ❶0xdf
#define NUL '\0'

int toUpper(char *srcPtr, char *destPtr)
{
  int count = 0;
  while (*srcPtr != NUL)
  {
    *destPtr = ❷*srcPtr & UPMASK;
    srcPtr++;
    destPtr++;
    count++;
  }
```

❸ *destPtr = *srcPtr;

❹ return count;
}

---

*Listing 16-3: The toUpper function*

To make sure that bit 5 is 0, we use a mask that has 0 in bit position 5 and 1 elsewhere ❶. While it's not the NUL character, we perform a bitwise AND with the character, which masks out bit 5 and allows all the other bits to remain the same in the result ❷. Don't forget to include the NUL character from the input text string ❸! Forgetting to do so is a common programming error that often does not show up during testing, because the byte in memory following where the output is being stored just happens to be 0x00 (the NUL character). Then if you change the length of the input text string, the next byte in memory may not be 0x00. The error might show up in a seemingly random way.

Although this function returns a count of the number of characters processed ❹, our main function does nothing with the value. A calling function doesn't need to use a returned value. I usually include a counting algorithm in functions like this for debugging purposes if needed.

Listing 16-4 shows the assembly language the compiler generates for the toUpper function.

```
        .file   "toUpper.c"
        .intel_syntax noprefix
        .text
        .globl  toUpper
        .type   toUpper, @function
toUpper:
        push    rbp
        mov     rbp, rsp
        mov     QWORD PTR -24[rbp], rdi ## save srcPtr
        mov     QWORD PTR -32[rbp], rsi ## save destPtr
        mov     DWORD PTR -4[rbp], 0    ## count = 0;
        jmp     .L2
.L3:
❶ mov     rax, QWORD PTR -24[rbp] ## load srcPtr
❷ movzx   eax, BYTE PTR [rax]     ## and char there
❸ and     eax, -33               ## and with 0xdf
        mov     edx, eax
        mov     rax, QWORD PTR -32[rbp] ## load destPtr
        mov     BYTE PTR [rax], dl      ## store new char
        add     QWORD PTR -24[rbp], 1   ## srcPtr++;
        add     QWORD PTR -32[rbp], 1   ## destPtr++;
        add     DWORD PTR -4[rbp], 1    ## count++;
.L2:
❹ mov     rax, QWORD PTR -24[rbp] ## load srcPtr
❺ movzx   eax, BYTE PTR [rax]     ## and char there
❻ test    al, al                 ## NUL char?
        jne     .L3                    ## no, loop back
        mov     rax, QWORD PTR -24[rbp] ## yes, load srcPtr
        movzx   edx, BYTE PTR [rax]     ## and char there
```

```
    mov     rax, QWORD PTR -32[rbp]  ## load destPtr
    mov     BYTE PTR [rax], dl       ## store NUL
    mov     eax, DWORD PTR -4[rbp]   ## return count;
    pop     rbp
    ret
    .size   toUpper, .-toUpper
    .ident  "GCC: (Ubuntu 9.3.0-17ubuntu1~20.04) 9.3.0 "
    .section        .note.GNU-stack,"",@progbits
```

*Listing 16-4: Compiler-generated assembly language for the toUpper function*

Before entering the while loop, toUpper loads the address of the source text string into rax ❶❹. The movzx instruction overwrites the address in rax with the byte stored at that address (BYTE PTR) and zeros the upper 56 bits of the register ❷❺. The and instruction ❸ uses the immediate data -33 = 0xdf, which is the mask to turn bit 5 to 0, thus making sure that the character is uppercase. This code sequence is repeated within the while loop for each character in the input text string that is not the NUL character ❻.

As explained, treating the characters as bit patterns rather than as numerical values works for both converting lowercase to uppercase and letting uppercase remain unchanged.

Listing 16-4 introduces another logic instruction, and ❸. We already saw the xor instruction in Chapter 11. Let's look at two more logical instructions, and and or.

## Logic Instructions

*Logic instructions* work bitwise. That is, they operate on the individual bits in the corresponding bit positions of the two operands. Two of the most common logic instructions are AND and OR.

### and—Logical AND

Performs a bitwise AND between two values.

and *reg1, reg2* performs bitwise AND between values in registers, *reg1* and *reg2*, which can be the same or different registers. The result is left in *reg1*.

and *reg, mem* performs bitwise AND between a value in a register and a value in memory, leaving the result in the register.

and *mem, reg* performs bitwise AND between a value in memory and a value in a register, leaving the result in memory.

and *reg, imm* performs bitwise AND between a value in a register and the constant *imm*, leaving the result in the register.

and *mem, imm* performs bitwise AND between a value in memory and the constant *imm*, leaving the result in memory.

The and instruction performs a bitwise AND between the source and destination values, leaving the result in the destination. The SF, ZF, and PF flags in the rflags register are set according to the result, the OF and CF flags are set to 0, and the AF flag is undefined.

### or—Logical Inclusive OR

Performs a bitwise inclusive OR between two values.

or *reg1, reg2* performs bitwise inclusive OR between values in registers, *reg1* and *reg2*, which can be the same or different registers. The result is left in *reg1*.

or *reg, mem* performs bitwise inclusive OR between a value in a register and a value in memory, leaving the result in the register.

or *mem, reg* performs bitwise inclusive OR between a value in memory and a value in a register, leaving the result in memory.

or *reg, imm* performs bitwise inclusive OR between a value in a register and the constant *imm*, leaving the result in the register.

or *mem, imm* performs bitwise inclusive OR between a value in memory and the constant *imm*, leaving the result in memory.

The or instruction performs a bitwise inclusive OR between the source and destination values, leaving the result in the destination. The SF, ZF, and PF flags in the rflags register are set according to the result, the OF and CF flags are set to 0, and the AF flag is undefined.

Next, we'll look at a way to write this same program directly in assembly language.

## Bit Masking in Assembly Language

We'll use the same masking algorithm in our assembly language version, but we'll use identifiers that make it easier to see what is taking place. Listing 16-5 shows the main function written in assembly language.

```
# upperCase.s
# Makes user alphabetic text string all upper case
        .intel_syntax noprefix
# Stack frame
        .equ    myString,-64
        .equ    canary,-8
        .equ  ❶ localSize,-64
# Useful constants
        .equ    upperMask,0xdf
        .equ  ❷ MAX,50                    # character buffer limit
        .equ    NUL,0
# Constant data
        .section  .rodata
        .align  8
prompt:
        .string "Enter up to 50 alphabetic characters: "
message:
        .string "All upper: "
newLine:
        .string "\n"
# Code
        .text
        .globl  main
        .type       main, @function
```

```
main:
        push    rbp                     # save frame pointer
        mov     rbp, rsp                # set new frame pointer
        add     rsp, localSize          # for local var.
        mov     rax, qword ptr fs:40    # get canary
        mov     qword ptr canary[rbp], rax

        lea     rdi, prompt[rip]        # prompt user
        call    writeStr

        mov     esi, MAX                # limit user input
        lea     rdi, myString[rbp]      # place to store input
        call    readLn

        lea     rsi, myString[rbp]      # destination string
        lea     rdi, myString[rbp]      # source string
        call    toUpper

        lea     rdi, message[rip]       # tell user
        call    writeStr

    ❸  lea     rdi, myString[rbp]      # result
        call    writeStr
        lea     rdi, newLine[rip]       # some formatting
        call    writeStr

        mov     eax, 0                  # return 0;
        mov     rcx, canary[rbp]        # retrieve saved canary
        xor     rcx, fs:40              # and check it
        je      goodCanary
        call    __stack_chk_fail@PLT    # bad canary
goodCanary:
        mov     rsp, rbp                # restore stack pointer
        pop     rbp                     # and caller frame pointer
        ret
```

*Listing 16-5: Assembly language version of the main function to convert lowercase alphabetic characters to uppercase*

We're allowing enough memory space for 50 characters ❷. Allowing another 8 bytes for the canary value totals 58 bytes, but we need to keep the stack pointer at a multiple of 16, so we allocate 64 bytes for our local variables ❶. We're passing the address of the char array as both the source and the destination to the toUpper function ❸, so it will replace the original values in the array with the new ones.

We'll use the same masking algorithm as the compiler when writing toUpper in assembly language but will structure the function differently. See Listing 16-6 for the code.

```
# toUpper.s
# Converts alphabetic characters in a C string to upper case.
# Calling sequence:
#   rdi <- pointer to source string
#   rsi <- pointer to destination string
```

```
#    returns number of characters processed.
        .intel_syntax noprefix

# Stack frame
        .equ    count,-4
        .equ    localSize,-16
# Useful constants
        .equ    upperMask,0xdf
        .equ    NUL,0
# Code
        .text
        .globl  toUpper
        .type   toUpper, @function
toUpper:
        push    rbp                     # save frame pointer
        mov     rbp, rsp                # set new frame pointer
    ❶ add     rsp, localSize          # for local var.

        mov     dword ptr count[rbp], 0
whileLoop:
        mov   ❷ al, byte ptr [rdi]      # char from source
        and     al, upperMask           # no, make sure it's upper
        mov     byte ptr [rsi], al      # char to destination
    ❸ cmp     al, NUL                 # was it the end?
        je      allDone                 # yes, all done
        inc     rdi                     # increment
        inc     rsi                     #       pointers
        inc     dword ptr count[rbp]    #       and counter
        jmp     whileLoop               # continue loop
allDone:
    ❹ mov     byte ptr [rsi], al      # finish with NUL
        mov     eax, dword ptr count[rbp] # return count

        mov     rsp, rbp                # restore stack pointer
        pop     rbp                     # and caller frame pointer
        ret
```

*Listing 16-6: The toUpper function, written in assembly language*

The compiler used the red zone on the stack for local variables, but I prefer creating an explicit stack frame ❶. Instead of saving the source and destination addresses that were passed to this function in the local variable area of the stack, we can simply use the registers that the addresses were passed in.

The compiler used the movzx instruction to zero the portion of the rax register that was not used for processing each character. I prefer using a byte portion of the rax register, al, to process a character since that's the correct size ❷. Keep in mind that this leaves the 56 high-order bits in rax as they were, but if we are consistent in using only al when processing the character in the algorithm, that will be irrelevant. It also seems more natural to me to use the cmp instruction instead of test to check for the termination character, NUL ❸. And, as explained earlier, don't forget to include the NUL character ❹.

*I do not know whether my assembly language solution is more, or less, efficient than what the compiler produced. In most cases, code readability is far more important than efficiency.*

---

**YOUR TURN**

1. Write a program in assembly language that converts all alphabetic characters to lowercase.

2. Write a program in assembly language that changes the case of all alphabetic characters to the opposite case.

3. Write a program in assembly language that converts all alphabetic characters to uppercase and to lowercase. Your program should also show the user's original input string after displaying both the uppercase and lowercase conversions.

---

## Shifting Bits

It's sometimes useful to be able to shift all the bits in a variable to the left or to the right. If the variable is an integer, shifting all the bits to the left one position effectively multiplies the integer by two, and shifting them one position to the right effectively divides it by two. Using left/right shifts to do multiplication/division by powers of two is very efficient.

### Shifting Bits in C

We'll discuss shifts by looking at a program that reads integers entered in hexadecimal from the keyboard and stores it as a long int. The program reads up to eight characters: '0'...'f'. Each character is in 8-bit ASCII code and represents a 4-bit integer, 0–15. Our program starts with a 64-bit integer that is 0. Starting with the most significant hexadecimal character, the first one entered by the user, the program converts the 8-bit ASCII code to its corresponding 4-bit integer. We'll shift the accumulated value of our 64-bit integer four bits to the left to make room for the next 4-bit integer and then add the new 4-bit integer value to the accumulated value.

Listings 16-7, 16-8, and 16-9 show the program.

---

```
/* convertHex.c
 * Gets hex number from user and stores it as a long int.
 */
#include <stdio.h>
#include "writeStr.h"
#include "readLn.h"
#include "hexToInt.h"

#define MAX 20
```

```
int main()
{
  char theString[MAX];
  long int theInt;

  writeStr("Enter up to 16 hex characters: ");
  readLn(theString, MAX);

  hexToInt(theString, &theInt);
  printf("%lx = %li\n", theInt, theInt);
  return 0;
}
```

*Listing 16-7: Program to convert hexadecimal to a* `long int`

The program allocates a `char` array for storing the user input character string and a `long int` to hold the converted value. The size of the `long int` data type depends on the operating system and hardware it's running on. In our environment, it's 64 bits. After reading the user's input string, the `main` function calls `hexToInt` to do the actual conversion, passing the addresses of the input text string and the variable where the result will be stored.

The `printf` function converts `theInt` back to character format for display on the screen. The `%lx` formatting code tells `printf` to display the entire `long int` (64 bits in our environment) in hexadecimal. The `%li` formatting code displays the `long int` in decimal.

```
/* hexToInt.h
 * Converts hex character string to long int.
 * Returns number of characters converted.
 */

#ifndef HEXTOINT_H
#define HEXTOINT_H
int hexToInt(char *stringPtr, long int *intPtr);
#endif
```

*Listing 16-8: Header file for the* `hexToInt` *function*

The header file declares the `hexToInt` function, which takes two pointers. The `char` pointer is the input, and the `long int` pointer is the location for the primary output. The `hexToInt` function also returns the number of characters that it converted as an `int` as a secondary output.

```
/* hexToInt.c
 * Converts hex character string to int.
 * Returns number of characters.
 */

#include "hexToInt.h"
#define GAP 0x07
#define INTPART 0x0f /* also works for lowercase */
#define NUL '\0'
```

```
int hexToInt(char *stringPtr, long int *intPtr)
{
  *intPtr = 0;
  char current;
  int count = 0;

  current = *stringPtr;
  while (current != NUL)
  {
    if (current > '9')
    {
    ❶ current -= GAP;
    }
  ❷ current = current & INTPART;
  ❸ *intPtr = *intPtr  4;
  ❹ *intPtr |= current;
    stringPtr++;
    count++;
    current = *stringPtr;
  }
  return count;
}
```

*Listing 16-9: Converting a string of hexadecimal characters to a* `long int`

First, we need to convert the hexadecimal character to a 4-bit integer.
The ASCII code for the numeric characters ranges from 0x30 to 0x39, and for
the uppercase alphabetic characters from 0x41 to 0x46. Subtracting this 0x07
gap from the alphabetic characters ❶ gives us the bit patterns 0x30, 0x31, ...,
0x39, 0x3a, ..., 0x3f for the characters entered. Of course, the user may enter
lowercase alphabetic characters, in which case subtracting 0x07 gives 0x30,
0x31, ..., 0x39, 0x5a, ..., 0x5f. Each hexadecimal character represents four bits,
and if we look at the low-order four bits after subtracting 0x07, they are the
same whether the user enters lowercase or uppercase alphabetic characters.
We can convert to a 4-bit integer by masking off the upper four bits with the
bit pattern 0x0f using the C bitwise AND operator, & ❷.

Next, we shift all the bits in the accumulated value four bits to the left
to make room for the next four bits represented by the hexadecimal character ❸. The left shift leaves 0s in the four least significant bit positions, so
we can copy the four bits in current into these positions with the bitwise OR
operation, | ❹.

Now let's look at the assembly language the compiler generates for the
hexToInt function, as shown in Listing 16-10.

```
        .file   "hexToInt.c"
        .intel_syntax noprefix
        .text
        .globl  hexToInt
        .type   hexToInt, @function
hexToInt:
        push    rbp
        mov     rbp, rsp
        mov     QWORD PTR -24[rbp], rdi ## save stringPtr
```

```
        mov     QWORD PTR -32[rbp], rsi  ## save intPtr
        mov     rax, QWORD PTR -32[rbp]
        mov     QWORD PTR [rax], 0       ## *intPtr = 0;
        mov     DWORD PTR -4[rbp], 0     ## count = 0;
        mov     rax, QWORD PTR -24[rbp]  ## load stringPtr
        movzx   eax, BYTE PTR [rax]      ## current = *stringPtr
        mov     BYTE PTR -5[rbp], al
        jmp     .L2
.L4:
        cmp     BYTE PTR -5[rbp], 57     ## current <= '9'?
        jle     .L3                      ## yes, skip
        movzx   eax, BYTE PTR -5[rbp]    ## no, load current
        sub     eax, 7                   ## subtract gap
        mov     BYTE PTR -5[rbp], al     ## store current
.L3:
  ❶ and     BYTE PTR -5[rbp], 15     ## current & 0x0f
        mov     rax, QWORD PTR -32[rbp]  ## load intPtr
        mov     rax, QWORD PTR [rax]     ## load *intPtr
  ❷ sal     rax, 4                   ## make room for 4 bits
        mov     rdx, rax
        mov     rax, QWORD PTR -32[rbp]
        mov     QWORD PTR [rax], rdx     ## store shifted value
        mov     rax, QWORD PTR -32[rbp]
        mov     rdx, QWORD PTR [rax]     ## load shifted value
  ❸ movsx   rax, BYTE PTR -5[rbp]    ## load new 4 bits
  ❹ or      rdx, rax                 ## add them
        mov     rax, QWORD PTR -32[rbp]
        mov     QWORD PTR [rax], rdx     ## store updated value
        add     QWORD PTR -24[rbp], 1    ## stringPtr++;
        add     DWORD PTR -4[rbp], 1     ## count++;
        mov     rax, QWORD PTR -24[rbp]
        movzx   eax, BYTE PTR [rax]      ## load next character
        mov     BYTE PTR -5[rbp], al     ## and store it
.L2:
        cmp     BYTE PTR -5[rbp], 0      ## NUL character?
        jne     .L4                      ## no, continue looping
        mov     eax, DWORD PTR -4[rbp]   ## yes, return count
        pop     rbp
        ret
        .size   hexToInt, .-hexToInt
        .size   hexToInt, .-hexToInt
        .ident  "GCC: (Ubuntu 9.3.0-17ubuntu1~20.04) 9.3.0"
        .section        .note.GNU-stack,"",@progbits
```

*Listing 16-10: Compiler-generated assembly language for the hexToInt function*

After subtracting the gap between the numeric and alphabetic characters, if necessary, the character is converted to a 4-bit integer with a masking
operation, leaving the result in the current variable in the stack frame ❶.
The accumulated value is then shifted four bit positions to the left to make
room for the new 4-bit integer value ❷.

These four bits are inserted into the vacated location in the accumulated value with an or instruction ❹, but like most arithmetic and logic
operations, it can be performed only on same-sized values. The accumulated

value is a 64-bit long int, so the 4-bit integer must be *type cast* to a 64-bit long int before inserting it into the 64-bit accumulated value. If the C compiler can figure out what type casting is needed from the C statement, it will do it automatically. Indeed, the compiler used the movsx instruction to extend the 8-bit value at -5[rbp] to a 64-bit value in rax ❸. The movsx instruction does sign extension, but since the masking operation made the high-order four bits of the 8-bit value all 0, the sign extension copies the 0 in bit number 7 into the 56 high-order bits of rax.

### movsx—Move with Sign-Extension

Copies (moves) an 8-bit or 16-bit value from memory or a register to a larger register width and copies the sign bit into the high-order bits in the destination register.

movsx *reg1, reg2* moves the value in *reg2* to *reg1*.

movsx *reg, mem* moves from a memory location to a register.

The movsx instruction extends the number of bits occupied by a value. The extension can be from 8 bits to 16, 32, or 64 bits, or from 16 bits to 32 or 64 bits. The movsx instruction does not affect the status flags in the rflags register.

### movsxd—Move with Sign-Extension Doubleword

Copies (moves) a 32-bit value from the memory 64-bit register and copies the sign bit into the high-order bits in the destination register.

movsxd *reg1, reg2* moves the value in *reg2* to *reg1*.

movsxd *reg, mem* moves from a memory location to a register.

The movsxd instruction extends the number of bits occupied by a value from 32 to 64 bits. The movsxd instruction does not affect the status flags in the rflags register.

Next, we'll look at the most common shift instructions.

## Shift Instructions

The *shift instructions* move all the bits in the destination location right or left. The number of bit places to shift is loaded into the cl register before the shift or expressed as an immediate value in the shift instruction. The CPU uses only the low-order five bits of the shift operand when shifting a 32-bit value, and it uses only the low-order six bits of the shift operand when shifting a 64-bit value.

### sal—Shift Arithmetic Left

Shifts bits logically to the left.

sal *reg,* cl shifts the bits in *reg* left by the number of places specified in cl.

sal *mem,* cl shifts the bits at the *mem* location left by the number of places specified in cl.

sal *reg, imm* shifts the bits in *reg* left by the number of places specified by *imm*.

sal *mem, imm* shifts the bits in *reg* left by the number of places specified by *imm*.

The bits on the right that are vacated by the left shift are filled with 0s. The last bit shifted out of the left (most significant) side of the destination operand is stored in CF in the rflags register. When the shift operand is 1, the OF is set to the exclusive OR of the CF and the bit that is shifted into the highest-order bit in the destination operand result; for larger shifts, the state of the OF is undefined.

### sar—Shift Arithmetic Right

Shifts bits arithmetically to the right.

sar *reg,* cl shifts the bits in *reg* right by the number of places specified in cl.

sar *mem,* cl shifts the bits at the *mem* location right by the number of places specified in cl.

sar *reg, imm* shifts the bits in *reg* right by the number of places specified by *imm*.

sar *mem, imm* shifts the bits in *reg* right by the number of places specified by *imm*.

The bits on the left that are vacated by the right shift are filled with a copy of the highest-order bit, thus preserving the sign of the value. The last bit shifted out of the right (least significant) side of the destination operand is stored in the CF flag.

**BE CAREFUL!** *Since the sar instruction copies the highest-order bit into the vacated bits, the result of shifting a negative value (in two's complement notation) can never be zero. For example, shifting –1 any number of bits to the right is still –1, but you might expect it to be 0.*

### shr —Shift Logical Right

Shifts bits logically to the right.

shr *reg,* cl shifts the bits in *reg* right by the number of places specified in cl.

shr *mem,* cl shifts the bits at the *mem* location right by the number of places specified in cl.

shr *reg, imm* shifts the bits in *reg* right by the number of places specified by *imm*.

shr *mem, imm* shifts the bits in *reg* right by the number of places specified by *imm*.

The bits on the left that are vacated by the right shift are filled with 0s. The last bit shifted out of the right (least significant) side of the destination operand is stored in the CF flag.

The manuals also define a shift logical left, shl, but this is just another name for the sal instruction.

Next, we'll take a similar approach to writing the hexadecimal-to-integer conversion program in assembly language as we did for the earlier case conversion C program. We'll use only the 8-bit portions of registers for converting each character.

## Shifting Bits in Assembly Language

Listing 16-11 shows the main function for the hexadecimal-to-integer conversion program written in assembly language.

```
# convertHex.s
        .intel_syntax noprefix
# Stack frame
        .equ    myString,-48
        .equ    myInt, -16
        .equ    canary,-8
        .equ    localSize,-48
# Useful constants
        .equ    MAX,20                  # character buffer limit
# Constant data
        .section .rodata
        .align  8
prompt:
        .string "Enter up to 16 hex characters: "
format:
        .string "%lx = %li\n"
# Code
        .text
        .globl  main
        .type       main, @function
main:
        push    rbp                     # save frame pointer
        mov     rbp, rsp                # set new frame pointer
        add     rsp, localSize          # for local var.
        mov     rax, qword ptr fs:40    # get canary
        mov     qword ptr canary[rbp], rax

        lea     rdi, prompt[rip]        # prompt user
        call    writeStr

        mov     esi, MAX                # get user input
        lea     rdi, myString[rbp]
        call    readLn

        lea     rsi, myInt[rbp]         # for result
        lea     rdi, myString[rbp]      # convert to int
        call    hexToInt
```

```
        mov     rdx, myInt[rbp]          # converted value
        mov     rsi, myInt[rbp]
        lea     rdi, format[rip]         # printf format string
        mov     eax, 0
        call    printf

        mov     eax, 0                   # return 0;
        mov     rcx, canary[rbp]         # retrieve saved canary
        xor     rcx, fs:40               # and check it
        je      goodCanary
        call    __stack_chk_fail@PLT     # bad canary
goodCanary:
        mov     rsp, rbp                 # restore stack pointer
        pop     rbp                      # and caller frame pointer
        ret
```

Listing 16-11: The main function for the program converting hexadecimal to long int in assembly language

There isn't anything new in the main function here, but we're using more meaningful labels and added comments to make it easier to read. As mentioned earlier, rather than type cast the char variables, we'll use the 8-bit portion of a register for our assembly language version of hexToInt, as in Listing 16-12.

```
# hexToInt.s
# Converts hex characters in a C string to int.
# Calling sequence:
#    rdi <- pointer to source string
#    rsi <- pointer to long int result
#    returns number of chars converted
            .intel_syntax noprefix

# Stack frame
            .equ    count,-4
            .equ    localSize,-16
# Useful constants
            .equ    GAP,0x07
            .equ    NUMMASK,0x0f             # also works for lowercase
            .equ    NUL,0
            .equ    NINE,0x39                # ASCII for '9'
# Code
            .text
            .globl  hexToInt
            .type   hexToInt, @function
hexToInt:
            push    rbp                      # save frame pointer
            mov     rbp, rsp                 # set new frame pointer
            add     rsp, localSize           # for local var.

    ❶ mov     dword ptr count[rbp], 0 # count = 0
    ❷ mov     qword ptr [rsi], 0       # initialize to 0
    ❸ mov     al, byte ptr [rdi]       # get a char
```

```
whileLoop:
        cmp     al, NUL                   # end of string?
        je      allDone                   # yes, all done
        cmp     al, NINE                  # no, is it alpha?
        jbe     numeral                   # no, nothing else to do
        sub     al, GAP                   # yes, numeral to alpha gap
numeral:
    ❹ and       al, NUMMASK               # convert to 4-bit int
        sal     qword ptr [rsi], 4        # make room
    ❺ or        byte ptr [rsi], al        # insert the 4 bits
        inc     dword ptr count[rbp]      # count++
        inc     rdi                       # increment string ptr
        mov     al, byte ptr [rdi]        # next char
        jmp     whileLoop                 # and continue
allDone:
        mov     eax, dword ptr count[rbp] # return count

        mov     rsp, rbp                  # restore stack pointer
        pop     rbp                       # and caller frame pointer
        ret
```

*Listing 16-12: Assembly language version of hexToInt function*

We're using three different sized variables in this function. The count variable, which shows the number of characters converted, is a 32-bit int ❶. Although our main function doesn't use this value, you'll get a chance to use it when it's Your Turn. Our conversion results in a 64-bit long int ❷. Both these variables are in memory, so we need to specify their size whenever we use them (dword ptr and qword ptr, respectively).

The character we are converting fits into a single byte, so we use the al portion of the rax register ❸. When doing this, the high-order 56 bits of the rax register can hold any bit pattern, but none of our operations on al will involve these high-order bits. The bit mask we're using will set the high-order four bits of the al register to 0 ❹, so the or instruction will insert only the four low-order bits of the al register into the low-order 4-bit portion of the result ❺.

Shifts are good for multiplying and dividing by powers of two, but we also need to be able to multiply and divide by any numbers. We'll look at multiplication and division of any integers in the next two sections, deferring fractional and floating-point values until Chapter 19.

---

**YOUR TURN**

1.  Modify the C main function in Listing 16-7 so it displays the number of hexadecimal characters converted. Use the assembly language hexToInt function in Listing 16-12 for the conversion.

2.  Write a program in assembly language that converts octal input to a long int.

---

# Multiplication

Of course, we need to be able to multiply arbitrary integers, not just by powers of two. It could be done using loops, but most general-purpose CPUs include multiply instructions.

## Multiplication in C

Let's modify the C program in Listings 16-7, 16-8, and 16-9 to convert numeric text strings into decimal integers. When converting from hexadecimal text strings, we shifted the accumulated value four bits to the left, thus multiplying it by 16. We'll use the same algorithm for converting decimal text strings but multiply by 10 instead of 16. Listings 16-13, 16-14, and 16-15 show the C program.

```
/* convertDec.c
 * Reads decimal number from keyboard and displays how
 * it's stored in hexadecimal.
 */

#include <stdio.h>
#include "writeStr.h"
#include "readLn.h"
#include "decToUInt.h"
#define MAX 20
int main()
{
  char theString[MAX];
  unsigned int theInt;

  writeStr("Enter an unsigned integer: ");
  readLn(theString, MAX);

  decToUInt(theString, &theInt);
❶ printf("\"%s\" is stored as 0x%x\n", theString, theInt);

  return 0;
}
```

*Listing 16-13: Program to convert a numeric text string into an unsigned decimal integer*

The main function for this decimal conversion program is almost the same as for the hexadecimal conversion program in the previous section. The primary difference is that we display the original text string entered by the user and show how the resulting unsigned int is stored in hexadecimal ❶.

The function to do the conversion, decToUInt, takes a pointer to the text string and a pointer to the variable for the primary output, and it returns the number of characters that were converted (Listing 16-14).

```
/* decToUInt.h
 * Converts decimal character string to unsigned int.
```

```
 * Returns number of characters.
 */

#ifndef DECTOUINT_H
#define DECTOUINT_H
int decToUInt(char *stringPtr, unsigned int *intPtr);
#endif
```

*Listing 16-14: Header file for the decToUInt function*

Listing 16-15 shows the implementation of the decToUInt function.

```
/* decToUInt.c
 * Converts decimal character string to unsigned int.
 * Returns number of characters.
 */

#include <stdio.h>
#include "decToUInt.h"
#define INTMASK 0xf

int decToUInt(char *stringPtr, unsigned int *intPtr)
{
  int radix = 10;
  char current;
  int count = 0;

  *intPtr = 0;
  current = *stringPtr;
  while (current != '\0')
  {
❶ current = current & INTMASK;
❷ *intPtr = *intPtr * radix;
❸ *intPtr += current;
    stringPtr++;
    count++;
    current = *stringPtr;
  }
  return count;
}
```

*Listing 16-15: The decToUInt function*

The first difference between this algorithm and the one for hexa-decimal is that we don't need to check for alphabetic characters because the ASCII code for the numeric characters is contiguous from 0 to 9. Since the low-order four bits of the ASCII code for the numerals is the same as the integer value it represents, we can simply mask off the high-order four bits ❶.

As we saw, when working with hexadecimal, we can easily make room for the new value by shifting the accumulating result, but this works only when the maximum of the new value is a power of two. When working with decimal, we need to multiply the accumulating result by 10 ❷, and then we need to add the new value ❸.

The compiler generates the assembly language for the decToUInt function, shown in Listing 16-16.

```
        .file    "decToUInt.c"
        .intel_syntax noprefix
        .text
        .globl   decToUInt
        .type    decToUInt, @function
decToUInt:
        push     rbp
        mov      rbp, rsp
        mov      QWORD PTR -24[rbp], rdi   ## save stringPtr
        mov      QWORD PTR -32[rbp], rsi   ## save intPtr
        mov      DWORD PTR -4[rbp], 10     ## radix = 10;
        mov      DWORD PTR -8[rbp], 0      ## count = 0;
        mov      rax, QWORD PTR -32[rbp]
        mov      DWORD PTR [rax], 0        ## *intPtr = 0;
        mov      rax, QWORD PTR -24[rbp]
        movzx    eax, BYTE PTR [rax]
        mov      BYTE PTR -9[rbp], al      ## load character
        jmp      .L2                       ## go to bottom
.L3:
        and      BYTE PTR -9[rbp], 15      ## convert to int
        mov      rax, QWORD PTR -32[rbp]
        mov      edx, DWORD PTR [rax]      ## load current value
        mov      eax, DWORD PTR -4[rbp]    ## load radix
❶ imul     edx, eax                  ## times 10
        mov      rax, QWORD PTR -32[rbp]
        mov      DWORD PTR [rax], edx      ## store 10 times current
        mov      rax, QWORD PTR -32[rbp]
        mov      edx, DWORD PTR [rax]      ## load 10 times current
❷ movsx    eax, BYTE PTR -9[rbp]     ## byte to 32 bits
❸ add      edx, eax                  ## add in latest value
        mov      rax, QWORD PTR -32[rbp]
        mov      DWORD PTR [rax], edx      ## *intPtr += current;
        add      QWORD PTR -24[rbp], 1     ## stringPtr++;
        add      DWORD PTR -8[rbp], 1      ## count++;
        mov      rax, QWORD PTR -24[rbp]
        movzx    eax, BYTE PTR [rax]
        mov      BYTE PTR -9[rbp], al      ## load next character
.L2:
        cmp      BYTE PTR -9[rbp], 0       ## NUL?
        jne      .L3                       ## no, keep going
        mov      eax, DWORD PTR -8[rbp]    ## yes, return count;
        pop      rbp
        ret
        .size    decToUInt, .-decToUInt
        .ident   "GCC: (Ubuntu 9.3.0-17ubuntu1~20.04) 9.3.0"
        .section      .note.GNU-stack,"",@progbits
```

Listing 16-16: Compiler-generated assembly language for the decToUInt function

The assembly language for the decToUInt function is similar to the assembly language for the hexToInt function shown in Listing 16-12. The primary differences are that the accumulated result is multiplied by the radix we're converting to, 10 for decimal, using the imul instruction ❶, and that the new value is type cast to be a 32-bit int ❷ before it's added to the accumulated result ❸.

The x86-64 instruction set includes both an unsigned multiply instruction, mul, and a signed one, imul. It may seem odd that the compiler is using the signed multiply instruction to convert the numeric text string to an unsigned int. We'll see the reason after looking at the details of the two instructions.

## Multiply Instructions

The signed multiply instruction can have one, two, or three operands:

### imul—Signed Multiply

Performs a signed multiply.

imul *reg* multiplies the integer in al, ax, eax, or rax by the integer in *reg*, leaving the result in ax, dx:ax, edx:eax, or rdx:rax, respectively.

imul *mem* multiplies the integer in al, ax, eax, or rax by the integer in *mem*, leaving the result in ax, dx:ax, edx:eax, or rdx:rax, respectively.

imul *reg1*, *reg2* multiplies the integer in *reg1* by the integer in *reg2*, leaving the result in *reg1*. *reg1* and *reg2* can be the same register.

imul *reg*, *mem* multiplies the integer in *reg* by the integer in *mem*, leaving the result in *reg*.

imul *reg1*, reg2, *imm* multiplies the integer in *reg2* by the integer *imm*, leaving the result in the destination *reg1*. *reg1* and *reg2* can be the same register.

imul *reg*, *mem*, *imm* multiplies the integer in *mem* by the integer *imm*, leaving the result in *reg*.

The width of the integers in registers or in memory must be the same. In the first form, the width of the result will be twice that of the integers being multiplied and will be sign-extended in the high-order portion. In the second and third forms, the $n$-bit destination is multiplied by the $n$-bit source and $n$ low-order bits left in the destination. In the last two forms $-128 \leq$ imm $\leq +127$, which is sign-extended to the same width as the source and destination registers before multiplying it by the $n$-bit source, leaving the $n$ low-order bits in the destination register.

In all but the first two forms, if the width of the result does not exceed the width or the two integers being multiplied, both the CF and OF in the rflags register are set to 0. If the width of the result exceeds the width of the two integers being multiplied, the high-order portion is lost, and both the CF and OF in the rflags register are set to 1.

### mul—Unsigned Multiply

Performs an unsigned multiply.

mul *reg* multiplies the integer in al, ax, eax, or rax by the integer in *reg*, leaving the result in ax, dx:ax, edx:eax, or rdx:rax, respectively.

mul *mem* multiplies the integer in al, ax, eax, or rax by the integer in *mem*, leaving the result in ax, dx:ax, edx:eax, or rdx:rax, respectively.

The width of the integers in registers or in memory must be the same. The width of the result will be twice that of the integers being multiplied and will not be sign-extended in the high-order portion.

When multiplying two $n$-bit integers, the product can be up to $2n$ bits wide. Without offering a formal proof here, you can probably be convinced by considering the largest 3-bit number, 111. Add 1 to get 1000. From 1000 × 1000 = 1000000, we can conclude that 111 × 111 ≤ 111111. More precisely, 111 × 111 = 110001.

The mul instruction and the single-operand forms of the imul instruction allow for the possibility of the full width of $2n$ for the product when multiplying two $n$-bit integers. When multiplying the 8-bit integer in al by an 8-bit integer, the 16-bit result is left in ax. For multiplying two 16-bit integers, the notation dx:ax means that the high-order 16 bits of the 32-bit result is stored in the dx register, and the low-order 16 bits in the ax register. Similarly, edx:eax means the high-order 32 bits of the 64-bit result are in edx and the low-order 32 bits in eax, and rdx:rax means the high-order 64 bits of the 128-bit result are in rdx and the low-order 64 bits in rdx. The 32-bit multiply, which uses edx:eax for the 64-bit result, also zeros the high-order 32 bits of both the rdx and rax registers, like most arithmetic instructions, so any data that might be in those parts of the registers would be lost.

It's important to remember that the portions of the rax and rdx registers (only rax for 8-bit multiply) used by the mul instruction and the single-operand forms of the imul instruction never appear as operands in the instruction. We can summarize the use of the mul and single-operand forms of the imul instructions in Table 16-1.

**Table 16-1:** Register Usage of mul and Single-Operand imul

| Multiplier | Multiplicand | Product | |
|---|---|---|---|
| Reg or mem size | Low-order | High-order | Low-order |
| 8 bits | al | ah | al |
| 16 bits | ax | dx | ax |
| 32 bits | eax | edx | eax |
| 64 bits | rax | rdx | rax |

The two's complement notation implies a fixed number of bits, but the mul instruction and the single-operand forms of the imul instruction extend the number of bits in the result. When we allow for a wider result, we need to distinguish between sign extension or not. For example, if 1111 is meant to represent 15 in a program and we convert it to eight bits, it should be 00001111. On the other hand, if it is meant to represent –1, then the 8-bit representation should be 11111111. The mul instruction doubles the width of the result with no sign extension, and the single-operand forms of the imul instruction that double the width of the result do extend the sign bit into the high-order bit positions.

In many cases, we know that the product will always fit within the same $n$-bit width of the multiplicand and multiplier. In these cases, the other four forms of imul provide more flexibility. But if we made a mistake and the product exceeds the $n$ bits allowed for it, the high-order bits are lost. The $n$-bit product is, of course, incorrect, which is noted by the CPU by setting both the OF and CF in the rflags register to 1.

In the two-operand forms of the imul instruction, if the result does not exceed the size of the two values being multiplied, it is correct whether it represents a signed integer (in two's complement notation) or an unsigned integer. With the three-operand forms of imul, the 8-bit immediate value is sign-extended to the same width as the other two operands before the multiplication, so the result is correct, both signed and unsigned, if it does not exceed the width of the other integer being multiplied.

Returning to the use of the imul instruction when converting to an unsigned integer in Listing 16-16 ❶, the result of the multiplication will be correct for both signed and unsigned integers as long as the result remains within 32 bits. As explained, a result exceeding 32 bits would be an error, and the compiler does not check for that possibility. What makes the result an unsigned integer is the way the integer is used in the program. In this program, the main function (Listing 16-13) treats it as an unsigned integer.

Next, we'll look at using multiplication in assembly language.

## Multiplication in Assembly Language

Our assembly language version of the main function for converting a decimal text string to an int, as shown in Listing 16-17, is similar to the C version.

```
# convertDec.s
        .intel_syntax noprefix
# Stack frame
        .equ    myString,-48
        .equ    myInt, -12
        .equ    canary,-8
        .equ    localSize,-48
# Useful constants
        .equ    MAX,11                  # character buffer limit
# Constant data
        .section  .rodata
        .align  8
prompt:
        .string "Enter an unsigned integer: "
format:
        .string "\"%s\" is stored as 0x%x\n"
```

```
# Code
        .text
        .globl  main
        .type     main, @function
main:
        push    rbp                     # save frame pointer
        mov     rbp, rsp                # set new frame pointer
        add     rsp, localSize          # for local var.
        mov     rax, qword ptr fs:40    # get canary
        mov     qword ptr canary[rbp], rax

        lea     rdi, prompt[rip]        # prompt user
        call    writeStr

        mov     esi, MAX                # get user input
        lea     rdi, myString[rbp]
❶ call    readLn

        lea     rsi, myInt[rbp]         # for result
        lea     rdi, myString[rbp]      # convert to int
❷ call    decToUInt

        mov     edx, myInt[rbp]         # converted value
        lea     rsi, myString[rbp]      # echo user input
        lea     rdi, format[rip]        # printf format string
        mov     eax, 0
        call      printf

        mov     eax, 0                  # return 0;
        mov     rcx, canary[rbp]        # retrieve saved canary
        xor     rcx, fs:40              # and check it
        je      goodCanary
        call    __stack_chk_fail@PLT    # bad canary
goodCanary:
        mov     rsp, rbp                # restore stack pointer
        pop     rbp                     # and caller frame pointer
        ret
```

*Listing 16-17: Assembly language version of the main function to convert a decimal number from a text string to an int*

After reading the user's input text string ❶, the main function calls the decToUInt function ❷, which converts the text string to the unsigned int that the string represents, as shown in Listing 16-18.

```
# decToUInt.s
# Converts decimal character string to unsigned 32-bit int.
# Calling sequence:
#   rdi <- pointer to source string
#   rsi <- pointer to int result
#   returns 0
        .intel_syntax noprefix
```

```
# Useful constants
        .equ    DECIMAL,10
        .equ    NUMMASK,0x0f
        .equ    NUL,0

# Code
        .text
        .globl  decToUInt
        .type   decToUInt, @function
decToUInt:
        push    rbp                       # save frame pointer
        mov     rbp, rsp                  # set new frame pointer

        mov     ❶ dword ptr [rsi], 0      # result = 0
        mov     al, byte ptr [rdi]        # get a char
whileLoop:
        cmp     al, NUL                   # end of string?
        je      allDone                   # yes, all done
      ❷ and     eax, NUMMASK              # no, 4-bit -> 32-bit int
      ❸ mov     ecx, dword ptr [rsi]      # current result
        imul  ❹ ecx, ecx, DECIMAL         # next base position
      ❺ add     ecx, eax                  # add the new value
      ❻ mov     dword ptr [rsi], ecx      # update result
        inc     rdi                       # increment string ptr
        mov     al, byte ptr [rdi]        # next char
        jmp     whileLoop                 # and continue
allDone:
        mov     dword ptr [rsi], ecx      # output result
        mov     eax, 0                    # return 0

        mov     rsp, rbp                  # restore stack pointer
        pop     rbp                       # and caller frame pointer
        ret
```

Listing 16-18: Assembly language version of decToUInt function

Instead of creating a local variable to hold the converted int, we'll use the memory location in the calling function, accessing it from the passed-in address ❶. We read the characters into the al register. Masking off all but the low-order four bits of the eax register type casts the 4-bit integer from the character in al to a 32-bit int ❷ so it can be added to the result ❺.

The destination operand of the imul instruction must be a register, so we need to load the result into a register for the multiplication operation ❸. Using the same register for one source operand and the destination operand multiplies the value in the register by the immediate value ❹. After adding in the new value in the ecx register, we store the new value back in the location of the result ❻.

Next, we'll discuss the inverse of multiplication, division.

# Division

When multiplying two $n$-bit numbers, we were concerned about the result being $2n$ bits wide. In division, the quotient will usually be narrower than the dividend. But division is complicated by the existence of a remainder, which needs to be stored someplace. When we describe the division instructions, you'll see that they start with a $2n$-bit-wide dividend and an $n$-bit-wide divisor and are limited to an $n$-bit quotient and an $n$-bit remainder.

We'll start with a C function that converts an int to the numerical text string it represents, the inverse of the earlier decToUInt function.

## Division in C

Our main function will read an unsigned integer from the user, add 123 to it, and show the sum. Our subfunction, intToUDec, will use a division algorithm to convert a 32-bit int to the text string that represents it so that the main function can display the sum. Listings 16-19, 16-20, and 16-21 show the program.

```
/* add123.c
 * Reads an unsigned int from user, adds 123,
 * and displays the result.
 */

#include "writeStr.h"
#include "readLn.h"
#include "decToUInt.h"
#include "intToUDec.h"
#define MAX 11
int main()
{
  char theString[MAX];
  unsigned int theInt;

  writeStr("Enter an unsigned integer: ");
  readLn(theString, MAX);
```

```
❶ decToUInt(theString, &theInt);
  theInt += 123;
  intToUDec(theString, theInt);

  writeStr("The result is: ");
  writeStr(theString);
  writeStr("\n");

  return 0;
}
```

*Listing 16-19: Program to add 123 to an unsigned integer*

The main function for this program is quite simple. We'll use the decToUInt function from earlier, either the C version (Listing 16-15) or assembly language version (Listing 16-18), to convert the user's input to an int ❶.

```
/* intToUDec.h
 * Converts an int to corresponding unsigned text
 * string representation.
 */

#ifndef INTTOUDEC_H
#define INTTOUDEC_H
void intToUDec(char *decString, unsigned int theInt);
#endif
```

*Listing 16-20: Header file for the intToUDec function*

The header file for the intToUDec function shows that the output, decString, is passed by pointer, and the input, theInt, is passed by value. Listing 16-21 shows the implementation of intToUDec.

```
/* intToUDec.c
 * Converts an int to corresponding unsigned text
 * string representation.
 */

#include "intToUDec.h"
#define ASCII 0x30
#define MAX 12
#define NUL '\0'

void intToUDec(char *decString, unsigned int theInt)
{
  int base = 10;
  char reverseArray[MAX];
  char digit;
  char *ptr = reverseArray;

❶ *ptr = NUL;  // start with termination char
  ptr++;
  do
  {
❷ digit = theInt % base;
```

```
❸ digit = ASCII | digit;
  *ptr = digit;
❹ theInt = theInt / base;
  ptr++;
} while (theInt > 0);
❺ do              // reverse the string
  {
    ptr--;
    *decString = *ptr;
    decString++;
  } while ❻ (*ptr != NUL);
}
```

*Listing 16-21: Function to convert a 32-bit unsigned int to its corresponding text string for display*

The algorithm we're using to find the characters that represent the unsigned int involves the repeated integer division of the unsigned int by the number base, 10 in this function. The % operator computes the remainder from the division, which will be the value of the low-order digit ❷. We convert this single digit to its ASCII character with an OR operation ❸ and append it the string we're creating. Now that we've converted the low-order digit, the / operator will perform an integer divide, effectively removing the low-order digit from theInt ❹.

Since this algorithm works from right to left, the characters are stored in reverse order. We need to reverse the order of the text string for the calling function ❺. Storing the NUL character first ❶ provides a way to know when the entire text string has been completely copied in reverse order ❻.

Next, we'll look at the assembly language generated by the compiler; see Listing 16-22.

```
          .file    "intToUDec.c"
          .intel_syntax noprefix
          .text
          .globl  intToUDec
          .type   intToUDec, @function
intToUDec:
          push    rbp
          mov     rbp, rsp
          sub     rsp, 64
          mov     QWORD PTR -56[rbp], rdi
          mov     DWORD PTR -60[rbp], esi
          mov     rax, QWORD PTR fs:40
          mov     QWORD PTR -8[rbp], rax
          xor     eax, eax
          mov     DWORD PTR -36[rbp], 10  ## base = 10;
          lea     rax, -20[rbp]           ## place to store string
          mov     QWORD PTR -32[rbp], rax
          mov     rax, QWORD PTR -32[rbp]
          mov     BYTE PTR [rax], 0
          add     QWORD PTR -32[rbp], 1
.L2:
          mov     ecx, DWORD PTR -36[rbp] ## load base
```

```
        mov     eax, DWORD PTR -60[rbp]  ## load the int
❶ mov     edx, 0                   ## clear high-order
        div     ecx
❷ mov     eax, edx                 ## remainder
❸ mov     BYTE PTR -37[rbp], al    ## store char portion
❹ or      BYTE PTR -37[rbp], 48    ## convert to char
        mov     rax, QWORD PTR -32[rbp]  ## pointer to string
        movzx   edx, BYTE PTR -37[rbp]   ## load the char
        mov     BYTE PTR [rax], dl       ## store the char
        mov     esi, DWORD PTR -36[rbp]  ## load base
        mov     eax, DWORD PTR -60[rbp]  ## load the int
❺ mov     edx, 0                   ## clear high-order
        div     esi
        mov     DWORD PTR -60[rbp], eax  ## store quotient
        add     QWORD PTR -32[rbp], 1    ## ptr++;
        cmp     DWORD PTR -60[rbp], 0    ## quotient > 0?
        jne     .L2                      ## yes, continue
.L3:
        sub     QWORD PTR -32[rbp], 1    ## no, reverse string
        mov     rax, QWORD PTR -32[rbp]
        movzx   edx, BYTE PTR [rax]
        mov     rax, QWORD PTR -56[rbp]
        mov     BYTE PTR [rax], dl
        add     QWORD PTR -56[rbp], 1
        mov     rax, QWORD PTR -32[rbp]
        movzx   eax, BYTE PTR [rax]
        test    al, al
        jne     .L3
        nop
        mov     rax, QWORD PTR -8[rbp]
        xor     rax, QWORD PTR fs:40
        je      .L4
        call    __stack_chk_fail@PLT
.L4:
        leave
        ret
        .size   intToUDec, .-intToUDec
        .ident  "GCC: (Ubuntu 9.3.0-17ubuntu1~20.04) 9.3.0"
        .section        .note.GNU-stack,"",@progbits
```

*Listing 16-22: Compiler-generated assembly language for the intToUDec function*

As you will see in the more detailed description of the div instruction coming up, we can divide a $2n$-bit number by an $n$-bit number. In our environment, an int is 32 bits. The div instruction assumes that we are dividing a 64-bit long int by a 32-bit int. The high-order 32 bits of the long int must be placed in edx, and the low-order 32 bits in eax, before the division. In many cases, the dividend is within the low-order 32 bits, but we need to be careful to fill in the full 64 bits of edx:eax by storing 0 in edx ❶.

After we have set up edx:eax, the div instruction will divide that 64-bit integer by the 32-bit integer in div's single operand, ecx in this example. The division will leave the remainder in the edx register ❷. By storing only the al portion of the rax register, the remainder is type cast as it's stored in the local char variable ❸ and then converted to an ASCII character ❹. We still need to divide the integer we're converting by 10 to effectively remove the low-order decimal digit. Before performing this division, we need to remember to zero edx ❺.

## Division Instructions

The x86-64 architecture provides two integer-divide instructions, signed and unsigned:

### idiv—Signed Divide

Performs a signed divide.

idiv *reg* divides the integer in ax, dx:ax, edx:eax, or rdx:rax by the integer in *reg*, leaving the quotient in al, ax, eax, or rax, and the remainder in ah, dx, edx, or rdx, respectively.

idiv *mem* divides the integer in ax, dx:ax, edx:eax, or rdx:rax by the integer in *mem*, leaving the quotient in al, ax, eax, or rax, and the remainder in ah, dx, edx, or rdx, respectively.

The division yields a signed integer quotient, truncated toward zero, and a remainder. The sign of the remainder is the same as the sign of the dividend. The states of the OF, SF, ZF, AF, PF, and CF flags in the rflags register are all undefined (can be either 0 or 1) after the idiv instruction is executed. If the quotient won't fit within the respective register (al, ax, eax, or rax), the instruction causes a system error.

### div—Unsigned Divide

Performs an unsigned divide.

div *reg* divides the integer in ax, dx:ax, edx:eax, or rdx:rax by the integer in *reg*, leaving the quotient in al, ax, eax, or rax, and the remainder in ah, dx, edx, or rdx, respectively.

div *mem* divides the integer in ax, dx:ax, edx:eax, or rdx:rax by the integer in *mem*, leaving the quotient in al, ax, eax, or rax, and the remainder in ah, dx, edx, or rdx, respectively.

The division yields an unsigned integer quotient, truncated toward zero, and a remainder. The states of the OF, SF, ZF, AF, PF, and CF flags in the rflags register are all undefined (can be either 0 or 1) after the idiv instruction is executed. If the quotient won't fit within the respective register (al, ax, eax, or rax), the instruction causes a system error.

If the divisor is 0 or the quotient is too large to fit into the destination register, the idiv and div instructions cause a type of system error called an *exception*. We'll look at exceptions in Chapter 21. For now, exceptions are handled by the operating system, which typically terminates the application with a somewhat cryptic error message.

It's important to remember that the portions of the rax and rdx registers (only rax for 8-bit divide) used by the divide instructions never appear as operands in the instruction. We can summarize register use of the div or idiv instruction in Table 16-2.

**Table 16-2:** Register Use of the div and idiv Instructions

| Divisor | Dividend | | Results | |
|---|---|---|---|---|
| Reg or mem size | High-order | Low-order | Remainder | Quotient |
| 8 bits | ah | al | ah | al |
| 16 bits | dx | ax | dx | ax |
| 32 bits | edx | eax | edx | eax |
| 64 bits | rdx | rax | rdx | rax |

Since the register names in Table 16-2 don't appear as part of the instruction's operands, a common programming error is to forget to set the high-order portion of the dividend to the correct value before executing a division instruction. For the div instruction, this usually means setting ah, dx, edx, or rdx to 0.

For the idiv instruction, you need to be careful to preserve the sign of the dividend before executing the instruction. For example, if you're using 32-bit integers and the dividend is −10 (= 0xfffffff6), you need to set edx to 0xffffffff to create −10 in 64 bits. The x86-64 instruction set includes four instructions that do not take any operands but extend the sign to the registers used in division, as shown in Table 16-3. When the dividend and divisor are the same size in your program, which is common, you should use the corresponding instruction from Table 16-3 immediately before an idiv instruction.

**Table 16-3:** Instructions to Sign-Extend an Integer for Signed Division

| Instruction | From | To, high-order | To, low-order |
|---|---|---|---|
| cbw | al | ah | al |
| cwd | ax | dx | ax |
| cdq | eax | edx | eax |
| cqo | rax | rdx | rax |

The / and % division operators in C and C++ follow the same rules for integers as the x86-64 div and idiv instructions: the quotient is truncated toward zero. This is not the case for all programming languages, which can create confusion when using signed division of integers.

For example, in Python the / operator computes the floating-point result. To get the integer part of a quotient, we need to use the *floor division* operator, //, which causes Python to apply the *floor* operation to the floating-point result. The floor of a real number, x, is the greatest integer that is less than or equal to x. So when the quotient is negative, the value in Python is one less than the value in C and C++. The % operator in Python gives a remainder value based on floor division for the quotient.

*The remarks here apply to Python 3. As of January 1, 2020, Python 2 is no longer supported.*

With signed division, the sign of the quotient is positive if both the dividend and divisor are of the same sign, and it's negative if they are of the opposite sign, like multiplication. But the sign of the remainder depends on how the quotient is truncated—toward zero as in C or toward the next lower signed integer as in Python. In all cases, when dividing $a$ by $b$,

$$r = a - b \times q$$

where $r$ is the remainder, and $q$ is the quotient. With truncation toward zero, the sign of the remainder is the same as the sign of the dividend, but with truncation toward the lower signed integer, the sign of the remainder is the same as that of the divisor. Proving it from this equation is a bit tricky, but you can probably be convinced if you plug in the values from Table 16-4 that I got for C and Python, where $a$ is the dividend, $b$ the divisor, $q$ the quotient, and $r$ the remainder.

**Table 16-4:** Dividing $a$ by $b$, C vs. Python 3

| | | C | | Python 3 | |
| --- | --- | --- | --- | --- | --- |
| $a$ | $b$ | $q$ | $r$ | $q$ | $r$ |
| 27 | 4 | 6 | 3 | 6 | 3 |
| 27 | −4 | −6 | 3 | −7 | −1 |
| −27 | 4 | −6 | −3 | −7 | 1 |
| −27 | −4 | 6 | −3 | 6 | −3 |

As you can see from this discussion, signed division can yield unexpected results. I try to design my algorithms to avoid signed division and adjust the sign after the result is computed.

The / and % are two separate operators in C, and the compiler generated a `div` instruction for the use of each C operation, as shown in Listing 16-22. Since the `div` instruction performs both operations, our assembly language version of `intToUDec` will use this fact.

### Division in Assembly Language

We didn't look at the compiler-generated assembly language for the C version of our `add123` program, as shown in Listing 16-19. It's similar to the assembly language version in Listing 16-23.

```
# add123.s
# Adds 123 to an int.
        .intel_syntax noprefix
# Stack frame
        .equ    myString,-32
```

```
        .equ    myInt, -12
        .equ    canary,-8
        .equ    localSize,-32
# Useful constants
    ❶ .equ    MAX,11                  # character buffer limit
# Constant data
        .section  .rodata
        .align  8
prompt:
        .string "Enter an unsigned integer: "
message:
        .string "The result is: "
endl:
        .string "\n"
# Code
        .text
        .globl  main
        .type     main, @function
main:
        push    rbp                     # save frame pointer
        mov     rbp, rsp                # set new frame pointer
        add     rsp, localSize          # for local var.
        mov     rax, qword ptr fs:40    # get canary
        mov     qword ptr canary[rbp], rax

        lea     rdi, prompt[rip]        # prompt user
        call    writeStr

        mov     esi, MAX                # get user input
        lea     rdi, myString[rbp]
        call    readLn

        lea     rsi, myInt[rbp]         # for result
        lea     rdi, myString[rbp]      # convert to int
    ❷ call    decToUInt

        mov     eax, dword ptr myInt[rbp]
    ❸ add     eax, 123
        mov     dword ptr myInt[rbp], eax

    ❹ mov     esi, myInt[rbp]         # the number
    ❺ lea     rdi, myString[rbp]      # place for string
        call    intToUDec

        lea     rdi, message[rip]       # message for user
        call    writeStr

        lea     rdi, myString[rbp]      # number in text
        call    writeStr

        lea     rdi, endl[rip]
        call    writeStr

        mov     eax, 0                  # return 0;
        mov     rcx, canary[rbp]        # retrieve saved canary
```

```
        xor     rcx, fs:40              # and check it
        je      goodCanary
        call    __stack_chk_fail@PLT    # bad canary
goodCanary:
        mov     rsp, rbp                # restore stack pointer
        pop     rbp                     # and caller frame pointer
        ret
```

Listing 16-23: Assembly language version of main function of program to add 123 to an unsigned integer

The main function for our program is probably familiar to you by now. Since unsigned integers can be as large as 4,294,967,295, we'll allow up to 11 characters as user input ❶, which includes the terminating NUL character. Before adding 123 to it, we need to convert the input integer from a text string to an unsigned int ❷.

The addition itself is a single instruction ❸. The sum is passed to the intToUDec function by value ❹, and the address of the input string is passed by pointer ❺.

We'll use the same algorithm in our assembly language version of intToUDec, as shown in Listing 16-24, but our implementation differs quite a bit from the compiler's version.

```
# intToUDec.s
# Creates character string that represents unsigned 32-bit int.
# Calling sequence:
#    rdi <- pointer to resulting string
#    esi <- unsigned int
        .intel_syntax noprefix

# Stack frame
        .equ    reverseArray,-32
        .equ    canary,-8
        .equ    localSize,-32
# Useful constants
        .equ    DECIMAL,10
        .equ    ASCII,0x30
        .equ    NUL,0

# Code
        .text
        .globl  intToUDec
        .type   intToUDec, @function
intToUDec:
        push    rbp                     # save frame pointer
        mov     rbp, rsp                # set new frame pointer
        add     rsp, localSize          # for local var.
        mov     rax, qword ptr fs:40    # get canary
        mov     qword ptr canary[rbp], rax

        lea     rcx, reverseArray[rbp]  # pointer
        mov     byte ptr [rcx], NUL     # string terminator
        inc     rcx                     # a char was stored
```

```
        mov      eax, esi                  # int to represent
        mov      r8d, DECIMAL              # base we're in
convertLoop:
    ❶ mov        edx, 0                    # for remainder
        div      r8d                       # quotient and remainder
    ❷ or         dl, ASCII                 # convert to char
    ❸ mov        byte ptr [rcx], dl        # append to string
        inc      rcx                       # next place for char
        cmp      eax, 0                    # all done?
        ja       convertLoop               # no, continue
reverseLoop:
        dec      rcx                       # yes, reverse string
        mov      dl, byte ptr [rcx]        # one char at a time
        mov      byte ptr [rdi], dl
        inc      rdi                       # pointer to dest. string
        cmp      dl, NUL                   # was it NUL?
        jne      reverseLoop               # no, continue

        mov      eax, 0                    # return 0;
        mov      rcx, canary[rbp]          # retrieve saved canary
        xor      rcx, fs:40                # and check it
        je       goodCanary
        call     __stack_chk_fail@PLT      # bad canary
goodCanary:
        mov      rsp, rbp                  # restore stack pointer
        pop      rbp                       # and caller frame pointer
        ret
```

*Listing 16-24: Assembly language version of intToUDec function*

The primary difference in our assembly language version is that we take advantage of knowing that the div instruction leaves the quotient in eax and the remainder in edx ❷. Since the conversion is base 10, we know that the remainder will always be in the range 0–9. Thus, the remainder can be easily converted to its corresponding numerical ASCII code ❷. Having appended the newly converted character to the text string we're creating ❸, the edx register is zeroed before the next time the div instruction is executed ❶.

Division takes more time than multiplication. People have invented algorithms for determining the low-order decimal digit without using division. One technique when dividing by a constant is to use the fact that shifting is much faster than division. For example, in our intToUDec function, we're dividing by 10. When dividing a number, $x$, by 10, consider the following equation:

$$\frac{x}{10} = \frac{2^n}{10} \times \frac{x}{2^n}$$
$$= \left(\frac{2^n}{10} \times x\right)\Big/_{2^n}$$

Now, if we compute the constant $2^n/10$, we can multiply $x$ by this new constant and then do the division by shifting the result of the multiplication $n$ bit positions to the right. The details are beyond the scope of this book, but you can see how this works by looking at the assembly language generated by the compiler, using the -01 optimization option for the intToUDec function in Listing 16-21.

---

**YOUR TURN**

1. Write the function intToSDec in assembly language that converts a 32-bit int to its text string representation. Your function should prepend negative numbers that have a negative sign but not prepend positive number with a plus sign. Hint: Your function could call the intToUDec function in Listing 16-24 to do most of the conversion.

2. Write the two functions, putInt and getInt, in assembly language. putInt takes one argument, a 32-bit signed integer, and displays it on the screen. getInt takes one argument, a pointer to a place for storing a 32-bit signed integer, which it reads from keyboard input. putInt should call your intToSDec function, and getInt should call your decToSInt function. Note: putInt and getInt will be used in subsequent chapters for displaying and reading integers.

3. Write a program in assembly language that allows a user to enter two signed decimal integers. The program will add, subtract, multiply, and divide the two integers. It will display the sum, difference, product, and quotient and remainder resulting from these operations.

---

## What You've Learned

**Bit masking**   We can use bitwise logic instructions to directly change bit patterns in variables.

**Bit shifting**   Bits in variables can be shifted left or right, effectively multiplying or dividing by multiples of 2.

**Mutliplication**   The signed multiply instruction has several forms, making it more flexible than the unsigned multiply instruction, which has only one form.

**Division**   Both the signed and unsigned divide instructions produce a quotient and a remainder. Signed integer division is somewhat complicated.

**Converting numbers between binary storage and character display**
Arithmetic operations are easier when numbers are stored in the binary system, but keyboard input and screen display use the corresponding character format.

We've covered ways to organize program flow and perform arithmetic or logic operations on data items. Organizing the data is another important part of designing computing algorithms. In the next chapter, we'll look at two of the most fundamental ways to organize data: arrays and records.

# 17

## DATA STRUCTURES

An essential part of programming is determining how to organize data. In this chapter, we'll look at two of the most fundamental ways of organizing data: arrays, which can be used for grouping only data items of the same data type; and records, which can be used for grouping data items of different data types.

As you will see, these ways of organizing data determine how we access the individual data items in each. Both require two addressing items to locate a data item. Since the data items are all the same type in an array, we can access an individual data item from knowing the name of the array plus the index number of the item. Accessing an individual data item in a record requires the name of the record and the name of the data item located in the record.

# Arrays

An *array* is a collection of data elements of the same data type, arranged in a sequence. We can access a single element in an array by using the name of the array together with an *index* value, which specifies the number of the element relative to the beginning of the array. We have used char arrays in previous chapters to store ASCII characters as text strings. Each element in the array was the same type, a char, which is one byte. In our applications, we were accessing each character in order, so we started with a pointer to the first char and simply incremented it by 1 to access each subsequent char. We didn't need an index to locate each char within the text string array.

In this chapter, we'll look at int arrays, which use four bytes for each data element in the array. If we started with a pointer to the first element, we would need to increment it by 4 to access each subsequent element. But it's much easier to use the array index number to access each individual element. You'll see how the index number is converted to an address offset to access an array element relative to the beginning of the array. You'll also see that C passes arrays to other functions differently from other data items.

## Arrays in C

We define an array in C by stating the element data type, giving the array a name, and specifying the number of elements in the array. Let's start with the example in Listing 17-1.

```
/* fill2XIndex.c
 * Allocates an int array, stores 2 X element number
 * in each element and prints array contents.
 */
#include <stdio.h>
#include "twiceIndex.h"
#include "displayArray.h"
#define N 10

int main(void)
{
❶ int intArray[N];

  twiceIndex(❷intArray, N);
  displayArray(intArray, N);
  return 0;
}
```

Listing 17-1: Filling an array with integers and then displaying the contents

As stated, we define an array by giving the data type of each element (int), a name for the array (intArray), and the number of elements in the array (N) ❶. This main function calls the twiceIndex function, which sets each element in the array to twice its index. For example, it stores the int 8 in array element number 4. It then calls displayArray, which prints the contents of the entire array in the terminal window.

One of the first things you might notice about the arguments we're passing to the functions is that it appears the array is being passed by value, since we give only its name in the argument list ❷. But since twiceIndex stores values in the array, it needs to know where the array is located in memory.

Usually, a programmer passes an input value to a function by value. But if the input consists of a large number of data items, copying them all into registers and onto the stack would be very inefficient, in which case it makes more sense to pass by pointer. Arrays almost always have many data items, so the designers of the C language decided to always pass them by pointer. When you give the name of the array as an argument to a function call, C will pass the address of the first element of the array.

We can see this explicitly by looking at the compiler-generated assembly language for this main function, as shown in Listing 17-2.

```
        .file   "fill2XIndex.c"
        .intel_syntax noprefix
        .text
        .globl  main
        .type   main, @function
main:
        push    rbp
        mov     rbp, rsp
        sub     rsp, 48         ## memory for array
        mov     rax, QWORD PTR fs:40
        mov     QWORD PTR -8[rbp], rax
        xor     eax, eax
❶ lea     rax, -48[rbp]   ## load address of array
        mov     esi, 10         ## number of elements
        mov     rdi, rax        ## pass address
        call    twiceIndex@PLT
❷ lea     rax, -48[rbp]   ## load address of array
        mov     esi, 10
        mov     rdi, rax        ## pass address
        call    displayArray@PLT
        mov     eax, 0
        mov     rdx, QWORD PTR -8[rbp]
        xor     rdx, QWORD PTR fs:40
        je      .L3
        call    __stack_chk_fail@PLT
.L3:
        leave
        ret
        .size   main, .-main
        .ident  "GCC: (Ubuntu 9.3.0-17ubuntu1~20.04) 9.3.0"
        .section        .note.GNU-stack,"",@progbits
```

Listing 17-2: Compiler-generated assembly language showing an array passed by pointer

In the assembly language, we can see the address of the array passed first to the twiceIndex function ❶ and then to the displayArray function ❷. The elements of the array are inputs to the displayArray function, so it does not need to know the address of the array, but it's much more efficient to pass the address than a copy of each of the array elements.

Next, we'll look at the subfunctions that store values in the array and display the contents of the array, as shown in Listings 17-3, 17-4, 17-6, and 17-7.

```
/* twiceIndex.h
 * Stores 2 X element number in each element.
 */

#ifndef TWICEINDEX_H
#define TWICEINDEX_H
void twiceIndex(int theArray[], int nElements);
#endif
```

*Listing 17-3: Header file for the twiceIndex function*

The int theArray[] syntax is equivalent to int *theArray, a pointer to an int. Using either syntax, C will pass the *address* of the first element of the array to the function. We need to pass the number of elements in the array separately.

```
/* twiceIndex.c
 * Stores 2 X element number in each array element.
 */
#include "twiceIndex.h"

void twiceIndex(int theArray[], int nElements)
{
  int i;

  for (i = 0; i < nElements; i++)
  {
    theArray[i] = 2 * i;
  }
}
```

*Listing 17-4: Function to store two times the index number in each element of an array*

The twiceIndex function uses a for loop to process the array, storing two times the index value in each element of the array. Let's look at the assembly language generated by the compiler for this function; see Listing 17-5.

```
        .file   "twiceIndex.c"
        .intel_syntax noprefix
        .text
        .globl  twiceIndex
        .type   twiceIndex, @function
twiceIndex:
        push    rbp
        mov     rbp, rsp
        mov     QWORD PTR -24[rbp], rdi ## save array address
        mov     DWORD PTR -28[rbp], esi ## and num of elements
        mov     DWORD PTR -4[rbp], 0    ## i = 0
        jmp     .L2
.L3:
        mov     eax, DWORD PTR -4[rbp]
```

```
❶ cdqe                                  ## to 64 bits
  lea      rdx, ❷0[0+rax*4]             ## element offset
❸ mov      rax, QWORD PTR -24[rbp]      ## array address
  add      rax, rdx                     ## element address
  mov      edx, DWORD PTR -4[rbp]       ## current i
  add      edx, edx                     ## 2 times i
  mov      DWORD PTR [rax], edx         ## store 2 times i
  add      DWORD PTR -4[rbp], 1         ## i++
.L2:
  mov      eax, DWORD PTR -4[rbp]
  cmp      eax, DWORD PTR -28[rbp]
  jl       .L3
  nop
  pop      rbp
  ret
  .size    twiceIndex, .-twiceIndex
  .ident   "GCC: (Ubuntu 9.3.0-17ubuntu1~20.04) 9.3.0"
  .section         .note.GNU-stack,"",@progbits
```

*Listing 17-5: Compiler-generated assembly language for the twiceIndex function*

The algorithm used by the compiler to access an array element is as follows: compute the offset of the element from the beginning of the array and then add that offset to the address of the beginning. This is an array of ints, so each element is four bytes. The compiler uses the register indirect with indexing addressing mode (described in Chapter 12) to compute the address offset of the int element ❷.

This addressing mode requires that all the registers be the same size. Since we're using 64-bit addressing in our environment, the 32-bit index value in eax must be extended to 64 bits before it can be used to compute the address offset. The compiler chose to do this with the cdqe instruction ❶ because the index variable, i, was declared as an int, which is signed by default.

The cdqe instruction doubles the size of the value in the eax register from 32 bits to the full 64 bits in the rax register. It copies the sign bit in eax into all the high-order 32 bits of rax, thus preserving the sign in the extended value. There are three such instructions like this, each of which operates on portions of the rax register:

**cbw, cwde, cdqe—Convert Byte to Word, Convert Word to Doubleword, Convert Doubleword to Quadword**

Doubles the size of the source operand using sign extension.

cbw copies bit number 7 in the al register into bits 15–8, doubling the size from al to ax and preserving the sign. Bits 63–16 are unaffected.

cwde copies bit number 15 in the ax register into bits 31–16, doubling the size from ax to eax and preserving the sign. Bits 63–32 are zeroed.

cdqe copies bit number 31 in the eax register into bits 63–32, doubling the size from eax to rax and preserving the sign.

These instructions work only on the rax register and do not affect the rflags register.

Once we have computed the 64-bit offset of the array element, we can get the address of the beginning of the array ❸ and add this offset to it to get the address of the array element. The algorithm used by the compiler doubles the value of the index by adding it to itself. It then stores this at the computed address of the array element.

After the array has been filled with data, the contents are displayed with the displayArray function, as shown in Listings 17-6 and 17-7.

```
/* displayArray.h
 * Prints array contents.
 */
#ifndef DISPLAYARRAY_H
#define DISPLAYARRAY_H
void displayArray(int theArray[], int nElements);
#endif
```

Listing 17-6: Header file for the displayArray function

```
/* displayArray.c
 * Prints array contents.
 */
#include "displayArray.h"
#include "writeStr.h"
#include "putInt.h"
void displayArray(int theArray[], int nElements)
{
  int i;

  for (i = 0; i < nElements; i++)
  {
    writeStr("intArray[");
    putInt(i);
    writeStr("] = ");
    putInt(theArray[i]);
    writeStr("\n");
  }
}
```

Listing 17-7: Function to display the contents of an int array

The displayArray function also uses a for loop to process each element of the array. We'll skip the compiler-generated assembly language for the displayArray function since it accesses the individual array elements using the same algorithm as twiceIndex (Listing 17-5).

We'll do things a little differently when writing this program directly in assembly language.

## Arrays in Assembly Language

Now we'll write our own assembly language function that fills an array with values. Our approach will be similar to the compiler's, but we'll use instructions that are a little more intuitive. Listing 17-8 shows our main function. It's similar to what the compiler generated (Listing 17-2) except that I have used meaningful names for the constants.

```
# fill2XIndex.s
# Allocates an int array, stores 2 X element number
# in each element and prints array contents.
        .intel_syntax noprefix
# Stack frame
        .equ    intArray,-48
        .equ    canary,-8
        .equ    localSize,-48
# Constant
        .equ    N,10
# Code
        .text
        .globl  main
        .type   main, @function
main:
        push    rbp                     # save frame pointer
        mov     rbp, rsp                # set new frame pointer
        add     rsp, localSize          # for local var.
        mov     rax, qword ptr fs:40    # get canary
        mov     qword ptr canary[rbp], rax

        mov     esi, N                  # number of elements
        lea     rdi, intArray[rbp]      # our array
        call    twiceIndex

        mov     esi, N                  # number of elements
        lea     rdi, intArray[rbp]      # our array
        call    displayArray

        mov     eax, 0                  # return 0;
        mov     rcx, canary[rbp]        # retrieve saved canary
        xor     rcx, fs:40              # and check it
        je      goodCanary
        call    __stack_chk_fail@PLT    # bad canary
goodCanary:
        mov     rsp, rbp                # restore stack pointer
        pop     rbp                     # and caller frame pointer
        ret
```

Listing 17-8: Filling an array and displaying its contents in assembly language

The main function here simply passes the address of the array and the number of elements in the array to the two functions, twiceIndex and displayArray, for processing the array.

Our assembly language version of twiceIndex, as shown in Listing 17-9, uses instructions that seem a little more intuitive than what the compiler used.

```
# twiceIndex.s
# Stores 2 X element number in each array element.
# Calling sequence:
#    rdi <- pointer to array
#    esi <- number of elements
        .intel_syntax noprefix

# Code
        .text
        .globl  twiceIndex
        .type   twiceIndex, @function
twiceIndex:
        push    rbp                  # save frame pointer
        mov     rbp, rsp             # set new frame pointer

        mov   ❶ ecx, 0               # index = 0
storeLoop:
        mov     eax, ecx             # current index
      ❷ shl     eax, 1               # times 2
      ❸ mov     [rdi+rcx*4], eax     # store result
        inc     ecx                  # increment index
        cmp     ecx, esi             # end of array?
        jl      storeLoop            # no, loop back

        mov     rsp, rbp             # restore stack pointer
        pop     rbp                  # and caller frame pointer
        ret
```

Listing 17-9: Assembly language function to store twice the index value in each array element

    We are using a register for the indexing variable ❶. Recall that when we are in 64-bit mode, storing a 32-bit value in a register zeros the entire high-order 32 bits of the register, so we don't need to extend the index value to 64 bits when using it as an address offset ❸. We also use a shift to multiply the index by 2 ❷ instead of adding it to itself.

    Our assembly language version of displayArray, as shown in Listing 17-10, uses the same approach to access the array elements as twiceIndex.

```
# displayArray.s
# Prints array contents.
# Calling sequence:
#    rdi <- pointer to array
#    esi <- number of elements
        .intel_syntax noprefix

# Stack frame
        .equ    nElements,-8
        .equ    localSize,-16
# Constant data
        .section  .rodata
```

```
          .align  8
format1:
          .string "intArray["
format2:
          .string "] = "
endl:
          .string "\n"
# Code
          .text
          .globl  displayArray
          .type   displayArray, @function
displayArray:
          push    rbp              # save frame pointer
          mov     rbp, rsp         # set new frame pointer
          add     rsp, localSize   # local variables
          push    rbx              # save, use for i
          push    r12              # save, use for array pointer

          mov     r12, rdi         # pointer to array
          mov     nElements[rbp], esi # number of elements

          mov     ebx, 0           # index = 0
printLoop:
          lea     rdi, format1[rip]    # start of formatting
          call    writeStr
          mov     edi, ebx             # index
          call  ❶ putInt
          lea     rdi, format2[rip]    # more formatting
          call    writeStr
          mov     edi, [r12+rbx*4]     # array element
          call    putInt               # print on screen
          lea     rdi, endl[rip]       # next line
          call    writeStr

          inc     ebx              # increment index
          cmp     ebx, nElements[rbp] # end of array?
          jl      printLoop        # no, loop back

          pop     r12              # restore registers
          pop     rbx
          mov     rsp, rbp         # yes, restore stack pointer
          pop     rbp              # and caller frame pointer
          ret
```

*Listing 17-10: Displaying the elements of an int array in assembly language*

Instead of using printf to display the contents of the array, we're using the putInt function that was developed in the last "Your Turn" in Chapter 16 ❶.

In the next section, we'll look at how to group items of different data types.

# Records

A *record* (or *structure*) allows a programmer to group several data items of possibly different data types together into a new programmer-defined data type. Each individual data item in a record is called a *field* or *element*. A field is often called a *member*, especially in object-oriented programming. We'll discuss C++ objects in the next chapter.

Since the fields in a record can have different sizes, accessing them is a bit more complex than accessing the data items in an array. We'll start with looking at how this is done, and then we'll look at how records are passed to other functions.

## Records in C

Let's start by looking at a program that defines a record, stores data in the fields of each record, and then displays the values, as shown in Listing 17-11.

```
/* recordField.c
 * Allocates a record and assigns a value to each field.
 */

#include <stdio.h>

int main(void)
{
❶ struct
  {
    char aChar;
    int anInt;
    char anotherChar;
❷ } x;

❸ x.aChar = 'a';
```

```
    x.anInt = 123;
    x.anotherChar = 'b';

    printf("x: %c, %i, %c\n",
           x.aChar, x.anInt, x.anotherChar);
    return 0;
}


#endif
```

*Listing 17-11: A single record using a struct variable in C*

We use the struct keyword to declare a record in C ❶. We define the fields of the record by using the usual C syntax: a data type followed by the field name. We can define a record by following its declaration with a name for the record ❷. We access the individual fields of a record by using the dot operator ❸.

We can learn how the record is stored in memory by looking at the compiler-generated assembly language for this function in Listing 17-12.

```
        .file   "recordField.c"
        .intel_syntax noprefix
        .text
        .section        .rodata
.LC0:
        .string "x: %c, %i, %c\n"
        .text
        .globl  main
        .type   main, @function
main:
        push    rbp
        mov     rbp, rsp
        sub     rsp, 16                 ## memory for record
        mov     BYTE PTR ❶-12[rbp], 97  ## x.aChar = 'a';
        mov     DWORD PTR -8[rbp], 123   ## x.anInt = 123;
        mov     BYTE PTR -4[rbp], 98     ## x.anotherChar = 'b';
        movzx   eax, BYTE PTR -4[rbp]    ## load x.anotherChar
        movsx   ecx, al                 ## to 32 bits
        mov     edx, DWORD PTR -8[rbp]   ## load x.anInt
        movzx   eax, BYTE PTR -12[rbp]   ## load x.aChar
        movsx   eax, al                 ## to 32 bits
        mov     esi, eax
        lea     rdi, .LC0[rip]
        mov     eax, 0
        call    printf@PLT
        mov     eax, 0
        leave
        ret
        .size   main, .-main
        .ident  "GCC: (Ubuntu 9.3.0-17ubuntu1~20.04) 9.3.0"
        .section        .note.GNU-stack,"",@progbits
```

*Listing 17-12: Accessing the fields of a C struct variable in memory*

Like other local variables, the record is allocated in the function's stack frame, so its fields are accessed relative to the stack frame pointer, rbp. The compiler computes the offset from the address in rbp to each field in the record ❶.

We show the layout in memory for the record in Figure 17-1, which shows the record after the values have been assigned to the three fields.

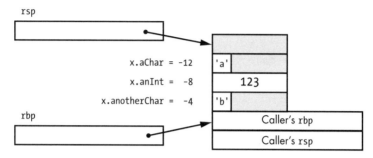

*Figure 17-1: Stack frame showing one record implemented as a C struct*

An int in our environment takes four bytes and must be aligned on a four-byte memory address. Although both the two char fields in this record take only one byte, the alignment requirement for the int field leads to the six "wasted" bytes, as shown in Figure 17-1. There are also four extra bytes in the stack frame to create proper stack pointer alignment, as described in "Variables on the Stack" in Chapter 11.

## Records in Assembly Language

Rather than compute the offset from rbp, we'll use a different technique in our assembly language version of accessing the fields of a record, as shown in Listing 17-13.

```
# recordField.s
# Allocates a record and assigns a value to each field.
        .intel_syntax noprefix
# Stack frame
        .equ    x,-12
        .equ    localSize,-16
# record offsets
    ❶ .equ    aChar,0
        .equ    anInt,4
        .equ    anotherChar,8
        .equ    recordSize,12
# Constant data
        .section  .rodata
        .align  8
message:
        .string "x: %c, %i, %c\n"
# Code
        .text
        .globl  main
```

```
            .type    main, @function
main:
            push    rbp                     # save frame pointer
            mov     rbp, rsp                # set new frame pointer
            add     rsp, localSize          # for local var.

    ❷ lea     rax, x[rbp]             # fill record
            mov     byte ptr aChar[rax], 'a'
            mov     dword ptr anInt[rax], 123
            mov     byte ptr anotherChar[rax], 'c'

            lea     rax, x[rbp]             # print record
            movzx   ecx, byte ptr anotherChar[rax]
            mov     edx, dword ptr anInt[rax]
            movzx   esi, byte ptr aChar[rax]
            lea     rdi, message[rip]
            mov     eax, 0
            call    printf@plt

            mov     eax, 0                  # return 0;
            mov     rsp, rbp                # restore stack pointer
            pop     rbp                     # and caller frame pointer
            ret
```

*Listing 17-13: Accessing record fields in assembly language.*

In our assembly language version, we first equate the field names with their respective offsets from the beginning of the record ❶. The diagram is Figure 17-1 is useful in coming up with these numbers. Then we can load the address of the beginning of the record ❷ and directly access the fields using their names.

Passing a record to another function raises additional issues. As you have seen, we need to specify the type of data that we are passing, but a record can have many fields, each of which can have a different data type. In the next section, we'll see how C solves this problem.

## Passing Records to Other Functions in C

Defining the fields every time we define another instance of a record is cumbersome. C allows us to define our own struct types using a *structure tag* (or simply *tag*), which serves as a synonym for the field definitions. Not only is this useful for defining multiple records of the same field composition, but it's necessary for passing records to other functions.

For example, we defined the struct variable x in Listing 17-11:

```
struct
  {
    char aChar;
    int anInt;
    char anotherChar;
} x;
```

Instead, if we create a tag for the fields in the struct like this,

```
struct aTag
  {
    char aChar;
    int anInt;
    char anotherChar;
  };
```

then we have created a new programmer-defined data type, struct aTag. We can then define variables of our new data type in the usual way:

```
struct aTag x;
```

We'll start by declaring our new struct  data type in a separate header file, as shown in Listing 17-14, so that it can be included in each file where it is used.

```
/* aRecord.h
 * Declaration of a record.
 */

#ifndef ARECORD_H
#define ARECORD_H
struct ❶aTag
{
  char aChar;
  int anInt;
  char anotherChar;
};
#endif
```

Listing 17-14: Declaration of a programmer-defined record data type in C

The tag for a record in C is a programmer-defined identifier placed immediately after the struct keyword in the record's declaration ❶. We can then use aTag to represent the record fields declared in Listing 17-14. Listing 17-15 shows how we can use the tag to define two records in a program.

```
/* records.c
 * Allocates two records, assigns a value to each field
 * in each record, and displays the contents.
 */

#include "aRecord.h"
#include "loadRecord.h"
#include "displayRecord.h"

int main(void)
{
❶ struct aTag x;
  struct aTag y;
```

```
    loadRecord(❷&x, 'a', 123, 'b');
    loadRecord(&y, '1', 456, '2');

    displayRecord(❸x);
    displayRecord(y);

    return 0;
}
```

*Listing 17-15: Program to load data into two records and then display the contents*

When defining a record variable, we need to follow the struct C keyword with our tag for the type of struct we're defining ❶. Since the loadRecord function will store data values in the record, we need to pass the address of the record ❷. We can use pass by value to pass a copy of the record to the displayRecord ❸ since it doesn't change the data values. But you'll see as we go through the details that it's common for programmers to use pass by pointer for records to avoid copying large amounts of data.

Both x and y are local variables in Listing 17-15, so they will be created on the stack, as shown in Listing 17-16.

```
        .file   "records.c"
        .intel_syntax noprefix
        .text
        .globl  main
        .type   main, @function
main:
        push    rbp
        mov     rbp, rsp
        sub     rsp, 32         ## memory for 2 records
        mov     rax, QWORD PTR fs:40
        mov     QWORD PTR -8[rbp], rax
        xor     eax, eax
    ❶ lea     rax, -32[rbp]    ## address of x record
        mov     ecx, 98         ## data to store in it
        mov     edx, 123
        mov     esi, 97
        mov     rdi, rax
        call    loadRecord@PLT
        lea     rax, -20[rbp]    ## address of y record
        mov     ecx, 50         ## data to store in it
        mov     edx, 456
        mov     esi, 49
        mov     rdi, rax
        call    loadRecord@PLT
    ❷ mov     rdx, QWORD PTR -32[rbp] ## 8 bytes of x
        mov     eax, DWORD PTR -24[rbp] ## 4 more bytes of x
        mov     rdi, rdx
        mov     esi, eax
        call    displayRecord@PLT
        mov     rdx, QWORD PTR -20[rbp] ## 8 bytes of y
        mov     eax, DWORD PTR -12[rbp] ## 4 more bytes of y
        mov     rdi, rdx
        mov     esi, eax
```

```
            call      displayRecord@PLT
            mov       eax, 0
            mov       rcx, QWORD PTR -8[rbp]
            xor       rcx, QWORD PTR fs:40
            je        .L3
            call      __stack_chk_fail@PLT
    .L3:
            leave
            ret
            .size     main, .-main
            .ident    "GCC: (Ubuntu 9.3.0-17ubuntu1~20.04) 9.3.0"
            .section          .note.GNU-stack,"",@progbits
```

*Listing 17-16: Compiler-generated assembly language for the program that stores values in two records*

As we specified, the compiler passes the address of each record to the loadRecord function ❶. However, the records are passed by value to the displayRecord function, so the compiler passes a copy of all 12 bytes in the record, including the unused bytes, to the function ❷.

Listings 17-17 and 17-18 show the loadRecord function header file and definition.

```
/* loadRecord.h
 * Loads record with data.
 */

#ifndef LOADRECORD_H
#define LOADRECORD_H
❶ #include "aRecord.h"
int loadRecord(struct aTag *aStruct, char x, int y, char z);
#endif
```

*Listing 17-17: Header file for the loadRecord function*

The argument list in Listing 17-17 shows how to use the tag for passing arguments to a function. The struct aTag syntax means that the data type of this argument is the C struct that has been declared with the tag, aTag. We need to #include the file where this tag is declared before using it in this file ❶.

The loadStruct function, as shown in Listing 17-18, introduces a useful C syntax for dealing with pointers to records.

```
/* loadRecord.c
 * Loads record with data.
 */

#include "loadRecord.h"

int loadRecord(struct aTag *aRecord, char x, int y, char z)
{
❶ (*aRecord).aChar = x;
❷ aRecord->anInt = y;        /* equivalent syntax */
  aRecord->anotherChar = z;
```

```
    return 0;
}
```

The argument passed to this function is a pointer to the record. We
need to dereference this pointer before accessing the individual fields in
the record it points to. Since the dot operator (.) has higher precedence
than the dereferencing operator (*), we need to use parentheses to do the
dereferencing before the field access ❶.

This pair of operations—dereference and then select a field—is so common and the syntax so cumbersome, the C language designers created an
alternative syntax, -> ❷. This performs exactly the same operations as the
other syntax but is more succinct.

Listing 17-19 shows the compiler-generated assembly language for
`loadRecord`.

```
        .file   "loadRecord.c"
        .intel_syntax noprefix
        .text
        .globl  loadRecord
        .type   loadRecord, @function
loadRecord:
        push    rbp
        mov     rbp, rsp
❶ mov     QWORD PTR -8[rbp], rdi  ## save address of record
        mov     DWORD PTR -16[rbp], edx ## save y
        mov     eax, ecx
        mov     edx, esi
        mov     BYTE PTR -12[rbp], dl   ## save x
        mov     BYTE PTR -20[rbp], al   ## save z
❷ mov     rax, QWORD PTR -8[rbp]   ## load address of record
        movzx   edx, BYTE PTR -12[rbp]  ## load x
        mov     BYTE PTR [rax], dl      ## store x
        mov     rax, QWORD PTR -8[rbp]  ## load address of record
        mov     edx, DWORD PTR -16[rbp] ## load y
        mov     DWORD PTR 4[rax], edx   ## store y
        mov     rax, QWORD PTR -8[rbp]  ## load address of record
        movzx   edx, BYTE PTR -20[rbp]  ## load z
        mov     BYTE PTR 8[rax], dl     ## store z
        mov     eax, 0
        pop     rbp
        ret
        .size   loadRecord, .-loadRecord
        .ident  "GCC: (Ubuntu 9.3.0-17ubuntu1~20.04) 9.3.0"
        .section        .note.GNU-stack,"",@progbits
```

*Listing 17-19: Compiler-generated assembly language for the* `loadRecord` *function*

For the `loadRecord` function, the compiler uses an algorithm for storing
data in the record fields that is essentially the same as it used in the `main`
function for storing data in Listing 17-11. It first saves the address of the
record in the red zone on the stack ❶. Then it retrieves this address before

storing the data in each field ❷, using the address offset from the declaration of the record in the *aRecord.h* file, Listing 17-14. Figure 17-1 shows these address offsets.

The displayRecord function is different because the record is passed by value, as shown in Listings 17-20 and 17-21.

```
/* displayRecord.h
 * Display contents of a record.
 */

#ifndef DISPLAYRECORD_H
#define DISPLAYRECORD_H
#include "aRecord.h"
void displayRecord(struct aTag aRecord);
#endif
```

*Listing 17-20: Header file for the `displayRecord` function*

```
/* displayRecord.c
 * Display contents of a struct.
 */

#include <stdio.h>
#include "displayRecord.h"

void displayRecord(struct aTag aRecord)
{
  printf("%c, %i, %c\n", aRecord.aChar,
         aRecord.anInt, aRecord.anotherChar);
}
```

*Listing 17-21: Function to display a record*

The algorithm that displays the contents of the fields in the record is straightforward. We simply pass the value in each field to the printf function. But when we look at the compiler-generated assembly language, as shown in Listing 17-22, we see that the algorithm requires a reconstruction of the record in the stack frame of the displayRecord function.

```
        .file   "displayRecord.c"
        .intel_syntax noprefix
        .text
        .section        .rodata
.LC0:
        .string "%c, %i, %c\n"
        .text
        .globl  displayRecord
        .type   displayRecord, @function
displayRecord:
        push    rbp
        mov     rbp, rsp
   ❶ sub     rsp, 16         ## memory for a record
        mov     rdx, rdi
```

```
       mov     eax, esi
❷ mov     QWORD PTR -16[rbp], rdx  ## 8 bytes of record
       mov     DWORD PTR -8[rbp], eax   ## another 4 bytes
❸ movzx   eax, BYTE PTR -8[rbp]     ## load anotherChar
       movsx   ecx, al                  ## extend to 32 bits
       mov     edx, DWORD PTR -12[rbp]  ## load anInt
       movzx   eax, BYTE PTR -16[rbp]   ## load aChar
       movsx   eax, al                  ## extend to 32 bits
       mov     esi, eax
       lea     rdi, .LC0[rip]
       mov     eax, 0
       call    printf@PLT
       nop
       leave
       ret
       .size   displayRecord, .-displayRecord
       .ident  "GCC: (Ubuntu 9.3.0-17ubuntu1~20.04) 9.3.0"
       .section        .note.GNU-stack,"",@progbits
```

*Listing 17-22: Compiler-generated assembly language for the displayRecord function*

For the displayRecord function, the compiler chose to create a stack frame ❶. It then copies the 12 bytes that make up the record from the registers they were passed in to the stack frame ❷. Once the record has been reconstructed in the local stack frame, the data in the individual fields is passed to the printf function for display on the screen ❸.

In the next section, we'll rewrite this program in assembly language and show the advantage of passing a record by pointer, even when it's an input.

## Passing Records to Other Functions in Assembly Language

Our approach to accessing the record fields in the loadRecord function will be similar to the compiler's. We'll use the address of the record (pass by pointer) in a register and use the field address offset to access it.

But we'll pass the record by pointer, instead of by value, to the displayRecord function. Although you could also do this in C, our assembly language version will clearly show the advantage of doing it this way.

We'll start with the main function in Listing 17-23.

```
# records.s
# Allocates two records, assigns a value to each field
# in each record, and displays the contents.
        .intel_syntax noprefix
# Stack frame
        .equ    x,-32
        .equ    y, -20
        .equ    canary,-8
        .equ    localSize,-32
# Constant data
        .section  .rodata
        .align  8
endl:
        .string "\n"
```

```
# Code
        .text
        .globl  main
        .type       main, @function
main:
        push    rbp                     # save frame pointer
        mov     rbp, rsp                # set new frame pointer
        add     rsp, localSize          # for local var.
        mov     rax, qword ptr fs:40    # get canary
        mov     qword ptr canary[rbp], rax

        mov     ecx, 'b'                # data to store in record
        mov     edx, 123
        mov     esi, 'a'
        lea     rdi, x[rbp]             # x record
        call    loadRecord

        mov     ecx, '2'                # data to store in record
        mov     edx, 456
        mov     esi, '1'
        lea     rdi, y[rbp]             # y record
        call    loadRecord

    ❶ lea     rdi, x[rbp]             # display x record
        call    displayRecord

        lea     rdi, y[rbp]             # display y record
        call    displayRecord

        mov     eax, 0                  # return 0;
        mov     rcx, canary[rbp]        # retrieve saved canary
        xor     rcx, fs:40              # and check it
        je      goodCanary
        call    __stack_chk_fail@PLT    # bad canary
goodCanary:
        mov     rsp, rbp                # restore stack pointer
        pop     rbp                     # and caller frame pointer
        ret
```

*Listing 17-23: Assembly language program to store data in two records and display their contents*

Our assembly language version of the main function is similar to the compiler-generated assembly language for our C version (Listing 17-16), except that we are passing the records to the displayRecord function by pointer ❶ instead of by value.

Next, we'll place the equates for the offsets of the fields in the record in a separate file, as shown in Listing 17-24, to make sure we use the same equates in all the files where the fields are accessed.

```
# aRecord
# Declaration of a record.
❶ # This record takes 12 bytes.
```

```
        .equ    aChar,0
        .equ    anInt,4
        .equ    anotherChar,8
```

*Listing 17-24: Record field offsets*

We're using the same offsets for the fields as the C version, as shown in Figure 17-1. Since the main function does not access the record fields directly, we didn't need the offsets in this file there. But we did need to know the total number of bytes used by the record ❶ when allocating space on the stack for each record.

The standard for the C language specifies some rules for the memory alignment of the fields in a struct, but the rules allow different compilers to use different values for the offsets to the fields. To help us interface assembly language functions with C functions, the standard specifies a macro in the *stddef.h* header file, offsetof, that will show the values that our compiler chose for the offsets in the C code. For example, this code

```
#include <stddef.h>
#include "aRecord.h"
--snip--
offsetof(struct aTag, anInt);
```

will return the value of the offset of anInt from the beginning of the struct. The man page for offsetof includes a more complete example of how to use it. I used both the offsetof macro and the assembly language generated by the compiler (Listing 17-19) to determine the values of the offsets.

The assembly language function to store data in a record (Listing 17-25) is similar to what the compiler generated from the C version (Listing 17-19).

```
# loadRecord.s
# Loads record with data.
# Calling sequence:
#   rdi <- pointer to record
#   esi <- 1st char
#   edx <- int
#   ecx <- 2nd char
        .intel_syntax noprefix
# Record field offsets
     ❶ .include  "aRecord"
# Code
        .text
        .globl  loadRecord
        .type   loadRecord, @function
loadRecord:
        push    rbp                     # save frame pointer
        mov     rbp, rsp                # set new frame pointer

     ❷ mov     aChar[rdi], esi       # 1st char field
        mov     anInt[rdi], edx       # int field
        mov     anotherChar[rdi], ecx # 2nd char field
```

```
        mov     rsp, rbp                # restore stack pointer
        pop     rbp                     # and caller frame pointer
        ret
```

*Listing 17-25: Assembly language version of the loadRecord function*

We're using the .include assembler directive to bring the record field names and their respective offsets into this function ❶. The .include assembler directive works like the #include C directive—it copies the text from the specified file into this source file before assembling the code.

Since this function does not call any other functions, we know that the address of the record that was passed to this function in rdi will not be changed. We can simply access each field using the field name with rdi as the base register ❷.

Passing a record by pointer to the displayRecord function, as shown in Listing 17-26, simplifies the function.

```
# displayRecord.s
# Displays contents of a record.
# Calling sequence:
#    rdi <- pointer to record
        .intel_syntax noprefix
# Record field offsets
        .include  "aRecord"
# Stack frame
        .equ    recordPtr,-16
        .equ    localSize,-16
# Useful constant
        .equ    STDOUT,1
# Constant data
        .section  .rodata
        .align  8
endl:
        .string "\n"
# Code
        .text
        .globl  displayRecord
        .type   displayRecord, @function
displayRecord:
        push    rbp                     # save frame pointer
        mov     rbp, rsp                # set new frame pointer
        add     rsp, localSize          # for local var.

   ❶ mov     recordPtr[rbp], rdi     # save record address

        mov     edx, 1                  # write one character
        mov     rax, recordPtr[rbp]     # address of record
        lea     rsi, aChar[rax]         # character located here
        mov     edi, STDOUT             # to screen
   ❷ call    write@plt
        lea     rdi, endl[rip]          # new line
        call    writeStr
```

```
mov     rax, recordPtr[rbp]     # address of record
mov     edi,anInt[rax]          # get the integer
call    putInt                  # write to screen
lea     rdi, endl[rip]
call    writeStr

mov     edx, 1                  # second character
mov     rax, recordPtr[rbp]     # address of record
lea     rsi, anotherChar[rax]
mov     edi, STDOUT
call    write@plt
lea     rdi, endl[rip]
call    writeStr

mov     rsp, rbp                # restore stack pointer
pop     rbp                     # and caller frame pointer
ret
```

*Listing 17-26: Assembly language version of displayRecord function*

This function calls other functions, which can change the contents of rdi, so we need to save the address of the record in our stack frame ❶ for accessing the individual record fields later in the function. Since the char fields hold a single character, we use the write function to display the contents of these fields ❷.

---

**YOUR TURN**

1. Modify the record declaration in Listing 17-14 so that the two char fields are adjacent to each other. Generate the assembly language for the main, loadRecord, and displayRecord functions in Listings 17-15, 17-18, and 17-21. Draw a diagram of the records in the stack frame similar to Figure 17-1.

2. Modify the C displayRecord function in Listings 17-20 and 17-21 to pass the record by pointer. Generate the assembly language file. How does this compare to the assembly language version in Listing 17-25?

## What You've Learned

**Arrays**   Collections of data items of the same data type, stored contiguously in memory.

**Processing arrays**   The CPU has an addressing mode for accessing an array element using an index value.

**Passing arrays**   In C, arrays are passed by pointer rather than by value.

**Records**   Collections of data items, possibly of different data types, stored together in memory, possibly with padding for address alignment.

**Accessing record fields**   The address with offset addressing mode can be used to access a record field.

**Passing records**   It's often more efficient to pass a record by pointer, even when it's an input.

In the next chapter, we'll discuss how C++ uses records to implement the object-oriented programming paradigm.

# 18

## OBJECT-ORIENTED PROGRAMMING

So far in this book, we have been using the procedural programming paradigm (see "Exploring Data Formats with C" on page 25). In this chapter, we'll take an introductory look at how object-oriented programming is implemented at the assembly language level.

In object-oriented programming, an object has a set of *attributes*, the data items that define the state of the object. These attributes can be changed or queried by a set of *methods* that are part of the object. A software solution typically consists of constructing *instances* of objects and then programming the sending of *messages* to the objects, which use the methods to act on the attributes.

We'll use C++, an object-oriented extension of C, to illustrate some of these concepts. Our discussion will show how a record can be used to store the attributes of an object and how methods are implemented as functions that are associated with the record.

Many other features of C++ are important for creating good object-oriented programming solutions, but we won't go into them in this book. For readers of this book, I think Josh Lospinoso's *C++ Crash Course* (No Starch Press, 2019) would be a good way to learn C++. If you want to dig into the design of C++ after learning how to use it, I recommend Bjarne Stroustrup's (the creator of C++) book, *The Design and Evolution of C++* (Addison-Wesley, 1994).

As usual, we'll start with looking at some assembly language generated by the C++ compiler.

## Objects in C++

A C++ object is declared by specifying a *class*, which adds a programmer-defined type to the program. A C++ class is very much like a C record, but in addition to the *data members* that define the attributes of the object, it can include functions as members of the class. In C++, we send a message to an object telling it to perform a method by calling a class *member function*.

We *instantiate* (create an instance of) an object by giving the class name along with a name for the object, just like defining a variable. For example, in the program we'll look at shortly, the C++ statement

```
fraction x;
```

instantiates an object named x that belongs to the fraction class.

C++ allows us to write two special member functions. The first is a *constructor* function for initializing an object to place it in a known state before sending messages to the object. The C++ compiler generates the code to call our constructor function automatically at the point where we instantiate an object. A constructor function has the same name as the class. It cannot have a return value, not even void. The *default constructor* takes no arguments, but we can also write constructors that take arguments, which allows us to have more than one constructor in a class.

We can also write a *destructor* function to release any resources that were allocated by a constructor. For example, a constructor might allocate memory from the heap, which the destructor would deallocate. (The heap is described in Chapter 10.) There can be only one destructor function, which has the same name as the class preceded by the ~ character. The destructor cannot have a return value and takes no arguments. The C++ compiler will generate the code to call the destructor automatically when program flow leaves the scope of the object.

We'll first look at a simple fraction class, whose attributes are a numerator and a denominator, that includes a constructor and destructor. If we don't supply constructor or destructor member functions, a C++ compiler will supply appropriate code to perform the construction and destruction of an object. Later in this chapter, we'll explore what our compiler does for us when we don't supply them.

We'll start with the declaration of our fraction class, which we'll place in a header file so it can be included in any file that uses the class, as shown in Listing 18-1.

```
❶ // fraction.hpp
   // Simple fraction class.

   #ifndef FRACTION_HPP
   #define FRACTION_HPP
   // Uses the following C functions
❷ extern "C" int writeStr(char *);
   extern "C" int getInt(int *);
   extern "C" int putInt(int);

❸ class fraction
   {
     ❹ int num;        // numerator
        int den;        // denominator
     ❺ public:
        ❻ fraction();      // default constructor
          ~fraction();     // default destructor
          void get();      // gets user's values
          void display();  // displays fraction
          void add(int);   // adds integer
   };
   #endif
```

*Listing 18-1: A simple fraction class*

Being an extension of C, nearly everything that can be done in C can also be done in C++. One of the additions in C++ is the // syntax for comments ❶. Like the # syntax in our assembly language, the remainder of the line is a comment, intended only for the human reader.

We'll be using some assembly language functions that we wrote earlier in the book, which follow the C calling conventions. As you'll see, the conventions for calling a function in C++ differ from C, so we need to tell the C++ compiler that we'll call these functions using the C conventions ❷.

The overall syntax of a class declaration ❸ is similar to a record declaration but includes the capability to include the methods of the class as member functions ❻. By default, data members and member functions declared within a class are in the *private scope* ❹: they can be accessed only by member functions of the same class. We'll place the attributes of our fraction class, num and den, in the private scope where they are defined as variables ❹. They can be accessed only by the member functions.

A class can also have a *public scope* for items that are to be accessed by entities outside the class ❺. We'll declare our member functions in the public scope so they can be called from outside the class ❻. C++ classes can have other levels of access, but we won't cover them in this book.

The struct keyword can also be used to declare a C++ class, but it does not have a default scope access protection. We would need to explicitly declare a private scope, as shown in Listing 18-2.

```
struct fraction
{
  private:
    int num;        // numerator
```

```
    int den;          // denominator
  public:
    fraction();       // constructor
    ~fraction();      // destructor
    void get();       // gets user's values
    void display();   // displays fraction
    void add(int);    // adds integer
};
```

*Listing 18-2: Our fraction class declared using the struct keyword*

I prefer using the class keyword because that emphasizes that there is more to it than a simple C record, but it's a personal choice. Next, we'll look at how to create objects and how to send messages to them.

## Using Objects in C++

To illustrate how to create an object and send messages to it, we'll use a simple program that allows a user to enter the numerator and denominator values of a fraction and then adds 1 to the fraction, shown in Listing 18-3. The program displays the state of the fraction before getting user input values and then again after adding 1 to the user's fraction.

```
// incFraction.cpp
// Gets a fraction from user and increments by 1.

#include "fraction.hpp"
int main(void)
{
❶ fraction x;

❷ x.display();
  x.get();
  x.add(1);
  x.display();
  return 0;
}
```

*Listing 18-3: Program to add 1 to a fraction*

An object is instantiated by using the class name and providing a name for the object, just like defining a variable ❶. The dot operator (.) is used to send a message to a method in the class ❷, which calls the respective member function in the class the object belongs to.

Next, we'll look at the assembly language generated by the C++ compiler to implement the main function in Listing 18-3. The C++ compiler is named **g++**. I used the following command to generate the assembly language in Listing 18-4:

```
g++ -fno-asynchronous-unwind-tables -fno-exceptions -fcf-protection=none -S \
-masm=intel incFraction.cc
```

This is the same as the command we've been using for C code except we've added the -fno-exceptions option. C++ provides an *exception* mechanism for dealing with runtime errors when they're detected. The compiler provides the information for this feature through assembler directives, which would tend to obscure the discussion here of how objects are implemented. The -fno-exceptions option turns off this feature.

```
        .file   "incFraction.cpp"
        .intel_syntax noprefix
        .text
        .globl  main
        .type   main, @function
main:
        push    rbp
        mov     rbp, rsp
        push    rbx
❶ sub     rsp, 24
        mov     rax, QWORD PTR fs:40
        mov     QWORD PTR -24[rbp], rax
        xor     eax, eax
❷ lea     rax, -32[rbp]     ## address of object
        mov     rdi, rax
        call    _ZN8fractionC1Ev@PLT  ## construct
        lea     rax, -32[rbp]     ## address of object
        mov     rdi, rax
        call    _ZN8fraction7displayEv@PLT
        lea     rax, -32[rbp]     ## address of object
        mov     rdi, rax
        call    _ZN8fraction3getEv@PLT
        lea     rax, -32[rbp]     ## address of object
        mov     esi, 1           ## integer to add
        mov     rdi, rax
        call    _ZN8fraction3addEi@PLT
        lea     rax, -32[rbp]     ## address of object
        mov     rdi, rax
        call    _ZN8fraction7displayEv@PLT
        mov     ebx, 0           ## return value
        lea     rax, -32[rbp]     ## address of object
        mov     rdi, rax
❸ call    _ZN8fractionD1Ev@PLT
        mov     eax, ebx         ## return 0;
        mov     rdx, QWORD PTR -24[rbp]
        xor     rdx, QWORD PTR fs:40
        je      .L3
        call    __stack_chk_fail@PLT
.L3:
        add     rsp, 24
        pop     rbx
        pop     rbp
        ret
        .size   main, .-main
        .ident  "GCC: (Ubuntu 9.3.0-17ubuntu1~20.04) 9.3.0"
        .section        .note.GNU-stack,"",@progbits
```

Listing 18-4: Compiler-generated assembly language showing the construction of an object, sending messages to it, and its destruction

The first thing to note is that x is an automatic local variable (Listing 18-3), so memory space is allocated on the stack for this fraction object in the function's prologue ❶. Then the address of this memory area ❷ is passed to a function, _ZN8fractionC1Ev, at the point where the object is instantiated. (Notice that rbx was pushed onto the stack before allocating the 24 bytes for the fraction object, making the correct offset here –32.)

If you look back at Listing 18-1, you can see that the C++ compiler has mangled the name of our constructor function, fraction, to be _ZN8fractionC1Ev. We saw the C compiler doing name mangling of a static local variable in Chapter 15. The purpose there was to distinguish between different static local variables with the same name in different functions defined in the same file.

C++ does name mangling to associate member functions with their class. If you look at the calls to the class member functions in Listing 18-4, you can see that they all begin with _ZN8fraction. Since function names are global in scope, including the class name allows us to define other classes in the program that have the same names for member functions. For example, we might have more than one class in a program that has a display member function. Name mangling identifies each display member function with the class it belongs to.

C++ name mangling also allows function overloading. If you look closely at how the compiler mangled our add member function, _ZN8fraction3addEi, you can probably figure out that the compiler's name mangling includes the number and types of arguments. In this example, the i at the end of the mangled name shows that the function takes a single int argument. This allows us to have more than one class member function with the same name but that differ in their number of arguments and their types, which is called *function overloading*. You'll get a chance to overload the default constructor when it's Your Turn.

There is no standard for how name mangling is done, so it could be different for each compiler. This means that all C++ code in a program must be compiled and linked using compatible compilers and linkers.

Next, look at the two instructions just before each call to a member function ❷. We can see that the address of the object is passed to each of them. This is a *hidden argument* that doesn't show up in the C++ code. We'll see how to access this address in a member function when we look inside the member functions later in the chapter.

Although it doesn't show in the C++ code that we write, the compiler generates a call to our destructor function at the point where program flow leaves the scope of the object ❸. In some more advanced programming techniques, we would call the destructor explicitly, but we won't cover them in the book. Most of time we let the compiler decide when to call the destructor.

We'll next look at the constructor and destructor and the other member functions of this fraction class.

## Defining Class Member Functions

Although it's common to put each C function in its own file, C++ source files are commonly organized to include all the functions in a class. Listing 18-5 shows the definitions of the member functions for our fraction class.

```
// fraction.cpp
// Simple fraction class.

#include "fraction.hpp"
// Use char arrays because writeStr is C-style function.
❶ char numMsg[] = "Enter numerator: ";
char denMsg[] = "Enter denominator: ";
char over[] = "/";
char endl[] = "\n";

❷ fraction::fraction()
{
  num = 0;
  den = 1;
}

fraction::~fraction()
{
  // Nothing to do for this object
}

void fraction::get()
{
  writeStr(numMsg);
  getInt(&num);

  writeStr(denMsg);
  getInt(&den);
}

void fraction::display()
{
  putInt(num);
  writeStr(over);
  putInt(den);
  writeStr(endl);
}

void fraction::add(int theValue)
{
  num += theValue * den;
}
```

Listing 18-5: Member function definitions for fraction class

Although C++ includes library functions for writing to the screen, the assembly language to call them is somewhat complex. Instead, we'll use our assembly language writeStr function, which follows C calling conventions. It works with C-style text strings, which we'll place in the global area ❶. This will allow us to concentrate on how objects are implemented in C++.

Membership in a class is specified by giving the name of the class followed by two colons (::) ❷. Constructors have the same name as the class and are used to do any initialization that may be required. For example, our constructor initializes the fraction object to be 0/1. In some designs they may need to do other things, such as allocate memory from the heap or open a file. They cannot have a return value.

Let's look at the assembly language generated by the C++ compiler for these member functions, as shown in Listing 18-6.

```
                .file    "fraction.cpp"
                .intel_syntax noprefix
                .text
                .globl   numMsg
                .data
                .align 16
                .type    numMsg, @object
                .size    numMsg, 18
numMsg:
                .string "Enter numerator: "
                .globl   denMsg
                .align 16
                .type    denMsg, @object
                .size    denMsg, 20
denMsg:
                .string "Enter denominator: "
                .globl   over
                .type    over, @object
                .size    over, 2
over:
                .string "/"
                .globl   endl
                .type    endl, @object
                .size    endl, 2
endl:
                .string "\n"
                .text
                .align 2
           ❶ .globl   _ZN8fractionC2Ev
                .type    _ZN8fractionC2Ev, @function
_ZN8fractionC2Ev:                       ## constructor
                push     rbp
                mov      rbp, rsp
           ❷ mov      QWORD PTR -8[rbp], rdi    ## this pointer
                mov      rax, QWORD PTR -8[rbp]    ## load addr of object
                mov      DWORD PTR [rax], 0       ## num= 0;
                mov      rax, QWORD PTR -8[rbp]
                mov      DWORD PTR 4[rax], 1      ## den = 1;
```

```
        nop
        pop     rbp
        ret
        .size   _ZN8fractionC2Ev, .-_ZN8fractionC2Ev
        .globl  _ZN8fractionC1Ev
❸ .set    _ZN8fractionC1Ev,_ZN8fractionC2Ev
        .align 2
❹ .globl  _ZN8fractionD2Ev
        .type   _ZN8fractionD2Ev, @function
_ZN8fractionD2Ev:                               ## destructor
        push    rbp
        mov     rbp, rsp
        mov     QWORD PTR -8[rbp], rdi    ## this pointer
        nop
        pop     rbp
        ret
        .size   _ZN8fractionD2Ev, .-_ZN8fractionD2Ev
        .globl  _ZN8fractionD1Ev
        .set    _ZN8fractionD1Ev,_ZN8fractionD2Ev
        .align 2
        .globl  _ZN8fraction3getEv
        .type   _ZN8fraction3getEv, @function
_ZN8fraction3getEv:
        push    rbp
        mov     rbp, rsp
        sub     rsp, 16
        mov     QWORD PTR -8[rbp], rdi    ## this pointer
        lea     rdi, numMsg[rip]
        call    writeStr@PLT
        mov     rax, QWORD PTR -8[rbp]
        mov     rdi, rax
        call    getInt@PLT
        lea     rdi, denMsg[rip]
        call    writeStr@PLT
        mov     rax, QWORD PTR -8[rbp]
        add     rax, 4
        mov     rdi, rax
        call    getInt@PLT
        nop
        leave
        ret
        .size   _ZN8fraction3getEv, .-_ZN8fraction3getEv
        .align 2
        .globl  _ZN8fraction7displayEv
        .type   _ZN8fraction7displayEv, @function
_ZN8fraction7displayEv:
        push    rbp
        mov     rbp, rsp
        sub     rsp, 16
        mov     QWORD PTR -8[rbp], rdi    ## this pointer
        mov     rax, QWORD PTR -8[rbp]
        mov     eax, DWORD PTR [rax]
        mov     edi, eax
        call    putInt@PLT
        lea     rdi, over[rip]
```

```
        call    writeStr@PLT
        mov     rax, QWORD PTR -8[rbp]
        mov     eax, DWORD PTR 4[rax]
        mov     edi, eax
        call    putInt@PLT
        lea     rdi, endl[rip]
        call    writeStr@PLT
        nop
        leave
        ret
        .size   _ZN8fraction7displayEv, .-_ZN8fraction7displayEv
        .align 2
        .globl  _ZN8fraction3addEi
        .type   _ZN8fraction3addEi, @function
_ZN8fraction3addEi:
        push    rbp
        mov     rbp, rsp
        mov     QWORD PTR -8[rbp], rdi       ## this pointer
        mov     DWORD PTR -12[rbp], esi
        mov     rax, QWORD PTR -8[rbp]
        mov     edx, DWORD PTR [rax]
        mov     rax, QWORD PTR -8[rbp]
        mov     eax, DWORD PTR 4[rax]
        imul    eax, DWORD PTR -12[rbp]
        add     edx, eax
        mov     rax, QWORD PTR -8[rbp]
        mov     DWORD PTR [rax], edx
        nop
        pop     rbp
        ret
        .size   _ZN8fraction3addEi, .-_ZN8fraction3addEi
        .ident  "GCC: (Ubuntu 9.3.0-17ubuntu1~20.04) 9.3.0"
        .section        .note.GNU-stack,"",@progbits
```

*Listing 18-6: Assembly language generated by the compiler for the fraction class member functions*

The main function calls _ZN8fractionC1Ev as the constructor for the fraction object (Listing 18-4), but the compiler names it _ZN8fractionC2Ev ❶. Then the compiler sets the _ZN8fractionC1Ev as equal to _ZN8fractionC2Ev ❸. (The .set assembler directive is the same as .equ.) The two different constructors are used to implement more advanced features of C++. In our simple example, they are the same.

Our main function calls _ZN8fractionD1Ev as the destructor. Similar to the constructor, the compiler named our destructor _ZN8fractionD2Ev and then made _ZN8fractionD2Ev equal to _ZN8fractionD2Ev ❹. Again, this allows for more complex destructors.

I said earlier that we can access the address of an object in a member function. C++ provides a special pointer variable named this that contains the object's address ❷. Most of the time we don't need to explicitly use the this pointer. When we use an object's data member in a member function, the compiler assumes that we mean the current object and uses the this pointer implicitly. This assumption also holds if we call another member function from within a member function. Some more advanced C++ programming techniques require the explicit use of the this pointer, but they are beyond the scope of this book.

The rest of the code in Listing 18-6 should be familiar to you, so we'll move on to show when we don't need to write a constructor or destructor.

---

**YOUR TURN**

Add another constructor to the C++ program in Listings 18-1, 18-3, and 18-5 that takes two integer arguments for initializing the fraction. Add an object that uses your second constructor. For example, fraction y(1,2); would create the fraction object initialized to 1/2. Modify the main function to display this second fraction object, get a new value for it, add an integer to the second object, and display it again.

---

## Letting the Compiler Write a Constructor and Destructor

If all we need is a default constructor to initialize data members, we don't even need to write a constructor or destructor. Bjarne Stroustrup and Herb Sutter maintain an excellent list of recommendations for writing C++. Their recommendation C.45 (*https://isocpp.github.io/CppCoreGuidelines/ CppCoreGuidelines#Rc-default/*) states: "Don't define a default constructor that only initializes data members; use in-class member initializers instead." They point out that the compiler will "generate the function" for us, which "can be more efficient." Most C++ books I've read give essentially the same advice.

In this section, we'll follow this advice. We'll modify the code from Listings 18-1, 18-3, and 18-5 by deleting our constructor and destructor. Then we'll use our knowledge of assembly language to see what the compiler has generated for us. Listing 18-7 shows our fraction class without a constructor or destructor, using *in-class member initializers* instead.

```
// fraction.hpp
// Simple fraction class.

#ifndef FRACTION_HPP
#define FRACTION_HPP
// Uses the following C functions
extern "C" int writeStr(char *);
extern "C" int getInt(int *);
extern "C" int putInt(int);

class fraction
{
❶ int num{0};            // numerator
   int den{1};            // denominator
  public:
   void get();            // gets user's values
```

```
        void display();        // displays fraction
        void add(int theValue); // adds integer
};
#endif
```

*Listing 18-7: fraction class from Listing 18-1 with the constructor and destructor removed*

Instead of using a constructor to initialize the data members in a fraction object, we'll initialize them using the *brace initialization* syntax of C++ ❶. C++ also allows the following syntaxes for data member initialization:

```
int num = 0;
int num = {0};
```

I like the brace initialization syntax because it conveys the message that the actual assignment to the variable doesn't take place until an object is instantiated, as we'll see shortly. The differences are discussed in Josh Lospinoso's book, cited at the beginning of this chapter.

We won't change the code in Listing 18-3, and we'll remove the constructor and destructor (fraction() and ~fraction()) from Listing 18-5. These changes give us the compiler-generated assembly language for the main function shown in Listing 18-8.

```
        .file   "incFraction.cpp"
        .intel_syntax noprefix
        .text
        .globl  main
        .type   main, @function
main:
        push    rbp
        mov     rbp, rsp
❶ sub     rsp, 16
        mov     rax, QWORD PTR fs:40
        mov     QWORD PTR -8[rbp], rax
        xor     eax, eax
❷ mov     DWORD PTR -16[rbp], 0    ## num = 0;
        mov     DWORD PTR -12[rbp], 1    ## den = 1;
        lea     rax, -16[rbp]
        mov     rdi, rax
        call    _ZN8fraction7displayEv@PLT
        lea     rax, -16[rbp]
        mov     rdi, rax
        call    _ZN8fraction3getEv@PLT
        lea     rax, -16[rbp]
        mov     esi, 1
        mov     rdi, rax
        call    _ZN8fraction3addEi@PLT
        lea     rax, -16[rbp]
        mov     rdi, rax
        call    _ZN8fraction7displayEv@PLT
        mov     eax, 0                  ## return 0;
❸ mov     rdx, QWORD PTR -8[rbp]
```

```
        xor     rdx, QWORD PTR fs:40
        je      .L3
        call    __stack_chk_fail@PLT
.L3:

        leave
        ret
        .size   main, .-main
        .ident  "GCC: (Ubuntu 9.3.0-17ubuntu1~20.04) 9.3.0"
        .section        .note.GNU-stack,"",@progbits
```

*Listing 18-8: Assembly language showing how the g++ compiler generates a constructor for our fraction object*

C++ creates the object in the stack frame, as it did when we wrote our own constructor ❶. But the compiler does not write a separate constructor function. Instead, it initializes the data members directly in the function where the object is instantiated ❷.

Since the only resource used by a fraction object is memory on the stack, the normal stack cleanup in the function epilogue deletes the object. Thus, the compiler doesn't need to do anything special to destruct our fraction object ❸.

Comparing the code in Listing 18-8 with that in Listing 18-4, we can see that the compiler has saved eight instructions, including two function calls. So it really did create a more efficient constructor for us. But the assembly language also shows us that it's more correct to say that the compiler generated an *inline constructor* rather than a constructor function. Of course, the C++ language specifications allow for other compilers to do this differently.

Finally, I'll point out that if we need another constructor that takes arguments, then we'll have to also supply our own default constructor. The compiler won't take care of the default construction for us.

The rest of the code in Listing 18-8 should be familiar to you, so we'll move on to looking at how we might implement objects directly in assembly language.

---

**YOUR TURN**

Remove the initialization of the num and den member functions from Listing 18-7. What effect does this have on the program? Hint: Look at the compiler-generated assembly language for the main function.

---

## Objects in Assembly Language

We probably would not be using assembly language for object-oriented programming, but the discussion in this section will help to ensure that we have a clear picture of how C++ implements objects.

We start with the offsets of the data members in a fraction object, as shown in Listing 18-9.

```
# fraction
# Declaration of fraction attributes.
# This object takes 8 bytes.
        .equ    num,0
        .equ    den,4
```

Listing 18-9: Offsets of the attribute values in the fraction class

The attributes of an object are implemented as a record, so the offsets to the object's data members are declared the same way as field offsets in a record. There are no assembler directives to make them private. The distinction between private and public is made by the high-level language, C++ in our case. It will be up to us to write our assembly language such that only class member functions access the data members.

Listing 18-10 shows the assembly language version of our main function.

```
# incFraction.s
# Gets numerator and denominator of a fraction
# from user and adds 1 to the fraction.
        .intel_syntax noprefix
# Stack frame
        .equ    x,-16
        .equ    canary,-8
        .equ    localSize,-16
# Constant data
        .section .rodata
        .align 8
# Code
        .text
        .globl  main
        .type   main, @function
main:
        push    rbp                     # save frame pointer
        mov     rbp, rsp                # set new frame pointer
        add     rsp, localSize          # for local var.
        mov     rax, qword ptr fs:40    # get canary
        mov     canary[rbp], rax

        lea     rdi, x[rbp]             # address of object
❶ call       fraction_construct      # construct it

        lea     rdi, x[rbp]             # address of object
        call    fraction_display        # display fraction

        lea     rdi, x[rbp]             # address of object
        call    fraction_get            # get fraction values

        mov     esi, 1                  # amount to add
        lea     rdi, x[rbp]             # address of object
        call    fraction_add            # add it
```

```
            lea     rdi, x[rbp]             # address of object
            call    fraction_display        # display fraction

            lea     rdi, x[rbp]             # address of object
            call    fraction_destruct       # delete fraction

            mov     eax, 0                  # return 0;
      ❷ mov     rcx, canary[rbp]
            xor     rcx, qword ptr fs:40
            je      goodCanary
            call    __stack_chk_fail@plt
goodCanary:
            mov     rsp, rbp                # restore stack pointer
            pop     rbp                     # and caller frame pointer
            ret
```

Listing 18-10: Assembly language program to add 1 to a fraction

When writing in C++, the constructor and destructor are called implicitly, but in assembly language we have to do it explicitly ❶. We won't mangle the names as much as the compiler. We'll simply prepend each member function name with fraction_.

Aside from the function name mangling, there's nothing unusual about this main function. Notice that we check the stack canary after calling the destructor since that call uses the stack ❷.

Next, we'll write the assembly language for the member functions, starting with the constructor in Listing 18-11.

```
# fraction_construct.s
# Initializes fraction to 0/1.
# Calling sequence:
#   rdi <- address of object
            .intel_syntax noprefix
            .include    "fraction"
# Code
            .text
            .globl  fraction_construct
            .type   fraction_construct, @function
fraction_construct:
            push    rbp                     # save frame pointer
            mov     rbp, rsp                # set new frame pointer
      ❶ mov     dword ptr num[rdi], 0   # initialize
            mov     dword ptr den[rdi], 1   #    fraction
            mov     rsp, rbp                # restore stack pointer
            pop     rbp                     # and caller frame pointer
            ret
```

Listing 18-11: Assembly language implementation of a constructor for our fraction class

Since we don't call any other functions from this function, we can use the rdi register as the this pointer for accessing the data members in the object ❶.

The destructor doesn't do anything in our fraction class, but we'll write one anyway for the sake of completeness, as shown in Listing 18-12.

```
# fraction_destruct.s
# Nothing to do here.
# Calling sequence:
#    rdi <- address of object
        .intel_syntax noprefix
        .include    "fraction"
# Code
        .text
        .globl  fraction_destruct
        .type   fraction_destruct, @function
fraction_destruct:
        push    rbp         # save frame pointer
        mov     rbp, rsp    # set new frame pointer
# Has nothing to do
        mov     rsp, rbp    # restore stack pointer
        pop     rbp         # and caller frame pointer
        ret
```

*Listing 18-12: A destructor for our fraction class*

Next, we'll write the fraction_display function, as shown in Listing 18-13.

```
# fraction_display.s
# Displays fraction.
# Calling sequence:
#    rdi <- address of object
        .intel_syntax noprefix
        .include    "fraction"
# Text for fraction_display
        .data
over:
        .string "/"
endl:
        .string "\n"
# Stack frame
   ❶ .equ     this,-16
        .equ    localSize,-16
# Code
        .text
        .globl  fraction_display
        .type   fraction_display, @function
fraction_display:
        push    rbp             # save frame pointer
        mov     rbp, rsp        # set new frame pointer
        add     rsp, localSize  # for local var.
        mov     this[rbp], rdi  # this pointer

        mov     rax, this[rbp]  # load this pointer
        mov     edi, num[rax]
        call    putInt

        lea     rdi, over[rip]  # slash
        call    writeStr
```

```
        mov     rax, this[rbp]      # load this pointer
        mov     edi, den[rax]
        call    putInt

        lea     rdi, endl[rip]      # newline
        call    writeStr

        mov     rsp, rbp            # restore stack pointer
        pop     rbp                 # and caller frame pointer
        ret
```

*Listing 18-13: The fraction_display function for our fraction class*

The fraction_display function calls other functions, any of which may
change the content of rdi, so we need to save the this pointer in our stack
frame ❶.

Listing 18-13 illustrates one of the reasons we're following the usual
custom of having a separate file for each function in assembly language. An
identifier defined by an .equ directive has file scope. Depending on what
other things need to go in the stack frame, the this pointer might need to
be in a different relative location in different functions. If we were to place
all the member functions in a single file, we would need to do some name
mangling to associate each this offset with its respective member function.
The C++ compiler figures out the numerical offset for the this pointer for
each member function separately, so the this name isn't used in the assembly language it generates.

Listings 18-14 and 18-15 show the fraction_get and fraction_add functions.

```
# fraction_get.s
# Gets numerator and denominator from keyboard.
# Calling sequence:
#   rdi <- address of object
        .intel_syntax noprefix
        .include    "fraction"
# Messages
        .data
numMsg:
        .string "Enter numerator: "
denMsg:
        .string "Enter denominator: "
# Stack frame
        .equ    this,-16
        .equ    localSize,-16
# Code
        .text
        .globl  fraction_get
        .type   fraction_get, @function
fraction_get:
        push    rbp                 # save frame pointer
        mov     rbp, rsp            # set new frame pointer
        add     rsp, localSize      # for local var.
        mov     this[rbp], rdi      # this pointer
```

```
        lea     rdi, numMsg[rip]    # prompt message
        call    writeStr
        mov     rax, this[rbp]      # load this pointer
        lea     rdi, num[rax]
        call    getInt

        lea     rdi, denMsg[rip]
        call    writeStr
        mov     rax, this[rbp]      # load this pointer
        lea     rdi, den[rax]
        call    getInt
        mov     rsp, rbp            # restore stack pointer
        pop     rbp                 # and caller frame pointer
        ret
```

*Listing 18-14: The fraction_get function for our fraction class*

```
# fraction_add.s
# Adds integer to fraction
# Calling sequence:
#   rdi <- pointer to object
#   esi <- int to add
        .intel_syntax noprefix
        .include    "fraction"
# Code
        .text
        .globl  fraction_add
        .type   fraction_add, @function
fraction_add:
        push    rbp                 # save frame pointer
        mov     rbp, rsp            # set new frame pointer
        mov     eax, den[rdi]       # load denominator
        imul    eax, esi            # denominator X int to add
        add     num[rdi], eax       # add to numerator
        mov     rsp, rbp            # restore stack pointer
        pop     rbp                 # and caller frame pointer
        ret
```

*Listing 18-15: The fraction_add function for our fraction class*

There is nothing remarkable about fraction_get or fraction_add. The fraction_get function calls other functions, so we need to place the this pointer in the stack frame. The rdi register is safe to use as the this pointer in fraction_add because it doesn't call any other functions.

---

**YOUR TURN**

Modify the assembly language program in Listings 18-9 through 18-15 so that it displays the fraction in "integer & fraction" format, where "fraction" is less than 1. For example, 3/2 would be displayed as 1 & 1/2.

---

# What You've Learned

**Class** The declaration of the data members that define the state of an object along with any member functions used to access these data members.

**Object in C++** A named area of memory that contains the data members declared in a class.

**Methods or member functions** The member functions declared in a class can be called to access the state of an object of the same class.

**Name mangling** The compiler creates member function names that include the function name, the class it belongs to, and the number and types of any arguments to the function.

**Constructor** A member function used to initialize an object.

**Destructor** A member function used to clean up resources that are no longer needed.

This has been a brief introduction to the way that C++ implements the basic object-oriented programming features.

So far in this book we have been using only integral values in our programs. In the next chapter, we'll look at how fractional values are represented in memory and some of the CPU instructions to manipulate them.

# 19

## FRACTIONAL NUMBERS

We have been using only integral values—integers and characters—in our programs. In this chapter, we'll look at how computers represent fractional numbers. We'll look at two ways to represent fraction values, *fixed-point* and *floating-point*.

We'll start by looking at fixed-point numbers, which will show how fractional values are represented in binary. As you will see, the number of bits we use for the integral part of the number limits the range of numbers we can represent. Using some bits for the fractional part simply allows us to divide that range into smaller portions.

This limitation on the range will lead us to a discussion of floating-point numbers, which allow for a much larger range but introduce other limitations. We'll discuss the format and properties of floating-point representation and then discuss the most common floating-point binary standard, IEEE 754. We'll end the chapter with a brief look at how floating-point numbers are processed in the x86-64 architecture.

# Fractional Values in Binary

Let's start by looking at the mathematics of fractional values. Recall from Chapter 2 that a decimal integer, $N$, is expressed in binary as follows:

$$N = d_{n-1} \times 2^{n-1} + d_{n-2} \times 2^{n-2} + \ldots + d_1 \times 2^1 + d_0 \times 2^0$$

where each $d_i = 0$ or $1$.

We can extend this to include a fractional part, $F$:

$$\begin{aligned} N.F &= d_{n-1} \times 2^{n-1} + d_{n-2} \times 2^{n-2} + \ldots + d_0 \times 2^0 + d_{-1} \times 2^{-1} + d_{-2} \times 2^{-2} + \ldots \\ &= d_{n-1}d_{n-2}\ldots d_0.d_{-1}d_{-2}\ldots \end{aligned}$$

where each $d_i = 0$ or $1$. Be careful to note the *binary point* between $d_0$ and $d_{-1}$ on the right side of this equation. All the terms to the right of the binary point are inverse powers of 2, so this portion of the number sums to a fractional value. Like the decimal point on the left side, the binary point separates the fractional part from the integral part of the number. Here's an example:

$$\begin{aligned} 1.6875_{10} &= 1.0_{10} + 0.5_{10} + 0.125_{10} + 0.0635_{10} \\ &= 1 \times 2^0 + 1 \times 2^{-1} + 0 \times 2^{-2} + 1 \times 2^{-3} + 1 \times 2^{-4} \\ &= 1.1011_2 \end{aligned}$$

Although any integer can be represented as a sum of powers of two, an exact representation of fractional values in binary is limited to sums of *inverse* powers of two. For example, consider an 8-bit representation of the fractional value 0.9. From

$$0.11100110_2 = 0.89843750_{10}$$
$$0.11100111_2 = 0.90234375_{10}$$

we can see the following:

$$0.11100110_2 < 0.9_{10} < 0.11100111_2$$

In fact,

$$0.9_{10} = 0.111001\overline{100}_2$$

where $\overline{1100}$ means this bit pattern repeats indefinitely.

Rounding fractional values in binary is simple. If the next bit to the right is 1, add 1 to the bit position where rounding. Let's round 0.9 to eight bits. From earlier, we see that the ninth bit to the right of the binary point is 0, so we do not add 1 in the eighth bit position. Thus, we use

$$0.9_{10} \approx 0.11100110_2$$

which gives a rounding error as follows:

$$\begin{aligned} 0.9_{10} - 0.11100110_2 &= 0.9_{10} - 0.8984375_{10} \\ &= 0.0015625_{10} \end{aligned}$$

# Fixed-Point Numbers

A *fixed-point number* is essentially a scaled integer representation, where the scaling is shown by the location of the *radix point*. The radix point separates the fractional part of a number from the integral part. We call it the *decimal point* in decimal numbers and the *binary point* in binary numbers. English-speaking countries commonly use a period; other regions typically use a comma.

For example, $1234.5_{10}$ represents $12345_{10}$ scaled by $1/10$; $10011010010.1_2$ is $100110100101_2$ scaled by a factor of $1/2$. When performing computations with fixed-point numbers, we need to be mindful of the location of the radix point.

Next, we'll look at scaling numbers with a fractional part that is an inverse power of two, in which case the fractional part can be represented exactly. Then we'll look at scaling fractional numbers in decimal to avoid the rounding errors described earlier.

## When the Fractional Part Is a Sum of Inverse Powers of Two

We'll start with a program that adds two measurements that are specified in inches. The fractional parts of inches are typically specified in inverse powers of 2: $1/2$, $1/4$, $1/8$, and so forth, which can be represented exactly in the binary system.

Our program will add two measurements that are specified to the nearest $1/16$ of an inch. We'll need four bits to store the fractional part, leaving 28 bits for the integral part.

When adding two numbers, we need to align their radix points. Listing 19-1 shows how we'll do this alignment when reading numbers from the keyboard.

```
# getLength.s
# Gets length in inches and 1/16s.
# Outputs 32-bit value, high 28 bits hold inches,
# low 4 bits hold fractional value in 1/16s.
# Calling sequence:
#    rdi <- pointer to length
        .intel_syntax noprefix
# Useful constant
        .equ    fractionMask, 0xf
# Stack frame
        .equ    lengthPtr,-16
    ❶ .equ    inches,-8
        .equ    fraction,-4
        .equ    localSize,-16
# Constant data
        .section .rodata
        .align  8
prompt:
        .string "Enter inches and 1/16s\n"
inchesPrompt:
        .string "        Inches: "
fractionPrompt:
        .string "     Sixteenths: "
```

```
# Code
        .text
        .globl  getLength
        .type   getLength, @function
getLength:
        push    rbp                             # save frame pointer
        mov     rbp, rsp                        # set new frame pointer
        add     rsp, localSize                  # for local var.

        mov     lengthPtr[rbp], rdi             # save pointer to output

        lea     rdi, prompt[rip]                # prompt user
        call    writeStr

        lea     rdi, inchesPrompt[rip]          # ask for inches
        call    writeStr
        lea     rdi, inches[rbp]                # get inches
        call  ❷ getUInt
        lea     rdi, fractionPrompt[rip]        # ask for 1/16's
        call    writeStr
        lea     rdi, fraction[rbp]              # get fraction
        call    getUInt

        mov     eax, dword ptr inches[rbp]      # retrieve inches
      ❸ sal     eax, 4                          # make room for fraction
        mov     ecx, dword ptr fraction[rbp]    # retrieve frac
      ❹ and     ecx, fractionMask               # make sure < 16
        add     eax, ecx                        # add in fraction
        mov     rcx, lengthPtr[rbp]             # load pointer to output
        mov     [rcx], eax                      # output

        mov     rsp, rbp                        # restore stack pointer
        pop     rbp                             # and caller frame pointer
        ret
```

*Listing 19-1: Function to read a number in inches and sixteenths of an inch from keyboard*

We allocate 32 bits for both the number of inches, and the number of sixteenths of an inch, each to be read as integers from the keyboard ❶. Notice that we're using the getUInt function to read each unsigned int ❷. This is a simple modification of the getInt function, which reads a signed int; we wrote getInt in Chapter 15.

We're using the four low-order bits to store the fractional part, so we shift the integral part four bits to the left to make room for adding in the fractional part ❸. Before adding the fractional part, we'll make sure that the user didn't enter a number that exceeds four bits ❹.

The scaling leaves 28 bits for the integral part. This limits the range of our numbers to be 0 to 268435455 15/16. This is sixteen times less than the 0 to 4294967295 range of a 32-bit integer, but the resolution is to the nearest 1/16.

Our function to display these measurements, as shown in Listing 19-2, shows both the integral and fractional parts.

```
# displayLength.s
# Displays length in inches and 1/16s.
# Calling sequence:
#    edi <- value with 1/16s in low-order 4 bits
        .intel_syntax noprefix
# Useful constant
        .equ   ❶ fractionMask, 0xf
# Stack frame
        .equ   length,-16
        .equ   localSize,-16
# Constant data
        .section .rodata
        .align  8
link:
        .string " "
over:
        .string "/16"
msg:
        .string "Total = "
endl:
        .string "\n"
# Code
        .text
        .globl  displayLength
        .type   displayLength, @function
displayLength:
        push    rbp                 # save frame pointer
        mov     rbp, rsp            # set new frame pointer
        add     rsp, localSize      # for local var.

        mov     length[rbp], rdi    # save input length
        lea     rdi, msg[rip]       # nice message
        call    writeStr

        mov     edi, length[rbp]    # original value
 ❷ shr     edi, 4              # integer part
        call    putUInt             # write to screen
        lea     rdi, link[rip]
        call    writeStr

        mov     edi, length[rbp]    # original value
 ❸ and     edi, fractionMask   # fraction part
        call    putUInt             # write to screen
 ❹ lea     rdi, over[rip]
        call    writeStr

        lea     rdi, endl[rip]
        call    writeStr

        mov     rsp, rbp            # restore stack pointer
        pop     rbp                 # and caller frame pointer
        ret
```

Listing 19-2: Function to display measurements in inches and sixteenths of an inch

We shift the number four bits to the right so that we can display the integral part as an integer ❷. Using a four-bit mask ❶, we mask off the integral part and display the fractional part as another integer ❸. And we add some text to show that this second integer is the fractional part ❹.

Listing 19-3 shows the `main` function.

```
# rulerAdd.s
# Adds two ruler measurements, to nearest 1/16 inch.
        .intel_syntax noprefix
# Stack frame
        .equ    x,-16
        .equ    y, -12
        .equ    canary,-8
        .equ    localSize,-16
# Constant data
        .section .rodata
        .align  8
endl:
        .string "\n"
# Code
        .text
        .globl  main
        .type   main, @function
main:
        push    rbp                     # save frame pointer
        mov     rbp, rsp                # set new frame pointer
        add     rsp, localSize          # for local var.
        mov     rax, qword ptr fs:40    # get canary
        mov     qword ptr canary[rbp], rax

        lea     rdi, x[rbp]             # x length
        call    getLength

        lea     rdi, y[rbp]             # y length
        call    getLength

        mov     edi, x[rbp]             # retrieve x length
❶ add     edi, y[rbp]             # add y length
        call    displayLength

        mov     eax, 0                  # return 0;
        mov     rcx, qword ptr canary[rbp]
        xor     rcx, qword ptr fs:40
        je      goodCanary
        call    __stack_chk_fail@plt
goodCanary:
        mov     rsp, rbp                # restore stack pointer
        pop     rbp                     # and caller frame pointer
        ret
```

*Listing 19-3: Program to add two measurements in inches and sixteenths of an inch*

If you look at the equation for representing fractional values in binary in the previous section, you can probably convince yourself that the integer add instruction will work for the entire number, including the fractional part ❶.

This example works nicely with binary numbers, but we mostly use decimal numbers in computations. As we saw earlier in this chapter, most fractional decimal numbers can't be converted to a finite number of bits and need to be rounded. In the next section, we'll discuss how to avoid rounding errors when using fractional decimal numbers.

## When the Fractional Part Is in Decimal

Let's think about how we've handled the fractional part in our fixed-point format here. When we read the integral part from the keyboard, we shifted it four bit positions to the left, leaving room to add the number of sixteenths to this int. We've effectively created a 32-bit number with the binary point between the fifth and fourth bits (bits numbered 4 and 3). This works because the fractional part is a sum of inverse powers of two.

Another way to think about how we handled fractions previously is that the four-bit shift multiplied the number by 16. We'll take this approach when working in decimal: multiply the numbers by multiples of 10 such that the smallest value becomes an integer.

We'll explore this approach with a program that adds two US dollar values to the nearest $1/100^{th}$ of a dollar. As with the ruler measurement program in Listings 19-1, 19-2, and 19-3, we'll start with the function to read money values from the keyboard, getMoney, as shown in Listing 19-4.

```
# getMoney.s
# Gets money in dollars and cents.
# Outputs 32-bit value, money in cents.
# Calling sequence:
#    rdi <- pointer to length
        .intel_syntax noprefix
# Useful constant
        .equ  ❶ dollar2cents, 100
# Stack frame
        .equ    moneyPtr,-16
        .equ    dollars,-8
        .equ    cents,-4
        .equ    localSize,-16
# Constant data
        .section .rodata
        .align  8
prompt:
        .string "Enter amount\n"
dollarsPrompt:
        .string "    Dollars: "
centsPrompt:
        .string "     Cents: "
# Code
        .text
        .globl  getMoney
        .type   getMoney, @function
getMoney:
        push    rbp                     # save frame pointer
        mov     rbp, rsp                # set new frame pointer
```

```
        add     rsp, localSize          # for local var.

        mov     moneyPtr[rbp], rdi      # save pointer to output

        lea     rdi, prompt[rip]        # prompt user
        call    writeStr

        lea     rdi, dollarsPrompt[rip] # ask for dollars
        call    writeStr
        lea     rdi, dollars[rbp]       # get dollars
  ❷ call    getUInt
        lea     rdi, centsPrompt[rip]   # ask for cents
        call    writeStr
        lea     rdi, cents[rbp]         # get cents
  ❸ call    getUInt

        mov     eax, dword ptr dollars[rbp] # retrieve dollars
        mov     ecx, dollar2cents           # scale dollars to cents
  ❹ mul     ecx
        mov     ecx, dword ptr cents[rbp]   # retrieve cents
        add     eax, ecx                    # add in cents
        mov     rcx, moneyPtr[rbp]          # load pointer to output
        mov     [rcx], eax                  # output

        mov     rsp, rbp                    # restore stack pointer
        pop     rbp                         # and caller frame pointer
        ret
```

*Listing 19-4: Function to read dollars and cents from the keyboard and convert to cents*

As with the ruler measurement program, we'll read the integral part ❷ and fractional part ❸ as integers. As explained, since the scaling is a multiple of 10, we need to multiply the integral part ❹ by the scaling factor ❶ instead of just shifting it.

The function to display the scaled numbers needs to invert the process to separate the integral and fractional parts. We'll do that in the displayMoney function, as shown in Listing 19-5.

```
# displayMoney.s
# Displays money in dollars and cents.
# Calling sequence:
#   edi <- money in cents
        .intel_syntax noprefix
# Useful constant
        .equ  ❶ cent2dollars, 100
# Stack frame
        .equ    money,-16
        .equ    localSize,-16
# Constant data
        .section .rodata
        .align 8
decimal:
        .string "."
msg:
```

```
          .string "Total = $"
zero:
          .string "0"
endl:
          .string "\n"
# Code
          .text
          .globl  displayMoney
          .type   displayMoney, @function
displayMoney:
          push    rbp                      # save frame pointer
          mov     rbp, rsp                 # set new frame pointer
          add     rsp, localSize           # for local var.

          mov     money[rbp], rdi          # save input money
          lea     rdi, msg[rip]            # nice message
          call    writeStr

          mov     edx, 0                   # clear high order
          mov     eax, money[rbp]          # convert money amount
          mov     ecx, cent2dollars        #      to dollars and cents
    ❷ div     ecx
    ❸ mov     money[rbp], edx          # save cents
          mov     edi, eax                 # dollars
          call    putUInt                  # write to screen
    ❹ lea     rdi, decimal[rip]
          call    writeStr

          cmp     dword ptr money[rbp], 10 # 2 decimal places?
          jae     twoDecimal               # yes
          lea     rdi, zero[rip]           # no, 0 in tenths place
          call    writeStr
twoDecimal:
          mov     edi, money[rbp]          # load cents
          call    putUInt                  # write to screen

          lea     rdi, endl[rip]
          call    writeStr

          mov     rsp, rbp                 # restore stack pointer
          pop     rbp                      # and caller frame pointer
          ret
```

*Listing 19-5: Function that displays cents as dollars and cents*

We used a scaling factor to move the decimal point two places to the right when reading the money values. Now we need to move the decimal point two places to the left to recover the fractional part. So we need to use the same scaling factor, 100 ❶.

Then the div instruction will leave the integral part in eax and the remainder (the fractional part) in edi ❷. We'll temporarily save the fractional part while we print the integral part ❸. As with the ruler measurement program, we print text to indicate the fractional part ❹.

Listing 19-6 shows the main function that adds two money amounts.

```
# moneyAdd.s
# Adds two money amounts in dollars and cents.
        .intel_syntax noprefix
# Stack frame
        .equ    x,-16
        .equ    y, -12
        .equ    canary,-8
        .equ    localSize,-16
# Constant data
        .section .rodata
        .align 8
endl:
        .string "\n"
# Code
        .text
        .globl  main
        .type   main, @function
main:
        push    rbp                       # save frame pointer
        mov     rbp, rsp                  # set new frame pointer
        add     rsp, localSize            # for local var.
        mov     rax, qword ptr fs:40      # get canary
        mov     qword ptr canary[rbp], rax

        lea     rdi, x[rbp]               # x amount
        call    getMoney

        lea     rdi, y[rbp]               # y amount
        call    getMoney

        mov     edi, x[rbp]               # retrieve x amount
❶ add     edi, y[rbp]               # add y amount
        call    displayMoney

        mov     eax, 0                    # return 0;
        mov     rcx, qword ptr canary[rbp]
        xor     rcx, qword ptr fs:40
        je      goodCanary
        call    __stack_chk_fail@plt
goodCanary:
        mov     rsp, rbp                  # restore stack pointer
        pop     rbp                       # and caller frame pointer
        ret
```

*Listing 19-6: Program to add money amounts using fixed-point numbers*

The money amounts we're using in the main function have been scaled to be integers, so we can use a simple add instruction to add them ❶.

Although fixed-point arithmetic allows us to preserve the full resolution of the numbers, the range of values is limited by the number of bits in the integral data type, 32 in this program. We've limited the range of the numbers in our program to be 0 to 42949672.95 but increased resolution to the nearest 0.01.

We have a more convenient notation for representing very large and very small numbers, which we'll explore next.

---

**YOUR TURN**

1. Enter the program in Listings 19-1, 19-2, and 19-3. Using the gdb debugger, examine the numbers stored in the x and y variables in main. Identify the integral and fractional parts.

2. Enter the program in Listings 19-4, 19-5, and 19-6. Using the gdb debugger, examine the numbers stored in the x and y variables in main. Identify the integral and fractional parts.

3. Enter the program in Listings 19-4, 19-5, and 19-6. Run the program, entering **$42949672.95** for one amount and **$0.01** for the other. What total does the program give?

4. Modify the program in Listings 19-4, 19-5, and 19-6 so it will work with both positive and negative values. You might need the getSInt and putSInt functions from Chapter 15. For a negative value, you'll need to enter both the dollars and cents amounts as negative numbers. What is the range of totals for this modification?

---

# Floating-Point Numbers

Let's begin with the most important concept in this section: *floating-point numbers* are not *real numbers*. Real numbers include the continuum of all numbers from $-\infty$ to $+\infty$. You already know that computers are finite, so there is certainly a limit on the largest values that can be represented, but the problem is worse than simply a limit on the magnitude.

As you will see in this section, floating-point numbers comprise a small subset of real numbers. There are significant gaps between adjacent floating-point numbers. These gaps can produce several types of errors. To make matters worse, these errors can occur in intermediate results, where they are difficult to debug.

## Floating-Point Representation

*Floating-point representation* is based on *scientific notation*. In floating-point representation, we have a sign and two numbers to completely specify a value: a *significand* and an *exponent*. A decimal floating-point number is written as a significand times 10 raised to an exponent. For example, consider these two numbers:

$$0.0010123 = 1.0123 \times 10^{-3}$$
$$-456.78 = -4.5678 \times 10^{2}$$

Notice that in floating-point representation, the number is *normalized* such that only one digit appears to the left of the decimal point. The exponent of 10 is adjusted accordingly. If we agree that each number is normalized and that we are working in base 10, then each floating-point number is completely specified by three items: significand, exponent, and sign. In the previous two examples:

$$10123, -3, \text{ and } + \text{ represent } +1.0123 \times 10^{-3}$$
$$45678, +2, \text{ and } - \text{ represent } -4.5678 \times 10^{+2}$$

The advantage of using floating-point representation is that, for a given number of digits, we can represent a larger range of values.

Let's look at how floating-point numbers are stored in a computer.

## IEEE 754 Floating-Point Standard

The most commonly used standard for storing floating-point numbers is IEEE 754 (*https://standards.ieee.org/standard/754-2019.html*). Figure 19-1 shows the general pattern.

Figure 19-1: General pattern for storing
floating-point numbers

Here, S is the sign of the number.

Like all storage formats, floating-point formats involve trade-offs between resolution, rounding errors, size, and range. The IEEE 754 standard specifies sizes from 4 to 16 bytes. The most common sizes used in C/C++ are float (four bytes) and double (eight bytes). The x86-64 architecture supports both sizes plus a 10-byte extended version that is similar to, but not part of, the IEEE 754 standard.

Figure 19-2 shows the number of bits specified for each of these three sizes.

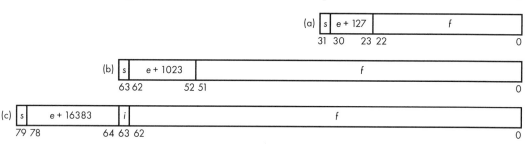

Figure 19-2: Number of bits for (a) C float, (b) C double, and (c) x86-64 extended version

The values in Figure 19-2 represent a floating-point number, *N*, stored in the normalized form.

$$N = (-1)^s \times 1.f \times 2^e$$

The first bit, *s*, is the sign bit, 0 for positive and 1 for negative.

As in decimal, the exponent is adjusted such that there is only one non-zero digit to the left of the binary point. In binary, though, this digit is always 1, giving 1.*f* as the significand. Since it's always 1, the integer part (1) is not stored in the IEEE 754 four- and eight-byte versions. It's called the *hidden bit*. Only the fraction part of the significand, *f*, is stored. The integer part, *i*, is included in the x86-64 extended 10-byte version.

The formats need to allow for negative exponents. Your first thought might be to use two's complement. However, the IEEE standard was developed in the 1970s, when floating-point computations took a lot of CPU time. Many algorithms in programs depend upon only the comparison of two numbers, and the computer scientists of the day realized that a format that allowed integer comparison instructions would result in faster execution times. So they decided to add an amount, a *bias*, to the exponent before storing it such that the most negative allowable exponent would be stored as 0. The result, a *biased exponent*, can then be stored as an unsigned int. As you can see in Figure 19-2, the bias is 127 for the 4-byte standard, 1023 for the 8-byte, and 16383 for the 10-byte.

The hidden bit scheme presents a problem—there is no way to represent 0. To address this and other issues, the IEEE 754 standard has several special cases:

**Zero value**    All the biased exponent bits and fraction bits are 0, allowing for both −0 and +0. This preserves the sign of a computation that converges to 0.

**Denormalized**    If the value to be represented is smaller than can be represented with all the biased exponent bits being 0, meaning that *e* has the most negative value possible, the hidden bit is no longer assumed. In this case, the amount of bias is reduced by 1.

**Infinity**    Infinity is represented by setting all the biased exponent bits to 1 and all the fraction bits to 0. Notice that this allows the sign bit to designate both +∞ and −∞, allowing us to still compare numbers that are out of range.

**Not a number (NaN)**    If the biased exponent bits are all 1 but the fraction bits are not all 0, this represents a value that is in error. This might be used to indicate that a floating-point variable doesn't yet have a value. A NaN should be treated as a program error.

An example of an operation that gives infinity is dividing a nonzero value by 0. An example that produces NaN is an operation that has an undefined result, like dividing 0 by 0.

Next, we'll discuss the x86-64 hardware used to work with floating-point numbers.

## SSE2 Floating-Point Hardware

Until the introduction of the Intel 486DX in April 1989, the *x87 floating-point unit* was on a separate chip, a *coprocessor*. It is now included on the

CPU chip, although it uses a somewhat different execution architecture than the *integer unit* in the CPU. It uses the 10-byte floating standard in Figure 19-2(c).

In 1997, Intel added *Multimedia Extensions* (*MMX*) to its processors, which include instructions that operate on multiple data items simultaneously— *single instruction, multiple data* (*SIMD*). Operations on single data items are called *scalar operations*. Operations on multiple data items in parallel are called *vector operations*, which are useful for many multimedia and scientific applications. We'll discuss only scalar operations in this book.

Originally, MMX performed only integer computations, but in 1998 AMD added the *3DNow!* extension to MMX, which includes floating-point instructions. Intel soon followed suit with the *Streaming SIMD Extension* (*SSE*) on the Pentium III in 1999, and AMD soon added SSE to give us *3DNow! Professional*. Several versions have evolved over the years—SSE, SSE2, SSE3, and SSE4. In 2011 Intel and AMD added *Advanced Vector Extensions* (*AVX*) for SIMD and floating-point operations.

The x86-64 architecture includes at least SSE2. Higher versions are available only on higher-level CPU chips. We'll discuss SSE2 in this book since it is the most common, and chips with more advanced versions still support SSE2. The only CPU chips that don't include at least SSE are some inexpensive 32-bit microcontrollers (for example, the Intel Quark), so we won't discuss the x87 architecture in this book.

Most of the SSE2 instructions operate on multiple data items simultaneously. There are SSE2 instructions for both integer and floating-point operations. Integer instructions operate on up to sixteen 8-bit, eight 16-bit, four 32-bit, two 64-bit, or one 128-bit integers at a time.

Vector floating-point instructions operate on all four 32-bit or both 64-bit floats in a register simultaneously. Each data item is treated independently. These instructions are useful for algorithms that do things like process arrays. One SSE2 instruction can operate on several array elements in parallel, resulting in considerable speed gains. Such algorithms are common in multimedia and scientific applications.

In this book we will consider only a few of the scalar floating-point instructions, which operate on only single data items. These instructions operate on either 32-bit (single-precision) or 64-bit (double-precision) values. The scalar instructions operate on only the low-order portion of the 128-bit xmm registers, with the high-order 64 or 96 bits remaining unchanged.

## xmm Registers

The SSE architecture added eight 128-bit registers to the CPU, which are separate from the general-purpose integer registers we've been using thus far in the book. SSE2 added a 64-bit mode, which adds eight more 128-bit registers with the register names xmm0, xmm1, …, xmm15. AVX extensions add wider registers, the 256-bit ymm0, ymm1, …, ymm15 and 512-bit zmm0, zmm1, …, zmm15 registers. In the AVX architecture, the register names xmm0, xmm1, …, xmm15 refer to the low-order 128 bits of the 256-bit ymm0, ymm1, …, ymm15 and 512-bit zmm0, zmm1, …, zmm15 registers.

Figure 19-3 shows a single xmm register and how its contents are arranged when copied into or from memory.

|  | | |
|---|---|---|
| Relative memory address | 00 | float0 |
| | 04 | float1 |
| | 08 | float2 |
| | 0c | float3 |

xmm register

| float3 | float2 | float1 | float0 |
|---|---|---|---|
| 127          96 | 95          64 | 63          32 | 31          0 |

*Figure 19-3: A single xmm register and its mapping into memory*

SSE also includes its own 32-bit status and control register, mxcsr. Table 19-1 shows the meanings of the bits in this register, and the default setting of each bit when the CPU is first powered on.

**Table 19-1:** The Bits in the mxcsr Register

| Bits | Mnemonic | Meaning | Default |
|---|---|---|---|
| 31:16 | | Reserved | |
| 15 | FZ | Flush to zero | 0 |
| 14:13 | RC | Rounding control | 00 |
| 12 | PM | Precision mask | 1 |
| 11 | UM | Underflow mask | 1 |
| 10 | OM | Overflow mask | 1 |
| 9 | ZM | Divide-by-zero mask | 1 |
| 8 | DM | Denormals operation mask | 1 |
| 7 | IM | Invalid operation mask | 1 |
| 6 | DAZ | Denormals are zero | 0 |
| 5 | PE | Precision flag | 0 |
| 4 | UE | Underflow flag | 0 |
| 3 | OE | Overflow flag | 0 |
| 2 | ZE | Divide-by-zero flag | 0 |
| 1 | DE | Denormal flag | 0 |
| 0 | IE | Invalid operation flag | 0 |

Bits 0–5 are set by SSE operations that result in the respective condition. They can cause exceptions, which are typically handled by the operating system. (You'll learn more about exceptions in Chapter 21.) Bits 7–12 are used to control whether the respective exception will occur in a process called *masking*. The RC bits are set to control the way a number is rounded, as shown in Table 19-2.

**Table 19-2:** Rounding Mode of Floating-Point Numbers

| RC | Rounding mode |
|----|---------------|
| 00 | Round to nearest value. If tied, choose even value. Default mode. |
| 01 | Round down, toward $-\infty$. |
| 10 | Round up, toward $+\infty$. |
| 11 | Truncate. |

A detailed description of each condition is beyond the scope of this book, but we'll look at one example to give you an idea of how they're used. A precision error is caused when a floating-point operation yields a result that cannot be represented exactly—for example, 1.0 divided by 3.0. The SSE unit rounds the result and sets the PE bit in the mxcsr register. In most cases, the precision error is acceptable, and we don't want the exception to occur. Setting the PM bit to 1 masks out this exception, and the program continues without involving the operating system in this error.

As you can see in Table 19-1, masking out a precision error is the default condition. If such an error is important in the program you're writing, you would need to unmask the PE error. The C standard library includes functions to work with the mxcsr register, which you can read about by using the man fenv command in a Linux terminal window. You'll get a chance to work with a divide-by-zero situation in assembly language when it's Your Turn.

Unlike the status flags set by integer instructions in the rflags register, there are no instructions to test the condition bits in the mxcsr register. Although most SSE instruction don't affect it, four comparison instructions, comisd, comiss, ucomisd, and ucomiss, do set the status flags in the rflags register. We're not using these instructions in this book, but they would allow us to use the conditional jump instructions based on floating-point comparisons.

Let's look at using the SSE hardware to perform floating-point computations.

## Programming with Floating-Point Numbers

The program in Listing 19-7 adds two floats and prints their sum. We'll use assembly language to make it easier for us to see what's going on and to examine numbers in the debugger.

```
# addFloats.s
# Adds two floats.
        .intel_syntax noprefix
# Stack frame
    ❶ .equ    x,-20
        .equ    y,-16
        .equ    z,-12
        .equ    canary,-8
        .equ    localSize,-32
# Constant data
        .section .rodata
```

```
prompt:
        .string "Enter a number: "
scanFormat:
        .string "%f"
printFormat:
        .string "%f + %f = %f\n"
# Code
        .text
        .globl  main
        .type   main, @function
main:
        push    rbp                     # save frame pointer
        mov     rbp, rsp                # set new frame pointer
        add     rsp, localSize          # for local var.
        mov     rax, qword ptr fs:40    # get canary
        mov     qword ptr canary[rbp], rax

        lea     rdi, prompt[rip]        # prompt for input
        mov     eax, 0
        call    printf@plt
        lea     rsi, x[rbp]             # read x
        lea     rdi, scanFormat[rip]
        mov     eax, 0
        call    __isoc99_scanf@plt

        lea     rdi, prompt[rip]        # prompt for input
        mov     eax, 0
        call    printf@plt
        lea     rsi, y[rbp]             # read y
        lea     rdi, scanFormat[rip]
        mov     eax, 0
        call    __isoc99_scanf@plt

    ❷ movss   xmm2, x[rbp]            # load x
        addss   xmm2, y[rbp]            # compute x + y
        movss   z[rbp], xmm2
    ❸ cvtss2sd xmm0, x[rbp]           # convert to double
        cvtss2sd xmm1, y[rbp]           # convert to double
        cvtss2sd xmm2, z[rbp]           # convert to double
        lea     rdi, printFormat[rip]
        mov     eax, 3                  # 3 xmm regs.
        call    printf@plt

        mov     eax, 0                  # return 0;
        mov     rcx, qword ptr canary[rbp]
        xor     rcx, qword ptr fs:40
        je      goodCanary
        call    __stack_chk_fail@plt
goodCanary:
        mov     rsp, rbp                # restore stack pointer
        pop     rbp                     # and caller frame pointer
        ret
```

*Listing 19-7: Program to add two numbers using floating-point variables*

The float data type is 32 bits ❶. All the computations using floating-point numbers are performed in the xmm registers ❷. The floating-point arguments to printf are also passed in xmm registers, but printf requires that they be passed as doubles ❸.

We see some SSE instructions in Listing 19-7, movss ❶, addss ❷, and cvtss2sd ❸:

### movss—Move Scalar Single-Precision Floating-Point

Copies (moves) a scalar single-precision 32-bit floating-point value from one location to another.

movss *xmmreg1, xmmreg2* moves from xmmreg2 register to xmmreg1 register.

movss *xmmreg, mem* moves from a memory location to an xmm register.

movss *mem, xmmreg* moves from xmmreg register to a memory location.

The movss instruction moves 32 bits using the low-order 32 bits of the specified xmm register(s). When the destination is an xmm register, the high-order 96 bits are not affected, except when moving from memory they are zeroed.

### addss—Add Scalar Single-Precision Floating-Point

Adds a scalar single-precision 32-bit floating-point value to another.

addss *xmmreg1, xmmreg2* adds the floating-point value in *xmmreg2* to the floating-point value in *xmmreg1*, leaving the result in *xmmreg1*.

addss *xmmreg, mem* adds the floating-point value in a memory location to the floating-point value in an xmm register.

addss *mem, xmmreg* adds the floating-point value in an xmm register to add the floating-point value in a memory location.

The result of the addition can cause an OE, UE, IE, PE, or DE exception. The addss instruction affects only the low-order 32 bits of the destination xmm register.

### cvtss2sd—Convert Scalar Single-Precision Floating-Point to Scalar Double-Precision

Converts a scalar single-precision 32-bit floating-point value to a double-precision 64-bit floating-point value.

cvtss2sd *xmmreg1, xmmreg2* converts the single-precision floating-point value in *xmmreg2* to the equivalent double-precision floating-point value, leaving the result in *xmmreg1*.

cvtss2sd *xmmreg, mem* converts the single-precision floating-point value in a memory location to the equivalent double-precision floating-point value, leaving the result in *xmmreg*.

The result of the conversion can cause an IE or DE exception. The cvtss2sd instruction affects only the low-order 64 bits of the destination xmm register.

## Floating-Point Arithmetic Errors

Most of the arithmetic errors we'll discuss here also exist with fixed-point arithmetic. Probably the most common arithmetic error is *rounding error*. This can occur for two reasons: either the number of bits available for storage is limited or the fractional values cannot be precisely represented in all number bases.

Both these limitations also apply to fixed-point representation. The difference with floating-point is that the CPU hardware can shift the significand of an arithmetic result, adjusting the exponent accordingly, causing bits to be lost. With integer arithmetic, any shifting of bits is explicit in the program.

It's easy to think of floating-point numbers as real numbers, but they're not. Most floating-point numbers are rounded approximations of the real numbers they represent. When using floating-point arithmetic, we need to be aware of the effects of rounding on our computations. If we don't pay close attention to the rounding effects, we might not notice any errors that could creep into our computations.

When computing with integers, we need to be aware of errors in the most significant places of the results: carry for unsigned integers and overflow for signed. With floating-point numbers, the radix point is adjusted to maintain the integrity of the most significant places. Most errors in floating-point are the result of any rounding in the low-order places that is needed to fit the value within the allocated number of bits. The errors in floating-point arithmetic are more subtle, but they can have important effects on the accuracy of our programs.

Let's run the program in Listing 19-7:

```
$ ./addFloats
Enter a number: 123.4
Enter a number: 567.8
123.400002 + 567.799988 = 691.200012
```

The arithmetic here doesn't look accurate. Before you go back to look for the bugs in Listing 19-7, let's bring in the debugger to see if we can figure out what's happening:

```
--snip--
(gdb) b 53
Breakpoint 1 at 0x11e4: file addFloats.s, line 53.
(gdb) r
Starting program: /home/bob/progs/chapter_19/addFloats_asm/addFloats
Enter a number: 123.4
Enter a number: 567.8

Breakpoint 1, main () at addFloats.s:53
53              call    printf@plt
```

I set a breakpoint at the call to printf and then ran the program, entering the same numbers we used earlier. Next, let's look at the numbers stored in the three variables, x, y, and z:

```
(gdb) i r rbp
rbp             0x7fffffffdee0      0x7fffffffdee0
```

```
(gdb) x/3xw 0x7fffffffdecc
0x7fffffffdecc: 0x42f6cccd        0x440df333        0x442ccccd
```

The x variable is located at 0x7fffffffdecc: 0x42f6cccd. From the IEEE 754 format shown previously, we see that the exponent is stored as $85_{16} = 133_{10}$, giving e = 6. Thus, x is stored as (writing the significand, including the hidden bit, in binary and the exponent part in decimal) 1.11101101100110011001101 $\times 2^6$ = 1111011.01100110011001101 = 123.40000152587890625. The f formatting character in the examine memory command shows us the memory contents in floating-point format:

```
(gdb) x/3fw 0x7fffffffdecc
0x7fffffffdecc: 123.400002        567.799988        691.200012
```

The display here is not as accurate as our hand computations, but it clearly shows that there is rounding error in all three numbers.

At this point in the program, x, y, and z have been loaded into the xmm0, xmm1, and xmm2 registers and converted to doubles. Let's look at those registers. Since the x86-84 uses little-endian order, the low-order values are displayed first in each {...} grouping:

```
(gdb) i r xmm0
xmm0            {v4_float = {0x0, 0x3, 0x0, 0x0}, v2_double = {0x7b, 0x0}, v16_
int8 = {0x0, 0x0, 0x0, 0xa0, 0x99, 0xd9, 0x5e, 0x40, 0x0, 0x0, 0x0, 0x0, 0x0,
0x0, 0x0, 0x0}, v8_int16 = {0x0, 0xa000, 0xd999, 0x405e, 0x0, 0x0, 0x0, 0x0},
v4_int32 = {0xa0000000, 0x405ed999, 0x0, 0x0}, v2_int64 = {0x405ed999a0000000,
0x0}, uint128 = 0x405ed999a0000000}
```

When using the info registers command, gdb shows us all possible uses of the xmm registers, but we can use the print command to tell gdb which usage to display. In our case, we're using the xmm registers to hold two doubles:

```
(gdb) p $xmm0.v2_double
$1 = {123.40000152587891, 0}
(gdb) p $xmm1.v2_double
$2 = {567.79998779296875, 0}
(gdb) p $xmm2.v2_double
$3 = {691.20001220703125, 0}
```

The print command displays more decimal places than the x command. We can also tell print to display the values as 64-bit ints.

```
(gdb) p/x $xmm0.v2_int64
$4 = {0x405ed999a0000000, 0x0}
(gdb) p/x $xmm1.v2_int64
$5 = {0x4081be6660000000, 0x0}
(gdb) p/x $xmm2.v2_int64
$6 = {0x40859999a0000000, 0x0}
```

Notice that the conversion from float to double simply adds 0s in the additional 28 bits in the low-order part of the significand. The conversion does not increase the number of significant bits.

Finally, we execute the rest of the program:

```
(gdb) cont
Continuing.
123.400002 + 567.799988 = 691.200012
[Inferior 1 (process 2547) exited normally]
(gdb)
```

The errors that occur from computing with rounded numbers can be subtle. We'll use our addFloats program in Listing 19-7 to illustrate some common errors.

---

**YOUR TURN**

1.  Modify the assembly language program in Listing 19-7 so that it performs the addition using doubles. Run it with the same numbers in my example. Does it give a more accurate result? Explain.

2.  Modify the assembly language program in Listing 19-7 so that it divides instead of adding. Try dividing by 0.0. The SSE instruction to divide floats is divss. What happens when you run it?

3.  Now, if your program in the previous exercise gave a result for the division, that means the divide-by-zero exception was masked out; modify the program so that ZE is no longer masked out. If it gave a core dump, ZE was not masked out; modify the program so that ZE is masked out. To modify the ZM bit in the mxcsr register, you need two instructions: stmxcsr *mem* stores a copy of the 32-bit mxcsr register in the memory location, *mem*, and ldmxcsr *mem* loads the 32-bit value at the memory location *mem* into the mxcsr register.

---

### Absorption

*Absorption* results from adding (or subtracting) two numbers of widely different magnitude. The value of the smaller number gets lost in the computation. Let's run our addFloats program under gdb to see how this occurs.

We'll set a breakpoint at the call to printf and run the program:

```
(gdb) run
Enter a number: 16777215.0
Enter a number: 0.1

Starting program: /home/bob/progs/chapter_19/addFloats_asm/addFloats
Breakpoint 1, main () at addFloats.s:53
53              call    printf@plt
```

The significand in a 32-bit float is 24 bits (don't forget the hidden bit), so I used 16777215.0 as one of the numbers. Then I used 0.1 as the fraction to be added to it.

Next, let's look at the numbers stored in the three variables, x, y, and z:

```
(gdb) i r rbp
rbp              0x7fffffffdee0      0x7fffffffdee0
(gdb) x/3xw 0x7fffffffdecc
0x7fffffffdecc: 0x4b7fffff          0x3dcccccd          0x4b7fffff
```

Let's look at the hexadecimal number in x, which is located at 0x7fffffff decc: 0x4b7fffff. From the IEEE 754 format shown earlier, we see that the exponent is stored as $96_{16} = 150_{10}$, giving e = 13. Thus, x is stored as 1.11111 111111111111111111 $\times 2^{13}$ = 1111111111111111111111.0 = $16777215.0_{10}$. Similarly, y is stored as 1.100110011001100110011001101 $\times 2^{-4}$ = 0.0001100110011001100110011001101 $\cong$ $0.100000001437_{10}$. Adding these two binary numbers gives 1111111111111111 1111111.0001100110011001100110011001101. The floating-point hardware in the CPU will round this to 24 bits to fit it into the IEEE 754 format, which cuts off the entire fractional portion. The small number in this example, 0.1, has been absorbed in this floating-point addition.

The absorption may not be obvious if we look at the numbers in gdb's floating-point format:

```
(gdb) x/3fw 0x7fffffffdecc
0x7fffffffdecc: 16777215            0.100000001         16777215
```

## Cancellation

Another type of error, *cancellation*, can occur when subtracting two numbers that differ by a small amount. Since floating-point notation preserves the integrity of the high-order portions, the subtraction will give 0 in the high-order portion of the result. If either of the numbers has been rounded, its low-order portion is not exact, which means that the result will be in error.

We'll use our addFloats program in Listing 19-7 to subtract by entering a negative number. Here's an example using two close numbers:

```
$ ./addFloats
Enter a number: 1677721.5
Enter a number: -1677721.4
1677721.500000 + -1677721.375000 = 0.125000
```

The relative error in this subtraction is (0.125 − 0.1) / 0.1 = 0.25 = 25%. We can see that the second number has been rounded from −1677721.4 to −1677721.375, which led to the error in the arithmetic.

Let's look at how these numbers are treated as floats:

$$x = 1.10011001100110011001100 \times 2^{20}$$
$$y = 1.10011001100110011001011 \times 2^{20}$$
$$z = 1.00000000000000000000000 \times 2^{-3}$$

Subtraction has caused the high-order 20 bits of x and y to cancel, leaving only three bits of significance for z. The rounding error in y carries through to cause an error in z.

Let's use two values that will not give a rounding error:

```
$ ./addFloats
Enter a number: 1677721.5
Enter a number: -1677721.25
1677721.500000 + -1677721.250000 = 0.250000
```

In this case, the three numbers are stored exactly:

$$x = 1.10011001100110011001100 \times 2^{20}$$
$$y = 1.10011001100110011001010 \times 2^{20}$$
$$z = 1.00000000000000000000000 \times 2^{-2}$$

The subtraction has still caused the high-order 20 bits of x and y to cancel and left only three bits of significance for z, but z is correct.

*Catastrophic cancellation* occurs when at least one of the floating-point numbers has a rounding error that causes an error in the difference. If both numbers are stored exactly, we get *benign cancellation*. Both types of cancellation cause a loss of significance in the result.

## Associativity

Probably the most insidious effects of floating-point errors are those that occur in intermediate results. They can show up in some sets of data but not in others. Errors in intermediate results even cause floating-point addition *not to be associative*: there are some values of the floats x, y, and z for which (x + y) + z is not equal to x + (y + z).

Let's write a simple C program to test for associativity, as shown in Listing 19-8.

```
/* threeFloats.c
 * Associativity of floats.
 */

#include <stdio.h>

int main()
{
  float x, y, z, sum1, sum2;

  printf("Enter a number: ");
  scanf("%f", &x);
  printf("Enter a number: ");
  scanf("%f", &y);
  printf("Enter a number: ");
  scanf("%f", &z);

❶ sum1 = x + y;
  sum1 += z;      /* sum1 = (x + y) + z */
  sum2 = y + z;
  sum2 += x;      /* sum2 = x + (y + z) */

  if (sum1 == sum2)
    printf("%f is the same as %f\n", sum1, sum2);
```

```
    else
        printf("%f is not the same as %f\n", sum1, sum2);

    return 0;
}
```

*Listing 19-8: Program to show that floating-point arithmetic is not associative*

Most programmers would do the addition in one statement, sum1 = (x + y) + z, but doing it in separate stages will allow us to look at the intermediate results in the debugger ❶. We'll start with some simple numbers:

```
$ ./threeFloats
Enter a number: 1.0
Enter a number: 2.0
Enter a number: 3.0
6.000000 is the same as 6.000000
```

The result seems reasonable. Let's try some slightly more interesting numbers:

```
$ ./threeFloats
Enter a number: 1.1
Enter a number: 1.2
Enter a number: 1.3
3.600000 is not the same as 3.600000
```

We'll use gdb to see if we can figure out what's going on here:

```
$ gdb ./threeFloats
--snip--

(gdb) b 18
Breakpoint 1 at 0x121f: file threeFloats.c, line 18.
(gdb) r
Starting program: /home/bob/progs/chapter_19/threeFloats_C/threeFloats
Enter a number: 1.1
Enter a number: 1.2
Enter a number: 1.3

Breakpoint 1, main () at threeFloats.c:18
18          sum1 = x + y;
(gdb) p x
$1 = 1.10000002
(gdb) p y
$2 = 1.20000005
(gdb) p z
$3 = 1.29999995
```

We can see that there is a rounding error in each number as it's stored. Let's step through each statement one at a time and look at how the sums build up:

```
(gdb) n
19          sum1 += z;
(gdb) p sum1
$4 = 2.30000019
```

Both x and y have rounding errors, and adding them introduces even more rounding error in their sum:

```
(gdb) n
20          sum2 = y + z;
(gdb) p sum1
$5 = 3.60000014
```

Next, we'll follow the buildup of sum2:

```
(gdb) n
21          sum2 += x;
(gdb) p sum2
$6 = 2.5
(gdb) n
22          if (sum1 == sum2)
(gdb) p sum2
$7 = 3.5999999
(gdb) cont
Continuing.
3.600000 is not the same as 3.600000
[Inferior 1 (process 2406) exited normally]
(gdb)
```

Using the debugger to look at the storage of each number and watching the sums build up allows us to see the effects of rounding errors in the float storage format. The %f format tells printf to display six decimal places, rounded as needed. So our program correctly tells us that 3.60000014 ≠ 3.5999999, but printf rounds both numbers to 3.600000.

---

**YOUR TURN**

Modify the C program in Listing 19-8 to use doubles. Does this make addition associative?

---

# Comments About Numerical Accuracy

Beginning programmers often see floating-point numbers as real numbers and thus think they are more accurate than integers. It's true that using integers carries its own set of problems: even adding two large integers can cause overflow. Multiplying integers is even more likely to produce a result that will overflow. And we need to take into account that integer division results in two values, the quotient and the remainder, instead of the one value that floating-point division gives us.

But floating-point numbers are not real numbers. As you've seen in this chapter, floating-point representations extend the range of numerical values but have their own set of potential inaccuracies. Arithmetically accurate results require a thorough analysis of your algorithm. These are some points to consider:

Try to scale the data such that integer arithmetic can be used.

Using doubles instead of floats improves accuracy and may actually increase the speed of execution. Most C and C++ library routines take doubles as arguments, so the compiler converts floats to doubles when passing them as arguments, as we saw in the call to printf in Listing 19-7.

Try to arrange the order of computations so that similarly sized numbers are added or subtracted.

Avoid complex arithmetic statements, which may obscure incorrect intermediate results.

Choose test data that stresses your algorithm. If your program processes fractional values, include data that has no exact binary equivalent.

The good news is that with today's prevalence of 64-bit computers, the range of integers is $-9,223,372,036,854,775,808 \leq N \leq +9,223,372,036,854,775,807$. And there are libraries available in many programming languages that allow us to use arbitrary-precision arithmetic in our programs. A good resource for finding one to use is *https://en.wikipedia.org/wiki/List_of_arbitrary-precision_arithmetic_software*.

We've looked at the primary causes of numerical errors when using floating-point numbers. For a more rigorous mathematical treatment of the topic, good starting points would be David Goldberg's paper, "What Every Computer Scientist Should Know About Floating-Point Arithmetic," ACM Computing Surveys, Vol 23, No 1, March 1991, and *https://en.wikipedia.org/wiki/Floating-point_arithmetic*. For an example of a programming technique to reduce rounding errors, you can read about the Kahan summation algorithm at *https://en.wikipedia.org/wiki/Kahan_summation_algorithm*.

# What You've Learned

**Binary representation of fractional values**   Fractional values in binary are equal to sums of inverse powers of two.

**Fixed point in binary**   The binary point is assumed to be between two specific bits.

**Floating-point numbers are not real numbers**   The gap between adjacent floating-point numbers varies according to the exponent.

**Floating-point is usually less accurate than fixed-point**   Rounding errors are commonly obscured by floating-point format normalization and can accumulate through multiple computations.

**IEEE 754**   The most common standard for representing floating-point values in a computer program. The integer part is always 1. The exponent specifies the number of bits included in, or excluded from, the integer part.

**SSE floating-point hardware**   A separate set of hardware in the CPU, with its own registers and instruction set, for working with floating-point numbers.

So far in this book, we have discussed programs that follow a step-by-step order of execution of instructions. But in some instances, an instruction cannot do anything meaningful with its operands—for example, when we divide by 0. As you saw earlier in this chapter, that can trigger an exception to the intended order of program execution. And we may want to allow outside events, like typing a key on the keyboard, to interrupt the ongoing program execution. After discussing input/output in Chapter 20, we'll look at interrupts and exceptions in Chapter 21.

# 20

## INPUT/OUTPUT

We'll look at the I/O subsystem in this chapter. The *I/O subsystem* is what programs use to communicate with the outside world, meaning devices other than the CPU and memory. Most programs read data from one or more input devices, process the data, and then write the results to one or more output devices.

Keyboards and mice are typical input devices; display screens and printers are typical output devices. Although most people don't think of them this way, devices such as magnetic disks, solid-state drives, USB sticks, and so forth, are also I/O devices.

We'll start the chapter by looking at some of the timing characteristics of I/O devices and how they compare to memory. Then we'll look at the interface between the CPU and I/O devices that we use to deal with the timing issues. Finally, we'll take a cursory look at how to program I/O devices.

# Timing Considerations

Since the CPU accesses memory and I/O over the same buses (see Figure 1-1, Chapter 1), it might seem that a program could access the I/O devices in the same way as memory. That is, it might seem that I/O could be performed by using the mov instruction to transfer bytes of data between the CPU and the specific I/O device. This can be done, but other issues must be taken into account in order to make it work correctly. One of the main issues lies in the timing differences between memory and I/O. Before tackling I/O timing, let's consider memory timing characteristics.

**NOTE**    *As I've pointed out, the three-bus description given in this book shows the logical interaction between the CPU and I/O. Most modern computers employ several types of buses. The way in which the CPU connects to the various buses is handled in hardware. A programmer generally deals only with the logical view.*

## Memory Timing

An important characteristic of memory is that its timing is relatively uniform and not dependent on external events. This means that memory timing can be handled by the hardware, so a programmer doesn't need to be concerned about memory timing. We can simply move data to and from memory with CPU instructions.

Comparing the two types of memory commonly used in computers, the access time for SRAM is 5–10 times as fast as DRAM, but SRAM costs more and takes up more physical space. As you learned in Chapter 8, DRAM is commonly used for the main memory, with SRAM used for the smaller cache memory. The combination of SRAM cache with DRAM main memory works well to ensure minimal time delays when the CPU accesses memory.

It's worth noting here that CPU speeds are still faster than memory, especially DRAM. Accessing memory—fetching an instruction, loading data, storing data—is typically the most important factor that slows program execution. There are techniques for improving cache performance, which improves memory access times. But employing such techniques requires a thorough understanding of the CPU and memory configuration of the system you're using, which is beyond the scope of this book.

## I/O Device Timing

Almost all I/O devices are much slower than memory. Consider a common input device, the keyboard. Typing at 120 words per minute is equivalent to 10 characters per second, or 100 milliseconds between each character. A CPU running at 2 GHz can execute approximately 200 million instructions during that time. This is to say nothing of the fact that the time intervals between keystrokes are very inconsistent. Many will be much longer than this.

Even a solid-state drive is slow compared to memory. For example, data can be transferred to and from a typical SSD at about 500 MBps. The transfer rate for DDR4 memory (commonly used for main memory) is around 20 GBps, some 40 times faster.

In addition to being much slower, I/O devices exhibit much more variance in their timing. Some people type very fast on a keyboard, some very slow. The required data on a magnetic disk might be just coming up to the read/write head, or it may have just passed by and we have to wait for nearly a full revolution of the disk for it to come under the head again.

Before discussing how to deal with I/O device timing, we'll look at some bus timing issues.

## Bus Timing

Although our overall view of the three major subsystems in Figure 1-1 shows only three buses connecting the subsystems, the large differences in timing between memory and the various I/O devices have led to different buses for accessing memory and I/O devices. Each bus design carries address, data, and control information, but they use different protocols and physical connections that are better matched to the speeds of the devices they connect to.

Most computers use a hierarchical bus structure that allows memory and other fast subsystems to be connected to the CPU through a fast bus, while connecting slower subsystems through slower buses. We can discuss the concepts by looking at a common arrangement for PCs up until around 2005, as shown in Figure 20-1.

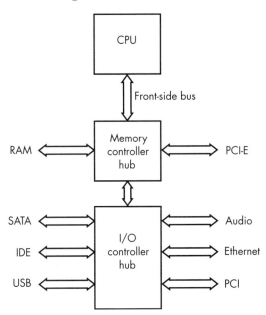

Figure 20-1: Typical bus control in a PC

The *memory controller hub* is often called the *northbridge*; it provides a fast communication pathway to the CPU through the *front-side bus*. In addition to providing a fast connection to main memory, the memory controller hub connects to fast I/O buses, like the PCI-E bus. The PCI-E bus provides a fast interface to devices like a graphics card. The *I/O controller hub* is often called the *southbridge*. It connects to slower I/O buses, like SATA, USB, and so forth.

As chip technology improves over the years, manufacturers are able to add more functionality to the CPU chip, which reduces cost and saves space and power. Intel included the functionality of the memory controller hub on the same chip as the CPU in 2008, and AMD included it in 2011. Manufacturers continue to move bus control hardware onto the same chip with the CPU.

These days, both Intel and AMD sell *system on a chip* (*SoC*) devices that use the x86-64 instruction set and include both memory control and I/O control on the same chip as the CPU. Of course, SoC devices provide a fixed set of I/O buses. Essentially all our mobile devices use an SoC for their computing power.

## Accessing I/O Devices

The CPU works with an I/O device through a *device controller*, the hardware that does the actual work of controlling the I/O device. For example, a keyboard controller detects which keys are pressed and converts this to a bit pattern that represents the key. It also detects whether a modifier key, like SHIFT or CTRL, is pressed and sets bits accordingly.

The device controller interfaces with the CPU through a set of registers. In general, the device controller provides the following types of I/O registers:

**Transmit**  Allows data to be written to an output device

**Receive**  Allows data to be read from an input device

**Status**  Provides information about the current state of the device, including the controller itself

**Control**  Allows a program to send commands to the controller to change the settings of the device and the controller

It's common for a device controller interface to have more than one register of the same type, especially control registers and status registers.

Writing data to an output device is very much like storing data in memory: you move the data from the CPU to the device controller *transmit register*. Where the output device differs is the timing. As discussed, memory timing is taken care of by the hardware, so a programmer doesn't need to be concerned about the timing when storing data in memory. However, an output device may not be ready to accept new data—it may be working on previously written data. This is where the *status register* comes into play. The program needs to check the status register of the device controller to see if it's ready to accept new data.

Reading data from an input device is like loading data from memory into the CPU: you move the data from the device controller *receive register*. Again, the difference is that an input device may not have new data, so the program needs to check the status register of the input device controller to see if it has new data.

Most I/O devices also need to be told what to do by sending commands to the *control register*. For example, after waiting for an output device controller to become ready for new data and then moving the data to the transmit register, some device controllers require that you tell them to output the data to the actual device. Or if you want to get data from an input device, some device controllers require that you request them to get an input. You can send such commands to the control register.

There are two ways that the CPU can access the I/O registers on a device controller: port-mapped I/O and memory-mapped I/O. The x86-64 architecture supports both techniques.

## Port-Mapped I/O

The x86-64 architecture includes a set of *I/O ports* that are numbered from 0x0000 to 0xffff. This port address space is separate from the memory address space. Using the I/O ports for input and output is called *port-mapped I/O*, or *isolated I/O*.

There are special instructions for accessing the I/O address space, in and out:

### in—Input from Port

Read from an I/O port.

in *reg*, *imm* reads byte(s) from I/O port number *imm*. *reg* can be al, ax, or eax.

in *reg*, dx reads byte(s) from the I/O port number specified in dx. *reg* can be al, ax, or eax.

The number of bytes read is one for al, two for ax, and four for eax. The in instruction does not affect the status flags in the rflags register.

### out—Output to Port

Write to an I/O port.

out *imm*, *reg* writes byte(s) to I/O port number *imm*. *reg* can be al, ax, or eax.

out dx, *reg* writes byte(s) to the I/O port number specified in dx. *reg* can be al, ax, or eax.

The number of bytes written is one for al, two for ax, and four for eax. The out instruction does not affect the status flags in the rflags register.

When using the in and out instructions, the CPU places the port number on the address bus, and a control signal on the control bus that selects the port address space instead of the program address space. This leaves the entire program address space available for programs. However, the x86-64 architecture's 64-bit addressing space provides plenty of room for us to use some of the addresses for I/O devices.

## Memory-Mapped I/O

It'll be easier to understand *memory-mapped I/O* if we first look at how memory is managed by Linux, and most other operating systems, when executing a program.

Programs run in a *virtual memory* address space, a technique that simulates a large memory with contiguous addressing from 0 to some maximum value. These are the addresses you see when using gdb—for example, the addresses in the rip and rsp registers. Although the x86-64 architecture allows 64-bit addressing, current CPU hardware implementations use only 48 bits for the address. This allows a maximum address of $2^{48}$ bytes (256 tebibytes) to execute programs in this virtual address space. But most computers have only around 4 to 16 gigabytes (or gibibytes) of *physical memory*, the actual RAM installed in the computer, and a program needs to be in physical memory to be executed.

**NOTE** *We commonly use the metric naming convention for specifying multiple-byte quantities that is based on powers of 10: kilobyte, megabyte, gigabyte, and so forth. The International Electrotechnical Commission (IEC) has also defined a naming convention that is based on powers of two: kibibyte, mebibyte, gibibyte, and so forth. For example, a kilobyte is 1,000 bytes, and a kibibyte is 1,024 bytes. You can read more about the naming conventions at https://en.wikipedia.org/wiki/Byte.*

The operating system manages the placement of programs in physical memory by dividing each program into *pages*. A typical page size is 4 kilobytes (or kibibytes). Physical memory is divided into the same size *page frames*. The page of the program that contains the code currently being executed by the CPU is loaded from the place where it's stored (for example, disk, DVD, USB stick) into a page frame of physical memory.

The operating system maintains a *page map table*, which shows where the page of the program is currently loaded in physical memory. Figure 20-2 shows the relationship between virtual memory and physical memory using the page map table.

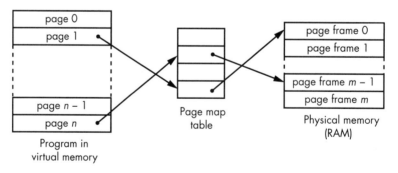

Figure 20-2: Relationship between virtual memory and physical memory

The CPU includes a *memory mapping unit*. When the CPU needs to access an item in memory, it uses the virtual address of the item. The memory mapping unit uses the virtual address as an index into the page map table to locate the page in physical memory, and from there, the item. If the requested page is not currently loaded into physical memory, the memory mapping unit generates a *page fault exception*, which calls a function in the operating system to load the page into physical memory and enter its location in the page map table. (You'll learn about exceptions in Chapter 21.)

Similar to mapping virtual memory to physical memory, virtual memory addresses can be mapped to I/O ports, giving us memory-mapped I/O. Once an I/O port has been associated with a memory address, the CPU instructions that access memory can be used to access the I/O port. One advantage is that you can usually write the I/O functions in a higher-level language like C. Using the in and out instructions requires you to use assembly language because compilers typically don't use these instructions.

Next, we'll take a look at how to approach I/O programming.

---

**YOUR TURN**

Pick two programs that you have written. Start each program with gdb in separate terminal windows. Set a breakpoint near the beginning of each program and run the program. When the program breaks, look at the addresses in the rip and rsp registers. Do the two programs appear to share the same memory space? Explain.

---

## I/O Programming

I/O devices differ widely in the amount of data they process and the speed with which they process it. For example, input from a keyboard is one byte at human typing speed, while input from a disk is several hundred megabytes per second. Depending on their inherent characteristics, I/O devices use different techniques for communicating with the CPU, and thus we need to program each of them accordingly.

### Polled I/O

*Polling* is the simplest way to do I/O and is often a sufficient method for small amounts of data. We first check the status register of the I/O device controller to determine the device's state. If the device is in a ready state, then we can read data from an input device or write data to an output device. Polling typically involves a loop that iterates, checking the device's status register in each iteration of the loop, until the device is in a ready state. This way of doing I/O is known as *polled I/O*, or *programmed I/O*.

The downside of polled I/O is that the CPU can be tied up for long periods of time while it waits for the device to become ready. This would probably be acceptable if the CPU were dedicated to running only one program on the system (for example, controlling your microwave oven). But it's not acceptable in the multiprogram environments of our laptop and desktop computers.

### Interrupt-Driven I/O

We could get more work out of the CPU if we could tell an I/O device to let us know when it's ready for data input or output and then use the CPU for something else. Many I/O devices include an *interrupt controller* that can send an interrupt signal to the CPU when the device has completed an operation or is ready to take on another operation.

An interrupt from an external device causes the CPU to call an *interrupt handler*, a function within the operating system that deals with the input or output from the interrupting device. We'll discuss the CPU features that allow it to call interrupt handlers in Chapter 21.

### Direct Memory Access

I/O devices that transfer large amounts of data at high speed often have the capability of *direct memory access (DMA)*. They have *DMA controllers* that can access main memory directly without the CPU. For example, when reading from a disk, the DMA controller accepts a memory address and a command to read data from the disk. When the DMA controller has read the data from the disk into its own buffer memory, it writes that data directly to main memory. When the DMA data transfer has completed, the controller sends an interrupt to the CPU, thus invoking the disk handler that notifies the operating system that the data is now available in memory.

Next, we'll look at some examples of how polling I/O might be done.

## Polled I/O Programming Algorithms

The operating system has complete control over the I/O devices on our computer, so it will not allow us to write applications that directly access an I/O device. The programs we're writing here are meant only to show the concepts, not to do anything useful. In fact, running them will elicit an error message from the operating system.

We'll look at some simple polling algorithms that show how we might program a *universal asynchronous receiver/transmitter (UART)* for I/O. This device performs parallel-to-serial conversion to transmit a byte of data one bit at a time. The output of a UART requires only one transmission line, which is placed at one of two voltage levels. A transmitting UART sends a string of bits by switching between the two voltage levels at a fixed rate. The receiving UART reads the bits one at a time and performs serial-to-parallel conversion to reassemble the byte that was sent to it. Both UARTs must be set at the same bit rate.

In the idle state, the transmitting UART places the high voltage on the transmission line. When a program outputs a byte to the UART, the transmitting UART switches the transmission line to the low voltage for the amount of time corresponding to the agreed-upon rate, thus sending a *start bit*.

The UART then uses a shift register to shift the byte one bit at a time, setting the voltage on the output line accordingly. Most UARTs start with the low-order bit. When the entire byte has been sent, the UART returns the output line to the idle state for at least one bit time, thus sending at least one *stop bit*.

Figure 20-3 shows how a UART with typical settings would send the two characters *m* and *n* that are encoded in ASCII.

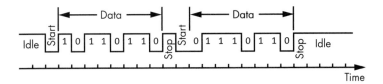

Figure 20-3: UART output to send the characters m and n

The receiving UART watches the transmission line, looking for a start bit. When it detects a start bit, it uses a shift register to reassemble the individual bits into a byte, which is provided to the receiving program as input.

We'll use the 16550 UART, a common type, for our programming example. The 16550 UART has 12 eight-bit registers, shown in Table 20-1.

**Table 20-1:** Registers of the 16550 UART

| Name | Address | DLAB | Purpose |
| --- | --- | --- | --- |
| RBR | 000 | 0 | Receiver buffer—input byte |
| THR | 000 | 0 | Transmitter holding—output byte |
| IER | 001 | 0 | Interrupt enable—set type of interrupt |
| IIR | 010 | x | Interrupt identification—show type of interrupt |
| FCR | 010 | x | FIFO control—set FIFO parameters |
| LCR | 011 | x | Line control—set communications format |
| MCR | 100 | x | Modem control—set interface with modem |
| LSR | 101 | x | Line status—show status of data transfers |
| MSR | 110 | x | Modem status—show status of modem |
| SCR | 111 | x | Scratch |
| DLL | 000 | 1 | Divisor latch, low-order byte |
| DLM | 001 | 1 | Divisor latch, high-order byte |

The addresses in Table 20-1 are offsets from the UART's base address. You probably noticed that some of the registers have the same offset. The address specifies a port to a register. The specific register being accessed through that port depends on what the program is doing with that port. For example, if the program reads from port 000, it's reading from the receiver buffer register (RBR). But if the program writes to port 000, it's writing to the transmitter holding register (THR).

The divisor latch access bit (DLAB) is a bit number 7 in the line control register (LCR). When it is set to 1, port 000 connects to the low-order byte of the 16-bit divisor latch value, and port 001 connects to the high-order byte of the divisor latch value.

The 16550 UART can be programmed for interrupt-driven I/O and direct memory access. It includes 16-byte first-in, first-out (FIFO) buffers on both the transmitter and the receiver ports. It can also be programmed to control a serial modem.

Older PCs typically connected the UART to a COM port. In past years, COM ports were often used to connect devices like a printer and a modem to the computer, but most PCs these days use USB ports for serial I/O. The 16550 UART on my desktop computer has a set of internal connection pins but no external connection port.

We'll assume that our UART is installed in a computer that uses memory-mapped I/O so that we can show the algorithms in C. To keep things simple, we'll do only polled I/O here, which requires these three functions:

**init_io**   Initializes the UART. This includes setting the parameters in the hardware such as speed, communications protocol, and so forth.

**charin**   Reads one character that was received by the UART.

**charout**   Writes one character to transmitted by the UART.

**WARNING**   *The code we'll discuss here is incomplete and does not run on any known computer. It's meant only to illustrate some basic concepts.*

## UART Memory-Mapped I/O in C

We will explore only a few features of the UART. Let's start with a file that provides symbolic names for the registers and some numbers we'll be using in our example program, as shown in Listing 20-1.

```
/* UART_defs.h
 * Definitions for a 16550 UART.
 * WARNING: This code does not run on any known
 *          device. It is meant to sketch some
 *          general I/O concepts only.
 */
#ifndef UART_DEFS_H
#define UART_DEFS_H
❶ /* register offsets */
#define RBR 0x00    /* receive buffer register   */
#define THR 0x00    /* transmit holding register */
#define IER 0x01    /* interrupt enable register */
#define FCR 0x02    /* FIFO control register     */
#define LCR 0x03    /* line control register     */
#define LSR 0x05    /* line status register      */
#define DLL 0x00    /* divisor latch LSB         */
#define DLM 0x01    /* divisor latch MSB         */

/* status bits */
#define RxRDY 0x01  /* receiver ready */
#define TxRDY 0x20  /* transmitter ready */

/* commands */
#define NOFIFO       0x00   /* don't use FIFO  */
#define NOINTERRUPT  0x00   /* polling mode    */
#define MSB38400     0x00   /* 2 bytes used to */
#define LSB38400     0x03   /* set baud 38400  */
#define NBITS        0x03   /* 8 bits          */
#define STOPBIT      0x00   /* 1 stop bit      */
```

```
  #define NOPARITY      0x00
❷ #define SETCOM        NBITS | STOPBIT | NOPARITY
❸ #define SETBAUD       0x80 | SETCOM
  #endif
```

*Listing 20-1: Definitions for a 16550 UART*

The ports to the registers are at fixed positions relative to the start of the mapped memory address of the UART. The UART might be used in another computer, where the mapping might begin at another base address, so we just define the offsets here ❶. These offsets, and the status and control bit settings, are taken from a 16550 datasheet. You can download one at *https://www.ti.com/product/TL16C550D/*.

Let's look at how I arrived at the value for the SETCOM control ❷. The communication parameters are set by writing a byte to the line status register. The number of bits in each data frame can range from 5 to 8. The datasheet tells us that setting bits 1 and 0 to 11 will specify 8 bits. Hence, I set NBITS to 0x03. Setting bit 2 to 0 specifies one stop bit, so STOPBIT = 0x00. We won't use parity, which is bit 3, so NOPARITY = 0x00. I OR these together to create the byte that sets the communication parameters. Of course, we really don't need the two 0 values, but specifying them makes our intent explicit.

*Baud* is a measure of the speed of communication, defined as the number of symbols per second. A UART uses only two voltage levels for communication, symbolically 0 or 1, or one bit. So for a UART, baud is equivalent to the number of bits transmitted or received per second. We need to set the DLAB bit to 1 to place our UART in the mode that allows us to set the baud ❸.

Next, we need a header file for declaring the functions, as shown in Listing 20-2.

```
/* UART_functions.h
 * Initialize, read, and write functions for an abstract UART.
 * WARNING: This code does not run on any known
 *          device. It is meant to sketch some
 *          general I/O concepts only.
 */
#ifndef UART_FUNCTIONS_H
#define UART_FUNCTIONS_H
void UART_init(unsigned char* UART);        /* initialize UART */
unsigned char UART_in(unsigned char* UART);        /* input */
void UART_out(unsigned char* UART, unsigned char c); /* output */
#endif
```

*Listing 20-2: Declarations of UART functions*

The header file in Listing 20-2 declares the three basic functions for using our UART. We won't cover the more advanced features of a UART in this book.

We'll place the definitions of these three functions in one file, as shown in Listing 20-3, because they would typically be used together.

```
/* UART_functions.c
 * Initialize, read, and write functions for an abstract UART.
 * WARNING: This code does not run on any known
 *          device. It is meant to sketch some
 *          general I/O concepts only.
 */

#include "UART_defs.h"
#include "UART_functions.h"

/* UART_init initializes the UART. */
❶ void UART_init(unsigned char* UART)
{
  unsigned char* port = UART;

❷ *(port+IER) = NOINTERRUPT;  /* no interrupts        */
  *(port+FCR) = NOFIFO;       /* no fifo              */
  *(port+LCR) = SETBAUD;      /* set frequency mode   */
  *(port+DLM) = MSB38400;     /* set to 38400 baud    */
  *(port+DLL) = LSB38400;     /*    with 2 bytes      */
  *(port+LCR) = SETCOM;       /* communications mode  */
}

/* UART_in waits until UART has a character then reads it */
unsigned char UART_in(unsigned char* UART)
{
  unsigned char* port = UART;
  unsigned char character;

❸ while ((*(port+LSR) & RxRDY) != 0)
  {
  }
  character = *(port+RBR);
  return character;
}

/* UART_out waits until UART is ready then writes a character */
void UART_out(unsigned char* UART, unsigned char character )
{
  unsigned char* port = UART;
  unsigned char status;
  while ((*(port+LSR) & TxRDY) != 0)
  {
  }
  *(port+THR) = character;
}
```

Listing 20-3: UART memory-mapped I/O function definitions in C

We pass each of the functions in Listing 20-3 a pointer to the UART
port ❶. We then access each of the UART registers through an offset from this
pointer ❷. Both the input and output functions wait until the UART is ready
for their respective action ❸. These functions illustrate an important advantage of memory-mapped I/O: they can be written in a high-level language.

We can see a potential downside of writing these functions in a high-level language by looking at the assembly language generated by the compiler, as shown in Listing 20-4.

```
            .file   "UART_functions.c"
            .intel_syntax noprefix
            .text
            .globl  UART_init
            .type   UART_init, @function
UART_init:
            push    rbp
            mov     rbp, rsp
            mov     QWORD PTR -24[rbp], rdi
            mov     rax, QWORD PTR -24[rbp] ## UART base address
            mov     QWORD PTR -8[rbp], rax
     ❶ mov     rax, QWORD PTR -8[rbp]  ## UART base address
            add     rax, 1                 ## IER offset
            mov     BYTE PTR [rax], 0      ## no interrupts
            mov     rax, QWORD PTR -8[rbp]
            add     rax, 2                 ## FCR offset
            mov     BYTE PTR [rax], 0      ## no FIFO
            mov     rax, QWORD PTR -8[rbp]
            add     rax, 3                 ## LCR offset
            mov     BYTE PTR [rax], -125   ## set baud mode
            mov     rax, QWORD PTR -8[rbp]
            add     rax, 1                 ## DLM offset
            mov     BYTE PTR [rax], 0      ## high byte
            mov     rax, QWORD PTR -8[rbp] ## DLL offset = 0
            mov     BYTE PTR [rax], 3      ## low byte
            mov     rax, QWORD PTR -8[rbp]
            add     rax, 3                 ## LCR offset
            mov     BYTE PTR [rax], 3      ## communications mode
            nop
            pop     rbp
            ret
            .size   UART_init, .-UART_init
            .globl  UART_in
            .type   UART_in, @function
UART_in:
            push    rbp
            mov     rbp, rsp
            mov     QWORD PTR -24[rbp], rdi
            mov     rax, QWORD PTR -24[rbp]
            mov     QWORD PTR -8[rbp], rax
            nop
.L3:
            mov     rax, QWORD PTR -8[rbp]  ## UART base address
            add     rax, 5                 ## LSR offset
            movzx   eax, BYTE PTR [rax]
            movzx   eax, al                ## load LSR
            and     eax, 1                 ## (*(port+LSR) & RxRDY)
     ❷ test    eax, eax
            jne     .L3
            mov     rax, QWORD PTR -8[rbp]
```

```
        movzx   eax, BYTE PTR [rax]      ## input character
        mov     BYTE PTR -9[rbp], al
        movzx   eax, BYTE PTR -9[rbp]    ## return character
        pop     rbp
        ret
        .size   UART_in, .-UART_in
        .globl  UART_out
        .type   UART_out, @function
UART_out:
        push    rbp
        mov     rbp, rsp
        mov     QWORD PTR -24[rbp], rdi
        mov     eax, esi
        mov     BYTE PTR -28[rbp], al
        mov     rax, QWORD PTR -24[rbp]
        mov     QWORD PTR -8[rbp], rax
        nop
.L6:
        mov     rax, QWORD PTR -8[rbp]   ## UART base address
        add     rax, 5                   ## LSR offset
        movzx   eax, BYTE PTR [rax]
        movzx   eax, al                  ## load LSR
        and     eax, 32                  ## (*(port+LSR) & TxRDY)
        test    eax, eax
        jne     .L6
        mov     rax, QWORD PTR -8[rbp]
        lea     rdx, 7[rax]
        movzx   eax, BYTE PTR -28[rbp]   ## load character
        mov     BYTE PTR [rdx], al       ## output character
        nop
        pop     rbp
        ret
        .size   UART_out, .-UART_out
        .ident  "GCC: (Ubuntu 9.3.0-17ubuntu1~20.04) 9.3.0"
        .section        .note.GNU-stack,"",@progbits
```

*Listing 20-4: Assembly language generated by the compiler for our UART functions*

We can see some inefficiencies in the code that the compiler generates.
The initialization function, UART_init, sends several commands to the UART's
control registers. The compiler computes the effective address of each control register ❶, and then it repeats this computation for each command.

Another inefficiency can be seen in the input function, UART_in. The algorithm uses the and instruction to check the receiver ready bit. The compiler
has then used the test instruction to determine if the result of the and instruction was 0 ❷. But the test instruction performs an AND operation to set the
status flags in the rflags register, which were already set by the and instruction.
In other words, the test instruction is redundant in this algorithm.

I stated earlier in this book that we won't be concerned about code
efficiency, and it may seem that saving a few CPU cycles when accessing
a slow I/O device is unimportant. But the algorithms we're looking at
here are often used within a device handler. Other I/O devices may interrupt the handler currently being executed, causing delays. Since it's not

possible to know the timing of external devices, it's a good idea to minimize the amount of time spent within a device handler. When writing a device handler, I often start with C. Then I generate the corresponding assembly language and check that for inefficiencies and inaccuracies.

More often, I write device handlers directly in assembly language. We'll look now at how these functions could be written directly in assembly language.

## UART Memory-Mapped I/O in Assembly Language

Having learned what the compiler generates for these three UART I/O functions, we can now try to do a better job directly in assembly language. This starts with the definitions of symbolic names for use in our assembly language functions, as shown in Listing 20-5.

```
# UART_defs
# Definitions for a 16550 UART.
# WARNING: This code does not run on any known
#          device. It is meant to sketch some
#          general I/O concepts only.

# register offsets
        .equ    RBR,0x00    # receive buffer register
        .equ    THR,0x00    # transmit holding register
        .equ    IER,0x01    # interrupt enable register
        .equ    FCR,0x02    # FIFO control register
        .equ    LCR,0x03    # line control register
        .equ    LSR,0x05    # line status register
        .equ    DLL,0x00    # divisor latch LSB
        .equ    DLM,0x01    # divisor latch MSB

# status bits
        .equ    RxRDY,0x01  # receiver ready
        .equ    TxRDY,0x20  # transmitter ready

# commands
        .equ    NOFIFO,0x00         # don't use FIFO
        .equ    NOINTERRUPT,0x00    # polling mode
        .equ    MSB38400,0x00       # 2 bytes used to
        .equ    LSB38400,0x03       # set baud 38400
        .equ    NBITS,0x03          # 8 bits
        .equ    STOPBIT,0x00        # 1 stop bit
        .equ    NOPARITY,0x00
        .equ    SETCOM,NBITS | STOPBIT | NOPARITY
        .equ    SETBAUD,0x80 | SETCOM
```

Listing 20-5: Assembly language symbolic names for UART functions

Listing 20-6 shows our assembly language version of the three UART I/O functions.

```
# UART_functions.s
# Initialize, read, and write functions for a 16550 UART.
```

```
        # WARNING: This code does not run on any known
        #          device. It is meant to sketch some
        #          general I/O concepts only.
                .intel_syntax noprefix

                .include "UART_defs"

# Intialize the UART
# Calling sequence:
#    rdi <- base address of UART
                .text
                .globl  UART_init
                .type   UART_init, @function
UART_init:
                push    rbp                     # save frame pointer
                mov     rbp, rsp                # set new frame pointer

            # no interrupts, don't use FIFO queue
        ❶ mov       byte ptr IER[rdi], NOINTERRUPT
                mov     byte ptr FCR[rdi], NOFIFO
            # set divisor latch access bit = 1 to set baud
                mov     byte ptr LCR[rdi], SETBAUD
                mov     byte ptr DLM[rdi], MSB38400
                mov     byte ptr DLL[rdi], LSB38400
            # divisor latch access bit = 0 for communications mode
                mov     byte ptr LCR[rdi], SETCOM


                mov     rsp, rbp                # yes, restore stack pointer
                pop     rbp                     # and caller frame pointer
                ret

# Input a single character
# Calling sequence:
#    rdi <- base address of UART
#    returns character in al register
                .globl  UART_in
                .type   UART_in, @function
UART_in:
                push    rbp                     # save frame pointer
                mov     rbp, rsp                # set new frame pointer

inWaitLoop:
        ❷ and       byte ptr LSR[rdi], RxRDY  # character available?
                jne     inWaitLoop              # no, wait
                movzx   eax, byte ptr RBR[rdi]  # yes, get it
                mov     rsp, rbp                # restore stack pointer
                pop     rbp                     # and caller frame pointer
                ret

# Output a single character in sil register
                .globl  UART_out
                .type   UART_out, @function
UART_out:
                push    rbp                     # save frame pointer
                mov     rbp, rsp                # set new frame pointer
```

```
outWaitLoop:
        and     byte ptr LSR[rdi], TxRDY    # ready for character?
        jne     outWaitLoop                 # no, wait
        mov     THR[rdi], sil               # yes, send it
        mov     rsp, rbp                    # restore stack pointer
        pop     rbp                         # and caller frame pointer
        ret
```

*Listing 20-6: Assembly language versions of UART I/O functions*

The functions are called with a pointer to the base address of the UART, so we can access the UART registers by using the register-indirect-with-offset addressing mode ❶. The compiler chose to use an add instruction to add the offset for each UART register access, which is less efficient.

Since we are using memory-mapped I/O here, we can use the and instruction to check the ready status without loading the contents of the UART's status register into a CPU general-purpose register ❷, which is what the compiler does. Our assembly language solution here may not be more efficient because the contents still must be loaded into the CPU (using a hidden register) before the and operation can be performed.

At the beginning of the chapter, I described I/O programming as being complex, but the code I've presented is fairly straightforward. The complexity comes when interfacing the I/O programming with the operating system, which is responsible for managing all the system resources. For example, we could have several programs running concurrently, all using the same keyboard. The operating system needs to keep track of which program gets the input from the keyboard at any moment in time.

The algorithms I've presented here are only a small part of the entire picture of I/O, but they should give you an introduction to the sorts of issues involved. Although memory-mapped I/O is the more common technique, the x86-64 also support port-mapped I/O, which we'll explore in the next section.

---

**YOUR TURN**

1.  Use the -c option to create object files from the code in Listings 20-3 and 20-7:

    ```
    gcc -c -masm=intel -Wall -g UART_echo.c
    gcc -c -masm=intel -Wall -g UART_functions.c
    ```

    Link the two object files with this command:

    ```
    ld -e myProg -o UART_echo UART_echo.o UART_functions.o
    ```

    *(continued)*

The UART address I give in this program is arbitrary. If you run the resulting program, the operating system should give you an error message. This exercise will only show whether all the functions fit together correctly.

```
/* UART_echo.c
 * Use a UART to echo a single character.
 * WARNING: This code does not run on any known
 *          device. It is meant to sketch some
 *          general I/O concepts only.
 */

#include "UART_functions.h"
#define UART0 (unsigned char *)0xfe200040 /* address of UART */

int myProg() {
  unsigned char aCharacter;

  UART_init(UART0);
  aCharacter = UART_in(UART0);
  UART_out(UART0, aCharacter);

  return 0;
}
```

*Listing 20-7: Program to check UART I/O functions. (Do not try to run this program.)*

2.  Enter the code in Listings 20-5 and 20-6. Assemble it and check for correctness by linking the resulting object file with the *UART_echo.o* object file from the previous "Your Turn" exercise.

## UART Port-Mapped I/O

Unlike memory-mapped I/O, we cannot treat the I/O port numbers as memory addresses. The arguments to the functions are numbers, not pointers, as shown in Listing 20-8.

```
/* UART_functions.c
 * Initialize, read, and write functions for a 16550 UART.
 * WARNING: This code does not run on any known
 *          device. It is meant to sketch some
 *          general I/O concepts only.
 */

#include <sys/io.h>
#include "UART_defs.h"
#include "UART_functions.h"

/* UART_init intializes the UART and enables it. */
void UART_init(unsigned short int UART)
{
```

```
❶ unsigned short int port = UART;

❷ outb(NOINTERRUPT, port+IER);    /* no interrupts        */
  outb(NOFIFO, port+FCR);         /* no fifo              */
  outb(SETBAUD, port+LCR);        /* set frequency mode   */
  outb(MSB38400, port+DLM);       /* set to 38400 baud    */
  outb(LSB38400, port+DLL);       /* 2 regs to set        */
  outb(SETCOM, port+LCR);         /* communications mode  */
}

/* UART_in waits until UART has a character then reads it */
unsigned char UART_in(unsigned short int UART)
{
  unsigned short int port = UART;
  unsigned char character;

  while ((inb(port+LSR) & RxRDY) != 0)
  {
  }
  character = inb(port+RBR);
  return character;
}

/* UART_out waits until UART is ready then writes a character */
void UART_out(unsigned short int UART, unsigned char character )
{
  unsigned short int port = UART;

  while ((inb(port+LSR) & TxRDY) != 0)
  {
  }
  outb(character, port+THR);
}
```

*Listing 20-8: UART port-mapped I/O function definitions in C*

The Linux programming environment provides a header file, *io.h*, that includes functions to use the I/O ports. The interface with our UART takes bytes, so we'll use inb and outb. You can read about these functions on their man page: man inb.

The algorithms for port-mapped I/O are the same as for memory mapped. But instead of accessing the port as a memory address, we use a number ❶. And we need to call the appropriate function to transfer bytes to and from the UART ❷.

When I tried to compile the file in Listing 20-8 by using the -masm=intel option, I got the following error messages:

```
$ gcc -c -masm=intel -Wall -g UART_functions.c
/usr/include/x86_64-linux-gnu/sys/io.h: Assembler messages:
/usr/include/x86_64-linux-gnu/sys/io.h:47: Error: operand type mismatch for
`in'
/usr/include/x86_64-linux-gnu/sys/io.h:98: Error: operand type mismatch for
`out'
```

I was puzzled so decided to look at the compiler-generated assembly language by changing the -c option to -S. I won't go through the entire file, but let's look at the first part of the compiler-generated assembly language, as shown in Listing 20-9.

```
        .file   "UART_functions.c"
        .intel_syntax noprefix
        .text
        .type   inb, @function
❶ inb:
        push    rbp
        mov     rbp, rsp
        mov     eax, edi
        mov     WORD PTR -20[rbp], ax
        movzx   eax, WORD PTR -20[rbp]
        mov     edx, eax
❷ #APP
# 47 "/usr/include/x86_64-linux-gnu/sys/io.h" 1
        inb dx,al
# 0 "" 2
#NO_APP
        mov     BYTE PTR -1[rbp], al
        movzx   eax, BYTE PTR -1[rbp]
        pop     rbp
        ret
        .size   inb, .-inb
        .type   outb, @function
outb:
        push    rbp
        mov     rbp, rsp
        mov     edx, edi
        mov     eax, esi
        mov     BYTE PTR -4[rbp], dl
        mov     WORD PTR -8[rbp], ax
        movzx   eax, BYTE PTR -4[rbp]
        movzx   edx, WORD PTR -8[rbp]
#APP
# 98 "/usr/include/x86_64-linux-gnu/sys/io.h" 1
        outb al,dx
# 0 "" 2
#NO_APP
        nop
        pop     rbp
        ret
        .size   outb, .-outb
        .globl  UART_init
        .type   UART_init, @function
UART_init:
        push    rbp
        mov     rbp, rsp
        sub     rsp, 24
        mov     eax, edi
```

```
        mov     WORD PTR -20[rbp], ax
        movzx   eax, WORD PTR -20[rbp]
        mov     WORD PTR -2[rbp], ax
        movzx   eax, WORD PTR -2[rbp]
        add     eax, 1
        movzx   eax, ax
        mov     esi, eax
        mov     edi, 0
        call    outb
        movzx   eax, WORD PTR -2[rbp]
        add     eax, 2
--snip--
```

*Listing 20-9: Some compiler-generated assembly language for the functions in Listing 20-8*

The first thing to note is that the compiler has included the assembly language for the inb and outb functions ❶. These functions are not part of the C standard library. They are meant to be used in the operating system code, not in applications programs. They are specific to the Linux kernel running on an x86-64 computer.

Next, we see that the actual in and out instructions are inserted into the code by macros ❷. The macros insert these two instructions in AT&T syntax (see AT&T Syntax at the end of Chapter 10):

```
        inb     dx, al          ## at&t syntax
        outb    al, dx
```

As we saw earlier in this chapter, the instructions are written in Intel syntax as follows:

```
        in      al, dx          ## intel syntax
        out     dx, al
```

The problem here is that the assembly language used in the Linux kernel is written using the AT&T syntax, whereas we're using the Intel syntax for assembly language. If we were to generate the assembly language without the -masm=intel option, all the assembly language would be in the AT&T syntax. If we use the C functions in *io.h* for port-mapped I/O, we cannot use the -masm=intel compiler option.

---

**YOUR TURN**

Rewrite the UART I/O functions in Listing 20-6 to use port-mapped I/O instead of memory-mapped I/O and assemble them. Modify *UART_echo.c* in Listing 20-7 to use your port-mapped I/O functions. The base port number on most PCs is 0x3f8. Compile *UART_echo.c* and link the two resulting object files to check for correctness.

---

# What You've Learned

**Memory timing**   Memory access is synchronized with the timing of the CPU.

**I/O timing**   I/O devices are much slower than the CPU and have a wide range of characteristics, so we need to program their access.

**Bus timing**   Buses are often arranged in a hierarchical manner to better match the differences in timing between various I/O devices.

**Port-mapped I/O**   In this technique, I/O ports have their own address space.

**Memory-mapped I/O**   In this technique, I/O ports are given a portion of the main memory address space.

**Polled I/O**   The program waits in a loop until the I/O device is ready to transfer data.

**Interrupt-driven I/O**   The I/O device interrupts the CPU when it is ready to transfer data.

**Direct memory access**   The I/O device can transfer data to and from main memory without using the CPU.

In the next chapter, you'll learn about the CPU features that allow it to maintain control over the I/O hardware and prevent application programs from accessing the hardware without going through the operating system.

# 21

## INTERRUPTS AND EXCEPTIONS

Thus far, we've viewed each application as having exclusive use of the computer. But like most operating systems, Linux allows multiple applications to be executing concurrently. The operating system manages the hardware in an interleaved fashion, providing each application, and the operating system itself, with the use of the hardware components it needs at any given time.

There are two issues here. First, for the operating system to carry out its management tasks, it needs to maintain control over the interaction between applications and hardware. It does this by using a system of privilege levels in the CPU that allows the operating system to control a gateway between applications and the operating system. Second, we saw near the end of the previous chapter that most I/O devices can interrupt the ongoing activity of the CPU when they are ready with input or ready to accept output. The CPU has a mechanism to direct I/O interruptions through this gateway and call functions that are under the control of the operating system, thus allowing the operating system to maintain its control over the I/O devices.

We'll start by looking at how the CPU uses privilege levels to enforce its control. Then we'll look at how the CPU reacts to an interrupt or exception, including the three ways to notify the CPU that its services are needed by an I/O device or an application: *external interrupt, exception,* or *software interrupt.* We'll end the chapter by discussing how applications can directly call upon services of the operating system by using a software interrupt.

## Privilege Levels

For the operating system to carry out its management tasks, it needs to maintain control over the interaction between applications and hardware. It does this by using a system of *privilege levels* in the CPU that the operating system uses to maintain a gateway between applications and the hardware. At any given time, the CPU is running in one of four possible privilege levels. Table 21-1 shows the levels, from most privileged to least.

**Table 21-1:** CPU Privilege Levels

| Level | Usage |
| --- | --- |
| 0 | Provides direct access to all hardware resources. Restricted to the lowest-level operating system functions, such as I/O devices and memory management. |
| 1 | Somewhat restricted access to hardware resources. Might be used by some library routines and software that control I/O devices not requiring full access to the hardware. |
| 2 | More restricted access to hardware resources. Might be used by some library routines and software that control I/O devices not requiring less access than level 1. |
| 3 | No direct access to hardware resources. Applications run at this level. |

Most operating systems use only levels 0 and 3, often called *supervisor mode* and *user mode,* respectively. The operating system, including hardware device drivers, runs in supervisor mode, and applications, including the library routines they call, run in user mode. Levels 1 and 2 are seldom used. Be careful not to confuse CPU privilege levels, a hardware feature, with operating system *file permissions,* a software feature.

Whenever the CPU accesses memory, it does so through a *gate descriptor.* This 16-byte record includes the privilege level for the page of memory being accessed. The CPU is allowed to access memory that is at a privilege level equal to or below the current privilege level of the CPU.

When the operating system first boots up, the memory allocated to it is at the highest privilege level, 0, and the CPU is running at privilege level 0. Memory allocated for I/O devices is also at privilege level 0.

When the operating system loads an application, it first allocates memory for the program at the lowest privilege level, 3. After the application is loaded, the operating system passes use of the CPU to the application while simultaneously changing the CPU to privilege level 3. With the CPU running at the lowest privilege level, the application cannot directly access any memory that belongs to the operating system or the I/O devices. The instructions that allow you to directly change privilege levels can be executed only at level 0. Applications can access operating system services only through a gate descriptor.

Next, we'll look at what the CPU does when an interrupt or exception occurs, including how gate descriptors are used.

## CPU Response to an Interrupt or Exception

An *interrupt* or *exception* is an event that causes the CPU to pause the execution of the current instruction stream and call a function, called an *interrupt handler, exception handler,* or simply *handler.* Handlers are part of the operating system. In Linux they can be either built into the kernel or loaded as separate modules as needed.

This transfer of control is similar to a function call but with some additional actions. In addition to pushing the contents of the `rip` register (the return address) onto the stack when responding to an interrupt or exception, the CPU also pushes the contents of the `rflags` register onto the stack. Handlers almost always need to be executed at a high privilege level—most often level 0 in Table 21-1—so there's also a mechanism for placing the CPU at the proper privilege level.

The calling address and privilege level of a handler, along with other information, are stored in a gate descriptor (also called a *vector*) by the operating system. Gate descriptors for interrupts and exceptions are stored in an array, the *interrupt descriptor table* (*IDT*), or *vector table*, at the location corresponding to their interrupt number. The x86-64 architecture supports 256 possible interrupts or exceptions, numbered 0–255. The first 32 (0–31) are pre-assigned in the CPU hardware for specific uses. For example, the first gate descriptor in the interrupt descriptor table, location 0, is for a divide-by-zero exception. The remaining 224 are available for the operating system to use for external interrupts and software interrupts.

In addition to transferring control to the hander-calling address, the CPU also switches to the privilege level specified in the gate descriptor for the interrupt or exception. The gate descriptor can tell the operating system to use a different stack than the application. Under certain conditions, the CPU will also push the application's stack pointer onto the operating system's stack. The CPU then moves the address of the interrupt handler from the gate descriptor into the `rip`, and execution continues from there.

Here's a summary of the actions taken by the CPU in response to an interrupt or exception:

1. Push the contents of the `rflags` register onto the stack.

2. Push the contents of the `rip` register onto the stack. Depending on the nature of an exception, the handler may or may not return to the current program after it has handled the exception.

3. Set the privilege level of the CPU to the level specified in the corresponding gate descriptor.

4. Load the address of the handler from the corresponding gate descriptor into the `rip` register.

A simple ret instruction at the end of the handler will not work correctly. There is another instruction, iret, that first restores the rflags register, the privilege level, and the stack pointer (if it was saved) being used by the code that was interrupted, and then restores the rip.

In some situations, it's not possible to continue the interrupted code. In such cases, the handler may be able to display an error message and pass control to the operating system. In other cases, the operating system itself stops running.

There is no universal agreement on how the two terms, *interrupt* or *exception*, are used. I'll follow the usage in the Intel and AMD manuals to describe the three ways to notify the CPU that the services of the operating system are needed by an I/O device or an application program: external interrupt, exception, or software interrupt.

## External Interrupts

An *external interrupt* is caused by hardware that is outside the CPU. The interrupt signal is sent to the CPU via the control bus. An external interrupt is *asynchronous* with CPU timing—it can occur while the CPU is in the middle of executing an instruction.

Keyboard input is an example of an external interrupt. It's impossible to know exactly when someone will press a key on the keyboard or how soon the next key will be pressed. For example, say a key is pressed in the middle of executing the first of the following two instructions:

```
cmp     byte ptr [ebx], 0
je      allDone
```

The operating system needs to use the CPU to read the character from the keyboard as soon as possible to prevent the character from being overwritten by the next key press, but first, the CPU needs to complete the execution of the currently executing instruction.

The CPU will acknowledge an interrupt only between the execution of instructions. In our example, the CPU will acknowledge the external interrupt after it has executed the cmp instruction. In "Instruction Execution Cycle" on page 180, you learned that the rip register gets updated to contain the address of the je instruction while the CPU is executing the cmp instruction. This is the address that gets pushed onto the stack so that the CPU can return to the je instruction in our program after the interruption has been handled.

The CPU then calls the keyboard handler to read the character from the keyboard. It's almost certain that the handler will change the rflags register. The action of the je instruction needs to be based on the results of the cmp instruction, not on whatever might have happened to the rflags register in the handler. Now we see why the CPU needs to save a copy of the rflags register when responding to an external interrupt.

## Exceptions

The next way to interrupt the CPU we'll consider is with an *exception*. Exceptions are typically the result of a number that the CPU cannot deal with. Examples include dividing by 0, accessing an invalid address, or attempting to execute an invalid instruction. In a perfect world, the application software would include all the checks that would prevent these errors from occurring. The reality is that no program is perfect, so some of these errors will occur.

When one of these errors does occur, it's the operating system's responsibility to take the appropriate action. Often, the best the operating system can do is to exit the application program and print an error message. For example, when I made an error in how I treated the call stack in one of my assembly language programs, I got the following message:

```
Segmentation fault (core dumped)
```

Like an external interrupt, a handler in the operating system needs to be called to deal with an exception. The more the handler knows about the state of the CPU when an exception occurs, the better it can determine the cause. So it's helpful to have the values in the rip and rflags registers passed to the exception handler. And, of course, the CPU needs to be placed in the highest privilege level since the handler is part of the operating system.

Not all exceptions are due to actual program errors. For example, when a program references an address in another part of the program that has not yet been loaded into memory, it causes a *page fault exception*. The operating system provides a handler that loads the appropriate part of the program from the disk into memory and then continues with normal program execution without the user even being aware of this event. In this case, the handler requires the values in the rip and rflags registers when the page fault occurs so they can be restored when control returns to the program.

## Software Interrupts

A *software interrupt* happens when we use an instruction to have the CPU act as though there were an external interrupt or exception. Why would a programmer want to purposely interrupt the program? The answer is to request the services of the operating system.

Applications are running at the lowest privilege level, so they can't directly call functions in the operating system. The interrupt/exception mechanism in the CPU includes the means for switching the privilege level of the CPU while calling a function. Thus, a software interrupt allows an application running at the lowest privilege level, 3, to call the functions within the operating system kernel, while simultaneously switching the CPU to the higher privilege level of the operating system. This mechanism allows the operating system to maintain control.

Programming interrupt and exception handlers is beyond the scope of this book, but we can look at how to use software interrupts in applications, which are running at the lowest privilege level, to call functions in the operating system, which can be run only at a higher privilege level.

## System Calls

A *system call*, often called a *syscall*, allows an application to directly invoke Linux kernel system tasks, such as performing I/O functions. Thus far in the book, we have used C wrapper functions in the C standard library (for example, write and read) to do system calls. These C wrapper functions take care of the privilege-level transition from application to operating system and back. In this section, we'll see how to use assembly language instructions to make system calls directly without using the C runtime environment.

We'll look at two mechanisms, int 0x80 and syscall. The int 0x80 instruction causes a software interrupt that uses the interrupt descriptor table. The syscall instruction was added as part of the 64-bit instruction set and is available only in 64-bit mode. It causes a somewhat different set of actions in the CPU, as we'll see shortly.

### The int 0x80 Software Interrupt

We can call any of the interrupt handlers installed in the interrupt descriptor table with the int instruction:

**int—Call to Interrupt Procedure**

Call an interrupt handler.

int *n* calls interrupt handler *n*.

*n* can be any number in the range 0 to 255. The details of how int calls the specified interrupt handler depend on the state of the CPU and are beyond the scope of this book, but the overall result is the same as though an external device had interrupted.

Although we won't write any interrupt handlers here, you probably realize that a handler needs to perform several actions to restore the CPU state before returning. All this is done with the iret instruction.

**iret—Interrupt Return**

Return from interrupt handler.

iret returns from interrupt handler.

The iret instruction restores the rflags register, the rip register, and CPU privilege level from the stack.

Linux uses interrupt descriptor number $128_{10}$ (= $80_{16}$) in the interrupt descriptor table to specify a handler that will direct the operating system to perform one of more than 300 functions. The specific operating system function is specified by a number in the eax register.

Most of these operating system functions take arguments. We pass in the arguments to an int 0x80 system call using registers, as shown in Table 21-2. Notice that the register usage for int 0x80 differs from that of function calls.

**Table 21-2:** Register Usage for int 0x80 System Call

| Syscall # | Arg 1 | Arg 2 | Arg 3 | Arg 4 | Arg 5 | Arg 6 |
|-----------|-------|-------|-------|-------|-------|-------|
| eax | ebx | ecx | edx | esi | edi | ebp |

The system call numbers are listed in the Linux file *unistd_32.h*. On my version of Ubuntu (20.04 LTS), I found the file at */usr/include/x86_64-linux -gnu/asm/unistd_32.h*. Table 21-3 shows three commonly used system call numbers, along with any required arguments.

**Table 21-3:** Some Linux Operations for the int 0x80 Instruction

| Operation | eax | ebx | ecx | edx |
|-----------|-----|-----|-----|-----|
| read | 3 | File descriptor | Address of place to store input | Number of bytes to read |
| write | 4 | File descriptor | Address of first byte to output | Number of bytes to write |
| exit | 1 | | | |

Many of the system calls have C wrapper functions, which allows you to determine the arguments from the man page for the function. If you look back at Listing 13-2 in Chapter 13, you'll see that the arguments to the write system call using int 0x80 are the same as the write C wrapper function.

Listing 21-1 provides an example of using the int 0x80 software interrupt to directly access operating system services.

```
# helloWorld-int80.s
# Hello World program
# ld -e myStart -o helloWorld3-int80 helloWorld3-int80.o

        .intel_syntax noprefix
# Useful constants
        .equ    STDOUT, 1        # screen
        .equ    WRITE, 4         # write system call
        .equ    EXIT, 1          # exit system call

        .text
        .section  .rodata        # read-only data
message:
        .string "Hello, World!\n"
        .equ    msgLength, .-message-1

# Code
        .text                    # code
        .globl  myStart
```

```
❶ myStart:
       ❷ mov    edx, msgLength        # message length
         lea    ecx, message[rip]     # message address
         mov    ebx, STDOUT           # the screen
       ❸ mov    eax, WRITE            # write the message
         int    0x80                  # tell OS to do it

         mov    eax, EXIT             # exit program
         int    0x80
```

*Listing 21-1: "Hello, World!" program using int 0x80 software interrupt.*

The C runtime environment requires that the first function in a program be named main. If you want to write a program that executes on its own, without using any of the C library routines, you're free to choose any name you want ❶. But instead of using gcc to link your program, you need to use ld explicitly and provide the name of your function with the -e option. For example, to assemble and link the program in Listing 21-1, use this:

```
$ as --gstabs -o helloWorld_int80.o helloWorld-int80.s
$ ld -e myStart -o helloWorld-int80 helloWorld-int80.o
```

We pass the number of the write system call to the int 0x80 handler in the eax register ❸. The arguments to the write system call are the same as those we used when we called the write C wrapper function in Listing 13-2 (Chapter 13), but we need to pass them in the registers specified in Table 21-2 ❷.

You might notice that we use only the 32-bit portions of the registers when calling the int 0x80 handler. This mechanism was designed for a 32-bit environment. Although it also works in our 64-bit environment, the 64-bit enhancement to the x86 architecture added an instruction for making a fast system call, which we'll discuss in the next section.

## The syscall Instruction

Besides adding more registers, the 64-bit enhancement to the x86 architecture added some instructions, one of which is the *fast system call*, syscall. The syscall instruction bypasses the interrupt descriptor table. It's the preferred method for making a system call in 64-bit mode:

**syscall—Fast System Call**

syscall moves contents of rip to rcx and then moves contents of the LSTAR register to rip. Moves rflags to r11. Switches to privilege level 0.

The LSTAR register is a special CPU register where the operating system stores the address of the syscall handler.

Unlike the int 0x80 instruction, syscall does not use the interrupt descriptor table or save information on the stack, thus saving several memory accesses. All its actions occur with registers in the CPU. That's why it's called *fast system call*. Of course, this means the syscall handler must save the contents of the rcx and r11 registers if it uses them, and then it restores them to their original values before returning.

Returning from a syscall handler is done with a sysret instruction, which moves r11 to rflags, moves rcx to rip, and sets the CPU privilege level to 3.

You must pass the arguments to the syscall system call in Linux in registers, as shown in Table 21-4. Be careful to note that the arguments are passed in different registers than with the int 0x80 system call.

**Table 21-4:** Register Usage for syscall System Call Instruction

| Syscall # | Arg 1 | Arg 2 | Arg 3 | Arg 4 | Arg 5 | Arg 6 |
|---|---|---|---|---|---|---|
| rax | rdi | rsi | rdx | r10 | r8 | r9 |

The system call numbers for syscall are listed in the Linux file *unistd_64.h*. On my version of Ubuntu (20.04 LTS), I found the file at */usr/include/x86_64 -linux-gnu/asm/unistd_64.h*. Table 21-5 shows several commonly used system call numbers.

**Table 21-5:** Some Linux Operations for the syscall Instruction

| Operation | rax | rdi | rsi | rdx |
|---|---|---|---|---|
| read | 0 | File descriptor | Address of place to store input | Number of bytes to read |
| write | 1 | File descriptor | Address of first byte to output | Number of bytes to write |
| exit | 60 | | | |

As with the int 0x80 instruction, you can determine the arguments for most system calls from the man page for their C wrapper function.

Listing 21-2 shows our "Hello, World!" program using the syscall instruction.

```
# helloWorld-syscall.s
# Hello World program
# ld -e myStart -o helloWorld3_int80 helloWorld3_int80.o
        .intel_syntax noprefix
# Useful constants
        .equ    STDOUT, 1           # screen
 ❶ .equ    WRITE, 1            # write system call
        .equ    EXIT, 60            # exit system call

        .text
        .section  .rodata          # read-only data
message:
        .string "Hello, World!\n"
        .equ    msgLength, .-message-1

# Code
        .text                       # code
        .globl  myStart
```

```
myStart:
        ❷ mov     rdx, msgLength        # message length
          lea     rsi, message[rip]     # message address
          mov     rdi, STDOUT           # the screen
          mov     rax, WRITE            # write the message
          syscall                       # tell OS to do it

          mov     rax, EXIT             # exit program
          syscall
```

*Listing 21-2: "Hello, World!" program using syscall instruction*

The commands to assemble and link the program in Listing 21-2 are as follows:

```
$ as --gstabs -o helloWorld_syscall.o helloWorld-syscall.s
$ ld -e myStart -o helloWorld-syscall helloWorld-syscall.o
```

This program performs only the write and exit operations, which are given symbolic names at the beginning of the code for readability ❶. It stores the arguments to the write operation in the correct registers before executing the syscall instruction ❷.

---

**YOUR TURN**

Write a program in assembly language that reads one character at a time from the keyboard and echoes that character on the screen. Your program should continue echoing characters until it reads a newline character. You may see your typed text displayed twice. If so, why?

---

## What You've Learned

**Privilege levels**   The operating system maintains control of the hardware by running applications at a lower CPU privilege level.

**Gate descriptor**   A record that contains the address of an interrupt handler and the CPU privilege settings for running the interrupt handler.

**Interrupt descriptor table**   An array of gate descriptors. The interrupt or exception number is the index into the array.

**External interrupts**   Other hardware devices can interrupt the regular execution cycle of the CPU.

**Exceptions**   Certain conditions in the CPU can cause the CPU to interrupt its regular execution cycle.

**Software interrupts**  Specific instructions that cause the CPU to interrupt its regular execution cycle.

**Interrupt handler**  A function in the operating system that gets called by the CPU when an interrupt or exception occurs.

`int 0x80`  The software interrupt used to perform a system call in Linux.

`syscall`  The instruction used to perform a fast system call in 64-bit Linux.

This has been a brief overview of interrupts and exceptions. The details are complex and require a thorough knowledge of the specific model of CPU you're working with.

This concludes my introduction to computer organization. I hope that it has provided you with the tools to further pursue any of the topics that interest you.

# INDEX

as options
    `-a` 246
    `--gstabs` 210
    `-l` 246
    `-o` 210
assembler
    algorithm 258–260
    data size notation 239
    directives 199–203
    local symbol table 258
    opcode table 259
    two-pass 258
assembler directive (pseudo op) 204
assembler directives
    `.align` 292
    `.ascii` 317
    `.asciz` 317
    `.bss` 291, 311
    `.byte` 318
    `.cfi` 199
    `.comm` 292
    `.equ` 230, 411
    `.file` 201
    `.globl` 202
    `.include` 392
    `.int` 315, 318
    `.intel_syntax` 203
    `.long` 315, 318
    memory allocation 317
    `.quad` 285
    `.rodata` 226, 230
    `.set` 404
    `.size` 292
    `.string` 317
    `.text` 202, 230
    `.type` 203, 292
    `.zero` 292
assembly language
    and machine language 195, 206
    comments 205
    compiler-generated 197–201
    data size directives 207
    label field 204
    operand field 204
    operation field 204
assembly listing 246
AT&T syntax 217
AVX (Advanced Vector Extensions) 428

# B

base 14
battery 90
baud 453
BCD (binary coded decimal) 23
big endian 35, 36
binary
    C syntax 12
binary and unsigned decimal 13–17
binary coded decimal (BCD) 23
binary digit 10
binary number system 13
binary point 417
bitmask 336
bit masking 335, 420
    in assembly language
        340–342, 359
    in C 336–339, 353
bits 10
    representing groups of 10–12
Boolean algebra
    basic operations of 57
    literal 60
    operator precedence 61
    term 60
Boolean algebra rules
    annulment value 63, 65
    associative 61
    commutative 63
    complement 65
    distributive 63
    idempotent 65
    identity value 62
    involution 63
Boolean expression minimization 71–86
    minimal product of sums 72
    minimal sum of products 72
    using algebraic manipulations 73
    using Karnaugh maps 76–84
Boolean expressions 60–66
Boolean functions 66–86
    canonical form 67
    canonical product 70
    canonical sum 68
    conjunctive normal form 70
    disjunctive normal form 68
    full conjunctive normal form 70
    full disjunctive normal form 68

floating-point arithmetic error 433–440
    absorption 435
    associativity 437
    cancellation 436
    man fenv 430
    rounding 433
floating-point numbers 425–427
    not real numbers 425
    programming with 430
    rounding mode 430
floating-point representation 425
    biased exponent 427
    double 426
    exponent 425
    float 426
    hidden bit 427
    significand 425
    x86-64 extended version 426
floor division, in Python 365
for loop 272
fractional values in binary 416
frame pointer 185, 209, 216, 298, 307
front-side bus 445
function
    epilogue 210
    epilogue, inside 232
    input to 289
    minimal processing 208–210
    output from 289
    prologue 210
    prologue, inside 231
    return value 294, 338
function arguments 289
    more than six 299–306
    pass by pointer 294
    pass by reference 294
    pass by value 294
    passing in C 294–303
    pass in registers 223–224
    pushing onto the stack 299
    in registers 296–298
    return value 294
    storing directly on the stack 303

# G

gate
    AND 59
    NOT 60
    OR 59
    XOR 86
gate descriptor 466
gcc options
    -c 196
    -E 196
    -fcf-protection=none 201
    -fno-asynchronous-unwind
        -tables 199
    -masm=intel 198
    -o 197
    -O0 198
    -S 196, 198
gdb 30
    as a learning tool 31
    breakpoint 32
    commands
        b 31
        c 31
        h 31
        i r 31
        l 31
        layout regs 212
        n 189
        q 35
        r 31
        s 189
        set disassembly-flavor 211
        si 189
        tui enable 212
        x 31
gdb debugger
    learning assembly
        language 210–216
    TUI mode 211–217
    viewing registers 188–193
    viewing stack frame 231–233
getInt 370
global offset table (GOT) 227, 260
global variables 290–293
Goldberg, David ("What Every
        Computer Scientist Should
        Know About Floating-Point
        Arithmetic") 440
GOT (global offset table) 227, 260
Gray code and Karnugh maps 79
Gray, Frank 79

integral data types  183
integral values  415
interpreter  3
interrupt controller  449
interrupt descriptor table (IDT)  467
interrupt-driven I/O  449
interrupt handler  450, 467
interrupt
    CPU response to  467–469
    handler  450, 467
    terminology  468
intToSDec  370
intToUDec  368
invert  60
I/O controller hub  445
I/O controller register
    control  446
    receive  446
    status  446
    transmit  446
I/O devices  443
    accessing  446–449
I/O functions
    decToSInt  360
    decToUInt  358
    hexToInt  360
    getInt  370
    intToSDec  370
    intToUDec  368
    putInt  370
    readLn  308
    writeStr  308
*io.h* header file  461
I/O, memory-mapped  447
I/O, port-mapped  447
I/O ports  447
I/O programming  449
isolated I/O  447
iteration  264, 267–275
    versus recursion  267, 320

## J

joule  99
jump
    conditional  265–267
    long  256

near  256
short  256
unconditional  264
jump instructions  256–257
jump table  283

## K

Kahan summation algorithm, link to  440
Karnaugh, Maurice  76
Karnaugh map  76–86, 154, 160

## L

latch  136–144
    D  142
    feedback in  136
    SR, gated  141
    SR using NAND gates  139
    SR using NOR gates  136
    SR with Enable  141
ld options
    -e  472
    -o  472
leaf functions  298
least significant digit  14
linker
    algorithm  260
    global symbol table  260
listing file, assembler  246
little-endian  34
locality of reference  167
logic circuit  113
    combinational  114
    sequential  114
loop control variable  267
looping  267–275
Lospinoso, Josh (*C++ Crash Course*)
    396, 406

## M

machine code
    looking at  246
    ModR/M byte  248
    opcode bytes  247
    operands  247
    REX prefix byte  250
    SIB byte  255

magnetic field 97
main function 28, 221
main memory 165–166, 175
    organization 166
mask 336
mass storage 164–165
Mealy state machine 136
memory
    addresses 19
    cache 164
    cost 164
    data storage 18–23
    hardware 168–176
    hierarchy 163–164
    layers 164
    main 164–166, 175
    nonvolatile 164
    offline 164
    page 448
    page frame 448
    page map table 448
    physical 448
    random access
        dynamic 175–176
        static 173–175
    read-write 172–173
    speed 164
    timing 444
    virtual 448
    volatile 165
memory controller hub 445
memory-mapped I/O 447
    in assembly language 457–459
    in C 452–457
memory mapping unit 448
memory segments
    bss 292
    characteristics 317
    data 202
    heap 202
    stack 202
    text 202
metal-oxide-semiconductor field-effect
    transistor (MOSFET) 101
minimum function
    assembly language 208
    C 197

Moore state machine 136
MOSFET (metal-oxide-semiconductor
    field-effect transistor) 101
    channel 101
    drain 101
    gate 101
    N-channel 102
    P-channel 103
    power consumption 104
    source 101
    switch 101–104
    switching time 104
most significant digit 14
multiplexer (MUX) 124–127, 172
multiplication, integer 352–359
    by powers of two 351
    register usage 356
    signed versus unsigned 356
MUX (multiplexer) 124–127, 172
mxcsr register 429

**N**

name mangling 313, 400
NAND gate, universal 108–110
negation 48, 57
newline character 23
NOR gate, universal 110
northbridge 445
NOT gate 105
numerical accuracy 440

**O**

object
    attribute 395
    instance 395
    instantiate 396
    message 395
    method 395
    using in C++ 398–400
object file 196, 202, 210
objects in assembly language 407–412
octal 11
    C syntax 12
octal digit, three bits 12
ohms 92
Ohm's law 92
one's complement 49

## W

watt  99

"What Every Computer Scientist
Should Know About Floating-
Point Arithmetic" (Goldberg,
David)  440

while loop  267–272

## X

x87 floating point unit  427

## Z

zero flag (ZF)  186

# RESOURCES

Visit *https://nostarch.com/introcomporg/* for errata and more information.

---

*More no-nonsense books from*  **NO STARCH PRESS**

**THE LINUX COMMAND LINE, 2ND EDITION**
**A COMPLETE INTRODUCTION**
*BY* WILLIAM SHOTTS
504 PP., $39.95
ISBN 978-1-59327-952-3

**C++ CRASH COURSE**
**A FAST-PACED INTRODUCTION**
*BY* JOSH LOSPINOSO
792 PP., $59.95
ISBN 978-1-59327-888-5

**THE ART OF 64-BIT ASSEMBLY, VOLUME 1**
**X86-64 MACHINE ORGANIZATION AND PROGRAMMING**
*BY* RANDALL HYDE
1032 PP., $79.99
ISBN 978-1-7185-0108-9

**EFFECTIVE C**
**AN INTRODUCTION TO PROFESSIONAL C PROGRAMMING**
*BY* ROBERT SEACORD
272 PP., $49.95
ISBN 978-1-7185-0104-1

**ALGORITHMIC THINKING**
**A PROBLEM-BASED INTRODUCTION**
*BY* DANIEL ZINGARO
408 PP., $49.95
ISBN 978-1-7185-0080-8

**HOW LINUX WORKS, 3RD EDITION**
**What Every Superuser Should Know**
*BY* BRIAN WARD
464 PP., $49.99
ISBN 978-1-7185-0040-2

---

**PHONE:**
800.420.7240 OR
415.863.9900

**EMAIL:**
SALES@NOSTARCH.COM
**WEB:**
WWW.NOSTARCH.COM